High Performance iOS Apps

Gaurav Vaish

Beijing · Boston · Farnham · Sebastopol · Tokyo

High Performance iOS Apps

by Gaurav Vaish

Copyright © 2016 Gaurav Vaish. All rights reserved.

Printed in the United States of America.

Published by O'Reilly Media, Inc., 1005 Gravenstein Highway North, Sebastopol, CA 95472.

O'Reilly books may be purchased for educational, business, or sales promotional use. Online editions are also available for most titles (*http://safaribooksonline.com*). For more information, contact our corporate/institutional sales department: 800-998-9938 or *corporate@oreilly.com*.

Editor: Courtney Allen
Acquisitions Editor: Brian Anderson
Production Editor: Nicole Shelby
Copyeditor: Jasmine Kwityn
Proofreader: Rachel Head

Indexer: Judy McConville
Interior Designer: David Futato
Cover Designer: Karen Montgomery
Illustrator: Rebecca Demarest

June 2016:   First Edition

Revision History for the First Edition
2016-06-10:   First Release

See *http://oreilly.com/catalog/errata.csp?isbn=9781491911006* for release details.

978-1-491-91100-6

[LSI]

This book is dedicated to Agryav Vaish, my son.

Table of Contents

Part I.   Getting Started

Part V.   iOS 9

Preface

You may already have an amazing iOS app, or be developing one. Everything looks great except for some kinks that prohibit users from giving the app that final fifth star or prevent you from releasing it.

Issues like a jitter when the user goes to the nth item in table view or the app hogging the network or consuming a lot battery are some of the visible symptoms that the user will be aware of. However, the problems lie somewhere deeper.

Tuning an app for performance is a never-ending task, especially with new app features, OS versions, third-party libraries, and device configurations. These are only some of the things that keep developers on their toes about app performance.

According to a study, about a quarter of users abandon an app if it does not load within 3 seconds, and about a third of users will tell others about their poor experience.

Users want apps that are fast, responsive, and do not hog resources. This book takes a look at various aspects that negatively impact use and outlines how you can tune *your* app for performance.

Who Should Read This Book

If you have been writing iOS apps and publishing them to the App Store, you have an implicit goal to make them better, faster, and more fluid—not to mention loved by your users. And if you are continuously looking for ways to achieve that goal, then this book is just for you.

You should already have working knowledge of Objective-C and iOS. This book is not about jump-starting with Objective-C or iOS, though the fundamentals will be revisited for completeness when necessary.

Why I Wrote This Book

iPhone OS 1 and iPhone 1 were launched in June 2007. During their early releases, developers were busy flushing out code and releasing apps for a wider audience. As the hardware, OS, networks, and overall ecosystem advanced over time—and as new user interface (UI) and engineering design patterns emerged—apps matured in functionality, stability, and performance.

More often than not, performance is an afterthought. And I can, to some degree, agree with that approach. After all, it is important to first get the functionality right, rather than worrying about performance. Thinking about optimizing early in the development lifecycle is more commonly referred to as *premature optimization*. But when poor performance hits, it hits hard.

The primary goal of this book is to show you how to write optimal code from an engineering perspective.

This book is not about theoretical computer science, data structures, and algorithms for faster execution of a task. You can find tons of literature on those topics. It covers best practices for implementing an app in such a manner that even in non-ideal conditions (low storage space, poor network, low battery, etc.), users still can use your app effectively and love using it. Generally, it will not be possible to optimize across all the parameters, but you'll be able to achieve the best trade-off considering the available options.

Navigating This Book

This book is organized in five parts. Each part is comprised of one or more chapters that detail the theme of the particular part. Each chapter begins with a brief abstract outlining the topics that will be covered.

Part I provides an overview of how to measure performance. Chapter 1 discusses the aspects that we want to optimize and outlines the parameters we want to measure as part of tracking app performance.

Part II reviews the key optimizations that are core to any app. Chapter 2 addresses memory management. It describes the memory management model and object reference types. It also discusses best practices for design patterns that impact memory consumption, namely singleton and dependency injection.

Chapter 3 covers energy and techniques for minimizing consumption. Chapter 4 provides an overview of concurrent programming. It describes the various options available and gives a comparative analysis.

Part III covers performance optimization techniques specific to iOS app development. Chapter 5 provides in-depth coverage of the application lifecycle. It details how lifecycle events can be utilized to ensure resources are used effectively.

Chapter 6 reviews optimization techniques specifically for the user interface. Chapter 7 and Chapter 8 deal with networking and data sharing, respectively. Chapter 9 provides an in-depth review of security. It describes how enhanced security can slow down an app and discusses what can be done for an effective trade-off.

Part IV reviews the non-code aspects of performance. Chapter 10 covers testing, and performance testing in particular. It also discusses continuous integration and automation.

Chapter 11 provides an overview of the tools you can use to measure performance during development. Chapter 12 discusses instrumentation and analytics, and how it can be used to collect performance-related data from apps in production.

Part V focuses on iOS 9. Chapter 13 provides an outline of the changes in this release and how they impact the code you write from the perspective of performance.

Code snippets are provided throughout the book where applicable. Several of these snippets can be used either as is or with minimal modifications in your app. Other snippets may need to be further adapted to suit your app.

Each chapter also provides a set of best practices associated with the topic. It may not always be possible to follow all of the best practices in a single app. The decisions of which ones you want to trade off against others will be based on your app's requirements.

Online Resources

This book refers to several online blogs, articles, tutorials, and other references. The links to those references are provided where applicable. Should you feel any reference has been missed out accidentally, feel free to contact the publisher or the author.

This book also references screenshots from several apps. The apps are copyright of their respective owners. The screenshots have been added for educational and illustrative purposes only.

Conventions Used in This Book

The following typographical conventions are used in this book:

Italic
Indicates new terms, URLs, email addresses, filenames, and file extensions.

`Constant width`

> Used for program listings, as well as within paragraphs to refer to program elements such as variable or function names, databases, data types, environment variables, statements, and keywords.

`Constant width bold`

> Shows commands or other text that should be typed literally by the user. It also highlights new code in program listings as compared to an earlier example that may have been shown.

`Constant width italic`

> Shows text that should be replaced with user-supplied values or by values determined by context.

 This icon signifies a general note.

 This icon signifies a tip or suggestion.

 This icon indicates a warning or a caution.

Using Code Examples

Supplemental material (code examples, exercises, etc.) is available for download at *https://github.com/gvaish/high-performance-ios-apps*.

This book is here to help you get your job done. In general, if example code is offered with this book, you may use it in your programs and documentation. You do not need to contact us for permission unless you're reproducing a significant portion of the code. For example, writing a program that uses several chunks of code from this book does not require permission. Selling or distributing a CD-ROM of examples from O'Reilly books does require permission. Answering a question by citing this book and quoting example code does not require permission. Incorporating a significant amount of example code from this book into your product's documentation does require permission.

We appreciate, but do not require, attribution. An attribution usually includes the title, author, publisher, and ISBN. For example: "*High Performance iOS Apps* by Gaurav Vaish (O'Reilly). Copyright 2016 Gaurav Vaish, 978-1-491-91100-6."

If you feel your use of code examples falls outside fair use or the permission given above, feel free to contact us at *permissions@oreilly.com*.

Safari® Books Online

 *Safari Books Online* is an on-demand digital library that delivers expert content in both book and video form from the world's leading authors in technology and business.

Technology professionals, software developers, web designers, and business and creative professionals use Safari Books Online as their primary resource for research, problem solving, learning, and certification training.

Safari Books Online offers a range of plans and pricing for enterprise, government, education, and individuals.

Members have access to thousands of books, training videos, and prepublication manuscripts in one fully searchable database from publishers like O'Reilly Media, Prentice Hall Professional, Addison-Wesley Professional, Microsoft Press, Sams, Que, Peachpit Press, Focal Press, Cisco Press, John Wiley & Sons, Syngress, Morgan Kaufmann, IBM Redbooks, Packt, Adobe Press, FT Press, Apress, Manning, New Riders, McGraw-Hill, Jones & Bartlett, Course Technology, and hundreds more. For more information about Safari Books Online, please visit us online.

How to Contact Us

Please address comments and questions concerning this book to the publisher:

O'Reilly Media, Inc.
1005 Gravenstein Highway North
Sebastopol, CA 95472
800-998-9938 (in the United States or Canada)
707-829-0515 (international or local)
707-829-0104 (fax)

We have a web page for this book, where we list errata, examples, and any additional information. You can access this page at *http://bit.ly/hp-ios-apps*.

To comment or ask technical questions about this book, send email to *bookquestions@oreilly.com*.

For more information about our books, courses, conferences, and news, see our website at *http://www.oreilly.com*.

Find us on Facebook: *http://facebook.com/oreilly*

Follow us on Twitter: *http://twitter.com/oreillymedia*

Watch us on YouTube: *http://www.youtube.com/oreillymedia*

Acknowledgments

Even though it might seem so at times, nobody writes a book alone.

I am grateful to have worked closely with Daryl Low, Distinguished Architect at Yahoo!, in developing the monetization SDK from the ground up. He provided guidance on several sections in the book. It has always been fun and exciting to work with him on prototypical apps just to test performance extremes or identify the root cause of an error.

I would like to thank Walter Pezzini, who heads mobile DevOps engineering at Yahoo. He provided key insights on my understanding of continuous integration and a delivery pipeline, and what it takes to build a high-quality system.

As an author, it is easy to assume a few things to be known by the reader that may not always be the case. A big thanks goes to Chris Devers, Laura Savino, and Niklas Saers for their reviews, which identified areas that I needed to clarify. Thanks for also providing feedback that helped elevate overall content quality.

I would like to acknowledge Renu Chandel, my wife, for her continuous push to force me to complete this book. It would not have been finished if not for her. Thanks for all the coffee!

Last, but not the least, thanks to O'Reilly Media for publishing this book.

This book would not have been complete without collective efforts from all of you. Thanks, team.

PART I

Getting Started

In the opening part, we define performance for mobile apps and identify the performance metrics—the factors that impact the overall user experience and your app's rating. We also identify the app-measurable counters that should be monitored and improved upon over time.

CHAPTER 1

Performance in Mobile Apps

This book assumes that you are an iOS developer and have been writing native iOS apps for a substantial amount of time—and that you now want to take the leap from being yet another iOS developer to the top of the league.

Consider the following statistics:[1]

- 79% of users retry an app *only once or twice* if it failed to work the first time.
- 25% of users abandon an app if it does not load *in 3 seconds.*
- 31% of users will *tell others* about their bad experience.

These numbers reemphasize the importance of optimizing your app for performance. Getting your app recognized in the users' view is not just about the functionality. It is about providing a smooth experience all throughout the interaction with the app.

For any particular task, there might be several apps available in the App Store to accomplish it. But users will stick to the one that is either indispensable or has no glitches and stands out from others in terms of performance.

Performance is impacted by many factors, including memory consumption, network bandwidth efficiency, and user interface responsiveness. We will first outline different types of performance characteristics, before moving on to ways of measuring them.

---

1 Hewlett Packard Enterprise Software Solutions, "3 keys to a 5-star mobile experience" (*http://bit.ly/3-keys-mobile*).

Defining Performance

From a technical standpoint, performance is, strictly speaking, a very vague term. When someone identifies an app as being a high-performing one, we don't necessarily know what that means. Does the app use less memory? Does it save money on network usage? Or does it allow you to work fluidly? The meaning can be multifaceted, and the implications abundant.

Performance can be related to one or more of the considerations that we discuss next. One part of these considerations is *performance metrics* (what we want to measure and monitor) while the other is about *measurement* (actually collecting the data).

We explore the measurement process in great depth in Chapter 11. Improving the usage of the engineering parameters is the crux of Part II and Part III of the book.

Performance Metrics

Performance metrics are the user-facing attributes. Each attribute may be a factor of one or more engineering parameters that can be measured.

Memory

Memory refers to the minimum RAM that the app requires to run, and the average and maximum memory that it consumes. Minimum memory puts a strong constraint on the hardware, whereas higher average or peak memory means more background apps are likely be killed.

Also, you must ensure that you do not leak memory. A gradual increase in memory consumption over time results in a higher likelihood of app crashes due to out-of-memory exceptions.

Memory is covered in depth in Chapter 2.

Power Consumption

This is an extremely important factor to tackle when writing performant code. Your data structures and algorithms must be efficient in terms of execution time and CPU resources, but you also need to take into account various other factors. If your app drains battery, rest assured that no one will appreciate it.

Power consumption is not just about calculating CPU cycles—it also involves using the hardware effectively. It is therefore important to not only minimize power consumption but also ensure that the user experience is not degraded.

We cover this topic in Chapter 3.

Initialization Time

An app should perform *just enough* tasks at the launch to initialize itself so that the user can work with it. Time taken to perform these tasks is the initialization time of the app. *Just enough* is an open-ended term—finding the right balance is dependent on your app's needs.

One option is to defer object creation and initialization until the app's first usage (i.e., until the object is needed). This is known as *lazy initialization*. This is a good strategy, but the user should not be kept waiting each time any subsequent task is performed.

The following list outlines some of the actions you may want to execute during your app's initialization, in no particular order:

- Check if the app is being launched for the first time.
- Check if the user is logged in.
- If the user is logged in, load previous state, if applicable.
- Connect to the server for the latest changes.
- Check if the app was launched with a deep link. If so, load the UI and state for the deep link.
- Check if there are pending tasks from the last time the app was launched. Resume them if need be.
- Initialize object and thread pools that you want to use later.
- Initialize dependencies (e.g., object-relational mapping, crash reporting system, and cache).

The list can grow pretty quickly, and it can be difficult to decide what to keep at launch time and what to defer to the next few milliseconds.

We cover this topic in Chapter 5.

Execution Speed

Once the user opens an app, the expectation is for it to work as quickly as possible. Any necessary processing should be handled in as little time as possible.

Consider a photo app, for example. A live preview is ideal for simple effects like changing brightness or contrast where the processing needs to happen within milliseconds.

This may require parallel processing for local computation or the ability to offload to the server for complex tasks. We will touch on this topic in Chapter 4, Chapter 6, and Chapter 7. Chapter 11 covers various related tools.

Responsiveness

Your app should be fast to respond to user interaction. Responsiveness is the result of all the optimizations and trade-offs that you have made in your app.

There may be multiple apps in the App Store to accomplish similar or related tasks. Given an array of options, the user will ultimately choose the app that is most responsive.

Parallel processing for optimal local execution is covered in Chapter 4. Best practices for implementing fluid interactions in your app are covered in Chapter 5 and Chapter 6. We explore testing your app in Chapter 10.

Local Storage

Any app that stores data on a server and/or has to refresh its data from an external source must plan for local storage for offline viewing capabilities.

For example, a mail app will be expected to at least show previously downloaded messages if the network is not present or the device is in offline mode.

Similarly, a news app should be able to show recently updated news for offline mode as well as an indicator showing which articles are new and unread.

However, loading from local storage and syncing the data should be painless and fast. This may require selecting not only the data to be cached locally but also the structure of the data, choosing from a host of options, as well as the frequency of sync.

If your app uses local storage, you should provide an option to clean it. Unfortunately, most of the apps in the market do not do so. What is more worrisome is that some of these apps consume storage in the hundreds of megabytes. Users frequently uninstall these apps to reclaim local storage. This results in a bad user experience, thereby threatening the app's success.

Looking at Figure 1-1, you will see that over 12 GB of space has been used and the user is left with only 950 MB. A large part of the data can be safely deleted from local storage. The app should provide an option for cache cleanup.

Figure 1-1. Disk usage

Always give the end user an option to clean up the local cache.

If the user has iCloud backup enabled, the app data will consume the user's storage quota. Use it prudently.

The topics that impact local storage are covered in Chapters 7, 8, and 9.

Interoperability

Users may use multiple apps to accomplish a task, which requires interoperability across them. For example, a photo album may be best viewed in a slideshow app but might require another app for editing it. The viewer app should be able to send a photo to the editor and receive the edited photo.

iOS provides multiple options for interoperability and sharing data across apps. `UIActivityViewController`, deep linking, and the `MultipeerConnectivity` framework are some of the options available on iOS.

Defining good URL structure for deep linking is as important as writing good code to parse it. Similarly, for sharing data using the share sheet, it is important to identify the exact content to be shared as well as to take care of security concerns that arise from processing content from an untrusted source.

It would be a really bad user experience if your app took a long time just to prepare data to be shared with a nearby device.

We discuss this in Chapter 8.

Network Condition

Mobile devices are used in varying network conditions. To ensure the best user experience, your app must work in all of the following scenarios:

- High bandwidth and persistent network
- Low bandwidth but persistent network
- High bandwidth but sporadic network
- Low bandwidth and sporadic network
- No network

It is acceptable to present the user with a progress indicator or an error message, but it is not acceptable to block indefinitely or let the app crash.

The screenshots in Figure 1-2 show different ways in which you can convey the message to the end user. The TuneIn app shows how much of the streaming content it has been able to buffer. This conveys to the user the expected wait time before the music can start. Other apps, such as the MoneyControl and Bank of America apps, just provide an indefinite progress bar, a more common style for non-streaming apps.

Figure 1-2. Different indicator types for poor network conditions or large data

We cover this topic in Chapter 7.

Bandwidth

People use their mobile devices on various network types with speeds ranging from hundreds of kilobits per second to tens of megabits per second.

As such, optimal use of bandwidth is another key parameter that defines your product's quality. In addition, if you have been developing your app using low-bandwidth conditions, running it in high-bandwidth conditions can produce different results.

In around 2010, my team and I were developing an app in India. In low-bandwidth conditions, the app's local initialization would happen long before initial responses from the server were available, and we tuned the app for those conditions.

However, the app was focused on the South Korean market, and when we tested it there, the results were extremely different. None of our optimizations worked, and we had to rewrite a large chunk of code that could have resulted in resource and data contention.

Planning for high performance does not always result in optimizations, but can result in trade-offs as well.

Chapter 7 covers best practices for optimally using bandwidth.

Data Refresh

Even if you do not have any offline viewing capabilities, you may still refresh periodically with data from the server. The rate at which you refresh and the amount of data transferred will affect overall data consumption. If the number of total bytes transferred is large, the user is bound to exhaust his data plan quickly. And if that value is large enough, you may have just lost a user.

In iOS 6.x and below, if your app is in the background, the app cannot refresh data. In iOS 7 onward, the app can use background app refresh for periodic refreshes. For live chat apps, a persistent HTTP or raw TCP connection may be more useful.

This is covered in Chapter 5 and Chapter 7.

Multiuser Support

A family might share a mobile device, or a user may have multiple accounts for the same application. For example, two siblings might share the same iPad for games. As another example, a family may want to configure one device to check each person's emails during vacation to minimize roaming costs, particularly during international travel. Similarly, one person may have multiple email accounts to be configured.

Whether you want to support multiple simultaneous users will be dependent on your product. But if you do decide to offer this feature, make sure to follow these guidelines:

- Adding a new user should be efficient.
- Updates across the users should be efficient.
- Switching between users should be efficient.
- User-data boundaries should be neat and without any bugs.

Figure 1-3 shows examples of two apps with multiuser support. The left shows the account selector for Google apps while the right shows the one for Yahoo apps.

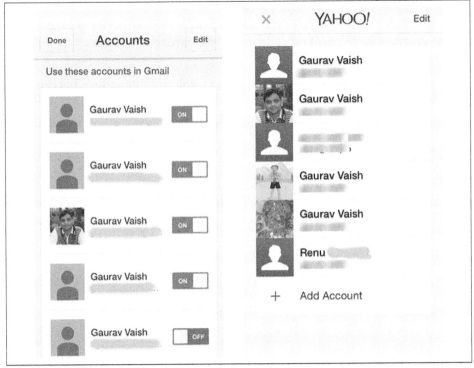

Figure 1-3. The Google and Yahoo apps both offer multiuser support

You will learn how to make your application secure for multiuser support and more in Chapter 9.

Single Sign-on

If you have created multiple apps that allow or require sign-in, it is always a good idea to support single sign-on (SSO). If a user logs in to one of your apps, it should be one-click sign-in to your other apps.

This process requires more than just sharing data across apps—you'll also need to share state, synchronize across your apps, and more. For example, if the user signs out using one of the apps, signout should also occur in all other apps where the user signed in using SSO.

In addition, the synchronization across the apps must be secure.

This is covered in Chapter 9.

Security

Security is paramount in a mobile app, particularly because sensitive information might be shared across apps. It is important to secure all communications, as well as both local and shared data.

Implementing security requires additional computation, memory, or storage, which is at odds with your end goal of striving for maximum speed and minimum memory and storage requirements.

As a result, you'll need to trade off between security and other factors.

Adding multiple layers of security degrades performance and may have a perceivable negative impact on user experience. Where you draw the line with security is app- and user demographics–determined. In addition, the hardware plays an important role: the options chosen will vary based on the computing capabilities of the device.

Security is covered in depth in Chapter 9.

Crashes

Apps can and do crash. Extreme optimizations can lead to crashes. Likewise, using native C code can lead to crashes.

A high-performing app will try to not only secure itself from crashes but also recover gracefully if a crash actually happens, particularly if it was in middle of an operation when the crash occurred.

Crash reporting, instrumentation, and analytics are covered in depth in Chapter 12.

App Profiling

There are two ways to profile your app to measure the parameters that we have discussed: sampling and instrumentation. Let's take a look at each.

Sampling

Sampling (or probe-based profiling), as the name implies, requires sampling the state at periodic intervals, generally with the help of tools. We explore these tools in "Instruments" on page 363. Sampling provides a great overall picture of the app, as it does not interfere with its execution. The downside of sampling is that it does not return 100% accurate details. If the sampling frequency is 10 ms, you will not know what happens for the 9.999 ms between the probes.

 Use sampling for initial performance explorations and to track CPU and memory utilization.

Instrumentation

Instrumentation—that is, modifying the code to log detailed information—provides more accurate results than sampling. This can be done proactively for critical sections, but can also be done reactively to troubleshoot problems found during profiling or through user feedback. We will discuss this process in more depth in "Instrumenting Your App" on page 15.

 Because instrumentation involves injecting extra code, it does impact app performance—it can take a toll on memory or speed (or both).

Measurement

Now that we have established the parameters we would like to measure and explored the types of profiling for measurement, let's run through the steps to implement it.

By measuring performance and identifying where you truly have problems, you can avoid the pitfall of premature optimization described by Donald Knuth:

The real problem is that programmers have spent far too much time worrying about efficiency in the wrong places and at the wrong times; premature optimization is the root of all evil (or at least most of it) in programming.[2]

Project and Code Setup

In the following sections, we will set up a project to be able to measure the parameters we've identified during development as well as production. There are three sets of tasks for project configuration, setup, and code implementation:

Build and release
Ensure that it is easy to build and release the app.

Testability
Ensure that your code works with both mock and real data, including isolated replication of real-world scenarios.

Traceability
Ensure that you can resolve errors by identifying where the problem happened and what the code was trying to do at that stage.

The following subsections take a look at each of these options.

Build and release

Until recently, build and release was an afterthought. But thankfully, with the urge to go nimble and agile, systems and tools have evolved. They are now sped up to pull in dependencies, to build and release the product for testing or for enterprise distribution, and/or to upload to iTunes Connect for public release.

In a blog post (*http://bit.ly/1U5NCJP*) published by Joel Spolsky in 2000, he asks the question, "Can you build your app in one click (from the source)?" The question still stands today. And the answer may define how quickly you can respond to improving quality and performance after defects or bottlenecks have been identified.

CocoaPods (*https://cocoapods.org*), written in Ruby, is the de facto dependency manager for Objective-C and Swift projects.[3] It integrates with Xcode command-line utilities for build and release.

---

2 Donald Knuth, "Computer Programming as an Art" (*http://bit.ly/knuth-art*).

3 At the time of writing, most of the objects released as CocoaPods are written in Objective-C. After all, Swift is relatively new compared to Objective-C.

Testability

All apps have multiple components that work together. A well-designed system supports *loose coupling* and *tight cohesion*, allowing you to replace any or all of a component's dependencies.

You should test each component in isolation by mocking out the dependencies. In general, there are two types of tests:

Unit tests
> Validate the operation of an individual unit of code in isolation. This is typically done in an environment that repeatedly calls methods with a variety of input data to assess how the code performs.

Functional tests
> Validate the operation of a component in the final integrated setup, either in the final shippable version of the software or in a reference app built specifically for test purposes.

We explore testing in detail in Chapter 10.

Traceability

During development, instrumentation allows us to prioritize performance optimizations, improve resilience, and provide debug information. Crash reporting focuses on collecting debug information from the production version of the software.

Crash Reporting Setup

Crash reporting systems collect debug logs for analysis. There are dozens of crash reporters available on the market. With no particular bias, Flurry (*http://www.flurry.com*) has been used in this book. The primary reason I chose Flurry is that crash reporting and instrumentation can be set up using one SDK. We discuss instrumentation in depth in Chapter 12.

To use Flurry, you'll need to set up an account at *www.flurry.com*, get an API key, then download and set up the Flurry SDK. Example 1-1 shows the code for the initialization.

Example 1-1. Configuring crash reporting in the app delegate

```
#import "Flurry.h"

- (BOOL)application:(UIApplication *)application
  didFinishLaunchingWithOptions:(NSDictionary *)launchOptions {

  [Flurry setCrashReportingEnabled:YES];
```

```
    [Flurry startSession:@"API_KEY"]; ❶
}
```

❶ Replace API_KEY with the one associated with your account (you'll find this in the Flurry dashboard).

 The crash reporting systems (CRS) will set the global exception handler using the NSSetUncaughtExceptionHandler method. If you have been using a custom handler, it will be lost.

If you want to keep your exception handler, set it after initializing the CRS. You can get the handler set by the CRS using the NSGetUncaughtExceptionHandler method.

Instrumenting Your App

Instrumenting your app is a very important step in understanding user behavior, but also—and more importantly for our purpose here—in identifying critical paths of the app. Injecting deliberate code to record key metrics is a good step toward improving app performance.

 It is a good idea to abstract and encapsulate any dependencies. This allows you to do a last-minute switch or even work with multiple systems simultaneously before making a final decision. It is especially useful in scenarios where there are multiple options available and you are in the evaluation phase.

As shown in Example 1-2, we will add a class called HPInstrumentation to encapsulate instrumentation. For now, we log in to the console using NSLog and send out the details to the server as well.

Example 1-2. Class HPInstrumentation wrapper for underlying instrumentation SDK

```
//HPInstrumentation.h
@interface HPInstrumentation : NSObject

+(void)logEvent:(NSString *)name;
+(void)logEvent:(NSString *)name withParameters:(NSDictionary *)parameters;

@end

//HPInstrumentation.m
@implementation HPInstrumentation

+(void)logEvent:(NSString *)name
{
    NSLog(@"%@", name);
```

```
    [Flurry logEvent:name];
}

+(void)logEvent:(NSString *)name withParameters:(NSDictionary *)parameters
{
    NSLog(@"%@ -> %@", name, params);
        [Flurry logEvent:name withParameters:parameters];
}
```

@end

We start with instrumenting three critical stages of our app lifecycle (see Example 1-3):

- Whenever the app comes to the foreground, indicated by a call to `application DidBecomeActive:`

- Whenever the app goes into the background, indicated by a call to `application DidEnterBackground:`

- If and when the app receives a low-memory warning, indicated by a call to `appli cationDidReceiveMemoryWarning:`

And just for fun, we add a button in the `HPFirstViewController` that will cause the app to crash when clicked.

Example 1-3. Basic instrumentation in the app delegate

```
- (void)applicationDidBecomeActive:(UIApplication *)application
{
    [HPInstrumentation logEvent:@"App Activated"];
}

- (void)applicationDidEnterBackground:(UIApplication *)application
{
    [HPInstrumentation logEvent:@"App Backgrounded"];
}

- (void)applicationDidReceiveMemoryWarning:(UIApplication *)application
{
    [HPInstrumentation logEvent:@"App Memory Warning"];
}
```

`App Activated`, `App Backgrounded`, and `App Memory Warning` are unique names that we have given to these events. You can choose any names that you are comfortable with. Numeric values are also fine.

Instrumentation should not be used as a logging alternative. Logging can be very verbose. Because it consumes the network's resources when reporting to the server, you should instrument only the bare minimum.

It is important that you instrument only the events that you and other members of the engineering or product teams are interested in (with enough data to support important reports).

The line between instrumentation and overinstrumentation is thin. Start with instrumenting for a few reports and increase the coverage over time.

Next, let's add a UI control so that we can generate a crash and then look at the crash report.

Figure 1-4 shows the UI for the crash button. Example 1-4 shows the code to link the Touch Up Inside event to the method crashButtonWasClicked:

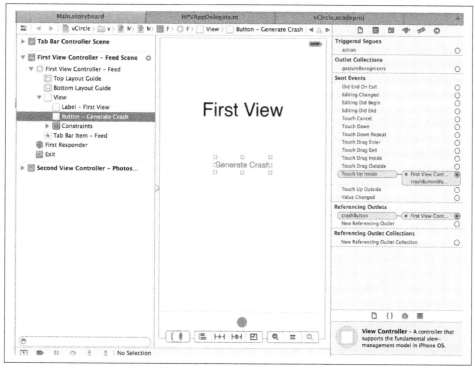

Figure 1-4. Add Generate Crash button in the storyboard

Example 1-4. Raising exception to generate a crash

```
- (IBAction)crashButtonWasClicked:(id)sender
{
    [NSException raise:@"Crash Button Was Clicked" format:@""];
}
```

Let's interact with the app to generate some events:

1. Install and launch the app.

2. Background the app.

3. Foreground it.

4. Repeat steps 2 and 3 a few times.

5. Tap the Generate Crash button. This will cause the app to crash.

6. Launch the app again. It is only now that the crash report will actually be sent to the server.

The first set of instrumentation events and crash reports can take a little while to be sent to the server and processed. You may have to wait for some time for the reports to appear on the Flurry dashboard. Then, go to the dashboard and take a look at these events and the crash report. You should see reports similar to the ones shown in the following screenshots, which were taken from the dashboard for my app.

Figure 1-5 shows the user sessions—that is, how many users opened the app at least once per day. Multiple launches may or may not be considered as part of the same session depending on the time elapsed between those launches.

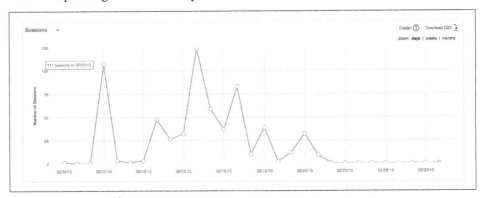

Figure 1-5. Report of user sessions

Figure 1-6 shows a detailed breakdown of each event instrumented. This report is more useful because it provides insights into the app usage (i.e., it pinpoints which parts of the app were more frequently used as compared to the others).

Event Summary Statistics					Explain ⊙ Download CSV ⬇
Event Name	Total Event Occurrences	Event Occurrences (Daily Avg) ▾	Unique Event Users (Daily Avg)	Events per Session (Daily Avg)	Analyses
App_Activate	240	8.28	0.82	0.95	⊙ ⅊ ⅊ ⟳ ▣ filter
Appear_Chxx	219	7.55	0.86	0.87	⊙ ⅊ ⅊ ⟳ ▣ filter
App_Background	102	3.52	0.52	0.40	⊙ ⅊ ⅊ ⟳ ▣ filter
SCR_DebugLog	38	1.31	0.17	0.15	⊙ ⅊ ⅊ ⟳ ▣ filter
SCR_ViewController	54	1.86	0.17	0.21	⊙ ⅊ ⅊ ⟳ ▣ filter
App_MemWarn	1	0.03	0.03	0.00	⊙ ⅊ ⅊ ⟳ ▣ filter
SCR_ViewController_Child	7	0.24	0.07	0.03	⊙ ⅊ ⅊ ⟳ ▣ filter
SCR_InteractiveNotification	19	0.66	0.07	0.08	⊙ ⅊ ⅊ ⟳ ▣ filter
FV_Ph_Strong	0	0.00	0.00	0.00	⊙ ⅊ ⅊ ⟳ ▣ filter
FV_Ph_Weak	0	0.00	0.00	0.00	⊙ ⅊ ⅊ ⟳ ▣ filter

Figure 1-6. Events—a more important report

If you look at the crash report in Figure 1-7, you will notice a "download" link for downloading the crash log. Go ahead and click that to download the log. Looks familiar, right?

Full Stack Trace

```
Full Stack Trace:
0   CoreFoundation       0x2fa3cecb <redacted> + 130
1   libobjc.A.dylib      0x3a1d7ce7 _objc_exception_throw + 38
2   CoreFoundation       0x2fa3ce0d -[NSException initWithCoder:] + 0
3   vCircle              0x0001833b -[HPVFirstViewController crashButtonWasClicked:] + 122
4   UIKit                0x322a36a7 -[UIApplication sendAction:to:from:forEvent:] + 90
5   UIKit                0x322a3643 -[UIApplication sendAction:toTarget:fromSender:forEvent:] + 38
6   UIKit                0x322a3613 -[UIControl sendAction:to:forEvent:] + 46
7   UIKit                0x3228ed5b -[UIControl _sendActionsForEvents:withEvent:] + 374
8   UIKit                0x322a305b -[UIControl touchesEnded:withEvent:] + 594
9   UIKit                0x322a2d2d -[UIWindow _sendTouchesForEvent:] + 528
10  UIKit                0x3229dc87 -[UIWindow sendEvent:] + 758
11  UIKit                0x32272e55 -[UIApplication sendEvent:] + 196
12  UIKit                0x32271521 <redacted> + 7120
13  CoreFoundation       0x2fa07faf <redacted> + 14
14  CoreFoundation       0x2fa07477 <redacted> + 206
15  CoreFoundation       0x2fa05c67 <redacted> + 630
16  CoreFoundation       0x2f970729 _CFRunLoopRunSpecific + 524
17  CoreFoundation       0x2f97050b _CFRunLoopRunInMode + 106
18  GraphicsServices     0x348df6d3 _GSEventRunModal + 138
19  UIKit                0x322d1871 _UIApplicationMain + 1136
20  vCircle              0x00018195 main + 116
21  libdyld.dylib        0x3a6d5ab7 <redacted> + 2
Crash Report Data: ⬇ download
Desym File: ⬆ upload a new desym file
```

Figure 1-7. The crash report—this is the most important report you'll work with

Viewing Crash Reports on iTunes Connect

Apple provides a service that allows you to download crash reports for the most recent app versions and builds that you distribute using TestFlight or the App Store. In theory, this should allow you to forgo using third-party crash reporting tools.

There is, however, a catch. Crash logs are not sent to Apple unless the user agrees to share crash data with app developers. TestFlight users automatically agree to share the crash data. However, for production apps (distributed via the App Store), sharing must be enabled by the user.

To do that, users must go into the Settings app, navigate to Privacy → Diagnostics & Usage, and select the Automatically Send option (see Figure 1-8).

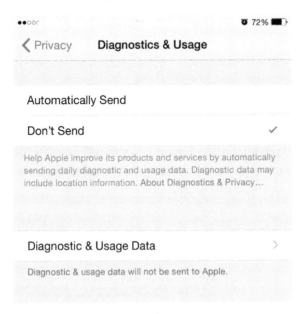

Figure 1-8. Device settings to send crash reports

There are two problems with this. First, users cannot set this option within your app —they need to go to the Settings app and then navigate to the specific setting. Second, and more importantly, this setting applies to all apps: users cannot choose specific apps to send crash reports for.

Using a third-party crash reporting tool ensures that you control the overall experience and user settings to send crash reports to the server.

Logging

Logging is an invaluable tool to know what is going on with an app.

There may only be subtle differences between logging and instrumentation. Instrumentation can be considered a subset of logging. Anything that is instrumented must also be logged.

Whereas instrumentation entails publishing key performance data for aggregated analysis, logging provides detailed information for tracing app behavior at various levels, such as debug, verbose, info, warning, and error. While logging typically runs throughout an app's execution lifecycle, instrumentation is added to particular sections of development interest.

Instrumentation data is sent to the server, whereas logging is local to the device.

For logging, we will use CocoaLumberjack, which is available via CocoaPods.

Example 1-5 shows the line to add to your Podfile to include the library. After making the change, run pod update to update the Xcode workspace.

Example 1-5. Podfile configuration for CocoaLumberjack

```
pod 'CocoaLumberjack', '~> 2.0'
```

CocoaLumberjack is an extensible framework that comes bundled with built-in *loggers* that can emit *messages* to various *destinations*. For example, use DDASLLogger to log to the Apple System Log (ASL)—the default location used by the NSLog method. Similarly, use DDFileLogger to log to a file. The loggers can be configured during app launch.

The macros DDLog<Level> can be used to log at a specific level. The higher the level, the more severe the message. The highest level is Error, while the lowest is Verbose. The minimum level for which the messages should actually be logged can be configured at a per-file level, per-Xcode-configuration level, per-logger level, or global level.

The following macros are available:

DDLogError
    Indicates an unrecoverable error

DDLogWarn
    Indicates a recoverable error.

DDLogInfo
    Indicates non-error information.

DDLogDebug
    Indicates data mostly useful for debugging.

DDLogVerbose
    Provides absolutely all details, predominantly to trace control flow during execution

The macros have the same signature as that of NSLog. This means that you can just replace NSLog with the appropriate DDLog<Level> call.

Example 1-6 shows representative code that configures and uses the library.

Example 1-6. Configuring and using CocoaLumberjack

```
//Setup
-(void)setupLogger { ❶

#if _DEBUG
    [DDLog addLogger:[DDASLLogger sharedInstance]]; ❷
#endif

    DDFileLogger fileLogger = [[DDFileLogger alloc] init]; ❸
    fileLogger.rollingFrequency = 60 * 60 * 24;
    fileLogger.logFileManager.maximumNumberOfLogFiles = 7;

    [DDLog addLogger:fileLogger]; ❹
}

//Using logger in some file

#if _DEBUG ❺
    static const DDLogLevel ddLogLevel = DDLogLevelVerbose;
#elsif MY_INTERNAL_RELEASE
    static const DDLogLevel ddLogLevel = DDLogLevelDebug;
#else
    static const DDLogLevel ddLogLevel = DDLogLevelWarn;
#end

-(void)someMethod {
  DDVerbose(@"someMethod has started execution"); ❻
  //...
  DDError(@"Ouch! Error state. Don't know what to do");
  //...
  DDVerbose(@"someMethod has reached its end state");
}
```

❶ The most likely place to call this method is `application:didFinishLaunchingWithOptions:`.

❷ Log to ASL only in debug mode, when connected to Xcode. You do not want these logs to be available on the device in production.

❸ The file logger, configured to create a new file every 24 hours (`rollingFrequency`) with a maximum of 7 files (`maximumNumberOfLogFiles`).

❹ Register the logger.

❺ Configure the log level (ddLogLevel) to an appropriate value. Here, we set up for maximum verbosity during development, less verbose (debug level) logging for internal releases (MY_INTERNAL_RELEASE is a custom flag), and only error logging for distribution builds.

❻ Log some messages. For the level DDLogLevelVerbose, all messages will be logged, whereas for DDLogLevelWarn, only the error messages will be logged.

The app delegate's application:didFinishLaunchingWithOp tions: callback is the recommended method to set up the logger.

Summary

In this chapter, we established the factors that contribute to app performance. One part of performance concerns user perception, while a larger chunk is actually making an app highly performant.

We looked at some of the key attributes that constitute and affect app performance. In the metrics involving measurement and tracking, these attributes are referred to as *key performance indicators*.

We looked at the concept of profiling and explored two broad categories of profiling techniques: sampling and instrumentation. We also looked at some code changes required to instrument our app. We then played around with the instrumented app, causing the events to be generated.

Finally, we added some boilerplate code for classes that will help in instrumentation and logging.

The chapters in the next part are focused on individual attributes that define performance. Each chapter begins by defining and reviewing the attribute, and then moves on to discuss potential problems and how to get them solved with actual code.

PART II

Core Optimizations

We will now explore the core optimizations for writing efficient apps using Objective-C. These optimizations form the foundation of any app, and they must go everywhere. It does not depend on what API you use, which tier of the app you are writing at, or what exactly you are trying to achieve—these optimizations run application-wide.

The optimizations we will discuss include the following:

- Memory management
- Energy
- Concurrent programming

CHAPTER 2

Memory Management

iPhone and iPad devices are resource-constrained on memory. An app may be terminated by the operating system if it crosses the established per-process limit.[1] As such, successfully managing memory plays a central role in implementing an iOS app.

At WWDC 2011, Apple revealed that about 90% of device crashes happened due to issues pertaining to memory management. And of these, the biggest causes are either bad memory access or memory leaks due to retain cycles.

Unlike the Java runtime (which uses garbage collection), iOS runtimes for Objective-C and Swift use reference counting. The downsides of using reference counting include possible overrelease of memory and cyclic references if the developer is not careful.

As such, it is important to understand how memory is managed in iOS.

In this chapter, we study the following:

- Memory consumption (i.e., how an app consumes memory)

- The memory management model (i.e., how the iOS runtime manages memory)

- Language constructs—we'll take a look at Objective-C constructs and the available features you can use

- Best practices for minimizing memory usage without degrading the user experience

---

1 iOS Developer Library, "Technical Note TN2151: Understanding and Analyzing iOS Application Crash Reports" (*http://apple.co/1YrGlHt*).

Memory Consumption

Memory consumption refers to the RAM that an app consumes.

The iOS virtual memory model does not include swap memory, which means that, unlike with desktop apps, the disk cannot be used to page memory. The end result is that the apps are restricted to available RAM, which is used not only by the app in the foreground but also by the operating system services and potentially also by background tasks being run by other apps.

There are two parts to memory consumption in an app: stack size and heap size. The following subsections take a closer look at each.

Stack Size

Each new thread in an app receives its own stack space consisting of both reserved and initially committed memory. The stack is freed when the thread exits. The maximum stack size for a thread is small, and among other things, it limits the following:

Maximum number of methods that can be called recursively
> Each method has its own stack frame and contributes to the overall stack space consumed. For instance, as shown in Example 2-1, if you call `main`, which in turn calls `method1` (which subsequently calls `method2`), there are three stack frames contributing a few bytes each. Figure 2-1 shows how a thread stack looks like over time.

> *Example 2-1. Call tree*

```
main() {
    method1();
}

method1() {
    method2();
}
```

Maximum number of variables that you can use within a method
> All variables are loaded on the method stack frame, and hence contribute to the stack space consumed.

Maximum number of views that you can nest in the view hierarchy
> Rendering a composite will invoke `layoutSubViews` and `drawRect` recursively across the complete hierarchy tree. If the hierarchy is deep, it may result in a stack overflow.

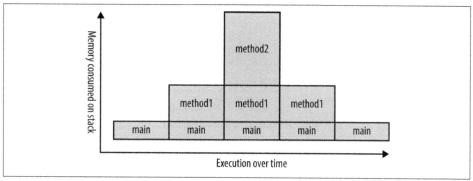

Figure 2-1. Stack with stack frame of each method

Heap Size

All threads of one process share the same heap. The total heap size available for an app is generally much lower than the device RAM. For example, an iPhone 5S may have 1 GB of RAM, but the maximum heap size allocated to an app may be 512 MB or even less. The app cannot control the heap allocated for it. It is managed by the operating system.[2]

Processes such as NSString, loading images, creating or consuming JSON/XML data, and using views will consume a lot of heap memory. If your app is an image-heavy one (something along the lines of the Flickr and Instagram apps), you will need to take special care to minimize average and peak memory usage.

Figure 2-2 shows a typical heap that may exist at some time in an app.

In Figure 2-2, the main thread started by the main method creates UIApplication. We assume that at some point in time the window comprises a UITableView that uses a UITableViewDataSource whose method tableView:cellForRowAtIndex: is called when a row must be rendered.

The data source has a reference to all the photos to be shown in a property named photos of type NSArray. If not implemented properly, this array can be huge, resulting in high peak memory usage. One solution is to always store a fixed number of images in the array and swap in and out as the user scrolls the view. This fixed number ber will determine your app's average memory usage.

---

2 Stack Overflow, "iOS Equivalent to Increasing Heap Size" (*http://stackoverflow.com/a/25369670*).

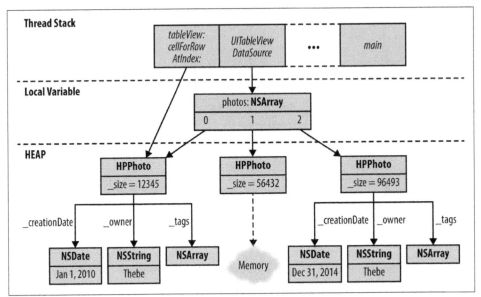

Figure 2-2. Heap demonstrating use of a model HPPhoto in a UITableViewDataSource

Each item in the array is of type HPPhoto, which represents a photo. HPPhoto stores data associated with the object—for example, image size, date of creation, owner, tags, web URL associated with the photo (not shown in the image), reference to local cache (not shown in the image), and so on.

All data related to objects created from classes is stored on the heap.

The class may have properties or instance variables (iVars) of value types such as int, char, or struct, but because the objects are created on the heap, they will consume only heap memory.

When objects are created and values assigned, they may be copied from stack to heap. Similarly, when values are used within a method, they may be copied from heap to stack. This may be an expensive operation. Example 2-2 highlights when the copy from stack to heap and vice versa happens.

Example 2-2. Heap versus stack

```
@interface AClass ❶

@property (nonatomic, assign) NSInteger anInteger; ❷
@property (nonatomic, copy) NSString *aString; ❸

@end

//some other class
```

```
-(AClass *) createAClassWithInteger:(NSInteger)i
    string:(NSString *)s { ❹

    AClass *result = [AClass new];
    result.anInteger = i; ❺
    result.aString = s; ❻
}

-(void) someMethod:(NSArray *)items { ❼
    NSInteger total = 0;
    NSMutableString *finalValue = [NSMutableString string];

    for(AClass *obj in items) {
        total += obj.anInteger; ❽
        [finalValue appendString:obj.aString]; ❾
    }
}
```

❶   The class AClass has two properties.

❷   anInteger is of type NSInteger, which is passed by value.

❸   aString is of type NSString *, which is passed by reference.

❹   The createAClassWithInteger:string: method (in some class that is not of relevance here) instantiates AClass. This method is provided with the values required to create the object.

❺   The value for i is on the stack. However, when assigned to the property, it must be copied to the heap because that is where result is stored.

❻   Although NSString * is passed by reference, the property is marked copy, which means that the value must be duplicated or cloned, depending on how the method [-NSCopying copyWithZone:] is implemented.

❼   someMethod: processes an array of AClass objects.

❽   When anInteger is used, its value must be copied to the stack before it can be processed. In this example, the value is added to total.

❾   When aString is used, it is passed by reference. In this example, appendString: uses the reference to the aString object.

It is a good idea to keep your memory requirements to not more than a percentage of available RAM. Though there is no hard rule to it, it is recommended to not use more than 80%–85%, leaving the remainder for core OS services.

Do not ignore `didReceiveMemoryWarning` signals.

Memory Management Model

In this section, we study how the iOS runtime manages memory and the effect it has on the code.

The memory management model is based on the concept of *ownership*. As long as an object is *owned*, the memory it uses cannot be reclaimed.

Whenever an object is created in a method, the method is said to *own* the object. If this object is returned from the method, then the caller is said to *claim the ownership*. The value can be assigned[3] to another variable, and the corresponding variable is likewise said to have claimed the ownership.

Once the task with the object is completed, you *relinquish* ownership. This process does not transfer ownership, but increases or decreases the number of owners, respectively. When the number of owners goes down to zero, the object is deallocated (*http://bit.ly/nsobject-dealloc*) and the memory is released.

This ownership count is more formally referred to as the *reference count*. When you manage it yourself, it is called *manual reference counting* (MRC). Although it is rarely used today, MRC is useful to understand. Modern-day apps use *automatic reference counting* (ARC), which we discuss in "Automatic Reference Counting" on page 39.

Example 2-3 demonstrates the basic structure of manual memory management using reference counting.

Example 2-3. Reference counting with manual memory management

```
NSString *message = @"Objective-C is a verbose yet awesome language"; ❶
NSString *messageRetained = [message retain]; ❷
[messageRetained release]; ❸
[message release]; ❹
NSLog(@"Value of message: %@", message); ❺
```

❶ Object created, ownership claimed by `message`, reference count of 1.

❷ Ownership claimed by `messageRetained`, reference count increases to 2.

---

3 The term *assigned* is used loosely here. We will explore it later.

---

❸ Ownership relinquished by messageRetained, reference count decreases to 1.

❹ Ownership relinquished by message, reference count decreases to 0.

❺ The value of message, strictly speaking, is undetermined. You may still get the same value as before because the memory may not have been reused or reset.

Example 2-4 demonstrates how methods affect the reference count.

Example 2-4. Reference count in methods

```
//part of a class Person
-(NSString *) address {
    NSString *result = [[NSString alloc]
            initWithFormat:@"%@\n%@\n%@, %@",
            self.line1, self.line2, self.city, self.state]; ❶
    return result;
}

-(void) showPerson:(Person *) p {
    NSString *paddress = [p address]; ❷

    NSLog(@"Person's Address: %@", paddress);

    [paddress release]; ❸
}
```

❶ Object first created; reference count of memory pointed to by result is 1.

❷ Reference count of memory referenced via paddress (referring to result) is still 1. The method showPerson: is the owner of the object it creates using the address button. It should not retain.

❸ Renounce the ownership; reference count goes down to 0.

If you look at Example 2-4, showPerson: does not know if address creates a new object or reuses one. However, it does know that the object would have been returned to it after incrementing the reference count by 1. As such, it does not retain the address. Once the job is completed, it releases it. If the object had a reference count of 1, it will become 0 and object will be dealloced.

Official Apple and LLVM documentation prefers the term *ownership*. The terms *ownership* and *reference count* are used interchangeably in the book.

Autoreleasing Objects

Autoreleasing objects allows you to relinquish the ownership of an object but defer its destruction. It is useful in scenarios in which you create an object in a method and want to return it. It helps in the management of an object's life in MRC.

In the strict sense of naming conventions of Objective-C, in Example 2-4, there is nothing to denote that the `address` method owns the returned string. The caller, `show Person:`, therefore has no reason to release the returned string, resulting in a potential memory leak. `[paddress release]` is a piece of code that has been added for illustrative purposes.

So, what is the correct code for the method `address`?

There are two possibilities:

- Do not use `alloc` or associated methods.
- Return an object with a deferred `release` message.

The first fix is easy to implement when working with `NSString`. The updated code is shown in Example 2-5.

Example 2-5. Fixed code for reference count in methods

```
-(NSString *) address {
    NSString *result = [NSString
            stringWithFormat:@"%@\n%@\n%@, %@",
            self.line1, self.line2, self.city, self.state]; ❶
    return result;
}

-(void) showPerson:(Person *) p {
    NSString *paddress = [p address];

    NSLog(@"Person's Address: %@", paddress);
    ❷
}
```

❶ Do not use the `alloc` method.

❷ Do not use the `release` method within the `showPerson:` method that does not create the entity.

However, this fix is not easy to apply when not working with `NSString`, as it is generally difficult to find the appropriate method that will serve the need. For example, when working with a third-party library or with a class that has multiple methods to create an object, it may not always be clear which method `retains` the ownership.

And this is where deferred destruction comes into play.

The NSObject protocol defines the message autorelease that can be used for deferred release. Use it when returning an object from a method.

The updated code using autorelease is given in Example 2-6.

Example 2-6. Reference counting using autorelease

```
-(NSString *) address
{
    NSString *result = [[[NSString alloc]
            initWithFormat:@"%@\n%@\n%@, %@",
            self.line1, self.line2, self.city, self.state]
        autorelease];
    return result;
}
```

The code can be analyzed as follows:

1. You own the object (NSString, in this case) returned by the alloc method.
2. To ensure no memory leak, you must relinquish the ownership before losing the reference.
3. However, if you use release, the object will be dealloced before return and the method, as a result, will return an invalid reference.
4. autorelease signifies that you want to relinquish ownership but at the same time allow the caller of the method to use the returned object before it is dealloced.

Use autorelease when creating an object and returning from a non-alloc method. It ensures that the object will be released and, if applicable, memory reclaimed once the caller method is done working with it.

Autorelease Pool Blocks

The autorelease pool block is a tool that allows you to relinquish ownership of an object but avoid it being dealloced immediately. This is a very useful feature when returning objects from a method.

It also ensures that the objects created within the block are dealloced as may be needed once the block is complete. This is useful when you need to create several objects. Local blocks can be created to dealloc the objects as early as possible and keep the memory footprint low.

An autorelease pool block is marked using `@autoreleasepool`.

If you open the *main.m* file in the sample project, you will notice the code shown in Example 2-7.

Example 2-7. @autoreleasepool block in main.m

```
int main(int argc, char * argv[]) {
    @autoreleasepool {
        return UIApplicationMain(argc, argv, nil,
            NSStringFromClass([HPAppDelegate class]));
        }
}
```

All objects that were sent an `autorelease` message within the block will be sent a `release` message at the end of the `autoreleasepool` block. More importantly, a `release` message will be sent for each `autorelease` call. This means that if an object was sent an `autorelease` message more than once, the `release` message will be sent more than once. This is good, as it will keep the reference count of the object down to the same as it was before the `autoreleasepool` block. If the count is 0, the object will be `dealloced`, keeping a low memory footprint.

If you look at the code in the `main` method, you'll see that the entire app is within the `autoreleasepool` block. This means that any `autorelease` object will be `dealloced` at the end, resulting in no memory leak.

Like other code blocks, `autoreleasepool` blocks can be nested, as shown in Example 2-8.

Example 2-8. Nested autoreleasepool blocks

```
@autoreleasepool {
 // some code
 @autoreleasepool {
  // some more code
        }
}
```

Because control passes from one method to another, it is uncommon to use nested `autoreleasepool` blocks in the same method. However, the called method may have its own `autoreleasepool` block for early object deallocations.

Autorelease Pool Blocks Are Omnipresent

The Cocoa framework expects code execution within an `autoreleasepool` block, or else `autorelease` objects are not released and the app starts leaking memory.

The AppKit and UIKit frameworks process each event-loop iteration within an `autoreleasepool` block. As a result, there is generally no need to create one yourself.

There are some occasions where you will likely want to create `autoreleasepool` blocks of your own. For example:

When you have a loop that creates lot of temporary objects
> Use an `autoreleasepool` block within the loop to deallocate the memory for each iteration. Although the eventual memory use before and after the iteration may still be the same, the maximum memory requirement for your app may be reduced by a large factor.
>
> Example 2-9 provides examples of bad as well as good code to write when using `autoreleasepool` blocks.

When you create a thread
> Each thread will have its own `autoreleasepool` block stack. The main thread starts with its own `autoreleasepool` because it comes from the generated code. However, for any custom thread, you have to create your own `autoreleasepool`.
>
> See Example 2-10 for sample code.

Example 2-9. Autorelease pool block in a loop

```
//Bad code ❶
{
    @autoreleasepool {
        NSUInteger *userCount = userDatabase.userCount;

        for(NSUInteger *i = 0; i < userCount; i++) {
            Person *p = [userDatabase userAtIndex:i];

            NSString *fname = p.fname;
            if(fname == nil) {
                fname = [self askUserForFirstName];
            }

            NSString *lname = p.lname;
            if(lname == nil) {
                lname = [self askUserForLastName];
            }
```

```
        //...
        [userDatabase updateUser:p];
      }
    }
}

//Good code ❷
{
    @autoreleasepool {
        NSUInteger *userCount = userDatabase.userCount;

        for(NSUInteger *i = 0; i < userCount; i++) {

            @autoreleasepool {
                Person *p = [userDatabase userAtIndex:i];

                NSString *fname = p.fname;
                if(fname == nil) {
                    fname = [self askUserForFirstName];
                }

                NSString *lname = p.lname;
                if(lname == nil) {
                    lname = [self askUserForLastName];
                }
                //...
                [userDatabase updateUser:p];
            }
        }
    }
}
```

❶ This code is bad because there is only one autoreleasepool and the memory cleanup happens after all the iterations of the loop are complete.

❷ In this case, there are two autoreleasepools. The inner autoreleasepool ensures that the memory cleanup happens after each iteration. This results in less memory requirements.

Example 2-10. Autorelease pool block in custom thread

```
-(void)myThreadStart:(id)obj {
    @autoreleasepool {
        //New thread's code
    }
}

//Somewhere else
{
    NSThread *myThread = [[NSThread alloc] initWithTarget:self
```

```
        selector:@selector(myThreadStart:)
        object:nil];

    [myThread start];
}
```

Automatic Reference Counting

Keeping track of `retain`, `release`, and `autorelease` is not easy. What is even more puzzling is determining where, when, and to whom to send these messages.

Apple introduced Automatic Reference Counting (ARC) at WWDC 2011 as a solution to this problem. Swift, the new language for iOS apps, also uses ARC. Unlike Objective-C, Swift does not support MRC.

ARC is a compiler feature.[4] It evaluates the lifetime requirements of the objects in the code and automatically injects appropriate memory management calls at compile time. The compiler also generates appropriate `dealloc` methods. This means that most of the difficulties related to keeping track of memory usage (e.g., ensuring that it is deallocated when not required) are eliminated.

Figure 2-3 demonstrates the relative development time with MRC versus ARC. Development with ARC is faster because of reduced code.

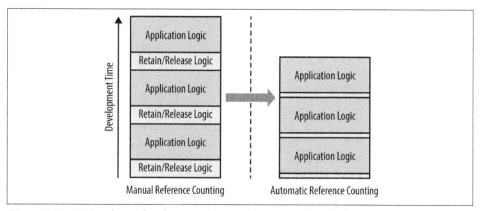

Figure 2-3. ARC reduces development time and prevents headaches

You'll need to ensure that ARC is enabled in the Xcode project settings, which is the default starting with Xcode 5 (see Figure 2-4).

---

4 The complete specification on Automatic Reference Counting is available on the LLVM site (*http://bit.ly/obj-c-arc*).

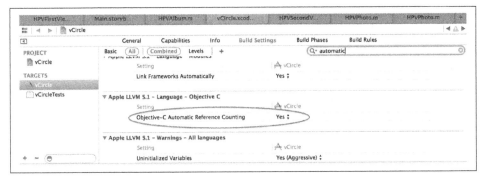

Figure 2-4. Project settings for ARC in Xcode

Working with Non-ARC Dependencies

It may be very difficult to find a dependency that does not use ARC or does not have an alternative solution.

But if you do happen to find such a dependency, you will need to disable ARC on one or more files.

To disable ARC, go to Targets → Build Phases → Compile Sources, select the files where ARC must be disabled, and add the compiler flag `-fno-objc-arc`, as shown in Figure 2-5.

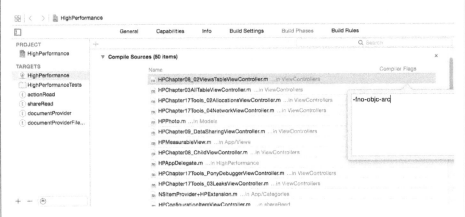

Figure 2-5. Disabling ARC on one file

The same option can be used to create a mixed-mode class where a category can be introduced for MRC code. The code in the category can be written in its own file and ARC can be disabled for that file.

Rules of ARC

ARC enforces a few rules that you must follow when writing your code. The intention of these rules is to provide a reliable memory management model. In some cases, they just enforce best practice, while in others they simplify the code or are direct corollaries of you not having to work directly with memory management.[5] These rules are enforced by the compiler, resulting in a compile-time error rather than a runtime crash. These are the compiler rules when working with ARC:

- You cannot implement or invoke `retain`, `release`, `autorelease`, or `retainCount` methods. This restriction is not only limited to working with objects but also with selectors. So, `[obj release]` or `@selector(retain)` are compile-time errors.

- You can implement `dealloc` methods but cannot invoke them. This restriction extends not only to other objects but also to the superclass when implementing one. `[super dealloc]` is a compile-time error.

  You can still use `CFRetain`, `CFRelease`, and related methods with Core Foundation–syle objects.

- You cannot use `NSAllocateObject` or `NSDeallocateObject`. Use `alloc` for creating objects. The runtime takes care of deallocation.

- You cannot use object pointers in C structs.

- There is no casual casting between `id` and `void *`. If necessary, you must do an explicit cast.

- You cannot use `NSAutoreleasePool`. Use `anautoreleasepool` block instead.

- You cannot use `NSZone` memory zones.

- You cannot have a property accessor name starting with `new`, to ensure interoperability with MRC. This is demonstrated in Example 2-11.

- Though something to avoid in general, you still can mix ARC and MRC code (we discussed this in "Working with Non-ARC Dependencies" on page 40).

Example 2-11. Accessor name with ARC enabled

```
//Not allowed
@property NSString * newTitle;

//Allowed
@property (getter=getNewTitle) NSString * newTitle;
```

---

5 iOS Developer Library, "Transitioning to ARC Release Notes" (*http://apple.co/1KfifW3*).

Keeping these rules in mind, we can update Example 2-5. The resultant code is shown in Example 2-12.

Example 2-12. Updated code with ARC enabled

```
-(NSString *) address
{
    NSString *result = [[NSString alloc] initWithFormat:@"%@\n%@\n%@, %@",
        self.line1, self.line2, self.city, self.state]; ❶
    return result;
}

-(void) showPerson:(Person *) p
{
    NSString *paddress = [p address];

    NSLog(@"Person's Address: %@", paddress);
        ❷
}
```

❶ There is no need for autorelease. You cannot call autorelease or retain on the object result.

❷ You cannot call release on paddress.

Reference Types

ARC introduced a new reference type: *weak references*. Understanding the available reference types is important to memory management. The supported types are:

Strong references
> A strong reference is the default reference created. Memory referred to by a strong reference cannot be relinquished. A strong reference increases the reference count by 1, resulting in extension of the object's lifetime.

Weak references
> A weak reference is a special reference that does not increase the reference count (and hence does not extend the object's lifetime). Weak references are a very important part of ARC-enabled Objective-C programming, as we explore later.

Other Types of References

Objective-C does not currently support other types of references. However, you may be interested in exploring the following other types:

Soft references

A soft reference is exactly like a weak reference, except that it is less eager to throw away the object to which it refers. An object that is only weakly reachable will be discarded at the next garbage collection cycle, but an object that is softly reachable will generally stick around for a while.

Phantom references

These are the weakest references in terms of strength, and are the first ones to be cleaned up. A phantomly referenced object is similar to a `dealloced` object, but without the memory actually being reclaimed.

These reference types do not have signifance in a reference count–based system. They are more suited for a garbage collector.

Variable Qualifiers

ARC also introduced four lifetime qualifiers for variables:

__strong

This is the default qualifier and does not need explicit mention. An object is kept in memory as long as there is a strong pointer to it. Consider it ARC's version of the `retain` call.

__weak

This indicates that the reference does not keep the referenced object alive. A weak reference is set to `nil` when there are no strong references to the object. Consider it ARC's version of an assignment operator, except with the added safety that the pointer is automatically set to `nil` when the object is `dealloced`.

__unsafe_unretained

This is similar to __weak except that the reference is *not* set to `nil` when there are no strong references to the object. Consider it ARC's version of an assignment operator.

__autoreleasing

Used for message arguments passed by reference using `id *`. It is expected that the method `autorelease` will have been called in the method where the argument is passed.

The syntax for using these qualifiers is as follows:

```
TypeName * qualifier variable;
```

The code in Example 2-13 shows these qualifiers in use.

Example 2-13. Using variable qualifiers

```
Person * __strong p1 = [[Person alloc] init]; ❶
Person * __weak p2 = [[Person alloc] init]; ❷
Person * __unsafe_unretained p3 = [[Person alloc] init]; ❸
Person * __autoreleasing p4 = [[Person alloc] init]; ❹
```

❶ Object created has a reference count of 1 and will not be `dealloced` until the point p1 is last referenced.

❷ Object created has a reference count of 0, will be immediately `dealloced` and p2 will be set to `nil`.

❸ Object created has a reference count of 1, will be immediately `dealloced` but p3 will *not* be set to `nil`.

❹ Object created has a reference count of 1 and will be automatically released once the method returns.

Property Qualifiers

Two new ownership qualifiers have been introduced for property declaration: `strong` and `weak`. In addition, the semantics of the `assign` qualifier have been updated. In all, there are now six qualifiers:

`strong`
> Default, indicates a __strong relationship.

`weak`
> Indicates a __weak relationship.

`assign`
> This is not a new qualifier, but the meaning has now changed. Before ARC, `assign` was the default ownership qualifier. With ARC enabled, `assign` now implies __unsafe_unretained.

`copy`
> Implies a __strong relationship. Additionally, it implies the usual behavior of copy semantics (*http://bit.ly/nsobject-copy*) on the setter.

`retain`
> Implies a __strong relationship.

`unsafe_unretained`
> Implies an __unsafe_unretained relationship.

Example 2-14 shows these qualifiers in action. Because `assign` and `unsafe_unre`
`tained` only copy over the value without any sanity check, they should only be used
for value types (`BOOL`, `NSInteger`, `NSUInteger`, etc.). They must be avoided for reference types, specifically pointers such as `NSString *` and `UIView *`.

Example 2-14. Using property qualifiers

```
@property (nonatomic, strong) IBOutlet UILabel *titleView;
@property (nonatomic, weak) id<UIApplicationDelegate> appDelegate;
@property (nonatomic, assign) UIView *danglingReference; ❶
@property (nonatomic, assign) BOOL selected; ❷
@property (nonatomic, copy) NSString *name;
@property (nonatomic, retain) HPPhoto *photo; ❸
@property (nonatomic, unsafe_unretained) UIView *danglingReference;
```

❶ Wrong usage of `assign` with a pointer.

❷ Correct usage of `assign` with a value.

❸ `retain` is a relic from the pre-ARC era and is rarely used in modern code. It is
added here for completeness.

Getting Your Hands Dirty

OK, now that we have learned a bit about the new lifetime qualifiers for variables and
properties, let's put them to use, update our project, and see the effects.

Photo Model

Let's create a class called `HPPhoto` that represents a photo in an album. A photo has a
`title`, a `url`, and a list of `comments`. We also override the method `dealloc` to see
what's going on behind the scenes.

Start by adding a new Objective-C class:

```
File → New → iOS → Cocoa Touch → Objective-C class
```

A typical declaration of the class is given in Example 2-15.

Example 2-15. Class HPPhoto

```
//HPPhoto.h
@interface HPPhoto : NSObject

@property (nonatomic, strong) HPAlbum *album;
@property (nonatomic, strong) NSURL *url;
@property (nonatomic, copy) NSString *title;
```

```
@property (nonatomic, strong) NSArray *comments;

@end

//HPPhoto.m
@implementation HPPhoto

-(void) dealloc
{
    DDLogVerbose(@"HPPhoto dealloc-ed");
}

@end
```

Storyboard Update

Add a label and four buttons to the view of the First View Controller in the story-board. The buttons will trigger creation of these variables while the label will be used to display the result. The final UI should look similar to that shown in Figure 2-6.

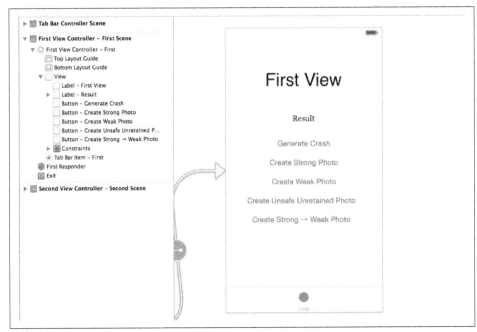

Figure 2-6. Updated view of First View Controller

We also add appropriate IBOutlet and IBAction references in the code, as shown in Example 2-16.

Example 2-16. Reference updates in HPFirstViewController.h

```
@interface HPFirstViewController : UIViewController

@property (nonatomic, strong) IBOutlet UILabel *resultLabel;

-(IBAction)createStrongPhoto:(id)sender;
-(IBAction)createStrongToWeakPhoto:(id)sender;
-(IBAction)createWeakPhoto:(id)sender;
-(IBAction)createUnsafeUnretainedPhoto:(id)sender;

@end
```

Method Implementations

For each method, we will do the following:

1. Create an instance of `HPPhoto` and assign it to a local reference.
2. Set the `title` of the photo.
3. In the `resultLabel`, display whether the reference is `nil` or not. If it is not `nil`, display the `title` as well.

Let's now look at the code for each method (Example 2-17 through Example 2-20). The implementation is largely the same for each of them, the only difference being the type of reference created. Note that we will not create a method to return the reference. We explore the reference within the method where the memory was allocated and the reference created. We also make ample use of `NSLog` to track the order of lifecycle events.

In addition, we cover a special case where a strong reference is assigned to a weak reference in order to see what happens to the object.

The results from the code are covered in "Output Analysis" on page 49.

Example 2-17. Implementation for createStrongPhoto:

```
-(IBAction)createStrongPhoto:(id)sender
{
    DDLogDebug(@"%s enter", __PRETTY_FUNCTION__);
        HPPhoto * __strong photo = [[HPPhoto alloc] init];
    DDLogDebug(@"Strong Photo: %@", photo);
        photo.title = @"Strong Photo";

        NSMutableString *ms = [[NSMutableString alloc] init];
        [ms appendString:(photo == nil ? @"Photo is nil" : @"Photo is not nil")];
        [ms appendString:@"\n"];
        if(photo != nil) {
                [ms appendString:photo.title];
```

```
    }
    self.resultLabel.text = ms;
    DDLogDebug(@"%s exit", __PRETTY_FUNCTION__);
}
```

Example 2-18. Implementation for createWeakPhoto:

```
-(IBAction)createWeakPhoto:(id)sender
{
    DDLogDebug(@"%s enter", __PRETTY_FUNCTION__);
        HPPhoto * __weak wphoto = [[HPPhoto alloc] init];
    DDLogDebug(@"Weak Photo: %@", wphoto);
        wphoto.title = @"Weak Photo";

        NSMutableString *ms = [[NSMutableString alloc] init];
        [ms appendString:(wphoto == nil ? @"Photo is nil" : @"Photo is not nil")];
        [ms appendString:@"\n"];
        if(wphoto != nil) {
                [ms appendString:wphoto.title];
        }
        self.resultLabel.text = ms;
        DDLogDebug(@"%s exit", __PRETTY_FUNCTION__);
}
```

Example 2-19. Implementation for createStrongToWeakPhoto:

```
-(void)createStrongToWeakPhoto:(id)sender
{
    DDLogDebug(@"%s enter", __PRETTY_FUNCTION__);
        HPPhoto * sphoto = [[HPPhoto alloc] init];
    DDLogDebug(@"Strong Photo: %@", sphoto);
        sphoto.title = @"Strong Photo, Assigned to Weak";

        HPPhoto * __weak wphoto = sphoto;
        DDLogDebug(@"Weak Photo: %@", wphoto);

        NSMutableString *ms = [[NSMutableString alloc] init];
        [ms appendString:(wphoto == nil ? @"Photo is nil" : @"Photo is not nil")];
        [ms appendString:@"\n"];
        if(wphoto != nil) {
                [ms appendString:wphoto.title];
        }
        self.resultLabel.text = ms;
    DDLogDebug(@"%s exit", __PRETTY_FUNCTION__);
}
```

Example 2-20. Implementation for createUnsafeUnretainedPhoto:

```
-(void)createUnsafeUnretainedPhoto:(id)sender
{
    DDLogDebug(@"%s enter", __PRETTY_FUNCTION__);
```

```
    HPPhoto * __unsafe_unretained wphoto = [[HPPhoto alloc] init];
  DDLogDebug(@"Unsafe Unretained Photo: %@", wphoto);
    wphoto.title = @"Strong Photo";

    NSMutableString *ms = [[NSMutableString alloc] init];
    [ms appendString:(wphoto == nil ? @"Photo is nil" : @"Photo is not nil")];
    [ms appendString:@"\n"];
    if(wphoto != nil) {
            [ms appendString:wphoto.title];
    }
    self.resultLabel.text = ms;
  DDLogDebug(@"%s exit", __PRETTY_FUNCTION__);
}
```

Output Analysis

The output is shown in Figure 2-7.

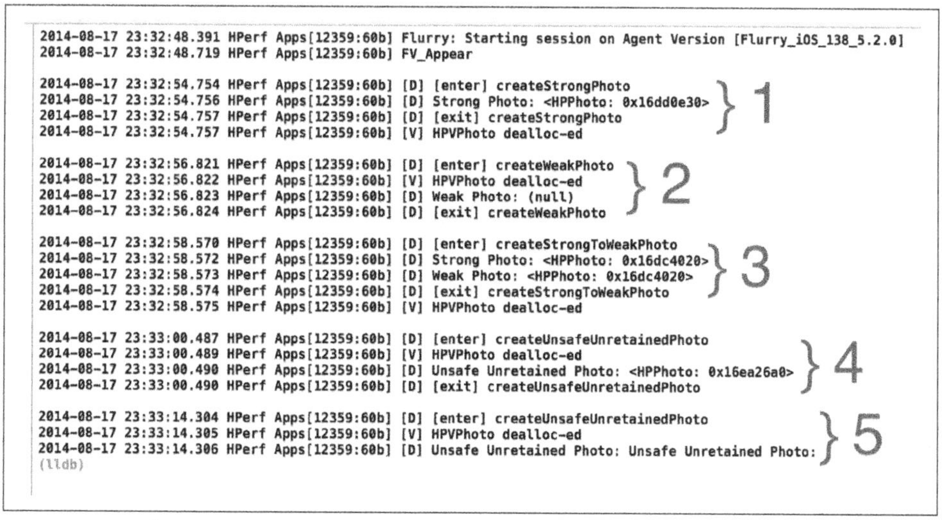
```
2014-08-17 23:32:48.391 HPerf Apps[12359:60b] Flurry: Starting session on Agent Version [Flurry_iOS_138_5.2.0]
2014-08-17 23:32:48.719 HPerf Apps[12359:60b] FV_Appear

2014-08-17 23:32:54.754 HPerf Apps[12359:60b] [D] [enter] createStrongPhoto
2014-08-17 23:32:54.756 HPerf Apps[12359:60b] [D] Strong Photo: <HPPhoto: 0x16dd0e30>
2014-08-17 23:32:54.757 HPerf Apps[12359:60b] [D] [exit] createStrongPhoto
2014-08-17 23:32:54.757 HPerf Apps[12359:60b] [V] HPVPhoto dealloc-ed

2014-08-17 23:32:56.821 HPerf Apps[12359:60b] [D] [enter] createWeakPhoto
2014-08-17 23:32:56.822 HPerf Apps[12359:60b] [V] HPVPhoto dealloc-ed
2014-08-17 23:32:56.823 HPerf Apps[12359:60b] [D] Weak Photo: (null)
2014-08-17 23:32:56.824 HPerf Apps[12359:60b] [D] [exit] createWeakPhoto

2014-08-17 23:32:58.570 HPerf Apps[12359:60b] [D] [enter] createStrongToWeakPhoto
2014-08-17 23:32:58.572 HPerf Apps[12359:60b] [D] Strong Photo: <HPPhoto: 0x16dc4020>
2014-08-17 23:32:58.573 HPerf Apps[12359:60b] [D] Weak Photo: <HPPhoto: 0x16dc4020>
2014-08-17 23:32:58.574 HPerf Apps[12359:60b] [D] [exit] createStrongToWeakPhoto
2014-08-17 23:32:58.575 HPerf Apps[12359:60b] [V] HPVPhoto dealloc-ed

2014-08-17 23:33:00.487 HPerf Apps[12359:60b] [D] [enter] createUnsafeUnretainedPhoto
2014-08-17 23:33:00.489 HPerf Apps[12359:60b] [V] HPVPhoto dealloc-ed
2014-08-17 23:33:00.490 HPerf Apps[12359:60b] [D] Unsafe Unretained Photo: <HPPhoto: 0x16ea26a0>
2014-08-17 23:33:00.490 HPerf Apps[12359:60b] [D] [exit] createUnsafeUnretainedPhoto

2014-08-17 23:33:14.304 HPerf Apps[12359:60b] [D] [enter] createUnsafeUnretainedPhoto
2014-08-17 23:33:14.305 HPerf Apps[12359:60b] [V] HPVPhoto dealloc-ed
2014-08-17 23:33:14.306 HPerf Apps[12359:60b] [D] Unsafe Unretained Photo: Unsafe Unretained Photo:
(lldb)
```


Figure 2-7. Lifetime qualifiers for variables

It's mostly self-explanatory, with some interesting observations:

1. A `__strong` reference (method `createStrongPhoto:`) ensures that the object is not destroyed until it goes out of scope. The object was `dealloced` only *after* the method completed.
2. A `__weak` reference (method `createWeakPhoto:`) does not contribute to the reference count. Because the memory was allocated in the method and pointed to a `__weak` reference, the reference count was 0 and the object was immediately `dealloced`, even before it could be used in the very next statement.

3. In the method `createStrongToWeakPhoto:`, even though the `__weak` reference does not increase the reference count, the `__strong` reference created earlier ensures that the object is not released before the method ends.

4. The results of the method `createUnsafeUnretainedPhoto:` are more interesting. Notice that the object was `dealloced` immediately, but because the memory was still not reclaimed, the reference was usable and did not result in an error.

5. However, when we call the method again, we see not only that the object has been `dealloced` but also that the memory has been reclaimed and repurposed. As such, using the reference resulted in an illegal access, causing the app to crash with a signal of `SIGABRT`. This is possible if the memory is reclaimed at a later time (after the object deallocation but before the object access).

Looking at Figure 2-8, you will notice that the memory was reclaimed just before the `title` property was set, resulting in an *unrecognized selector sent to instance* error because the memory is gone and may be now used by some other object.

```
<UIKit/UIView.h> may also be helpful.
2014-08-24 15:51:40.709 HPerf Apps[85481:60b] FV_Appear
2014-08-24 15:51:43.512 HPerf Apps[85481:60b] FV_Ph_UU
2014-08-24 15:51:43.513 HPerf Apps[85481:60b] [D] [enter] createUnsafeUnretainedPhoto
2014-08-24 15:51:43.513 HPerf Apps[85481:60b] [V] HPVPhoto dealloc-ed
2014-08-24 15:51:43.513 HPerf Apps[85481:60b] [D] Unsafe Unretained Photo: <HPPhoto:
0x10ea32180>
2014-08-24 15:51:43.513 HPerf Apps[85481:60b] -[__NSCFString setTitle:]: unrecognized
selector sent to instance 0x10ea32180
```

Figure 2-8. __unsafe_unretained crash

Zombies

Zombie objects are a debugging feature to help catch memory errors.

Normally when an object's reference count drops to 0 it is freed immediately, but that makes debugging difficult. If zombie objects are enabled, instead of the object's memory being instantly freed, it's just marked as a zombie. Any further attempts to use it will be logged, and you can track down where in the code the object was used past its lifetime.

`NSZombieEnabled` is an environment variable that controls whether the Core Foundation runtime will use zombies. `NSZombieEnabled` should not be left in place permanently, as by default no objects will ever be truly deallocated, which will cause your app to use tremendous amounts of memory. Specifically, remember to disable `NSZom bieEnabled` for archived release builds.

To set the NSZombieEnabled environment variable, navigate to Product → Scheme → Edit Scheme. Choose the Run section on the left, and the Diagnostics tab on the right. Select the Enable Zombie Objects entry, as shown in Figure 2-9.

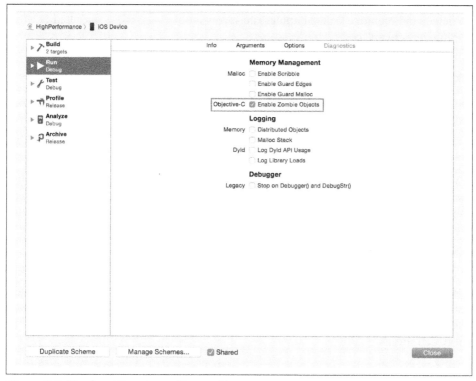

Figure 2-9. Xcode settings to enable zombies

Rules of Memory Management

Now that we know the details of these lifetime qualifiers, it is important to review some basic rules of memory management.

As per Apple's official documentation, there are four basic rules of memory management:

- You *own* any object you create, using, for example, new, alloc, copy, or mutable Copy.

- You *can take ownership* of any object using retain in MRC or a __strong reference in ARC.

- You *must relinquish ownership* of an owned object when you no longer need it using release in MRC. It's not necessary to do anything special in ARC. The ownership will be relinquished after the last reference to the owned object (i.e., the last line in a method).

- You *must not relinquish ownership* of any object that you do not own.

To help avoid memory leaks or app crashes, you should keep these rules handy when writing Objective-C code.

Retain Cycles

One of the biggest gotchas with reference counting is that it cannot handle cyclic references, or what are known as *retain cycles* in Objective-C. In this section, we look at common scenarios where retain cycles may be introduced and best practices to avoid them.

If you closely look at the rules described in the previous section, you'll see that they are nothing more than the implementation of reference counting. A claim of ownership increments the reference count, whereas relinquishing ownership decrements the reference count. When the reference count goes down to zero, the object is `dealloced` and the memory is released.

In our app, the `HPAlbum` entity may have a `coverPhoto` and an array of `photos` to represent the album's cover photo and other photos associated with it. Similarly, `HPPhoto` may represent a photo that belongs to an `album`, apart from having other attributes (e.g., the URL, title, comments, etc.). Example 2-21 shows representative code for the entity definitions.

Example 2-21. Retain cycle

```
@class HPPhoto;

@interface HPAlbum : NSObject

@property (nonatomic, copy) NSString *name;
@property (nonatomic, strong) NSDate *creationTime;
@property (nonatomic, copy) HPPhoto *coverPhoto; ❶
@property (nonatomic, copy) NSArray *photos; ❷

@end


@interface HPPhoto : NSObject

@property (nonatomic, strong) HPAlbum *album; ❸
@property (nonatomic, strong) NSURL *url;
@property (nonatomic, copy) NSString *title;
@property (nonatomic, copy) NSArray *comments;
```

@end

❶ HPAlbum has a strong reference to the coverPhoto, of the type HPPhoto.

❷ It also has references to several other HPPhoto objects within the photos array.

❸ HPPhoto has a strong reference to the album to which it belongs.

Let's take a simple scenario of one album with two photos: p1 (the cover photo) and p2. The reference count is as follows:

- p1 has strong references in photos and coverPhoto. The reference count is 2.
- p2 has a strong reference in photos. The reference count is 1.
- album has strong references in both p1 and p2. The reference count is 2.

We discussed strong references earlier, in "Reference Types" on page 42.

To start with, let's also say that these objects are created in some method named crea teAlbum. Even if the objects are never used after a certain point, the memory will not be released because the reference count never goes down to 0. Figure 2-10 demonstrates this relationship.

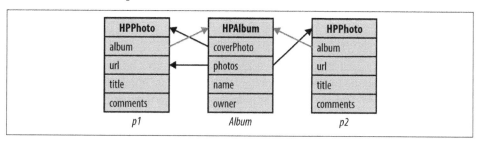

Figure 2-10. Album and photo references

Rules to Avoid Retain Cycles

The previous section demonstrated where retain cycles may be introduced. In this section, we review the rules for writing code that avoids retain cycles:

- An object should not have a strong reference to (retain) its parent. Use *weak references* to refer to the parent (see "Reference Types" on page 42).

  In the previous scenario, a photo is *contained* in an album, and we can consider the photo as the child. As such, the reference from a photo to its album should be weak. A weak reference does not contribute toward reference count.

  The updated reference count becomes:

1. `p1` has strong references in `photos` and `coverPhoto`. The reference count is 2.

2. `p2` has a strong reference in `photos`. The reference count is 1.

3. `album` does not have any strong references. The reference count is 0.

   As such, when the `album` object is no longer used, it is `dealloced`. Once the `album` is freed, the reference counts of `p1` and `p2` drop to 0 and they are `dealloced`.

- As a corollary, a hierarchical child object should retain an ancestor.

- Connection objects should not retain their target. The target should be regarded as the owner. Connection objects include:

1. Objects that use delegates. The delegate should be considered to be the target, and hence, the owner.

2. As a corollary of the previous guideline, objects with a target and an action. An example would be a `UIButton`; it invokes the action method on its target. The button should not retain its target.

3. Observed items in the observer pattern. The observer is the owner and observes changes on the observed item.

- Use definitive destroy methods to terminate the cycles.

   In the case of a doubly linked list, there will be retain cycles by definition. Similarly, retain cycles will exist in a circular linked list.

   In such cases, when you know that the object will never be used (when the head of the list is about to go out of scope), write code to break the links in the list. Create a method (say, `delink`) that *unlinks* itself from the next item in the list. Do this recursively using a visitor pattern to avoid infinite recursion.

Common Scenarios for Retain Cycles

There are more than a handful of common scenarios that can result in retain cycles. For example, using threads, timers, simple blocks, or delegates might result in retain cycles. Let's explore each of these scenarios and the steps that need to be taken to prevent the retain cycles.

Delegates

Delegates are probably the most common place for introducing retain cycles. At app start, it's common to retrieve the latest data from the server and update the UI. A similar refresh may be triggered when, for example, the user taps the refresh button.

Consider this specific scenario: a view controller that shows a list of records and has a refresh button that refreshes the list upon tap.

For the implementation, let there be two classes: `HPDataListViewController` for the UI and `HPDataUpdateOp` to simulate the network call. Example 2-22 shows the code for the view controller, and Example 2-23 shows the code for the update operation.

Example 2-22. App refresh invocation

```
//HPDataListViewController.h
@interface HPDataListViewController : UIViewController  ❶

@property (nonatomic, strong) HPDataUpdateOp *updateOp;  ❷
@property (nonatomic, strong) BOOL refreshing;

- (IBAction)onRefreshClick:(id)sender;

@end

//HPDataListViewController.m
@implementation HPDataListViewController

//Code of viewDidLoad omitted for brevity

- (IBAction)onRefreshClicked:(id)sender {  ❸
    DDLogDebug(@"%s enter", __PRETTY_FUNCTION__);  ❹
    if([self.refreshing == NO]) {
        self.refreshing = YES;
        if(self.updateOp == nil) {
            [self.updateOp = [[HPDataUpdateOp new];
        }
        [self.updateOp startWithDelegate:self
            withSelector:@selector(onDataAvailable:)];  ❺
    }
    DDLogDebug(@"%s exit", __PRETTY_FUNCTION__);  ❹
}

- (void)onDataAvailable:(NSArray *)records {  ❻
    //Update UI using latest records
    self.refreshing = NO;
    self.updateOp = nil;
}

@end
```

❶ `HPDataListViewController` shows data in a list.

❷ `updateOp` is the network operation that fetches the records.

❸ The method called when the user taps the `refreshButton`.

❹ Log to monitor the execution sequence.

❺ The updateOp method can invoke a callback when the results are available.

❻ onDataAvailable is the callback method. It updates the view controller state and UI.

Example 2-23. Update operation

```
//HPDataUpdateOp.m
@implementation HPDataUpdateOp

-(void)startWithDelegate:(id)delegate withSelector:(SEL)selector {
 dispatch_async(
  dispatch_get_global_queue(DISPATCH_QUEUE_PRIORITY_DEFAULT, 0), ^{ ❶
        //perform some operation ❷
                dispatch_async(dispatch_get_main_queue(), ^{ ❸
                if([delegate respondsToSelector:selector]) {
                        [delegate performSelector:selector
     withObject:[NSArray arrayWithObjects:nil]; ❹
                }
        });
        });
}

-(void)dealloc {
        DDLogDebug(@"%s called", __PRETTY_FUNCTION__);
}

@end
```

❶ All long-running tasks should be done outside of the main thread.

❷ Let's say it took 2 seconds for the operation.

❸ Once results are available, switch the context back to the main thread, and...

❹ ... invoke the selector.

If you look at the method onRefreshClicked, it passes self to updateOp. At the same time, HPDataListViewController holds a reference to updateOp. This is where the cyclic reference is created.

For the solution, one option is to not have updateOp as a property but instead to create an instance of HPDataUpdateOp in the onRefreshClicked: method, so that updateOp holds a reference to the HPDataListViewController object, but not vice versa. The updated code is shown in Example 2-24.

Example 2-24. App refresh without property

```
- (IBAction)onRefreshClicked:(id)sender {
    DDLogDebug(@"%s enter", __PRETTY_FUNCTION__);
    if(self.refreshing == NO) {
        self.refreshing = YES;
        HPDataUpdateOp *updateOp = [[HPDataUpdateOp new]; ❶
        [updateOp startWithDelegate:self withSelector:@selector(onDataAvailable:)];
    }
    DDLogDebug(@"%s exit", __PRETTY_FUNCTION__);
}
```

❶ Create a local variable so that it is not retained.

This does solve the problem of introducing a retain cycle, but it presents another problem. The updateOp object is never referenced elsewhere, and as a result, the moment control exits the onRefreshClicked: method, its reference count goes down to 0 and it may be dealloced immediately. The output is shown in Figure 2-11.

```
2014-09-01 22:59:43.330 HPerf Apps[29264:60b] [D] [onRefreshClicked] enter
2014-09-01 22:59:43.331 HPerf Apps[29264:60b] [D] [onRefreshClicked] exit
2014-09-01 22:59:43.332 HPerf Apps[29264:60b] [D] [FriendsUpdateOp::dealloc] called
```

Figure 2-11. Result using local variable

HPDataUpdateOp, as demonstrated here, is simplistic. Typically, the app will have a network queue on which the update operation will be queued for execution. And it is possible that by the time the operation is complete, the user may have moved to a different view controller. If that is the case, ideally the view controller should be dealloced immediately, but because it is being used by the operation, it will not be. Now imagine this being true for several view controllers being *retained* by these operations on the queue. This does not create retain cycles, but does increase peak memory requirements. And this is also a definite bug, because if there is no view controller, the operation should ideally release the object.

So, strictly speaking, this doesn't work either. What's the cause? The issue is the strong reference to the HPDataListViewController object being held by the HPDataUpdateOp. But it cannot be weak either, because then there may be no link between these objects at all.

The solution is to have a strong reference to the operation in the delegate (which is the view controller in our case) and a weak reference to the delegate in the operation.

When the operation is ready to invoke the callback method, it should get the strong reference to the delegate.

Additionally, we should introduce a cancel method in HPDataUpdateOp that can be called when the view controller is about to be dealloced. Example 2-25 shows the updated code to this effect.

Example 2-25. Final HPDataListViewController and HPDataUpdateOp

```
//HPDataListViewController
-(IBAction)onRefreshClicked:(id)sender {
 DDLogDebug(@"%s enter", __PRETTY_FUNCTION__);
        self.updateOp = [[HPDataUpdateOp new]; ❶
        [self.updateOp startUsingDelegate:self
            withSelector:@selector(onDataAvailable:)];
        DDLogDebug(@"%s exit", __PRETTY_FUNCTION__);
}

-(void)onDataAvailable:(NSArray *)records {
 DDLogDebug(@"%s called", __PRETTY_FUNCTION__);
        self.resultLabel.text = @"[- onDataAvailable] called";
        self.updateOp = nil; ❷
}

-(void)dealloc {
 DDLogDebug(@"%s called", __PRETTY_FUNCTION__);
        if(self.updateOp != nil) {
                [self.updateOp cancel]; ❸
        }
}

//HPDataUpdateOp.h
@protocol HPDataUpdateOpDelegate <NSObject>

-(void)onDataAvailable:(NSArray *)records;

@end

@interface HPDataUpdateOp

@property (nonatomic, weak) id<HPDataUpdateOpDelegate> delegate; ❹

-(void)startUpdate;
-(void)cancel;

@end

//HPDataUpdateOp.m
@implementation HPDataUpdateOp
-(void)startUpdate {
        dispatch_async(
```

```
          dispatch_get_global_queue(DISPATCH_QUEUE_PRIORITY_DEFAULT, 0), ^{
                     //perform network call, and then report the result
        //NSArray *records = ...
                     dispatch_async(dispatch_get_main_queue(), ^{
          id<HPDataUpdateOpDelegate> delegate = self.delegate; ❺
          if(!delegate) { ❻
                               return;
                     } else { ❼
                               [delegate onDataAvailable:records];
                     }
                });
        });
}

-(void)cancel { ❽
 //cancel inflight network request
        self.delegate = nil;
}
```

❶ Use property for the operation. Operation is *owned* by the view controller.

❷ Set property to nil once job is done. Enables deallocation of the operation object.

❸ Cancel operation if view controller is about to be dealloced.

❹ Operation keeps a weak reference to the callback delegate.

❺ Try to get a strong reference for the delegate.

❻ If the original object is still around…

❼ … use that to report onDataAvailable.

❽ The cancel operation explicitly calls for the callback objects to be dereferenced.

In essence, we implemented the first rule of "Rules to Avoid Retain Cycles" on page 53. HPDataListViewController is the owner, while HPDataUpdateOp is the object owned (i.e., the child in the ownership hierarchy).

Figure 2-12 shows the result when the response is ready before the user navigates back. Figure 2-13 shows the output when the user navigates back before the response is available.

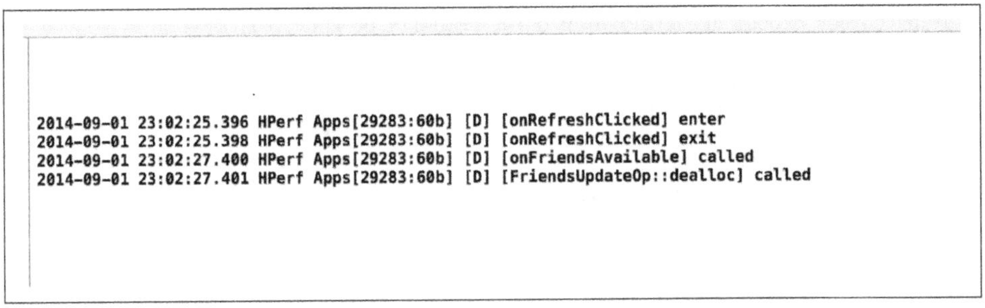

```
2014-09-01 23:02:25.396 HPerf Apps[29283:60b] [D] [onRefreshClicked] enter
2014-09-01 23:02:25.398 HPerf Apps[29283:60b] [D] [onRefreshClicked] exit
2014-09-01 23:02:27.400 HPerf Apps[29283:60b] [D] [onFriendsAvailable] called
2014-09-01 23:02:27.401 HPerf Apps[29283:60b] [D] [FriendsUpdateOp::dealloc] called
```

Figure 2-12. Result using updated code with view controller available after operation completes

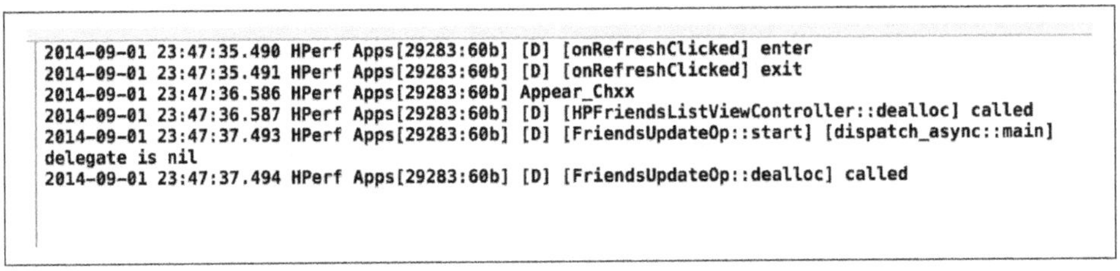

```
2014-09-01 23:47:35.490 HPerf Apps[29283:60b] [D] [onRefreshClicked] enter
2014-09-01 23:47:35.491 HPerf Apps[29283:60b] [D] [onRefreshClicked] exit
2014-09-01 23:47:36.586 HPerf Apps[29283:60b] Appear_Chxx
2014-09-01 23:47:36.587 HPerf Apps[29283:60b] [D] [HPFriendsListViewController::dealloc] called
2014-09-01 23:47:37.493 HPerf Apps[29283:60b] [D] [FriendsUpdateOp::start] [dispatch_async::main]
delegate is nil
2014-09-01 23:47:37.494 HPerf Apps[29283:60b] [D] [FriendsUpdateOp::dealloc] called
```

Figure 2-13. Result using updated code with view controller deallocated before operation completes

Although this might seem straightforward, it becomes more complicated as the execution goes through various layers and results in a complex object graph. It is very important to ensure that you do not *retain* the references in the lowest layers of networking, database, and storage that are used by the higher layers of the user interface (i.e., the layers whose usage *creates* objects).

Blocks

Similar to the problem that arises out of improper use of delegate objects is that of *capturing* outer variables when using blocks.

Consider the simple code in Example 2-26.

Example 2-26. Variable capturing using blocks

```
-(void)someMethod {
    SomeViewController *vc = [[SomeViewController alloc] init];
    [self presentViewController:vc animated:YES
        completion:^{
            self.data = vc.data;
            [self dismissViewControllerAnimated:YES completion:nil];
        }];
}
```

Unfortunately, this again results in long-lived objects—the child view controller will not die off because it is shown to the user, and the parent view controller will not clean up because it is *captured* in the *completion* block. In a scenario where SomeView Controller may perform long-running tasks such as image processing or complex view rendering, with the parent view controller memory not cleared, the application may run the risk of low memory.

The solution, shown in Example 2-27, is similar to what we discussed in the previous section.

Example 2-27. Variable capturing using blocks

```
-(void)someMethod {
    SomeViewController *vc = [[SomeViewController alloc] init];

    __weak typeof(self) weakSelf = self; ❶

    [self presentViewController:vc animated:YES
        completion:^{
            typeof(self) theSelf = weakSelf; ❷

            if(theSelf != nil) { ❸
                theSelf.data = vc.data; ❹
                [theSelf dismissViewControllerAnimated:YES completion:nil];
            }
        }];
}
```

❶ Grab a weak reference.

❷ Grab the strong reference from the weak. Note that __strong is implicit. It increases the reference count...

❸ ...but only if it was not already nil. If so...

❹ ...proceed with subsequent operations.

Threads and timers

Inappropriate use of NSThread and NSTimer objects can also result in retain cycles. Some common ways of running async operations include the following:

- Using dispatch_async on the *global queue*, unless you write advanced code to manage custom queues
- Using NSThread to spin off async executions whenever and wherever you want

- Using `NSTimer` to execute a piece of code periodically

Consider a news app with a UI that shows the newsfeed of the logged-in user and autorefreshes it every 2 minutes.

Example 2-28 presents some commonly used code for performing a periodic update.

Example 2-28. Using NSTimer

```
@implementation HPNewsFeedViewController

-(void)startCountdown {
 self.timer = [NSTimer scheduledTimerWithTimeInterval:120
  target:self
  selector:@selector(updateFeed:)
  userInfo:nil repeats:YES];
}

-(void)dealloc {
    [self.timer invalidate];
}

@end
```

The retain cycle in Example 2-28 is obvious—the object retains the timer and the timer retains the object. Similar to the case of Example 2-22, we cannot solve the problem by not having a property. In fact, we will need the property so that it can be `invalidated` later.

For our code, the run loop (*http://bit.ly/objc-run-loop*) will also `retain` the timer and will not `release` it until `invalidate` is called.

This creates a secondary retained reference to the timer object, resulting in a retain cycle even without an explicit reference in our code.

> NSTimer objects result in indirect references held by the runtime. These are strong references, resulting in the reference count of the target going up not by 1 but by 2. You must `invalidate` the timer to remove the reference.

For a moment, assume that the code in Example 2-28 belongs to a *view controller* and the view controller is created several times in the app because of user interaction. Imagine the amount of memory leaked.

And don't get excited if you use `NSThread`. Exactly the same problem happens here as well. There are two solutions to the problem:

- Include a deterministic call to `invalidate`.
- Split the code into separate classes.

Let's explore both.

Do not rely on `dealloc` to clean up these objects. Why? If a retain cycle has been established, `dealloc` will never be called and the timers will never be `invalidated`. Because the run loop keeps track of *live* timers and threads, they are never destroyed by just `niling` their references in the code. To solve this, you can create a custom method that will perform this cleanup in a more deterministic manner.

For the case of a view controller, a good place to call this method is when the user moves away from the view controller, either by pressing the Back button or by taking any other action (the point is that the class knows when this happens). Let's call this method `cleanup`. An implementation is provided in Example 2-29.

Example 2-29. Cleaning up NSTimer

```
-(void)didMoveToParentViewController:(UIViewController *) parent { ❶
 if(parent == nil) {
  [self cleanup];
 }
}

-(void)cleanup {
 [self.timer invalidate];
}
```

❶ `didMoveToParentViewController` is called whenever the view controller moves into or out of the `parent` view controller.

In Example 2-29, we do the cleanup when the user navigates out from this view controller into its parent by overriding the `didMoveToParentViewController:` method. This call is far more deterministic than the `dealloc` call.

The other way out is to change the target of the Back button, as shown in Example 2-30.

Example 2-30. Cleaning up by intercepting the Back button

```
-(id)init {
    if(self = [super init]) {
        self.navigationItem.backBarButtonItem.target = self;
        self.navigationItem.backBarButtonItem.action
            = @selector(backButtonPressDetected:); ❶
    }
    return self;
```

```
}

-(void)backButtonPressDetected:(id)sender {
    [self cleanup]; ❷
    [self.navigationController popViewControllerAnimated:TRUE];
}
```

❶ Intercept the Back button press of the navigation controller.

❷ Clean up before popping up the view controller.

The next, cleaner option is to split the task ownership into multiple classes—a *task* class that actually performs the action, and the *owner* class that executes the task.

The latter option is preferred because:

- It is cleaner and has well-defined ownership of responsibilities.
- The *task* can be reused across multiple *owners* whenever needed.

We can break the previous code into two classes: HPNewsFeedViewController shows the latest feed, and HPNewsFeedUpdateTask runs periodically and checks for the latest feed that is fed into the view controller.

To this effect, the refactored code will now be as shown in Example 2-31.

Example 2-31. Refactored code for using timers

```
//HPNewsFeedUpdateTask.h
@interface HPNewsFeedUpdateTask

@property (nonatomic, weak) id target; ❶
@property (nonatomic, assign) SEL selector;

@end

//HPNewsFeedUpdateTask.m
@implementation HPNewsFeedUpdateTask

-(void)initWithTimeInterval:(NSTimeInterval)interval
    target:(id)target selector:(SEL)selector { ❷

    if(self = [super init]) {
        self.target = target;
        self.selector = selector;

        self.timer = [NSTimer scheduledTimerWithTimeInterval:interval
            target:self selector:@selector(fetchAndUpdate:)
            userInfo:nil repeats:YES];
    }
```

```
        return self;
}

-(void)fetchAndUpdate:(NSTimer *)timer { ❸
    //Retrieve feed
    HPNewsFeed *feed = [self getFromServerAndCreateModel];
    __weak typeof(self) weakSelf = self; ❹

    dispatch_async(dispatch_get_main_queue(), ^{
        __strong typeof(self) sself = weakSelf;
        if(!sself) {
            return;
        }

        if(sself.target == nil) {
            return;
        }

        id target = sself.target; ❺
        SEL selector = sself.selector;

        if([target respondsToSelector:selector]) {
            [target performSelector:selector withObject:feed];
        }
    });
}

-(void)shutdown { ❻
    [self.timer invalidate];
    self.timer = nil;
}
@end

//HPNewsFeedViewController.m
@implement HPNewsFeedViewController

-(void)viewDidLoad { ❼
    self.updateTask = [HPNewsFeedUpdateTask initWithTimeInterval:120
        target:self selector:@selector(updateUsingFeed:)];
}

-(void)updateUsingFeed:(HPNewsFeed *)feed { ❽
    //update the UI
}

-(void)dealloc { ❾
    [self.updateTask shutdown];
}
@end
```

Let's take a look at a detailed analysis of HPNewsFeedUpdateTask:

1. The `target` property ❶ is weakly referenced. It is the `target` that instantiates the task here and *owns* it.

2. `initWithTimeInterval:` ❷ is the preferred method to be used. It takes the necessary inputs and starts the timer.

3. The `fetchAndUpdate:` method ❸ is executed periodically.

4. When using async blocks, we must ensure that we do not introduce a retain cycle. We have a __weak reference ❹ to be used inside the block.

5. In the method `fetchAndUpdate:` ❼, the local variables for the `target` and the `selector` are created before calling `respondsToSelector:` and performing the operation.

    This is done to avoid a race condition arising during the following possible sequence of execution:

    a. Invoking [`target respondsToSelector:selector`] in some thread A.

    b. Changing either `target` or `selector` in some thread B.

    c. Invoking [`target performSelector:selector withObject:feed`] in thread A. With this code, even if either `target` or `selector` is changed, `performSelector` will be called on the correct `target` and `selector`.

6. The `shutdown` method ❺ invalidates the timer. The run loop deferences it, resulting in it being the only reference held by the *task* object.

On the usage side, `HPNewsFeedViewController` uses `HPNewsFeedUpdateTask`. The controller is not referenced by any object other than its parent controller. So, when the user navigates out of the controller (say, when the Back button is pressed), the reference count goes down to zero and it is `dealloced`. This in turn causes the update task to be shut down, which causes the timer to be `invalidated`, triggering the `dealloc` chain across all the associated objects (including the `timer` and the `updateTask`).

Let's now look at an analysis of the `HPNewsFeedViewController` code in Example 2-31:

1. In the `viewDidLoad` method ❼, the task is initialized, which internally triggers the timer.

2. The `updateUsingFeed:` method ❽ is the callback invoked periodically by the `HPNewsFeedUpdateTask` object.

3. `dealloc` ❽ is responsible for invoking the `shutdown` method on the task, which internally `invalidates` the timer. Note that `dealloc` is deterministic here because the object is not referenced anywhere else.

When using `NSTimer` and `NSThread`, always use a layer of indirection with deterministic invalidation. The indirection layer ensures a weak link, causing the owner object to be `dealloced` when not used in the app.

Observers

Apart from using delegates and callbacks for subscribing to changes for more complex data, there are two built-in options available for listening to changes in the system. They are termed *built-in* because the observee does not keep track of observers by writing any custom code—the runtime provides support to manage them. These options are:

- Key-value observing
- The notification center

Key-value observing

Objective-C allows adding observers on any `NSObject` subclassed object using the method `addObserver:forKeyPath:options:context:`. The observer gets a notification in the method `observeValueForKeyPath:ofObject:change:context:`. The method `removeObserver:forKeyPath:context:` can be used to unregister or remove the observer. This is known as *key-value observing* (KVO).

This is an extremely useful feature, especially for the purposes of debugging, to keep track of an object that may be shared across various sections of your app (e.g., user interface, business logic, persistence, and networking).

An example of such an object may be a custom class that keeps the details of the current state of the app—for example, whether the identity of the user is logged in or not, the user that is logged in, items in the shopping cart in an ecommerce app, or the user to whom the last message was sent in a messaging app. For debugging, you may add an observer to this object to keep track of any changes or updates.

KVO is also useful in bidirectional data binding. The views allow attaching delegates to respond to user interactions that can result in model updates. KVO can be used for the reverse binding to update the UI whenever the model is updated.

From the official documentation (*http://apple.co/1IBd0lC*):

> The key-value observing `addObserver:forKeyPath:options:context:` method does not maintain strong references to the observing object, the observed objects, or the context. You should ensure that you maintain strong references to the observing, and observed, objects, and the context as necessary.

This means that the observer must live long enough to continue to monitor the changes. You should take extra care in deciding where you would like the observer to be dereferenced last for memory relinquishment.

Example 2-32 implements KVO using a central `ObserverManager` class that returns an `ObserverObserveeHandle` that can be referred to by the owner. When the observation initiator (the view controller in the example) needs to observe a `keyPath`, it invokes the `addObserverToObject:forKey:` method and stores the `ObserverObserveeHandle`, which is `dealloced` when the view controller is. The handle removes the observer during deallocation.

Essentially, we are trying to solve a similar problem of reference routing as that encountered in the case of `NSTimer`. However, there is a weak reference established, and as such the observer may be `dealloced` prematurely if not handled appropriately.

Example 2-32. Key-value observer

```
@interface ObserverObserveeHandle

@property (nonatomic, strong) MyObserver *observer;
@property (nonatomic, strong) NSObject *obj;
@property (nonatomic, copy) NSString *keyPath;

-(id)initWithObserver:(MyObserver *)observer
 target:(NSObject *)obj
 keyPath:(NSString *)keyPath;

@end

@implementation ObserverObserveeHandle

-(id)initWithObserver:(MyObserver *)observer
 target:(NSObject *)obj
 keyPath:(NSString *)keyPath {
  //Omitted for brevity
}

-(void)removeObserver {
 [self.obj removeObserver:self forKeyPath:self.keyPath context:nil];
 self.obj = nil;
}

-(void)dealloc {
 [self removeObserver];
}
@end

@interface ObserverManager
//Omitted for brevity
```

```
@end

@implementation ObserverManager
NSMutableArray *observers;

+(ObserverObserveeHandle)addObserverToObject:(NSObject *)obj
 forKey:(NSString *)keyPath {
 MyObserver *observer = [[MyObserver alloc] init];
 [obj addObserver:observer forKeyPath:keyPath
   options:(NSKeyValueObservingOptionNew | NSKeyValueObservingOptionOld)
   context:NULL];

 ObserverObserveeHandle *details = [[ObserverObserveeHandle alloc]
   initWithObserver:observer target:obj keyPath:keyPath];
 [observers addObject:details];

 return details;
}

@interface SomeViewController

@property (nonatomic, strong) IBOutlet UILabel *resultLabel;
@property (nonatomic, strong) ObserverObserveeHandle *resultLabelMonitor;

@end

@implementation SomeViewController

-(void)viewDidLoad {
 self.resultLabelMonitor = [ObserverManager
   addObserverToObject:self.nameTextField
   forKey:@"text"];
}

@end
```

 Whenever you add a key-value observer to a target, the target must have a life at least as long as that of the observer because it should be possible to remove the observer from the target. This can result in the target having a longer life than originally intended, and is something to watch out for.

Example 2-32 seems to provide a great solution because it takes away the burden of cleanup by utilizing well-written code that is bound not to fail. There is, however, still a gotcha. The catch with this code is that for all notifications to the observer, the exact same piece of code executes (i.e., the code defined in the MyObserver class).

How can we solve this problem? Think about it. Hint: use *blocks*. And in the block, if you need to invoke a method that uses `self`, do not forget to create a weak reference to `self` before referring to it internally in the block.

As such, the code for registering the observer may be updated to that shown in Example 2-33.

Example 2-33. Key-value observer with block

```
@implementation SomeViewController

-(void)viewDidLoad
{
    __weak typeof(self) weakSelf = self;
    self.resultLabelMonitor = [ObserverManager
        addObserverToObject:self.nameTextField
        forKey:@"text" block:^(NSDictionary *changes) {

            typeof(self) sSelf = weakSelf;
            if(sself) {
                NSLog(@"Text changed to %@",
                    [changes objectForKey:NSKeyValueChangeNewKey]);

                //use sSelf if need be
                sSelf.resultLabel.text = @"Name changed";
            }
        }];
}

@end
```

Notification center

The second option is to use the notification center. An object can register as an observer with the notification center (an `NSNotificationCenter` object) and receive `NSNotification` objects. Similar to the key-value observer, the notification center does not keep a strong reference to the observer. This means that we are not responsible for ensuring that the observer is not `dealloced` earlier or later than intended.

The solution pattern is similar to what we discussed in the previous subsection.

Returning Errors

When working with methods that take `NSError **` parameters and fill in the error variable if there is one, always use the `__autoreleasing` qualifier. The most common place to use this pattern is when you need to process an input and return a value with a possibility of error.

A typical method will have a signature similar to that shown in Example 2-34.

Example 2-34. Returning errors

```
-(Matrix *)transposeMatrix:(Matrix *)matrix error:(NSError * __autoreleasing *) error
{
    //process
    //if error
    *error = [[NSError alloc] initWithDomain:@"transpose" code:123 userInfo:nil];
}
```

Pay close attention to the syntax. The keyword __autoreleasing is squeezed between the two asterisks. Always remember this:

```
NSError * __autoreleasing *error;
```

As you will notice, the variable and property qualifiers play an important role in helping with the life cycle management of an object and ensuring the object's precise lifetime—neither too short nor too long. Whenever in doubt, go back to the drawing board, get back to the basics, and define your properties and variables accordingly. At times, you may need to create properties with strong references and lengthen the life, while at other times you may need to use weak references and ensure appropriate memory usage and no memory leaks.

Weak Type: id

There are several cases where we use the type id. It is not uncommon to see this used in the Cocoa framework itself. For example, in the Xcode-generated code, the IBAction methods have a parameter of type id to denote the sender.

Another scenario is working with objects in an NSArray.[6] Consider the code in Example 2-35.

Example 2-35. Using an object in an NSArray

```
@interface HPDataListViewController
    : UITableViewController <UITableViewDataSource, UITableViewDelegate>

@property (nonatomic, copy) NSArray *input;

@end

@implementation HPDataListViewController

-(void)tableView:(UITableView *)tableView
    didSelectRowAtIndexPath:(NSIndexPath *)indexPath
```

---

6 iOS 9 introduces lightweight generics for Objective-C collections for interoperability with Swift. See iOS Developer Library, "Lightweight Generics" (*http://apple.co/1Otxtuh*).

```
{
    NSUInteger value = [self.input objectAtIndex:indexPath.row].someProperty;
    //proceed
}
```

@end

In the method `tableView:didSelectRowAtIndexPath:`, we expect the array `input` to consist of objects of some type—let's call it `ClassX`—that has a property `someProperty`.

This code looks great, and if you try it out, you will most likely get the correct result. We know that as long as the object at the corresponding index responds to the `someProperty` selector, this code will work as intended. But if the object does not respond to the selector it may result in an app crash.

It is assumed that the compiler does not need to know the type information, because the runtime will know which object and method to invoke. But the fact is that the compiler does require a fair bit of detail—specifically, it must know the sizes of all the parameters and the type of the return value so that it can have correct instruction sets for pushing and popping the values on to and off of the stack. For example, if the method takes two parameters of type `int`, 8 bytes need to be pushed to the stack.

Normally, we do not need to take any steps for this to happen, though. The compiler obtains the parameter information by looking at the name of the method we are trying to invoke, searching through the included headers for methods matching the invoked method name, and then getting the parameter lengths from the first matching method it finds.

The good part is that this works most of the time. It fails when there are multiple classes that have exactly the same method signature (i.e., name and parameters).

Consider a scenario in which, at compile time, the compiler zeros in not on the `ClassX` class but say, for example, the `ClassY` object. The method may not return an `NSUInteger`, but maybe an `NSInteger` or even an `NSString`. In another scenario where we expect an `NSUInteger`, it may return a reference to an object that we are supposed to `invalidate` or `cleanup` ourselves (e.g., `CGColor` or `CGContext`), resulting in a memory leak.

Solution to the Problem

Why does the type mismatch happen? How can the compiler be so naïve? It does the hard work of resolving the object for the message to be sent. The compiler is responsible for generating accurate instructions (i.e., the correct values to pass to the `objc_msgSend` method).

Fortunately, it is not hard to solve the problem of incorrect type matching by the compiler. There are two parts to the solution.

First, we must configure the compiler to report an error if it finds multiple matches for selectors on id objects. This is controlled by the Strict Selector Matching setting, which is turned off by default. It corresponds to the -Wstrict-selector-match flag passed to the compiler. Turn it on to generate warnings when the compiler finds two selectors that have different parameter or return types.

Figure 2-14 shows the project settings in Xcode.

Figure 2-14. Xcode settings for strict selector matching

There are a few issues related to the use of this option:

- Built-in frameworks will result in several warnings, even though the majority of them will never cause you any trouble.
- You will still not be able to catch issues when working with a class rather than an object.
- It will not help if you did not import the header with the correct definition.

That brings us to the second part of the solution: give enough information to the compiler to generate messages against correct types. You can do that by using a strong type (ClassX in our case). Example 2-36 shows the changes to be made to the code.

Example 2-36. Using strong types

```
-(void)tableView:(UITableView *)tableView
    didSelectRowAtIndexPath:(NSIndexPath *)indexPath

{
    ClassX *item = (ClassX *) [self.input objectAtIndex:indexPath.row];
    NSUInteger value = item.someProperty;
    //Proceed
}
```

In a nutshell, when working with methods that are commonly named, be sure to avoid using id. Use a specific class instead.

Object Longevity and Leaks

The longer the objects live in memory, the higher are the chances of memory never being cleaned up. Avoid long-lived objects as much as possible. Of course, you will need references to key operations all over your code, and you will not want to waste time re-creating them each time. Due diligence must be done on their usage.

One of the most common scenarios of long-lived objects is singletons. Loggers are a good example of this—they are created once but never destroyed. We discuss these kinds of scenarios in depth in the next section.

Another scenario is using global variables. Global variables are dreaded in programming.

For a variable to qualify as global, it must meet the following criteria:

- It is not owned by another object.
- It is not a constant.
- There is exactly one in the entire app, not just per app component.

If a variable does not meet these requirements, it should not be made into a global variable.

Complex object graphs provide fewer opportunities for reclaiming memory, and hence increase the risk of crashes due to memory exhaustion. App responsiveness can suffer if the main execution thread is forced to wait for subthread operations such as network or database access.

Singletons

The singleton pattern is a design pattern that restricts the instantiation of a class to one object. In practice, the instantiation occurs near the start of the app and the object never dies.

Having an object that has a very long life compared to the overall life of the app is never a good idea. And if the object becomes the source of other objects (more like a service locator), there is risk of memory buildup if the locator is not correctly implemented.

Singletons are necessary—there is no doubt about it. But how they are implemented plays an important role in determining how they will be used.

Before we fully discuss the problems that singletons introduce, let's take a step back to better understand what singletons are and why we really need them.

Singletons are useful when exactly one object is needed to coordinate actions across the system. We need singletons in several scenarios:

- Queuing operations (e.g., logging and instrumentation)
- Shared resource access (e.g., cache)
- Pooling constrained resources (e.g., thread pool or connection pool)

Singletons, once built up and ready to use, continue to live until the app is shut down. Loggers, instrumentation services, and the cache are good examples of singletons.

More importantly, these singletons are generally initialized at app startup, as other components that intend to use them get them ready. This increases the app load time.

What is the way out? There is no one solution that can be used. The memory constraints become visible as you start integrating more and more off-the-shelf solutions, especially if you do not have their source code.

Here are some guidelines that you can use:

- Avoid singletons as much as possible.
- Identify the sections that need memory—for example, an in-memory-buffer for instrumentation (used before flushing to the server).

  Look for ways to minimize the memory overhead. Note that you will have to trade off with something else. If you keep the buffer smaller, you will have to make more frequent server trips.
- Avoid object-level properties as much as possible, as they will stay with the object forever. Try to use local variables.

Dependency Injection

Singletons may not be avoidable, but it is at least possible to avoid using them directly.

You should avoid writing code like that shown in Example 2-37.

Example 2-37. Improper use of dependencies

```
-(void)someMethod {
    XXSomeClass *obj = [XXSomeClass sharedInstance]; ❶
    NSString *someValue = [obj operation:@"some parameter"];
```

```
    //proceed
}
```

❶   someMethod uses XXSomeClass for the operation method.

In Example 2-37, someMethod depends on an external class XXSomeClass that it does not control to manage app settings. It works great, but it poses a few problems:

- If the class XXSomeClass needs some initialization, someMethod assumes that it is already done. However, the fact that it uses XXSomeClass is not known to the upstream methods using someMethod, which may leave XXSomeClass uninitialized.

- If the class XXSomeClass holds on to some resources, it will continue to do so even when the sharedInstance is no longer used anywhere else.

To avoid such pitfalls, use *dependency injection* (DI), which in essence is about passing down the dependencies wherever needed. Depending on the scope of the dependency, it can be *injected* using a custom initializer or by invoking a method.

If the dependency object is used in several places in the dependent class, the best place to inject is a custom initializer. If it is required in only a couple of operations and it is OK to possibly provide different instances for the operations, inject per-method.

The updated code in Example 2-38 illustrates both options for injecting the dependencies: it uses Typhoon (*http://typhoonframework.org*) and Objection (*http://objection-framework.org*), two popular and actively developed DI frameworks.

Example 2-38. Updated code using dependency injection

```
@interface MyClass

-(instancetype)initWithSomeClass:(XXSomeClass *)someClass; ❶

-(void)someMethod;
-(void)anotherMethodWithAnotherClass:(AnotherClass *)anotherClass; ❷

@end

@interface MyClass ()

@property (nonatomic, strong) XXSomeClass *someClass;

@end

@implementation MyClass

-(instancetype)initWithSomeClass:(XXSomeClass *)someClass {
    if(self = [super init]) {
```

```
        self.someClass = someClass;
    }
    return self;
}

-(void)someMethod { ❸
    NSString *someValue = [self.someClass operation:@"some parameter"];
    //proceed
}

-(void)anotherMethodWithAnotherClass:(AnotherClass *)anotherClass { ❹
    NSString *someValue = [self.someClass operation:@"some parameter"];
    NSString *anotherValue = [anotherClass anotherOp:@"another parameter"];
    //proceed
}

@end
```

❶ Custom initializer that requires an XXSomeClass object to be passed.

❷ anotherMethodWithAnotherClass uses the AnotherClass object, and requires it to be passed as a parameter.

❸ someMethod now uses the property someClass to invoke the method operation.

❹ anotherMethodWithAnotherClass can now use someClass as well as another object of type AnotherClass to complete its task.

Finding Mystery Retains

A class may have been well designed, and the objects well retained, and there may or may not be memory leaks. It may, however, be a good idea to be able to get the reference graph. This brings us to the question, is it possible to find all the retains on an object?

The answer lies in the pre-ARC method retain. All we have to do is get the count of the method invocation. ARC does not allow you to override or call it, but you can temporarily disable ARC for the project (see Figure 2-15 for the details).

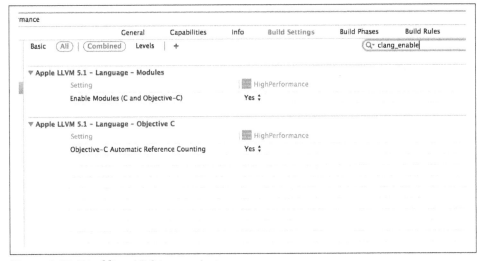

Figure 2-15. Disabling ARC in a project

Then, add the code given in Example 2-39 to all your custom classes. The code not only logs the call to the `retain` method but also prints the call stack so that you can get details of where exactly it has been invoked, and not only how many times.

Example 2-39. Use retain to get the reference count

```
#if !__has_feature(objc_arc)
-(id) retain
{
    DDLogInfo(@"%s %@", __PRETTY_FUNCTION__, [NSThread callStackSymbols]);
        return [super retain];
}
#endif
```

Best Practices

By following these best practices, you will largely avoid any trouble with memory leaks, retain cycles, and large memory requirements (you may want to print out a copy of this section to hang in your workstation for quick reference):

- Avoid huge singletons. Specifically, do not have *God objects* (i.e., objects that do too much or have too much state information). This is an *antipattern*, a common solution pattern that gets counterproductive sooner rather than later.

  Helper singletons like *loggers*, *instrumentation services*, and *task queues* are good, but *global state objects* are bad.

- Use `__strong` references to *child* objects.

- Use __weak references to *parent* objects.

- Use __weak references to *off-the-graph* objects such as delegates.

- For scalar properties (`NSInteger`, `SEL`, `CGFloat`, etc.), use the `assign` qualifier.

- For block properties, use the `copy` qualifier.

- When declaring methods with `NSError **` parameters, use `__autoreleasing` with the correct syntax: `NSError* __autoreleasing *`.

- Avoid directly referencing outer variables in a block. `weakify` them outside the block and then `strongify` them inside the block. See the `libextobjc` library (*https://github.com/jspahrsummers/libextobjc*) for helper macros `@weakify` and `@strongify`.

- Follow these guidelines for deterministic cleanup:

  — Invalidate timers.

  — Remove observers (specifically, unregister for notifications).

  — Unlink callbacks (specifically, `nil` any `strong` delegates).

Memory Usage in Production

Note that whatever setup you do to your Xcode, it will work only when debugging the app on a device. You really do not know what additional variations may arise until the app has gone live and been used by tens of thousands of users, if not millions.

To be able to profile your app in varying scenarios, use instrumentation. Send periodic information about your app to the server—memory consumed, especially if it grows beyond a threshold, along with a breadcrumb navigation trail is a great option.

As an example, if the memory consumption is beyond 40 MB, you may want to send the details of what screens the user navigated to and key operations performed. Another option is to keep track of memory consumption and log it locally at periodic intervals, and then upload the data to the server. You can use the code in Example 2-40 to find the memory used as well as the available memory.

 Instrument your app to include the memory used, as well as other statistics, on low-memory warnings, and send this information to the server on app relaunch. Use this data to identify common scenarios and/or corner cases where the app runs out of memory.

Example 2-40. Track available memory and memory used

```
//HPMemoryAnalyzer.m
```

```
#import <mach/mach.h>

vm_size_t getUsedMemory() {
 task_basic_info_data_t info;
 mach_msg_type_number_t size = sizeof(info);
 kern_return_t kerr = task_info(mach_task_self(), TASK_BASIC_INFO,
  (task_info_t) &info, &size);

 if(kerr == KERN_SUCCESS) {
  return info.resident_size;
 } else {
  return 0;
 }
}

vm_size_t getFreeMemory() {
 mach_port_t host = mach_host_self();
 mach_msg_type_number_t size = sizeof(vm_statistics_data_t) / sizeof(integer_t);
 vm_size_t pagesize;
 vm_statistics_data_t vmstat;

 host_page_size(host, &pagesize);
 host_statistics(host, HOST_VM_INFO, (host_info_t) &vmstat, &size);

 return vmstat.free_count * pagesize;
}
```

Memory Profiling Using Instruments

You can use the Xcode Instruments tool to profile your app's memory usage. The Instruments tool is covered in greater depth in "Instruments" on page 363. We are specifically interested in the Allocations (see "Allocations" on page 369) and Leaks ("Leaks" on page 372) instruments.

Summary

Now that you have a deeper understanding of how memory is managed by the iOS runtime and the basic rules to avoid retain cycles (the single largest source of memory leaks), you can now minimize your app's memory consumption and lower its average and peak memory requirements.

You can use zombies to keep track of overreleased objects, which are one of the most common sources of app crashes.

The code in this chapter can be used to track memory usage in production, not just in the test lab.

CHAPTER 3

Energy

With mobile devices becoming ubiquitous, battery life has become an important factor influencing which devices consumers ultimately purchase. Similarly, power consumption is an important factor that influences the decision of whether to install an app.

Each hardware component on the device consumes power. The primary consumer of power is the CPU, but that is only one side of the system. A well-written app is vigilant about using energy sparingly. Apps that drain the battery quickly tend to get deleted by users.

Aside from the CPU, noteworthy hardware components that consume battery life include network hardware, Bluetooth, GPS, and the microphone, accelerometer, camera, speaker, and screen.

In this chapter, we focus on key areas that contribute to power consumption and how we can minimize the consumption. We will learn how to write an app that is aware of the battery level of the device and its charging state. We will also learn how to analyze power, CPU, and resource usage in an iOS app.

CPU

The central processing unit (CPU) is the primary hardware used by an app, either when it is directly being used by the user or indirectly, during background operations and when processing push notifications.

The processors used for the iPhone (5, 5S, and 6) and iPad (3, 4, and Air) are either dual-core or tri-core. See Table 3-1 for the complete list. The Geekbench scores reflect the relative computing speed of the processors on these popular and recent iOS devices.

Table 3-1. iOS device and processor

Device	Processor	Cores	Address size	CPU clock	Geekbench single-core	Geekbench multi-core[a]
iPhone 5	A6	2	32 bit	1.3 GHz	569	950
iPhone 5S	A7	2	64 bit	1.3–1.4 GHz	1400	2524
iPhone 5C	A6	2	32 bit	1.3 GHz	689	1243
iPhone 6	A8	2	64 bit	1.4 Ghz	1621	2899
iPhone 6 Plus	A8	2	64 bit	1.4 Ghz	1619	2902
iPhone 6S	A9	2	64 bit	1.8 Ghz	2487	4327
iPhone 6S Plus	A9	2	64 bit	1.8 Ghz	2478	4330
iPad 3	A5X	2	32 bit	1 Ghz	261	495
iPad 4	A6X	2	32 bit	1.4 Ghz	781	1422
iPad Air	A7	2	64 bit	1.4 Ghz	1462	2636
iPad Air 2	A8X	3	64 bit	1.5 Ghz	1815	4502

[a] https://browser.primatelabs.com/ios-benchmarks

The more the app computes, the more energy it consumes. The older-generation devices consume more power for the same set of operations. The quantum of computation depends on various factors:

- Processing to be done on the data (e.g., applying formatting to the text)
- Size of data to be processed—larger displays allow your software to present more information in a single view, which in turn means more data to be handled
- Algorithms and data structures used to process the data
- Number of times an update is to be performed, particularly if the data update results in the app state or UI updating (push notifications received by the app may also result in a data update, and if the user has the app open, you may need to update the UI as well)

There is no single rule to reduce the execution on the device. A lot depends on the nature of the operation. The following are a few best practices that you can adapt to your app:

Use the optimal algorithm for the scenario

For example, when sorting, prefer insertion sort over merge sort when the list has less than 43 entries, but use quicksort for more than 286 entries. Prefer dual-pivot quicksort over traditional single-pivot quicksort.

If the app receives data from the server, minimize the need for processing on the client side

For example, if a piece of text needs to be rendered on the client side, cleanse the data on the server.

In one project I worked on, the server returned text that contained HTML tags because the service was implemented primarily for desktop use. Instead of stripping down the HTML tags on the client, we implemented that on the server, thereby reducing the processing time and computation needs on the device.

In another project, we realized that if there was a considerable gap between each time a user opened the app, the number of records that needed synchronization on the device would be fairly high. Instead of the server sending updates as would happen in normal app usage, we configured it to send a binary database file that would replace the existing one on the device. This not only ensured optimal network usage but also minimized the computation needed to merge records on the local device.

Optimize ahead-of-time (AOT) processing
The disadvantage of just-in-time (JIT) processing is that it may force the user to wait for an operation. But aggressive AOT processing may result in wasted computations. The exact quantum of AOT processing required is very app- and device-dependent.

For example, when rendering a list of records in a `UITableView`, it is not advisable to process all the records when loading the list. Based on the cell height, if the device can render N records, $3N$ or $4N$ may be an appropriate calculation to use for the number of records to be loaded. Similarly, if the user scrolls down fast, do not load the records immediately—instead, delay until the scrolling speed goes below a threshold. The exact threshold value will be determined by the processing time required for each cell and the complexity of the cell UI (e.g., if it has multiple images or has video).

Profile energy consumption
Measure energy consumed (see "Profiling for Energy Use" on page 102) across all devices of your target audience. Identify the areas where more energy is consumed and find options to reduce it.

Network

Intelligent management of network access makes your app more responsive and helps conserve battery life. If no network connection is available, you should defer further attempts to access the network until a connection has been restored.

In addition, avoid bandwidth-heavy operations, such as video streaming, unless a WiFi connection is available because cellular radio systems (LTE, 4G, 3G, etc.) are known to consume more battery than WiFi radio. This is because LTE devices use multi-input, multi-output (MIMO) technology that uses multiple concurrent signals and can maintain two LTE links. Similarly, all cellular data connections periodically scan for stronger signals.

We therefore need to:

- Check if an appropriate network connection is available before any network operation.
- Continually monitor network availability and respond appropriately when the connection status changes.

Apple has provided sample code (*http://apple.co/1Q3gRKL*) to check and monitor changes to network status. If your project uses CocoaPods, use Tony Million's `Reacha bility` pod (*https://github.com/tonymillion/Reachability*).

Example 3-1 demonstrates adding a simple method (`isAPIServerAvailable`) to your code and using it before actually making a call.

Example 3-1. Check for network status

```
//Helper API
-(BOOL)isAPIServerReachable {
  Reachability *r = [Reachability reachabilityWithHostname:@"api.yourdomain.com"]; ❶

  return r.isReachable;❷
}

//Actual networking operation
-(void)performNetworkOperation:(NSDictionary *)params
    completion:(void (^)(NSError *, id)) completion { ❸

if(!self.isAPIServerReachable) {
    [self enqueueRequest:params completion:completion]; ❹

    NSError *err = [[NSError alloc] initWithDomain:@"network"
        code:kErrorCodeNetworkUnreachable userInfo:nil];
    completion(err, nil); ❺
  } else {
    [self doNetworkOperation:params completion:completion]; ❻
  }
}
```

❶ Check the reachability of your server domain.

❷ Feel free to use `isReachableViaWiFi` or `isReachableViaWWAN` (3G, 4G, EDGE, etc.) for further optimization.

❸ The `completion` callback is provided with the result of type `id` (operation-specific) or an error of type `NSError *`.

❹ Enqueue the operation. The implementation of the queue method is not shown here.

❺ kErrorCodeNetworkUnreachable is a constant defined somewhere in your app.

❻ If the network is available, fire the request immediately.

Similarly, to implement the second step (monitoring the network status and executing the queue when available), you can use the code given in Example 3-2.

Example 3-2. Monitor for network and process queue

```
//HPNetworkOps.h
@property (nonatomic, readonly) BOOL isAPIServerReachable;

//HPNetworkOps.m

@property (nonatomic, strong) Reachability *reachability;
@property (nonatomic, strong) NSOperationQueue *networkOperationQueue;

-(id)init {
    if(self = [super init]) {
        self.reachability = [Reachability
                reachabilityWithHostname:@"api.yourdomain.com"];
        self.reachability.reachableOnWWAN = NO;

        self.networkOperationQueue = [[NSOperationQueue alloc] init];
        self.networkOperationQueue.maxConcurrentOperationCount = 1;

        [[NSNotificationCenter defaultCenter] addObserver:self
            selector:@selector(networkStatusChanged:)
            name:kReachabilityChangedNotification object:nil];
    }
    return self;
}

-(void)networkStatusChanged:(Reachability *)reachability {
    if(!reachability.isReachableViaWiFi) {
        self.networkOperationQueue.suspended = YES;
    } else {
        self.networkOperationQueue.suspended = NO;
    }
}

-(BOOL)isAPIServerReachable {
  return self.reachability.isReachableWiFi;
}

-(void)performNetworkOperation:(NSDictionary *)params
    completion:(void (^)(NSError *, id)) completion {
```

```
    [self enqueueRequest:params completion:completion];
}

-(void)enqueueRequest:(NSDictionary *)params
    completion:(void (^)(NSError *, id)) completion
{
    NSURLRequest *req = ...;
    AFHTTPRequestOperation *op =
        [[AFHTTPRequestOperation alloc] initWithRequest:req];

    [op setCompletionBlockWithSuccess:^(AFHTTPRequestOperation *op, id res){
        completion(nil, res);
    } failure:^(AFHTTPRequestOperation *operation, NSError *error) {
        completion(error, nil);
    }];

    [self.networkOperationQueue addOperation:op]
}
```

The code in Example 3-2 can be analyzed as follows:

- The class HPNetworkOps has a property isAPIServerReachable that can be used
  to check if the network is available or not.

  Depending on the app, the state of the app, and the task, you may use this flag to
  proceed or block app interaction using a heads-up display (HUD).

- The class has private properties reachability and networkOperationQueue.

  — reachability is used to monitor the status. It is configured to track changes
    for WiFi networks only.

  — networkOperationQueue keeps operations in the queue. The queue is config-
    ured to execute only one operation at a time.

- The notification receiver (networkStatusChanged) suspends or resumes the
  queue based on the network availability.

- The performNetworkOperation implementation has been updated to always
  route network operations to the queue.

- The method enqueueRequest:completion: actually enqueues the network operation.

  In this example, the AFHTTPRequestOperation operation from the AFNetworking
  pod (*https://github.com/AFNetworking/AFNetworking*) has been used. Feel free to
  use any other operation or create your own.

In the previous code, NSOperationQueue has been used for demonstration. You may
use a more sophisticated queue for additional control. As an extreme, you may want

to persist pending network operations so that you can sync the changes with the server whenever the network is available later.

Note that `NSOperationQueue` does not pause or suspend any executing operation. A suspended queue merely means that the subsequent operations will not be executed until the queue is resumed. As the Apple Developer Docs state:

> Operations are removed from the queue only when they finish executing. However, in order to finish executing, an operation must first be started. Because a suspended queue does not start any new operations, it does not remove any operations (including cancelled operations) that are currently queued and not executing.

 Use queue-based networking requests so as to not bombard your server with multiple simultaneous requests. Use at least two queues: one for heavy image downloads, which generally are non-critical, and another for critical data calls. See "Operations and Queues" on page 110 for more details on working with operations.

Additionally, as a good citizen, you should update the network activity indicator—turn it on after adding the operation to the queue and turn it off when the response is available. Use the method `setNetworkActivityIndicatorVisible:` defined in the `UIApplication` class.

Location Manager and GPS

It is important to understand that location services including both the GPS (or GLONASS) and the WiFi hardware, requires significant battery power.

Calculating location using GPS requires determination of two pieces of information:

Time lock
Each GPS satellite broadcasts a unique 1,023-bit pseudorandom number every millisecond, for a data rate of 1.024 Mbps. The GPS receiver chip must align to the correct slot to lock time with the satellite.

Frequency lock
The GPS receiver must calculate any signal skew from Doppler shift due to the relative motion between the satellite and the receiver.

Locking on to a satellite typically takes up to 30 seconds, and locks must be obtained for each satellite in range of the receiver. The more satellites that can be fixed, the more accurately location can be determined.

Calculating position in this manner requires constant use of the CPU and GPS hardware, which together can rapidly run down the battery.

GPS Precision Code

The precision code for each satellite, better known as the P-code, is actually 6.1871×10^{12} bits long, which is about 720 GB. It is transmitted at 10.23 Mbps and repeats once a week.

More interestingly, this P-code is only a subset of a master P-code that is approximately 2.34×10^{14} bits long, which is about a whopping 26.7 TB.

Now that you understand the complex nature of GPS locking, you'll see that the need to use it with caution cannot be emphasized enough, particularly if your app relies heavily on maps.

Let's look at basic best practices to follow for minimizing power usage (your users will appreciate that your app has been optimized for this).

Example 3-3 shows typical code for initializing `CLLocationManager` and receiving location updates efficiently.

Example 3-3. Using location manager

```
//HPLocationViewController.h
@interface HPLocationViewController : UIViewController <CLLocationManagerDelegate>

@property (nonatomic, strong) CLLocationManager *manager;

@end

//HPLocationViewController.m
@implementation HPLocationViewController

-(void)viewDidLoad
{
    self.manager = [[CLLocationManager alloc] init]; ❶
    self.manager.delegate = self;
}

-(IBAction)enableLocationButtonTapped:(id)sender
{
    self.manager.distanceFilter = kCLDistanceFilterNone; ❷
        self.manager.desiredAccuracy = kCLLocationAccuracyBest; ❸

    if(isIOS8()) {❹
        [self.manager requestWhenInUseAuthorization]; ❺
    }

    [self.manager startUpdatingLocation];
```

```
}

-(void)locationManager:(CLLocationManager *)manager
    didUpdateLocations:(NSArray *)locations
{
    CLLocation *loc = [locations lastObject];
    //work with the location
}

@end
```

❶ We're not using dependency injection, but here the manager is not only owned by the view controller but also managed and configured.

❷ Initialize the manager for all distance changes.

❸ Initialize the manager for maximum accuracy.

❹ isIOS8 is a helper method omitted here for brevity. It returns true when the app runs on iOS 8 and above.

❺ This is an iOS 8–specific API to request permissions to use location services only when the app is in use.

Optimal Initialization

As you may have noticed in Example 3-3, there are two parameters that play an important role before you call the startUpdatingLocation method:

distanceFilter
  The distance filter will cause the manager to notify the delegate about location Manager:didUpdateLocations: events only if the device has moved by the minimum distance. The distance is in SI units (meters).

  This does not help reduce GPS receiver usage but does impact the processing that your app will do, and hence indirectly reduces CPU usage.

desiredAccuracy
  The accuracy parameter has a direct impact on the number of antennas to be used, and hence the battery consumption. Choose the accuracy level based on the specific needs of the app. The accuracy, in decreasing order of precision, is defined by these constants:

kCLLocationAccuracyBestForNavigation
  Best accuracy level for navigation use.

`kCLLocationAccuracyBest`

Finest accuracy level possible for the device.

`kCLLocationAccuracyNearestTenMeters`

Accurate to the nearest 10 meters. Use this when you are not interested in every meter that a person walks (comes in handy when you want to measure block distances, for example).

`kCLLocationAccuracyHundredMeters`

Accurate to the nearest 100 meters (when computing distances, the value may be in multiples of 100 m).

`kCLLocationAccuracyKilometer`

Accurate to the nearest kilometer. Useful when there is a need to calculate rough distance between two points of interest that may be hundreds of kilometers apart (e.g., if the computed distance from your home in San Francisco to Disneyland in Anaheim is off by a few hundred meters, it would not be much of an issue).

`kCLLocationAccuracyThreeKilometers`

Accurate to the nearest 3 kilometers. Use this for really long distances (it should not cause much trouble if the distance computed between your home in London, England, and the Taj Mahal in India is off by a few kilometers).

The distance filter is a software-layer filter, while accuracy level impacts the physical antennas being used.

Having a higher distance filter will only impact the interval when the `locationManager:didUpdateLocations:` callback of the delgate is invoked. On the other hand, a finer accuracy level means more active antennas, which results in higher energy consumption.

Turn Off Inessential Features

Decide when you need to track location changes. Invoke `startUpdatingLocation` when you need to track and `stopUpdatingLocation` when you do not.

Consider a messaging app where the user may have enabled sharing her location with friends. If your app intends to send only the name of the city, you should get the location once and then turn location tracking off by calling `stopUpdatingLocation`. You should turn it on again after an interval. This can be a fixed interval (e.g., 60 seconds or even 5 minutes), or a dynamically computed interval (i.e., compute the approximate time it would take to cross the city limits using the previously obtained coordinates and speed).

Location tracking should also be turned off if the app is in the background or the user is not chatting with anyone—say, while exploring the media gallery, browsing the friend list, or changing the settings in the app.

An even better solution is to give the end user an option to turn off inessential features. As an example, the Waze app provides the option of turning off all activities from the app (see Figure 3-1).

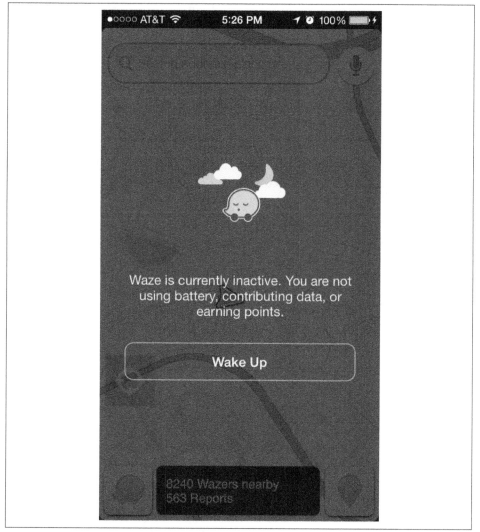

Figure 3-1. Waze with location tracking turned off

Use Network Only If Essential

For energy efficiency, iOS keeps the wireless network hardware turned off as much as possible. When an app needs to make a network connection, iOS will use this opportunity to allow background apps to share this network session, so that low-priority events such as push notifications, retrieving email, and so on can be processed.

The upshot is that whenever your app makes a network connection, the network hardware will remain active for several seconds after your app is finished with the connection. Each of these bursts of network traffic can consume a full percentage point of battery life.

To minimize this problem, your software needs to make sparing use of the network. It should attempt to process network access in periodic bursts rather than a continually active data stream so that the network hardware can be turned back off.

Background Location Services

`CLLocationManager` provides an alternative method for listening to location updates. `startMonitoringSignificantLocationChanges` helps you track movement for longer distances. The exact value is internally determined and is independent of the `distanceFilter`.

Use this mode to track movement when your app enters the background (unless it's a navigation app and you want fine details even when the screen is locked). A typical behavior will be to `startMonitoringSignificantLocationChanges` when the app is backgrounded and to `startUpdatingLocation` when foregrounded. Example 3-4 presents sample code that you can use in your app.

Example 3-4. Monitoring versus significant change monitoring

```
//App delegate
- (void)applicationDidEnterBackground:(UIApplication *)application
{
    [self.locationManager stopUpdatingLocation];
    [self.locationManager startMonitoringSignificantLocationChanges];
}

- (void)willEnterForeground:(UIApplication *)application
{
    [self.locationManager stopMonitoringSignificantLocationChanges];
    [self.locationManager startUpdatingLocation];
}
```

Unlike in iOS 7, the method startUpdatingLocation no longer requests the user's permission to use location data in iOS 8. You must use requestWhenInUseAuthorization and/or requestAlway sAuthorization.

NSTimers, NSThreads, and Location Services

Any timers or threads are suspended when an app is backgrounded. But if you have requested location updates when your app is backgrounded, the app will be woken for an infinitesimal duration each time the updates are sent to it. And for that duration, the threads and timers will also come to life again.

The killer here is if you happen to do any network operations during that time, as this will turn on all data-related antennas (i.e., WiFi, LTE/4G/3G).

It is always tricky to control this situation. The best option is to use the NSURLSession class. We discuss this further in "Networking API" on page 237.

Restart After App Kill

Last but not least, your app may be killed if it is backgrounded and another app needs resources. If that is the case, whenever a location change happens, the app will be restarted but you will need to reinitiate monitoring. The options in application:did FinishLaunchingWithOptions: have an entry corresponding to the key UIApplica tionLaunchOptionsLocationKey if this happens. See Example 3-5 for sample code.

Example 3-5. Reinitiate monitoring if app is killed

```
-(void)application:(UIApplication *)app
    didFinishLaunchingWithOptions:(NSDictionary *)launchOptions
{
    if(launchOptions[UIApplicationLaunchOptionsLocationKey]) { ❶
        [self.manager startMonitoringSignificantLocationChanges]; ❷
    }
}
```

❶ Detect if the app was restarted due to location changes after it was killed for lack of resources.

❷ If so, start monitoring for location changes. Otherwise, start monitoring at a later appropriate time.

Screen

The screen is a big power hog. The larger the screen, the greater the power consumption. Of course, if your app is in the foreground and the user interacts with it, there is bound to be screen and battery use.

However, there are options for optimizing the screen use.

Animation

Wise use of animation is a beaten-down concept. Nevertheless, it is mentioned here for completeness.

One simple rule to follow: animate when the app is in the foreground, and pause your animations whenever the app goes to the background. In general, you can listen to `UIApplicationWillResignActiveNotification` or `UIApplicationDidEnterBack groundNotification` notification events to pause or stop your animations and `UIApplicationDidBecomeActiveNotification` notification events to resume animations.

Video Play

During video play, it is a good idea to force the screen to be awake. To do so, use the property `idleTimerDisabled` on the `UIApplication` object. Once set to `YES`, it will prevent the screen going to sleep, which is exactly what you want.

As with animations, you can respond to the app notifications to release and obtain locks.

Multiple Screens

There is more to utilizing the screen than wake-lock or animation pause/resume.

What if the device is connected to an external display (using AirPlay or an HDMI connector)? Most apps usually just allow it to be default-handled by the OS, which does nothing more than mirror the device on the external display.

But more can be done. If you are playing a movie or running some animations, you can move that out of the device screen on to the external screen and just leave basic controls on the device screen. This will help reduce screen updates on the device, thereby preserving battery life. The Apple developer website provides a simple example on using an external display (*http://apple.co/1jauUnu*). It is not uncommon to connect an iPhone or iPad to a car's display screen using a cable or to an AppleTV using AirPlay.

Typical code for handling this scenario would involve the following steps:

1. During launch, detect the number of screens.

   If the count is more than one, switch.

2. Listen to screen connect and disconnect notifications.

   If a new screen has been added, switch.

   If all external screens have been removed, revert to default display.

Example 3-6 shows how you can use multiple screens to your benefit.

Example 3-6. Using multiple screens

```
//HPMultiScreenViewController.m
@interface HPMultiScreenViewController ()

@property (nonatomic, strong) UIWindow *secondWindow;

@end

@implementation HPMultiScreenViewController

-(void)viewDidLoad
{
    [super viewDidLoad];
    [self registerNotifications];
}

-(void)viewDidAppear:(BOOL)animated
{
    [super viewDidAppear:animated];
    [self updateScreens];
}

-(void)viewDidDisappear:(BOOL)animated
{
```

```
    [super viewDidDisappear:animated];
    [self disconnectFromScreen];
}

-(void)disconnectFromScreen
{
    if(self.secondWindow != nil) {
        //Disconnect links and set up for memory relinquishment
        self.secondWindow.rootViewController = nil;
        self.secondWindow.hidden = YES;
        self.secondWindow = nil;
    }
}

-(void)updateScreens
{
    NSArray *screens = [UIScreen screens];
    if(screens.count > 1) {
        UIScreen *secondScreen = (UIScreen *)[screens objectAtIndex:1];
        CGRect rect = secondScreen.bounds;
        if(self.secondWindow == nil) {
            self.secondWindow = [[UIWindow alloc] initWithFrame:rect];
            self.secondWindow.screen = secondScreen;

            HPScreen2ViewController *svc = [[HPScreen2ViewController alloc] init];
            //Set other properties of svc to initialize it completely
            svc.parent = self;
            self.secondWindow.rootViewController = svc;
        }
        self.secondWindow.hidden = NO;
    } else {
        [self disconnectFromScreen];
    }
}

-(void)dealloc
{
    [self unregisterNotifications];
}

-(void)screensChanged:(NSNotification *)notification
{
    [self updateScreens];
}

-(void)registerNotifications
{
    NSNotificationCenter *nc = [NSNotificationCenter defaultCenter];
    [nc addObserver:self
            selector:@selector(screensChanged:)
        name:UIScreenDidConnectNotification object:nil];
        [nc addObserver:self
```

```
        selector:@selector(screensChanged:)
    name:UIScreenDidDisconnectNotification object:nil];
}

-(void)unregisterNotifications
{
    [[NSNotificationCenter defaultCenter] removeObserver:self];
}

@end
```

In Example 3-6, the `HPMultiScreenViewController` is the view controller with the video or animation UI.

In this example, we use another helper view controller, `HPScreen2ViewController`, that can communicate with its `parent` view controller and send appropriate messages upon user interaction. A detailed description of each method is given next:

`viewDidLoad`

Because this method is called once and only once in the lifecycle of the view controller, this is the best place to register the observers to the `UIScreenDidConnect Notification` (screen connected) and `UIScreenDidDisconnectNotification` (screen disconnected) notifications.

Whenever a new screen is added or an existing one removed, we call the method `screensChanged:`, where we update the UI.

`viewDidAppear:`

Because the view can appear or disappear several times—or, to be more specific, a user can move into or move out the view controller multiple times—we use this method to update the screens.

The first time a user enters into the view controller, the UI is adjusted, looking at the number of screens currently available. Similarly, if the user moves out of this view controller into some other view controller and then returns to it, the number of screens may have changed. As such, they may require adjustments.

`viewDidDisappear:`

When the user moves out of this view controller, you may want to update the UI on another screen as well. Use this method to do so.

In our case, we remove the `secondWindow` from the screen (via the `disconnect FromScreen` method).

In a more sophisticated app, you may continue playing the video on the external screen while the user is free to perform more complex operations, such as reordering the playlist or performing a media search, on the device screen.

Figure 3-2 shows a mock UI of how such an app will look when in use.

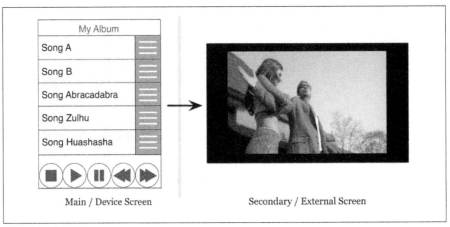

Figure 3-2. Multiple-screen UI

disconnectFromScreen
> We call this method to remove the secondWindow from the screen.

updateScreens
> This is where the real magic happens, although the example has been kept very simple for the purpose of demonstration.
>
> In this method, we check the total number of screens, and if it is greater than 1, we attach a new window to the second screen. In the real world, you can scan through all the screens and decide what to do on each—it can be as simple as replicating the UI on all of them.
>
> If the number of screens is 1, we invoke disconnectFromScreen.

dealloc
> Called once when view controller is about to be destroyed, we use this method to unregister for the screen notifications.

screensChanged:
> This method calls updateScreens whenever the app gets a notification about a screen being disconnected.

registerNotifications
> This method adds observers to the UIScreenDidConnectNotification and UIScreenDidDisconnectNotification notifications.

unregisterNotifications
> This method removes observers.

In a real-world app, the HPScreen2ViewController will consist of the UI that a user can interact with to control, for example, the movie player. You will also switch the controllers between the screens. Example 3-7 shows how you can achieve this.

Example 3-7. Swap UI across screens

```
-(void)swapScreens(UIWindow *)currentWindow newWindow:(UIWindow *)newWindow
{
    NSArray *screens = [UIScreen screens];

    UIScreen *deviceScreen = [screens objectAdIndex:0];
    UIScreen *extScreen = [screens objectAdIndex:1];

    //Optionally, you can set the bounds appropriately
    currentWindow.screen = extScreen;
    newWindow.screen = deviceScreen;
}
```

 It may be a little awkward to have controls on one screen and display on the other, but it allows for the display to be uninterrupted, and if the controls are standard buttons (for play, pause, resume, stop, etc.), it is not such a bad experience.

Of course, you do not want to use this approach in an interactive game where the touch controls are on the game screen. If you do, the users will be very unhappy, as it will be practically impossible to control the game dynamics from a blank screen.

Other Hardware

When the app is backgrounded, release any locks obtained on the hardware:

- Bluetooth
- Camera
- Speaker, unless the app is a music app
- Microphone

The specifics of these hardware options are not covered here, but the rules remain the same—start interaction with the hardware only when the app is in the foreground and stop the interaction when it goes to the background.

The exceptions here may be the speaker and Bluetooth radio. If you are working on a music, radio, or other audio-related app, continue to use the speaker even if the app goes to the background. Do not keep the screen on for audio-only purposes. Similarly, continue to use Bluetooth radio if the app has an unfinished transaction, such as file transfer with another device.

Battery Level and State-Aware Code

A smart app will take into consideration the battery level and its state to determine if it should actually be doing a resource-intensive operation. Another value of interest is the charging status, indicating whether or not the device is charging.

Use the UIDevice instance to retrieve the batteryLevel and batteryState (the charging status). You can use the code in Example 3-8 directly in your app. The method shouldProceedWithMinLevel: takes a minimum battery level that is required to proceed with a given operation that you intend to perform. The level is a floating-point number in the range of 0–100 (100 signifies a full battery).

Example 3-8. Conditional processing using battery level and charging status

```
-(BOOL)shouldProceedWithMinLevel:(NSUInteger)minLevel
{
    UIDevice *device = [UIDevice currentDevice];
    device.batteryMonitoringEnabled = YES;

    UIDeviceBatteryState state = device.batteryState;
    if(state == UIDeviceBatteryStateCharging ||
        state == UIDeviceBatteryStateFull) { ❶
        return YES;
    }

    NSUInteger batteryLevel = (NSUInteger) (device.batteryLevel * 100); ❷
    if(batteryLevel >= minLevel) {
        return YES;
    }
    return NO;
}
```

❶ Any operation can be performed during charging or when the device is fully charged.

❷ The batteryLevel returned by UIDevice is in the range 0.00–1.00.

Similarly, you can also retrieve the CPU utilized by your app. It's probably not useful information when your app is running, but for completeness, the code is given in Example 3-9.

Example 3-9. CPU used by the app

```
-(float)appCPUUsage {
 kern_return_t kr;
        task_info_data_t info;
        mach_msg_type_number_t infoCount = TASK_INFO_MAX;

        kr = task_info(mach_task_self(), TASK_BASIC_INFO,
                        (task_info_t)info, &infoCount);
        if (kr != KERN_SUCCESS) {
                return -1;
        }

        thread_array_t          thread_list;
        mach_msg_type_number_t thread_count;
        thread_info_data_t      thinfo;
        mach_msg_type_number_t thread_info_count;
        thread_basic_info_t     basic_info_th;

 kr = task_threads(mach_task_self(), &thread_list, &thread_count);
        if (kr != KERN_SUCCESS) {
                return -1;
        }

        float tot_cpu = 0;
        int j;

        for (j = 0; j < thread_count; j++) {
                thread_info_count = THREAD_INFO_MAX;
                kr = thread_info(thread_list[j], THREAD_BASIC_INFO,
                                (thread_info_t)thinfo, &thread_info_count);
                if (kr != KERN_SUCCESS) {
                        return -1;
                }

                basic_info_th = (thread_basic_info_t)thinfo;

                if (!(basic_info_th->flags & TH_FLAGS_IDLE)) {
                        tot_cpu += basic_info_th->cpu_usage /
                                (float)TH_USAGE_SCALE * 100.0;
                }
        }

        vm_deallocate(mach_task_self(), (vm_offset_t)thread_list,
                thread_count * sizeof(thread_t));
        return tot_cpu;
}
```

Alert the user if the battery level is low, and request the user's permission to execute battery-intensive operations—only proceed if the user agrees.

Always use an indicator to show the progress of a long-running task, whether it is about computation being done on the device or merely downloading some content. Providing users with an estimate of how long the task will take to complete helps them decide whether it's necessary to continue charging the device.

Profiling for Energy Use

Use Xcode Instruments to track CPU usage of your app during development. The tool is discussed in greater depth in Chapter 11. The template that will be of interest is Activity Monitor (see "Activity Monitor" on page 367). It gives a fairly good measure of relative energy consumption, as the CPU is the primary consumer of power.

To get a real sense of how much energy your app uses, use Monsoon Solutions's Power Monitor (*https://www.msoon.com/LabEquipment/PowerMonitor*). The steps to use this tool are as follows:

1. Open the case of the iOS device and find the power pins behind the battery.

2. Attach the pins from the Power Monitor device.

3. Run the app.

4. Measure the power consumption.

Figure 3-3 shows the Power Monitor tool connected with an iPhone's battery pins.

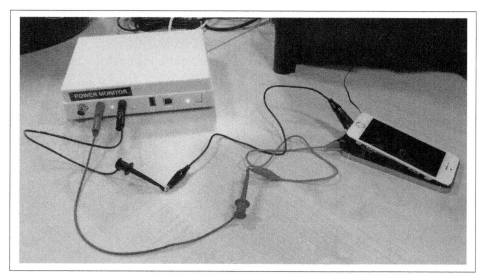

Figure 3-3. Power Monitor connected to iPhone 5S (image courtesey of Bottle of Code)

The Power Monitor tool comes with software that can track the power usage over time. The data is presented visually as a graph, as illustrated in Figure 3-4.

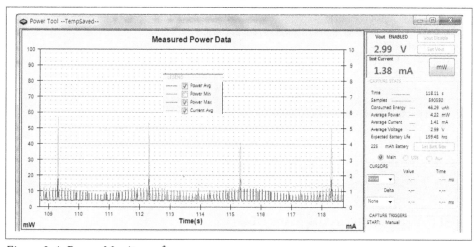

Figure 3-4. Power Monitor software

Best Practices

There are some best practices for ensuring prudent use of power. Follow these guidelines for an energy-efficient app:

- Minimize hardware use—in other words, start interaction with the hardware as late as possible and stop once the task is complete.
- Check the battery level and charging status before starting intensive tasks.
- If the battery level is low, prompt the user to determine whether the task should really be executed, and proceed only if the user agrees.
- Alternatively, include a setting to let the user define a threshold battery level below which the app should prompt the user before executing intensive operations.

Example 3-10 shows sample code for using the threshold battery level to prompt the user. The configuration for the threshold values is given in Figure 3-5.

Example 3-10. Prompt before intensive operation if battery level is low

```
-(IBAction)onIntensiveOperationButtonClick:(id)sender {

NSUserDefaults *defaults = [NSUserDefaults standardUserDefaults];
        BOOL prompt = [defaults boolForKey:@"promptForBattery"];
        int minLevel = [defaults integerForKey:@"minBatteryLevel"];

        BOOL canAutoProceed = [self shouldProceedWithMinLevel:minLevel];
        if(canAutoProceed) {
                [self executeIntensiveOperation];
        } else {
    if(prompt) {
    UIAlertView *view = [[UIAlertView alloc] initWithTitle:@"Proceed"
                        message:@"Battery level below minimum required. Proceed?"
                            delegate:self cancelButtonTitle:@"No"
     otherButtonTitles:@"Yes", nil];
     [view show];
    } else {
                    [self queueIntensiveOperation];
            }
        }
}

- (void)alertView:(UIAlertView *)alertView
  clickedButtonAtIndex:(NSInteger)buttonIndex {

  if(buttonIndex == 0) {
        [self queueIntensiveOperation];
        } else {
                [self executeIntensiveOperation];
        }
}
```

The code in Example 3-10 can be explained as follows:

- The `onIntensiveOperationButtonClick:` method is executed on the tap of a button (or by any other logic). This method is supposed to fire the intensive operation.

- The settings consist of two entries: `promptForBattery` (which may be a toggle switch in the app settings indicating whether or not to prompt in case of low battery conditions) and `minBatteryLevel` (which may be a slider ranging from 0 to 100, indicating the minimum battery level—in this case, user-selectable). See Figure 3-5 for the app settings UI.

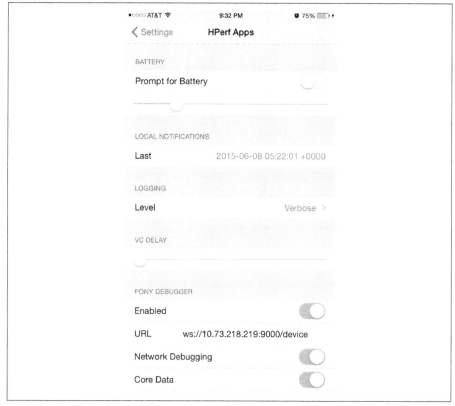

Figure 3-5. App settings for threshold battery level and prompt options

In a real-world app, the threshold will be a predetermined value set by the app developer based on the complexity and intensity of the operations. Different intensive operations may have different minimum battery level requirements.

- Before you actually execute the intensive operation, check whether the current level is good enough and/or the phone is charging. That is my logic to determine if we can proceed or not, as given in Example 3-8. You may have a different variant—minimum level *and* also charging.

- If we are good to proceed, we execute immediately (here, by calling some `execu teIntensiveOperation` method in the class).

- Otherwise, if the user has opted to `promptForBattery`, he is prompted.

  Or, if the user has not opted to be prompted, we queue the intensive operation for later execution (here, calling some `queueIntensiveOperation` method in the class).

- On the prompt, if user selects `Ok`, we invoke `executeIntensiveOperation`. We invoke `queueIntensiveOperation` otherwise.

Summary

With users carrying their mobile devices with them most of the time, it is important to write code that minimizes power consumption. It is not always possible to find a socket for the mobile device charger, and not all users carry a portable charger.

When it is not possible to reduce the complexity of the task that needs to be executed (e.g., processing an image or drawing a chart), having an option that is sensitive to the battery level and appropriately prompts the user will make the user feel good about the app. Your users *will* appreciate it.

In the next chapter, we discuss options and best practices for executing multiple tasks concurrently. The work we did in this chapter to optimize memory use and minimize power consumption will provide inputs to subsequent topics as we further develop those options.

CHAPTER 4

Concurrent Programming

iOS devices have two or three CPU cores (see Table 3-1). This means, even if the main thread (the UI thread) is busy updating the screen, the app can still be doing more computations in the background without the need for any context switch.

In this chapter, we explore various options for making the best use of the available CPU cores, and we'll learn how to optimize performance using concurrent programming. We will discuss the following topics:

- Creating and managing threads
- The Great Central Dispatch (GCD) abstraction
- Operations and queues

We will cover best practices and techniques for writing thread-safe, highly performant code.

Threads

A *thread* is a sequence of instructions that can be executed by a runtime.

Each process has at least one thread. In iOS, the primary thread on which the process is started is commonly referred to as the *main thread*. This is the thread in which all UI elements are created and managed. All interrupts related to user interaction are ultimately dispatched to the UI thread where the handler code is written—your IBAc tion methods are all executed in the main thread.

Cocoa programming does not allow updating UI elements from other threads. This means that whenever the app executes background threads for long operations such as network or other processing, the code must perform a context switch to the main thread to update the UI—for example, the progress bar indicating the task progress or the label indicating the outcome of the process.

The Cost of Threads

However great it may look to have several threads in the app, each thread has a cost associated with it that impacts app performance. Each thread not only takes some time during creation but also uses up memory in the kernel as well as the app's memory space.[1]

Kernel Data Structures

Each thread consumes approximately 1 KB of memory in kernel space. The memory is used to store the data structures and attributes pertaining to the thread. This is wired memory and cannot be paged.

Stack Size

The main thread stack size is 1 MB and cannot be changed. Any secondary thread is allocated 512 KB of stack space by default. Note that the full stack is not immediately created. The actual stack size grows with use. So, even if the main thread has a stack size of 1 MB, at some point in time, the actual stack size may be much smaller.

Before a thread starts, the stack size can be changed. The minimum allowed stack size is 16 KB, and the size must be a multiple of 4 KB. The sample code in Example 4-1 shows how you can configure the stack size before starting a thread.

Example 4-1. Change thread stack size

```
+(NSThread *)createThreadWithTarget:(id)target selector:(SEL)selector
        object:(id)argument stackSize:(NSUInteger)size {

    if( (size % 4096) != 0) {
        return nil;
    }
    NSThread *t = [[NSThread alloc] initWithTarget:target
        selector:selector object:argument];
    t.stackSize = size;

    return t;
}
```

---

1 iOS Developer Library, "Thread Costs" (*http://apple.co/1EukJhy*).

Creation Time

A quick test on an iPhone 6 Plus running iOS 8.4 showed average thread creation time (not including the start time) ranged between 4,000–5,000 μs, which is about 4–5 ms.

The time taken to actually start a thread after creation ranged from anywhere between 5 ms to well over 100 ms, averaging about 29 ms. That can be a lot of time, especially if you start multiple threads during app launch.

The elongated time for thread start can be attributed to several context switches that have overheads.

For brevity, the code for these computations has been omitted here. For details, see the `computeThreadCreationTime` method in the code on GitHub (*http://bit.ly/1OmXgWU*). Figure 4-1 shows the output from that code.

Figure 4-1. Thread creation time

GCD

The Grand Central Dispatch (GCD) API (*http://bit.ly/apple-gcd*) is comprised of core language features, runtime libraries, and system enhancements for concurrent code execution.

We will not get into the fundamentals of using GCD, as that is not the purpose of this book. You most likely already have a fair background working with GCD constructs, but if you need a review of GCD fundamentals, check out Ray Wenderlich's "Multithreading and Great Central Dispatch on iOS for Beginners Tutorial" (*http://bit.ly/1VG7JNE*).

However, for completeness, we will run through a quick list of what GCD provides:

- Task or dispatch queues, which allow execution on the main thread, concurrent execution, and serial execution
- Dispatch groups, which allow tracking execution of a group of tasks, irrespective of the underlying queue they are submitted on
- Semaphores
- Barriers, which allow creating synchronization points in a concurrent dispatch queue
- Dispatch object and source management, which allow low-level management and monitoring
- Asynchronous I/O, using either file descriptors or channels

GCD handles thread creation and management well. It also helps you to keep the total number of threads in your app under control and not cause any leaks.

 While most apps will generally perform well using GCD alone, there are specific cases when you should consider using NSThread or NSOperationQueue. In the scenarios where your app has multiple long-running tasks to be executed concurrently, it is better to take control of the thread creation. If your code takes longer to complete, you may soon hit the limit of 64,[2,3] the maximum GCD thread pool size.

Be wary about using dispatch_async and dispatch_sync lavishly too, as it can lead to app crashes.[4] Although 64 threads might look like a reasonably high number for a mobile app, the app may hit the limit sooner than later.

Operations and Queues

The next set of abstractions available for managing tasks in iOS programming is operations and operation queues.

NSOperation encapsulates a task and its associated data and code, whereas NSOperationQueue controls execution of one or more of such tasks in a FIFO order.

NSOperation and NSOperationQueue both provide control over the number of threads that get created. You control the number of queues formed. You also control

---

2 Stack Overflow, "Number of Threads Created by GCD?" (*http://bit.ly/1hsGU1S*).

3 Stack Overflow, "Workaround on the Threads Limit in Grand Central Dispatch?" (*http://bit.ly/1FZUKEN*).

4 Stack Overflow, "GCD Dispatch Concurrent Queue Freeze with 'Dispatch Thread Soft Limit Reached: 64' in Crash Log" (*http://bit.ly/1N1VHvY*).

the number of threads in each queue, using the maxConcurrentOperationCount property.

These two options sit somewhere in between using NSThread (where it is left to the developer to manage all concurrency) and GCD (where the OS manages concurrency).

Here's a quick comparison of the NSThread, NSOperationQueue, and GCD APIs:

GCD
- Highest abstraction.
- Two queues are available out of the box: main and global.
- Can create more queues (using dispatch_queue_create).
- Can request exclusive access (using dispatch_barrier_sync and dispatch_barrier_async).
- Manages underlying threads.
- Hard limit on 64 threads created.

NSOperationQueue
- No default queues.
- App manages the queues it creates.
- Queues are priority queues.
- Operations can have different priorities (use the queuePriority property).
- Operations can be cancelled using the cancel message. Note that cancel is merely a flag. If an operation is under execution, it may continue to execute.
- Can wait for an operation to complete (use the waitUntilFinished message).

NSThread
- Lowest-level construct, gives maximum control.
- App creates and manages threads.
- App creates and manages thread pools.
- App starts the threads.
- Threads can have priority. OS uses this for scheduling their execution.
- No direct API to wait for a thread to complete. Use a mutex (e.g., NSLock) and custom code.

NSOperationQueue is multicore-safe. It is safe to use a shared queue and submit tasks from multiple threads without having to worry about queue corruption.

Thread-Safe Code

All throughout our software engineering lives, we are told to always write thread-safe code—meaning that if multiple threads execute the same instruction sets concurrently, there should not be any negative side effects.

There are two broad techniques for achieving this:

- Do not have a modifiable shared state.
- If you cannot avoid using a modifiable shared state, make your code thread-safe.

These techniques are easier said than done. There are a number of choices available to accomplish them.

Because an app will have a modifiable shared state, we need to establish best practices for application state management and modifications.

One basic rule that drives these best practices is "Preserve invariants in the code."[5]

Atomic Properties

Atomic properties are a great start to making your application state thread-safe. If a property is atomic, the modification or retrieval is guaranteed to be atomic.

This is important because it prevents two threads from simultaneously updating a value, which otherwise could result in a corrupted state. The thread that is modifying the property must complete before the other thread can proceed.

All properties are atomic by default. As a best practice, use atomic explicitly where this is appropriate. To mark a property otherwise, use the nonatomic attribute. Example 4-2 demonstrates both atomic and nonatomic properties.

Example 4-2. Atomic and nonatomic properties

```
@property (atomic) NSString *firstName; ❶
@property (nonatomic) NSString *department; ❷
```

---

5 Stack Overflow, "What Is an Invariant?" (*http://bit.ly/1NtKQgI*).

---

❶ Atomic property

❷ Nonatomic property

Because atomic properties have overheads, it is advisable not to overuse them. For example, when it can be guaranteed that a property will never be accessed from more than one thread at any time, it is better to mark it nonatomic.

One such scenario is working with IBOutlets. @property (**nonatomic,** readwrite, strong) IBOutlet UILabel *nameLabel should be preferred over @property (**atomic,** readwrite, strong) IBOutlet UILabel *nameLabel because we know that UIKit allows manipulating UI elements from only the main thread. Because access will be in one designated thread, marking the property atomic will only add overhead without bringing any value.

Synchronized Blocks

Even if the properties are marked atomic, the eventual code using them may not be thread-safe. An atomic property only prohibits concurrent modification. Assuming that we have an entity HPUser that can be updated using an operation HPOperation, let's have a look at Example 4-3.

Example 4-3. Using atomic properties across threads

```
//An entity (partial definition)
@interface HPUser

@property (atomic, copy) NSString *firstName;
@property (atomic, copy) NSString *lastName;

@end


//A service class (declaration omitted for brevity)
@implementation HPUpdaterService

-(void)updateUser:(HPUser *)user properties:(NSDictionary *)properties {
    NSString *fn = [properties objectForKey:@"firstName"];
    if(fn != nil) {
        user.firstName = fn;
    }
    NSString *ln = [properties objectForKey:@"lastName"];
    if(ln != nil) {
        user.lastName = ln;
    }
}
```

@end

Let's consider that the `updateUser:properties:` method is called whenever the user pulls down to refresh and data is available from the server. It may also be called by a sync task that executes periodically.

So, at some point in time, there is a possibility that multiple responses will attempt to update the user profile concurrently—maybe on two cores or just using time-slicing.

Consider the scenario where two responses in different threads try to update the user with the names "Bob Taylor" and "Alice Darji." Without atomic updates on the properties `firstName` and `lastName`, the order of execution is not guaranteed and the final result can be any combination, including "Alice Taylor" and "Bob Darji."

This example is only demonstrative but enforces the point that atomic properties are not enough to make code thread-safe.

This brings us to the next best practice: all related state updates should be batched in a single transaction.

Use the `@synchronized` directive to create a mutex and enter a critical section, which can only be executed by one thread at any point in time. The code may be updated as shown in Example 4-4.

Example 4-4. Thread-safe blocks

```
@implementation HPUpdaterService

-(void)updateUser:(HPUser *)user properties:(NSDictionary *)properties {
    @synchronized(user) { ❶
        NSString *fn = [properties objectForKey:@"firstName"];
        if(fn != nil) {
            user.firstName = fn;
        }
        NSString *ln = [properties objectForKey:@"lastName"];
        if(ln != nil) {
            user.lastName = ln;
        }
    }
}

@end
```

❶ Acquire a lock against the `user` object. All related changes are now handled together with no possibility of race conditions.

With this change, the final name of the user will be either "Bob Taylor" or "Alice Darji."

 Note that overuse of the @synchronized directive can slow down your app, as only one thread can execute within the critical section at any time.

For our case, we chose user as the object to acquire a lock on. Thus, the upda teUser:properties: method can be called from multiple threads for as many users as necessary, and it will execute with high concurrency as long as the user objects are not the same. The result is code implemented for high-concurrency use with guards against data corruption.

 The object on which the lock is acquired is key to well-defined critical sections. As a rule of thumb, select the object whose state will be accessed or modified as the reference for the mutex.

So far, so good. But what should the strategy be for reading the properties? What if you needed to display the full name of the HPUser object while it is being modified?

Locks

Locks are the basic building blocks to enter a critical section. atomic properties and @synchronized blocks are higher-level abstractions available for easy use.

There are three kinds of locks available:

NSLock

This is a low-level lock. Once a lock is acquired, the execution enters the critical section and no more than one thread can execute concurrently. Release the lock to mark the end of the critical section.

Example 4-5 shows an example of using NSLock.

Example 4-5. Using NSLock

```
@interface ThreadSafeClass () {
  NSLock *lock; ❶
}
@end

-(instancetype)init {
```

```
  if(self = [super init]) {
   self->lock = [NSLock new]; ❷
  }
  return self;
 }

 -(void)safeMethod {
  [self->lock lock]; ❸

  //Thread-safe code ❹

  [self->lock unlock]; ❺
 }
```

❶   The lock is declared as a `private` field. Another option is to make it a prop-
      erty.

❷   Initialize the lock.

❸   Acquire the lock to enter the critical section.

❹   In the critical section, a maximum of one thread can execute at any time.

❺   Release the lock to mark the end of the critical section. Another thread can
      now acquire the lock.

NSLock must be unlocked from the same thread where it was locked.

NSRecursiveLock

NSLock does not allow `lock` to be called more than once without first calling
`unlock`. NSRecursiveLock, as the name indicates, *does* allow `lock` to be called
more than once before it is `unlocked`. Each `lock` call must be matched with an
equal number of `unlock` calls before the lock can be considered released for
another thread to acquire.

NSRecursiveLock is useful when you have a class with multiple methods that use
the same lock to synchronize and one method invokes the other. Example 4-6
shows an example of using it.

Example 4-6. Using NSRecursiveLock

```
@interface ThreadSafeClass () {
 NSRecursiveLock *lock; ❶
}
@end

-(instancetype)init {
```

```
  if(self = [super init]) {
   self->lock = [NSRecursiveLock new];
  }
  return self;
}

-(void)safeMethod1 {
  [self->lock lock]; ❷

  [self safeMethod2]; ❸

  [self->lock unlock]; ❻
}

-(void)safeMethod2 {
  [self->lock lock]; ❹

  //Thread-safe code

  [self->lock unlock]; ❺
}
```

❶ The NSRecursiveLock object.

❷ safeMethod1 acquires the lock.

❸ It calls method safeMethod2.

❹ safeMethod2 acquires a lock on the already-acquired lock.

❺ safeMethod2 releases the lock.

❻ safeMethod1 releases the lock. Because each lock call is now matched with a corresponding unlock, the lock is now released and ready to be acquired by another thread.

NSCondition

There are cases when there is a need to coordinate execution across threads. For example, a thread may want to wait until another thread has results ready. NSCondition can be used to atomically release a lock and let it be obtained by another waiting thread, while the original thread waits.

A thread can wait on a condition that releases the lock. Another thread can signal the condition by releasing the same lock and awakening the waiting thread.

The standard producer–consumer problem can be solved using NSCondition. Example 4-7 shows the code to implement the solution to this problem.

Example 4-7. Using NSCondition

```
@implementation Producer

-(instancetype)initWithCondition:(NSCondition *)condition
 collector:(NSMutableArray *)collector { ❶
 if(self = [super init]) {
  self.condition = condition;
  self.collector = collector;
  self.shouldProduce = NO;
  self.item = nil;
 }
 return self;
}

-(void)produce {
 self.shouldProduce = YES;
 while(self.shouldProduce) { ❷
  [self.condition lock]; ❸
  if(self.collector.count > 0) {
   [self.condition wait]; ❹
  }
  [self.collector addObject:[self nextItem]]; ❺
  [self.condition signal]; ❻
  [self.condition unlock]; ❼
 }
}
@end

@implementation Consumer

-(instancetype)initWithCondition:(NSCondition *)condition
 collector:(NSMutableArray *)collector { ❽
 if(self = [super init]) {
  self.condition = condition;
  self.collector = collector;
  self.shouldConsume = NO;
  self.item = nil;
 }
 return self;
}

-(void)consume {
 self.shouldConsume = YES;
 while(self.shouldConsume) { ❾
  [self.condition lock]; ❿
```

```
  if(self.collector.count == 0) {
   [self.condition wait]; ⓫
  }
  id item = [self.collector objectAtIndex:0];
  //process item
  [self.collector removeItemAtIndex:0]; ⓬
  [self.condition signal]; ⓭
  [self.condition unlock]; ⓮
 }
}
@end

@implementation Coordinator

-(void)start {
 NSMutableArray *pipeline = [NSMutableArray array];
 NSCondition *condition = [NSCondition new]; ⓯
 Producer *p = [Producer initWithCondition:condition
   collector:pipeline];
 Consumer *c = [Consumer initWithCondition:condition
   collector:pipeline]; ⓰
 [[NSThread initWithTarget:self selector:@SEL(startProducer)
  object:p] start];
 [[NSThread initWithTarget:self selector:@SEL(startCollector)
  object:c] start]; ⓱
 //once done
 p.shouldProduce = NO;
 c.shouldConsume = NO; ⓲
 [condition broadcst]; ⓳
}

@end
```

❶ The initializer for the producer needs the NSCondition object to coordinate with and a collector to push produced items to. It is initially set to not produce (shouldProduce = NO).

❷ The producer will produce while shouldProduce is YES. Another thread should set it to NO for the producer to stop producing.

❸ Obtain the lock on the condition to enter the critical section.

❹ If the collector already has some not-consumed items, wait, which blocks the current thread until the condition is signaled.

❺ Add the produced nextItem to the collector for it to be consumed.

❻ signal another waiting thread, if any. This is an indicator that an item has been produced, and added to the collector, and is available to be consumed.

❼ Release the lock.

❽ The initializer for the consumer needs the NSCondition object to coordinate with and a collector to push produced items to. It is initially set to not consume (shouldConsume = NO).

❾ The consumer will consume while shouldConsume is YES. Another thread should set it to NO for the consumer to stop consuming.

❿ Obtain the lock on the condition to enter the critical section.

⓫ If the collector has no items, wait.

⓬ Consume the next item in the collector. Ensure that it is removed from the collector.

⓭ signal another waiting thread, if any. This is an indicator that an item has been consumed and removed from the collector.

⓮ Release the lock.

⓯ The Coordinator class readies the input data for the producer and consumer (specifically, the collector and the condition).

⓰ Set up the producer and consumer.

⓱ Start production and consumption tasks in different threads.

⓲ Once completed, set the producer and consumer to stop producing and consuming, respectively.

⓳ Because the producer and consumer threads may be waiting, broadcast, which is essentially signaling *all* waiting threads, unlike signal, which affects only one of the waiting threads.

Use Reader–Writer Locks for Concurrent Reads and Writes

We started this section with two choices for achieving thread safety. We discuss best practices to safeguard against concurrent writes in this section and talk about immutable entities in the next section.

We already learned that `atomic` properties safeguard against inconsistent updates and are overcautious about it. If multiple threads attempt to read a property, the synthesized code allows access to only one thread at a time. Having an `atomic` property will therefore slow down the app.

This can be a big bottleneck, especially if the state is shared across various components and may need to be accessed from multiple threads. An example of this is a *cookie* or *access token* after login. It can change periodically but will be required by all network calls made to the server.

Another use case for such a scenario is the *cache*. A cache entry can be used anywhere in the app and may be updated upon specific user actions or otherwise.

Essentially, we need a mechanism for concurrent reads but exclusive writes. That brings us to the topic of *reader–writer* locks. They are also known as *multiple readers/ single-writer* or *multireader* locks.

A reader–writer lock allows concurrent access for read-only operations, while write operations require exclusive access. This means that multiple threads can read the data in parallel but an exclusive lock is needed to modify the data.

GCD barriers allow creating a synchronization point within a concurrent dispatch queue. When GCD encounters a barrier, the corresponding queue delays the execution of the block until all blocks submitted before the barrier are finished executing. And then, the block submitted via a barrier executes exclusively. We shall call this block a *barrier block*. Subsequently, the queue continues with its normal execution behavior.

Figure 4-2 demonstrates the effect that barriers have on execution in a multithreaded environment. Blocks 1 through 6 can execute concurrently across multiple threads in the app. However, the barrier block executes exclusively. The only constraint that must be satisfied is that all executions must happen on the same concurrent queue.

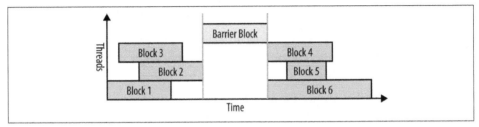

Figure 4-2. Dispatch blocks and barriers

To implement this behavior, we need to follow these steps:

1. Create a concurrent queue.

2. Execute all reads using dispatch_sync on this queue.

3. Execute all writes using dispatch_barrier_sync on the same queue.

You can use the code in Example 4-8 to implement a high-throughput thread-safe model.

Example 4-8. Thread-safe, high-throughput model

```
//HPCache.h
@interface HPCache

+(HPCache *)sharedInstance;

-(id)objectForKey:(id) key;
-(void)setObject:(id)object forKey:(id)key;

@end

//HPCache.m
@interface HPCache ()

@property (nonatomic, readonly) NSMutableDictionary *cacheObjects;
@property (nonatomic, readonly) dispatch_queue_t queue;

@end

@implementation HPCache

-(instancetype)init {
    if(self = [super init]) {
            _cacheObjects = [NSMutableDictionary dictionary];
            _queue = dispatch_queue_create(kCacheQueueName,
        DISPATCH_QUEUE_CONCURRENT); ❶
    }
    return self;
```

```
}

+(HPCache *)sharedInstance {
        static HPCache *instance = nil;

        static dispatch_once_t onceToken;
        dispatch_once(&onceToken, ^{
                instance = [[HPCache alloc] init];
        });
        return instance;
}

-(id)objectForKey:(id<NSCopying>)key {
        __block id rv = nil;

        dispatch_sync(self.queue, ^{ ❷
                rv = [self.cacheObjects objectForKey:key];
        });

        return rv;
}

-(void)setObject:(id)object forKey:(id<NSCopying>)key {
        dispatch_barrier_async(self.queue, ^{ ❸
                [self.cacheObjects setObject:object forKey:key];
        });
}

@end
```

❶ Create a custom DISPATCH_QUEUE_CONCURRENT queue.

❷ Use dispatch_sync (or dispatch_async) for operations that do not modify state.

❸ Use dispatch_barrier_sync (or dispatch_barrier_async) for operations that may modify state.

Notice that the properties have been marked nonatomic because there is custom code to manage thread safety using a custom queue and barrier.

Use Immutable Entities

This all looks great. But what if there is a need to access state while it is being modified?

For example, what if the cache is being purged but part of the state needs to be used immediately because the user performed an interaction? What if there were a more effective mechanism for state management than multiple components trying to update it simultaneously?

Your team should follow these best practices:

- Use immutable entities.
- Support them with an updater subsystem.
- Allow observers to receive notifications on data changes.

This creates a decoupled, scalable system to manage application state. Let's go through one of the several possible ways to implement this.

The first step is to clearly define the models. For our case study, we define the following three entities:

HPUser

> Represents a user in the system. A user has a unique id, name broken down into firstName and lastName, gender, and dateOfBirth.

HPAlbum

> Represents a photo album. A user may have zero or more albums. An album has a unique id, owner, name, creationTime, description, link to coverPhoto (the cover photo of the album), and likes (users that liked the album).

HPPhoto

> Represents a photo in an album. An album may have zero or more photos. A photo has a unique id, album to which it belongs, user (the person who uploaded the photo), caption, url, and size (width and height).

Example 4-9 shows the code for the entity definitions.

Example 4-9. Entities for the case study, representing a user, an album, and a photo

```
@interface HPUser

@property (nonatomic, copy) NSString *userId;
@property (nonatomic, copy) NSString *firstName;
@property (nonatomic, copy) NSString *lastName;
@property (nonatomic, copy) NSString *gender;
@property (nonatomic, copy) NSDate *dateOfBirth;
@property (nonatomic, strong) NSArray *albums;

@end

@class HPPhoto;

@interface HPAlbum
```

```
@property (nonatomic, copy) NSString *albumId;
@property (nonatomic, strong) HPUser *owner;
@property (nonatomic, copy) NSString *name;
@property (nonatomic, copy) NSString *description;
@property (nonatomic, copy) NSDate *creationTime;
@property (nonatomic, copy) HPPhoto *coverPhoto;

@end

@interface HPPhoto

@property (nonatomic, copy) NSString *photoId;
@property (nonatomic, strong) HPAlbum *album
@property (nonatomic, strong) HPUser *user;
@property (nonatomic, copy) NSString *caption;
@property (nonatomic, strong) NSURL *url;
@property (nonatomic, copy) CGSize size;

@end
```

There are multiple ways to define the model and mechanisms to populate the data. Two of the more common options are:

- Using a custom initializer
- Using a builder pattern

Each option has its advantages.

Using a custom initializer may mean a long method name, which can result in a nasty call. Think about the method `initWithId:firstName:lastName:gender:birthday:`. And this is when we have used only a few of the available attributes in our model. The initializer bloats if five more attributes were added.

Custom initializers also pose backward compatibility problems. A newer model with more attributes will never be backward compatible. However, this also ensures that the app using the updated version of the model knows right at compile time that things have changed.

Using a builder means managing an extra class for it. It will only have setter methods. The builder will also need parallel storage (properties or otherwise) to store all the data needed by the model. The builder will, eventually, use an initializer.

Any update to the model will require a corresponding change to the builder and its backing properties.

The builder pattern is preferred, as it enables backward compatibility and does not break the app even if there are more attributes added to the model. The extra attributes in the later versions of the model will continue to have their default values.

Using the second option, the code looks similar to that given in Example 4-10. This is code adapted from Klaas Pieter's idea of implementing the builder pattern using blocks (*http://www.annema.me/the-builder-pattern-in-objective-c*).

Example 4-10. Immutable entity using builder

```
//HPUser.h
@interface HPUserBuilder ❶

@property (nonatomic, copy) NSString *userId;
@property (nonatomic, copy) NSString *firstName;
@property (nonatomic, copy) NSString *lastName;
@property (nonatomic, copy) NSString *gender;
@property (nonatomic, copy) NSDate *dateOfBirth;
@property (nonatomic, strong) NSArray *albums;

-(HPUser *)build;

@end

@interface HPUser ❷

//properties

+(instancetype) userWithBlock:(void (^)(HPUserBuilder *))block;

@end

@interface HPUser () ❸

-(instancetype) initWithBuilder:(HPUserBuilder *)builder;

@end


@implementation HPUserBuilder

-(HPUser *) build { ❹
    return [[HPUser alloc] initWithBuilder:self];
}

@end

@implementation HPUser
-(instancetype) initWithBuilder:(HPUserBuilder *)builder { ❺

    if(self = [super init]) {
        self.userId = builder.userId;
        self.firstName = builder.firstName;
        self.lastName = builder.lastName;
        self.gender = builder.gender;
```

```
        self.dateOfBirth = builder.dateOfBirth;
        self.albums = [NSArray arrayWithArray:albums];
    }
    return self;
}

+(instancetype) userWithBlock:(void (^)(HPUserBuilder *))block { ❻
    HPUserBuilder *builder = [[HPUserBuilder alloc] init];
    block(builder);
    return [builder build];
}

@end


//Building the object, an example
-(HPUser *) createUser { ❼
    HPUser *rv = [HPUser userWithBlock:^(HPUserBuilder *builder) {
        builder.userId = @"id001";
        builder.firstName = @"Alice";
        builder.lastName = @"Darji";
        builder.gender = @"F";

        NSCalendar *cal = [NSCalendar currentCalendar];
        NSDateComponents *components = [[NSDateComponents alloc] init];
        [components setYear:1980];
        [components setMonth:1];
        [components setDay:1];
        builder.dateOfBirth = [cal dateFromComponents:components];

        builder.albums = [NSArray array];
    }];

    return rv;
}
```

❶ The builder.

❷ The model with the class method userWithBlock:. Example 4-9 has all the prop-
    erties declared.

❸ Private extension to the model—the custom initializer.

❹ Implementation of the build method.

❺ Implementation of the custom initializer of the model.

❻ Implementation of the userWithBlock: method.

❼ A sample use of the builder to create the object.

Note that the preceding code has a few advantages:

- The model is always backward compatible. A new version of the model-builder with extra attributes will not break the `createUser` code.
- The builder can be created directly. The consumer of the model can instantiate the builder and call the `build` method to create the model object.
- The builder creation and handling can be left to the core. The consumer of the model can use the class method `userWithBlock:` and does not need to either instantiate or call the `build` method by itself.

Have a Central State Updater Service

The next thing that we need an updater service to update is the client state. The updater service may require connecting to the server, validating the update before performing a local update—for example, adding or updating a record, confirming a friend request, or uploading a photo. From the UI perspective, in the interim, you may show a progress bar or some other indicator to keep the user informed about the status of the change of the state.

For our case, let's have `HPUserService`, `HPAlbumService`, and `HPPhotoService` classes for servicing `HPUser`, `HPAlbum`, and `HPPhoto` objects, respectively.

Updating state is tricky because it is immutable. Paradoxical, isn't it? One option is to let the state builder take an input state that can be subsequently modified.

To do that for `HPUser`, we can create a helper initializer on `HPUserBuilder` that takes an input object.

The code in Example 4-11 shows an updated `HPUserBuilder` class to support modifications to an earlier created `HPUser` object, and an `HPUserService` class to retrieve and update the objects. Similar infrastructure will exist for `HPAlbum` and `HPPhoto` entities. This code demonstrates the services for user and album entities for the following two scenarios:

- Retrieving data from the server resulting in an update to local state
- Updating local and remote states, for example, upon a user interaction

Example 4-11. Services for user and album objects

```
//HPUserBuilder.h
@interface HPUserBuilder
```

```
-(instancetype) initWithUser:(HPUser *)user;

@end

@interface HPUserBuilder

-(instancetype) initWithUser:(HPUser *)user { ❶
    if(self = [super init]) {
        self.userId = builder.userId;
        self.firstName = user.firstName;
        self.lastName = user.lastName;
        self.gender = user.gender;
        self.dateOfBirth = user.dateOfBirth;
        self.albums = user.albums;
    }
    return self;
}

@end

//HPUserService.h
@interface HPUserService

+(instancetype)sharedInstance; ❷
-(void)userWithId:(NSString *)id completion:(void (^)(HPUser *))completion;
-(void)updateUser:(HPUser *)user completion:(void (^)(HPUser *))completion;

@end

//HPUserService.m
@interface HPUserService

@property (nonatomic, strong) NSMutableDictionary *userCache; ❸

@end

@implementation HPUserService

-(instancetype) init { ❹
    if(self = [super init]) {
        self.userCache = [NSMutableDictionary dictionary];
    }
    return self;
}

-(void)userWithId:(NSString *)id completion:(void (^)(HPUser *))completion { ❺
    //Check in local cache or fetch from server
    HPUser *user = (HPUser *)[self.userCache objectForKey:id];
    if(user) {
        completion(user);
    }
```

```
    [[HPSyncService sharedInstance] fetchType:@"user"
        withId:id completion:^(NSDictionary *data) { ❻
        //Use HPUserBuilder, parse data and build
        HPUser *userFromServer = [builder build];
        [self.userCache setObject:userFromServer forKey:userFromServer.userId];
        callback(userFromServer);
    }];
}

-(void)updateUser:(HPUser *)user completion:(void (^)(HPUser *))completion { ❼
    //May require update to server
    [[HPSyncService sharedInstance] updateType:@"user"
        //Use HPUserBuilder, parse data and build
        HPUser *updatedUser = [builder build];

        [self.userCache setObject:updatedUser forKey:updatedUser.userId]; ❽
        [HPAlbumService updateAlbums:updatedUser.albums]; ❾
        completion(updatedUser);
    }];
}

@end
```

❶ HPUserBuilder now has another custom initializer. It takes an HPUser object as a parameter and initializes itself with the values from the user object. The state can be modified using property setters and a new object can finally be built using the build method. Note that although the state has been modified, the old object has not been modified. This also means that if the old object is being used in another entity (e.g., a view controller), it has to be replaced. We will explore state change notifications in the next section.

❷ HPUserService follows a singleton pattern here and is available using sharedIn stance. The code has been omitted for brevity, but we know how to implement good and safe singletons. It is not advisable to use a singleton entity or service levels, as it results in tight coupling and also interferes with mocking frameworks. A configurable factory is preferred over using singletons. The factory may create a disposable singleton. We will revisit this topic in Chapter 10.

❸ As a quick prototype, the service also holds on to the cache of user objects created. However, it is definitely not a good idea to mix state with the cache logic. Always keep the state separate from any other *intelligent* code. You want to keep the models as dumb as possible.

❹ The HPUserService initializer has been overridden to initialize the cache. This is a stopgap solution, as the focus of our discussion is about how immutable objects can serve better than mutable objects whose state can be changed from different parts of the app. In a real-world app, the service object will have access to the state, which can be used as input for any processing or be updated, and to underlying network operations to keep the server in sync.

❺ A user with a given `id` can be retrieved using `userWithId:completion:`. If the object exists in the local state, it is returned. Otherwise, it may contact the server and retrieve the details. Once ready, the `completion` callback is used to notify the caller that the object is available.

❻ Availability of a sync service, `HPSyncService`, is assumed here. The service retrieves data from the server. It is also assumed that the server sends a JSON object[6] that is deserialized into an `NSDictionary`. The code for extracting properties and populating the builder has been omitted. Once the data is available, we also update the local cache so that further server trips can be avoided.

❼ User state can be updated using the `updateUser:completion:` method.

❽ Updating local state may require syncing changes to the server.

❾ Once the server has been notified, the local cache is updated. Because the user object holds albums, the album service is used to update the related albums as well. Specifically, the associated `owner` object must now point to the updated user object. The old user object must be up for `dealloc`. Note that the solution presented here is not scalable: what if other entities also need to update themselves? We will fix this problem momentarily.

One of the points to note in the entities is their cross-references. The user has a list of albums, and each album has an owner. Similarly, an album has a list of photos, and each photo has its container album. And we have not even modeled the comments on a photo, which may comprise when the comment was made, the content, and the user who wrote it.

Regardless of whether they are strong or weak, creating immutable objects with such cross-references has been purposefully omitted here. We need the user object to be ready before the album can be created, and vice versa. It is a catch-22 situation.

The way out is to keep the objects mutable unless specifically marked immutable. This is known as *popsicle immutability*.[7] For this, you may have a special method, say,

---

6 You may want to explore other formats, such as Protobuf, Thrift, or Avro.

7 Stack Overflow, "How to Design an Immutable Object with Complex Initialization" (*http://bit.ly/1FuVRGI*).

freeze or markImmutable. To be able to use this structure, you will need custom set-ters that will first check if the object is immutable before allowing any changes.

We can now solve the deadlock. We allow HPAlbum to be modifiable until we set its owner. We create the HPUser object and set the owner of the HPAlbum object. Subse-quently, we call the method freeze on the HPAlbum object. After all albums are cre-ated, we assign them to albums property of the HPUser object. Finally, we call the method freeze on the HPUser object.

Code to this effect is shown in Example 4-12. HPUser has been updated to have read/write properties and be mutable until it is marked immutable. And guess what—for most common use cases, you will probably never need a builder because the proper-ties are read/write.

Example 4-12. Popsicle-immutable entities

```
//HPUser.h
@interface HPUser

@property (nonatomic, copy) NSString *userId; ❶
@property (nonatomic, copy) NSString *firstName;
-(void) freeze; ❷

@end

//HPUser.m
@interface HPUser ()

@property (nonatomic, copy) BOOL frozen; ❸

@end

@implementation HPUser

@synthesize userId = _userId; ❹
@synthesize firstName = _firstName;

-(void) freeze { ❺
    self.frozen = YES;
}

-(void) setUserId:(NSString *)userId { ❻
    if(!self.frozen) {
        self->_userId = userId;
    }
}

-(void) setFirstName:(NSString *)firstName {
    if(!self.frozen) {
        self->_firstName = firstName;
```

```
        }
    }

    //... Other setters omitted

@end

//Creating objects
-(HPUser *)sampleUser { ❼
    HPUser *user = [[HPUser alloc] init];
    user.userId = @"user-1";
    user.firstName = @"Bob";
    user.lastName = @"Taylor";
    user.gender = @"M";

    HPAlbum *album1 = [[HPAlbum alloc] init];
    album1.owner = user; ❽
    album1.name = @"Album 1";
    //... other properties
    [album1 freeze]; ❾

    HPAlbum *album2 = [[HPAlbum alloc] init];
    album2.owner = user;
    album2.name = @"Album 2";
    //... other properties
    [album2 freeze]; ❿

    user.albums = [NSArray arrayWithObjects:album1, album2, nil];
    [user freeze]; ⓫

    return user;
}
```

❶ The properties are no longer readonly. They are readwrite (implicit).

❷ We add the method freeze, which marks an object immutable. Objects are mutable by default.

❸ A flag to track the immutability state of the object.

❹ Because we are going write custom setters, we need to @synthesize and tell the compiler about the backing iVar to use.

❺ Implementation of the method freeze marks the object immutable.

❻ Custom setters. First, check if the object is mutable. If yes, update. If not, do not update. You may want to throw an exception during development time to ensure legitimate invocations and identify any bad code.

❼ Sample code to demonstrate the use of the new API.

❽ A user is assigned as the album's owner. At this point, both objects are mutable.

❾ `HPAlbum` object marked immutable.

❿ `HPUser` object marked immutable. Notice how the line just before this can make use of the immutable album objects.

Although the objects may be mutable for a while, we ensure that the mutability is short-lived and restricted only to the thread that created an object. Before the objects are pushed from the creation method to the shared app state, you must ensure that they are marked immutable.

State Observers and Notifications

The previous section left us with an unanswered question: how do we update dependents if an object is updated? Or, put differently, what are the best options to track state changes?

To track changes, you have the following options:

- KVO
- The notification center
- A custom solution

We looked at the first two options briefly in Chapter 2. KVO is great for tracking changes in object properties. But using our approach, this does not work because the objects are immutable and we replace the entire object. As such, the observer will never receive any callbacks.

The notification center is a great option. It serves a useful purpose and would suffice for most of the parts. But the challenge is scaling for the complex scenarios that an app will eventually have—for example, filtering update notifications by album ID or bubbling up the changes to the UI directly if possible.

That's where a custom solution is needed. And to make that happen, we will switch our style to *reactive programming*.

Reactive Programming is programming with asynchronous data streams.[8] Streams are cheap and ubiquitous, anything can be a stream: variables, user inputs, properties, caches, data structures, etc.

---

8 The introduction to Reactive Programming you've been missing (*http://bit.ly/1U1VBd8*).

The ReactiveCocoa library (*http://bit.ly/reactive-cocoa*) enables reactive programming in Objective-C. It not only allows observers on arbitrary state but also has advanced category extensions for bubbling them all the way up to UI elements (UILabel, for example) or responding to interactive views (UIButton, for example).

Functional Reactive Programming and ReactiveCocoa

An app generally consumes, generates, and updates data. *Reactive programming* is a programming paradigm that enables expressing data flows without having to worry about side effects or impact on other tasks under execution in parallel.

The core idea behind reactive programming is representation of a value over a period of time. Data flows that use these dynamic values will result in values that change over time.

Functional reactive programming (FRP) is enabling reactive programming using the building blocks of functional programming like map, reduce, filter, merge, etc.

ReactiveCocoa is inspired by FRP. Because various components of an app work in cohesion, there is a strong relationship between the state that they work with and update. As such, creating a decoupled cohesive reactive system is very important.

We will use ReactiveCocoa to notify observers about any model changes. The observers can be created anywhere.

For illustrative purposes, we will add a notification during each user creation and update operation. We will also add an observer in the album service to monitor any changes to the owner (user) and, for completeness, in the UI to monitor changes to the albums list for a user. Example 4-13 shows the relevant parts of the code.

Example 4-13. Observers and notifications

```
//HPUserService.m
-(RACSignal *)signalForUserWithId:(NSString *)id { ❶
    @weakify(self);
    return [RACSignal
        createSignal:^RACDisposable *(id<RACSubscriber> subscriber) { ❷
        @strongify(self);
        HPUser *userFromCache = [self.userCache objectForKey:id];
        if(userFromCache) {
            [subscriber sendNext:userFromCache];
            [subscriber sendCompleted];
        } else {
            //Assuming HPSyncService also follows FRP style
            [[[HPSyncService sharedInstance]
                loadType:@"user" withId:id]
                subscribeNext:^(HPUser *userFromServer) {
```

```
                        //Also update local cache and notify
                        [subscriber sendNext:userFromServer];
                        [subscriber sendCompleted];
                    } error: ^(NSError *error) {
                        [subscriber sendError:error];
                    }];
            }

        return nil;
    }]
}

-(RACSignal *)signalForUpdateUser:(HPUser *)user { ❸
    @weakify(self);
    return [RACSignal
        createSignal:^RACDisposable *(id<RACSubscriber> subscriber) { ❹
        //Update the server
        [[[HPSyncService sharedInstance]
            updateType:@"user" withId:user.userId value:user]
            subscribeNext:^(NSDictionary *data) {
                //Use HPUserBuilder, parse data and build
                HPUser *updatedUser = [builder build];

                @strongify(self);
                var oldUser = [self.userCache objectForKey:updatedUser.userId];
                [self.userCache setObject:updatedUser forKey:updatedUser.userId];
                [subscriber sendNext:updatedUser];
                [subscriber sendCompleted];
                [self notifyCacheUpdatedWithUser:updatedUser old:oldUser]; ❺
            } error: ^(NSError *error) {
                [subscriber sendError:error];
            }];
    }];
}

-(void)notifyCacheUpdatedWithUser:(HPUser *)user old:(HPUser *)oldUser { ❻
    NSDictionary *tuple = {
        @"old": oldUser,
        @"new": user
    };
    [NSNotificationCenter.defaultCenter
        postNotificationName:@"userUpdated" object:tuple]; ❼
}

-(RACSignal *)signalForUserUpdates:(id)object { ❽
    return [[NSNotificationCenter.defaultCenter
        rac_addObserverForName:@"userUpdated" object:object] ❾
        flattenMap:^(NSNotification *note) {
            return note.object;
        }];
}
```

```
//At some other place in app
-(void)retrieveAUser:(NSString *)userId { ❿
    [[[HPUserService sharedInstance]
        signalForUserWithId:userId]
        subscribeNext:^(HPUser *user) { ⓫
            //process user, maybe update UI
        } error:^(NSError *) {
            //show error to user
        }];
}

-(void)updateAUser:(HPUser *)user { ⓬
    [[[HPUserService sharedInstance]
        signalForUpdateUser:user]
        subscribeNext:^(HPUser *user) { ⓭
            //process user, maybe update UI
        } error:^(NSError *) {
            //show error to user
        }];
}

//Listening for user updates
-watchForUserUpdates { ⓮
    [[[HPUserService sharedInstance]
        signalForUserUpdates:self] ⓯
        subcribeNext:^(NSDictionary *tuple) { ⓰
            //Do something with the values
            HPUser *oldUser objectForKey:@"old";
            HPUser *newUser objectForKey:@"new";
        }];
}
```

❶ The method `signalForUserWithId` does not take in a block as a parameter but returns a promise that can be chained. The `@weakify` and `@strongify` macros that were first introduced in "Best Practices" on page 78 have been used here.

❷ The code for the signal is pretty much the same as the original code in `userWithId:` but this time using `RACSubscriber` and a promise.

It is assumed that the method `loadType:withId` in the class `HPSyncService` also returns a promise, an `RACSignal`.

❸ The method `signalForUpdateUser:` updates an `HPUser` object.

❹ This creates the `RACSignal`.

❺ When the user is updated, you need to not only inform the immediate subscriber, but also notify observers about updates to the cache.

❻ `notifyCacheUpdatedWithUser:old:` broadcasts about user object changes.

❼ `NSNotificationCenter` has been used here for simplicity. This method may not be exposed to the `HPUserService` users. It is an extension method.

❽ The method published (in the *HPUserService.h* file) is `signalForUserUpdates:`.

❾ It uses the `rac_addObserverForName` category extension provided by the ReactiveCocoa framework to subscribe to `userUpdated` notifications. It also extracts the actual `NSDictionary`, comprised of the `old` and `new` user objects from the underlying `NSNotification` object.

❿ The `retrieveAUser:` method demonstrates sample code to retrieve a user.

⓫ The `subscribeNext:` block is where the `user` object is received.

⓬ The `updateAUser:` method demonstrates sample code to update a user.

⓭ The `subscribeNext:` block is where the `user` object is received.

⓮ The `watchForUserUpdates:` method shows sample code to watch for changes in the user cache.

⓯ It uses the method `signalForUserUpdates:` to listen to notifications about changes to the user cache.

⓰ The `subscribeNext:` block is given the `NSDictionary` of `old` and `new` objects.

The advantage is that if in the future the implementation of `signalForUserUp dates:` changes to not use `NSNotificationCenter`, it will not result in changes all the way up to `watchForUserUpdates:`.

The primary motive for using this library is that it already has what we need to implement a decoupled, scalable, self-contained, general-purpose system for observing for changes. More importantly, it provides promises for chaining (using `RACSignal`) that allow us to write code in a style that is more understandable and maintainable. It also provides simpler solutions for interacting with the UI elements—something that we will use as we continue to build on these concepts in upcoming chapters. In a nutshell, it provides a lot of boilerplate code that we would otherwise have had to write ourselves, and a lot more.

Making Facebook's News Feed 50% Faster on iOS

In 2012, Facebook migrated its News Feed from HTML5 to a native iOS app to optimize performance. But over time, as other sections—including Groups, Pages, and Timeline—were moved to native, the News Feed degraded in performance. Instrumentation showed that the root cause was the data layer.[9]

The model layer was thus rewritten based on three principles:

- Immutability
- Denormalized storage
- Asynchronous, opt-in consistency

This also meant moving away from the Core Data framework, which guarantees strong data consistency but comes at the cost of performance.[10]

Prefer Async over Sync

In the previous section, we learned that we should prefer promises. This section provides some deeper discussion of asynchronous code.

There is a big and more impactful reason to always prefer async over sync. And it has to do with synchronization. In "Use Reader–Writer Locks for Concurrent Reads and Writes" on page 121, we discussed using dispatch barriers and learned about how `dispatch_sync` can be used for concurrent reads.

Let's briefly analyze the code in Example 4-14.

Example 4-14. Using dispatch-sync in the real world

```
//Case A
dispatch_sync(queue, ^() {
    dispatch_sync(queue, ^() {
        NSLog(@"nested sync call");
    });
});

//Case B
```

---

9 Facebook, "Making News Feed Nearly 50% Faster on iOS" (*http://bit.ly/faster-fb-ios*).

10 "Facebook's iOS Architecture - @Scale 2014 - Mobile" (*http://bit.ly/fb-ios-arch*).

```
-(void) methodA1 {
    dispatch_sync(queue1, ^() {
        [objB methodB];
    });
}

-(void)methodA2 {
    dispatch_sync(queue1, ^() {
        NSLog(@"indirect nested dispatch_sync");
    });
}

-(void) methodB {
    [objA methodA2];
}
```

In Example 4-14, Case A demonstrates a hypothetical scenario in which a nested dis
patch_sync is invoked using the same dispatch queue. This results in a deadlock. The
nested dispatch_sync cannot dispatch into the queue because the current thread is
already on the queue and will not release the lock.

Case B demonstrates a more likely scenario. A class has two methods (methodA1 and
methodA2) that use the same queue. The former method calls a methodB on some
object, which in turns calls the latter. The end result is a deadlock. The otherwise useful method dispatch_get_current_queue has long since been deprecated.[11]

One option is to use the dispatch_queue_set_specific and dispatch_get_spe
cific methods (*http://bit.ly/1NOj8fo*), but you will realize that the code gets murky
pretty soon.

For thread-safe, deadlock-free, and maintainable code, using an async style is highly
recommended. And there is nothing better than using promises. ReactiveCocoa (see
"Functional Reactive Programming and ReactiveCocoa" on page 135) introduces the
FRP style in Objective-C. dispatch_async does not suffer from this behavior.

PromiseKit

PromiseKit (*https://github.com/mxcl/PromiseKit*) is another library that supports
using promises. And it does that even better because it helps you avoid the *rightward
drift*.

---

11 dispatch_get_current_queue, Developer Tools Manual Page (*http://apple.co/1RPh8SH*).

Compare the code in Examples 4-15 and 4-16.

Example 4-15. Promise with rightward drift

```
[[[[
    [[HPNetworkService sharedInstance] promise:rq1]
        subcribeNext:^(id data1) {
            return [[HPNetworkService sharedInstance] promise:rq2];
        }]
    subscribeNext:^(id data2) {
        return [[HPNetworkService sharedInstance] promise:rq3];
    }]
    subscribeNext:^(id data3) {
        // three indents deep here
        // look at the opening brackets '[[[['
    }]
}];
```

Example 4-16. Promise with no rightward drift

```
[NSURLConnection promise:rq1].then(^(id data1){
    return [NSURLConnection promise:rq2];
}).then(^(id data2){
    return [NSURLConnection promise:rq3];
}).then(^(id data3){
    // yay! the code looks consecutive!
});
```

Notice that in Example 4-15, if multiple promises need to be chained, there's a chain of opening brackets ([), and if you are a one bracket per indentation per line programmer, the code suddenly looks to have too much right drift. On the other hand, in Example 4-16, it is always indented on the first column.

PromiseKit also provides elegant error handling. Exploring PromiseKit is highly recommended.

Summary

It is impossible to envision any app without concurrent programming. Operations as simple as animation require multitasking. All long-running tasks (such as networking and I/O) must always be done in a background thread.

With an in-depth analysis on various available options (namely threads, GCD, and operations and queues) in hand, you should now be able to select the one that works best in your specific scenario.

Choosing the right option to make your code thread-safe is key to the correctness of the app's state. Using mutexes to synchronize access to code blocks is as important as creating high-throughput reads with protected writes using reader–writer locks.

Now that you are familiar with the core optimization techniques for memory management, energy use, and concurrent programming discussed in this part of the book, you should be able to optimize the model and business logic layers of your app.

iOS Performance

Part II built up the foundation for creating a performant app—an app that is cognizant of resource utilization and that follows key best practices for optimization. Although our discussion was centered on iOS app development, the general principles apply to any Objective-C app.

The chapters in this part take a closer look at the options and techniques that are specific to iOS app development. We will explore the following topics:

- Application lifecycle
- User interface
- Networking
- Data sharing
- Security

CHAPTER 5

Application Lifecycle

An iOS app starts with a call to the `UIApplicationMain` method, with a reference to the `UIApplicationDelegate` class. The delegate receives application scope events and has a definitive lifecycle with the `application:didFinishLaunchingWithOptions:` method indicating the application startup. It is in this method that initialization of key components such as crash reporting, network, logging, and instrumentation happen. In addition, there may be one-time initialization during the first launch or restoring of previous state for subsequent launches.

The app window has a `rootViewController` that drives the user interface presented to the user. The corresponding `UIViewController` object also has a definitive lifecycle.

A flurry of activities during application startup has an impact on initial load time, which must be minimized for a better user experience. However, the tasks should not be removed to the extent that operations after app launch take much longer, as this will only further annoy users.

This chapter takes a deep dive into the application lifecycle. We will compare what app developers use an event callback for versus its primary intent and its impact on app performance. We also review some techniques, tips, and tricks that we can use to keep our users happy.

We will explore the `UIViewController` lifecycle in Chapter 6.

App Delegate

The app delegate will, generally, be the first object to be created in your app. It is this class that gets inputs from the environment into the app, including app launch details, remote notifications, deep links, and more.

If you need to refresh your understanding of app structure and execution state, check out *http://apple.co/1IV94sL*.

Figure 5-1 shows the application delegate callbacks during execution state transitions.

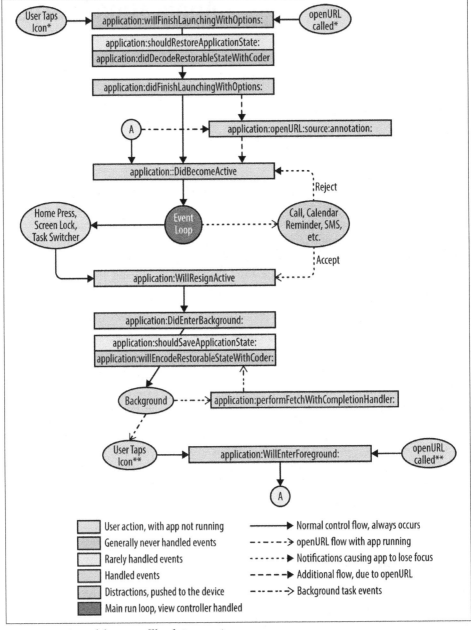

Figure 5-1. App delegate callback invocations

While it may appear complex, there shouldn't be any surprises in Figure 5-1, except perhaps for the methods `application:didDecodeRestorableStateWithCoder:` and `application:willEncodeRestorableStateWithCoder:`, which are rarely handled. Apps generally have their own local application state management and restore from there. These methods have been added for completeness.

The diagram does not enlist several other event callbacks. Specifically, callbacks related to push notifications have been omitted. They will be explored later, in "Push Notifications" on page 169.

What we will do is take one callback at a time, dissect it, review code commonly written in the callback, and determine if there is a better way to approach it.

Application Launch

The (in)famous `application:didFinishLaunchingWithOptions:` method is where your app's startup brain lies. You cannot go wrong with it—absolutely no crashes are expected here, lest the app become unusable until the next upgrade, which the user may rarely do unless the app is indispensable.

It is in this method where you load all dependencies and initialize your app core. And it is in this method where you want to spend the minimum time during startup—you do not want the user to be waiting for the UI to come up. You do not want your app to be labeled clumsy, bulky, or slow, and you definitely don't want it to receive bad ratings in the App Store.

There are four types of application launches possible:

First launch

> The first app start after installation. During this, there is no previous state to be used. There is no local cache.
>
> This means one of two things—either there is no content to load (and thus, there is a reduced load time), or the initial data needs to be download from the server (which could potentially involve a long load time).
>
> Upon first launch of the app, you may choose to provide an app walkthrough summarizing the app's capabilities and its usage. Figure 5-2 shows the Dropbox walkthrough as an example.

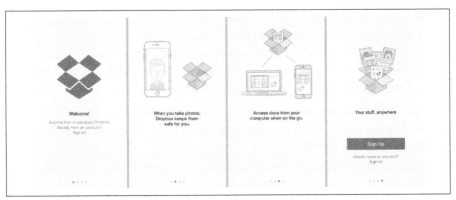

Figure 5-2. Dropbox walkthrough

Cold start

This is a subsequent app start. During this, there may be old state to restore from —for example, highest achieved level in a game, chat log in a messaging app, last synchronized articles in a news app, credentials for a previously logged-in user, or just the flag that the user has already taken the walkthrough.

Figure 5-3 shows the Facebook app at cold start. Notice how it quickly loads the cached posts while it synchronizes with the server for updates.

Warm (re)start

This is when the user switches to the app after it was backgrounded but not suspended or killed. In this scenario, it does not go through the launch callbacks but rather goes directly to the `applicationDidBecomeActive:` callback (or optionally, `application:openURL:source:annotation:`) when the user taps on the icon or returns to the app through a deep link (see "Deep Linking" on page 252).

Generally, this case is no different from a continued execution of the app, except it may or may not get some additional events to the view controller—something that we will explore later in this chapter.

Figure 5-3. Facebook app at cold start

Launch after upgrade

This is when the user launches the app after an upgrade. Generally, launching after an upgrade is no different from a cold start. However, the semantics change the moment there are changes to local storage—schema, content, or pending synchronization from the previous version, or even when the internal API/dependency defaults change.

First Launch

In general, the app may perform multiple tasks during the first launch:

- Load application defaults (NSUserDefaults, bundled config, etc.)
- Check for private/beta releases
- Initialize app identifiers, including but not limited to the Identifier for Vendor (IDFV) for anonymous users, Identifier for Advertiser (IDFA), and so on
- Initialize crash reporting system
- Set up A/B testing
- Set up analytics
- Set up networking using operations or GCD
- Set up UI infrastructure (navigation, themes, initial UI)
- Show login prompt or load latest content and other updates from the server
- Set up in-memory cache (e.g., image cache)

These tasks are only indicative of what an app may do on first launch. Some of these tasks may be executed on subsequent launches as well. The point is that these tasks can quickly add up, which will in turn slow down the app launch.

If we were to introduce these tasks in our app, the code might look similar to that given in Example 5-1.

Example 5-1. App startup code

```
-(BOOL)application:(UIApplication *)application
    didFinishLaunchingWithOptions:(NSDictionary *)launchOptions { ❶

    NSString *deviceId = [[[UIDevice currentDevice]
            identifierForVendor] UUIDString]; ❷

    NSUserDefaults *defaults = [NSUserDefaults standardUserDefaults];
    BOOL firstLaunch = ![defaults boolForKey:@"appLaunched"]; ❸
    if(firstLaunch) {
        [defaults setBool:YES forKey:@"appLaunched"]; ❹
        [defaults synchronize];

        //Register device to the server ❺
    }

    //set up A/B testing using device ID ❻

    //... more setup ❼
    [Flurry startSession:@"API_KEY"];
    [[NSURLCache sharedURLCache] setMemoryCapacity:(8 * 1024 * 1024)];
```

```
    [[NSURLCache sharedURLCache] setDiskCapacity:(50 * 1024 * 1024)];
    [SDImageCache sharedImageCache].maxCacheSize = 8 * 1024 * 1024;

    NSString *accessToken = nil; ❽
    if(!firstLaunch) {
        accessToken = [defaults stringForKey:@"accessToken"];
    }
    if(accessToken) { ❾
        //user is logged in
    } else {
        if(firstLaunch) { ❿
            //first launch
        } else { ⓫
            //user not logged in
        }
    }

    return YES;
}


-(BOOL)applicationDidBecomeActive:(UIApplication *)application { ⓬

#ifdef RELEASE_BETA ⓭
    [[BITHockeyManager sharedHockeyManager]
        configureWithIdentifier:@"API_KEY"];
    [[BITHockeyManager sharedHockeyManager] startManager]; ⓮
#endif
}
```

❶ The `application:didFinishLaunchingWithOptions:` callback, called once per app start.

❷ Grab the IDFV to uniquely track this device.

❸ Determine whether this is the first launch or if the app was launched earlier.

❹ Set the flag indicating that the app has already been launched earlier.

❺ You can send the ID to the server for anonymous registration or for tracking what is generally referred to as the *unique users or devices* count.

❻ Some subsystems may require the ID—for example, for A/B testing.

❼ A lot more setup: analytics, network cache, image cache, etc.

❽ Access token used to track the user login.

❾ If the access token is set, the user was already logged in. If the user changed the password or logged out remotely from another device, the token needs to be refreshed. The code is omitted for brevity.

❿ If the access token is not available, it may be that this is the first launch of the app, for which you may want to bring up the app walkthrough, or that the user did not log in during the previous app session.

⓫ If the user did not log in but it is not the first launch, you may want to bring up the login form directly.

⓬ Some of the configuration can be delayed until the app comes to the foreground (is active).

Note, however, that this callback is invoked each time the app returns from the background, not just during launch. As such, ensure that you do not introduce repetitive delays by running animations that might annoy the user.

⓭ RELEASE_BETA is not a standard flag. It is a custom flag that has been introduced here to differentiate between App Store builds versus private launches. Multiple configurations/targets may need to be created for this to work, as shown in Figure 5-4.

⓮ In this example, HockeyKit (*http://hockeyapp.net*) setup has been done. Your app may do different tasks.

Note that this is not an exhaustive list by any means. Other tasks such as initializations related to ads, logging, app-install attributions, single sign-on, and so on have not been shown here. A lot depends on app requirements and structure.

 Although each subsystem may be individually performant, their performance may drop when used together. For example, if multiple components attempt to simultaneously read from the filesystem, it will result in an overall sluggishness.

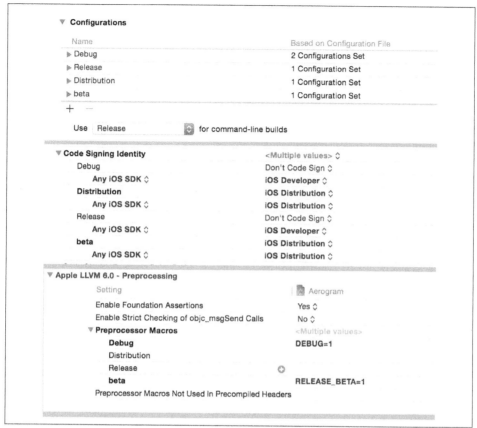

Figure 5-4. Multiple configurations

This brings us to the scenario posed earlier—these subsystem initializations can take substantial time and may have dependencies on one another. For example, themes may depend on A/B tests or data sync may depend on token validation (a.k.a. login).

How can we optimize the performance if these (possibly mandatory) initializations add up to a long initialization time?

There is no *definite* answer to this. The approach is to take a step back, identify what is the bare minimum required to show the app UI, and proceed from there.

You'll need to follow these concrete steps to split down the task list for more effective performance:

1. Identify what must be executed before the UI can be shown.

   If the app is being launched for the first time, there is no need to load any user preferences such as theme, refresh interval, cache size, and so on. There will be no custom values. It is OK to let the initial cache grow wild, as we know that it will not grow beyond a fraction of the final intended limit.

The crash reporting system should be the first one to be initialized.

2. Order the tasks.

   Ordering is very important—not only because the tasks may have interdependencies but also because it may save you precious user time.

   For example, if you trigger access token validation early, other tasks may execute in parallel because the validation process will require making a network call. As such, the *clock time* taken to complete the overall process may be less as compared to when the validation is done later and the app has to wait for the response.

3. Split the tasks into two categories—tasks that must execute in the main thread only and tasks that can execute in other threads—and execute them accordingly.

   It is possible to further split the tasks that can be executed in a non-main thread into those that can be executed concurrently and those that cannot be.

4. Other tasks can either be executed after the UI is loaded or may be fired asynchronously.

   Delay initialization of other subsystems, such as loggers and analytics. It may be possible to *queue* operations (e.g., writing log messages or tracking events) until these subsystems are completely initialized, which may happen late in the app's life.

As you may notice, there is no fixed solution. A lot depends on what control you have over these subsystems. With a bunch of third-party solutions available for these subsystems—crash reporting, A/B testing, instrumentation and analytics, networking, image cache—the exact answer to the question of how best to optimize load time depends on what options you choose and the amount of leeway you have with them.

For your app dependencies, if you have the code and you know the fix, provide a patch. By contributing to the community, you will help others who have faced similar issues.

If you purchased the license, be proactive and reach out to the company—you should receive a response. If not, do not hesitate to drop it and seek out an alternative. In the end, it is your app that the user interacts with. Third-party SDKs do not count in the eyes of the user.

As an example, if you find that the analytics SDK needs to capture a lot of data (e.g., OS version, app version, device info, etc.) or load some config from the local cache, you may want to look for an option to initialize it asynchronously off the main

thread, enqueue all the events in a queue (this can be as simple as an NSMutable
Array), and dump them all once initialized.

If you have the code, it is easy to patch. If not, you may have to maintain your own
queue. The only catch is that some of the events may have incorrect timestamps and
locations. Depending on your particular case, it might be OK for timestamps to be off
by a few milliseconds or locations by a few meters. If the exact timestamp or location
precision is crucial (i.e., if the SDK will not perform well in the event of inaccuracy),
it might be time to look for an alternative.

The code in Example 5-2 shows one of the possible strategies for minimizing the load
time. The example provides the necessary steps to initialize the analytics SDK asynchronously when the code is not available.

Some SDKs may require initialization in the main thread. Keep an eye on that, as it
directly impacts your app load time.

Example 5-2. App load time optimization

```
//HPInstrumentation.m

@interface HPInstrumentation () ❶

@property (nonatomic, copy) BOOL initialized;
@property (nonatomic, strong) NSMutableArray *events;
@property (nonatomic, strong) dispatch_queue_t queue;

-(void)markInitialized;
+(void)logEventImpl:(NSString *)name;

@end

static HPInstrumentation *_instance; ❷

@implementation HPInstrumentation

+(HPInstrumentation *)sharedInstance { ❸
    return _instance;
}

+(void)setSharedInstance:(HPInstrumentation *)instance { ❹
    _instance = instance;
}

+(void)logEvent:(NSString *)name { ❺
    [[HPInstrumentation sharedInstance] logEventImpl:name];
}

-(instancetype)initWithAPIKey:(NSString *)apiKey { ❻
    if(self = [super init]) {
```

```
        self.initialized = NO;
        self.events = [NSMutableArray array];
        self.queue = dispatch_queue_create("com.m10v.queue.analytics",
            DISPATCH_QUEUE_CONCURRENT);

        dispatch_async( ❼
            dispatch_get_global_queue(DISPATCH_QUEUE_PRIORITY_DEFAULT, 0), ^{
                [Flurry startSession:apiKey];
                dispatch_sync_barrier(self.queue, ^{ ❽
                    for(NSDictionary *name in self.events) {
                        [Flurry logEvent:name];
                    }
                    self.events = nil; ❾
                    self.initialized = YES;
                });
            });
    }
    return self;
}


-(void)logEventImpl:(NSString *)name { ❿
    dispatch_sync(self.queue, ^{ ⓫
        if(self.initialized) { ⓬
            [Flurry logEvent:name withParameters:params];
        } else {
            [self.events addObject:name];
        }
    });
}

@end

//HPAppDelegate.m
-(BOOL)application:(UIApplication *)application
    didFinishLaunchingWithOptions:(NSDictionary *)launchOptions {
    HPInstrumentation *analytics = [[HPInstrumentation alloc]
        initWithAPIKey:@"API_KEY"]; ⓭

    [HPInstrumentation setSharedInstance:analytics]; ⓮
    [HPInstrumentation logEvent:@"App Launched"]; ⓯
}
```

❶ HPInstrumentation is a wrapper on the underlying instrumentation API. It keeps events in memory until the underlying SDK, in this case Flurry, is initialized.

❷ Because we now need some coordination from initialization until the underlying SDK is ready, a pseudo-singleton model is preferred. The `_instance` is the singleton instance, which can be set or reset.[1]

❸ The getter for the shared/single instance. This is a public method (declared in the *.h* file).

❹ The setter for the shared/single instance. This is also a public method.

Note that by making the setter available for any code to use, you leave it open to abuse. As such, this must be done with caution.

❺ The public class method to set log events does not change, making the update backward compatible.

As for the implementation, it uses a non-public instance method, `logEventImpl`.

❻ Custom initializer for the class.

❼ Apart from initializing the state, it calls `dispatch_async` to initialize the underlying SDK[2] (the Flurry SDK, in this case).

❽ Once the underlying SDK has been initialized, flush all the queued events.[3] Use a queue to obtain a write lock to ensure that while the events list is being flushed, no other events can be added to the list.

❾ Free up the memory.

❿ The implementation method `logEventImpl`.

⓫ Use the same `queue` as in step 8. Obtain a read lock to allow concurrent writes.

⓬ Add to the events list if the SDK has not been initialized, or else log directly to the underlying SDK.

⓭ `HPInstrumentation` is instantiated once, in the app delegate.

---

1 The singleton pattern is about having one instance of the entity. There can be multiple ways to implement it. Application-wide nonresettable singletons, as we discussed in Chapter 2, should be avoided as much as possible.

2 Implicit assumption—the SDK can initialize in a non-main thread.

3 Another implicit assumption—rate of generation of new events is much lower than the speed of flushing events. If not, you are probably using analytics for the wrong purpose. Think again.

⑭ Set the shared instance.

⑮ To log, use the class method `logEvent`. No changes are required here.

Note that the implementation in Example 5-2 is only one of various available options.

A better option is to use a delegate approach. The initial delegate adds to the list while the other uses the actual SDK. Example 5-3 provides sample code that might be used for initialization and the switch.

The implementation follows the state design pattern. The advantage of this approach is that it makes it easy to manage the underlying implementations.

Example 5-3. Initialization using delegate

```
-(instancetype)initWithAPIKey:(NSString *)apiKey {
    //... same code for setup

    self.delegate = [[HPInstrumentationUseList alloc] init]; ❶

    //Code below is for after initialization
    dispatch_sync_barrier(self.queue, ^{
        for(NSDictionary *name in self.delegate.events) { ❷
            [Flurry logEvent:name];
        }
        self.delegate = [[HPInstrumentationUseSDK alloc] init]; ❸
    });
}

-(void)logEventImpl:(NSString *)name {
    dispatch_sync(self.queue, ^{
        [self.delegate logEvent:name]; ❹
    });
}
```

❶ To start with, `delegate` points to an object that enqueues events in a list.

❷ Once ready, flush the enqueued events...

❸ ... and change the `delegate` to point to an object that uses the analytics SDK.

❹ `logEventImpl` is simpler—it logs using the `delegate`. It does not need to make any decision on what the current state is (`initialized` or not).

Cold Start

We have had a glimpse of the tasks to execute during app launch. The tasks executed during cold start change only slightly, but this may have a huge impact.

One of the more important tasks to execute is loading from previous state. In our app, the first screen shown to the user (after login) is the feed. If the user logged in on a previous launch and data was synced, we may want to load the previously cached user's feed.

We will discuss local cache options in depth in Chapters 7 and 8. Here it is assumed that we choose some option that can perform basic CRUD operations on the records. In this section, we discuss how to put that option to good use.

To accomplish the task of showing the user's feed, one would fire a request to the server for recent updates and concurrently load from the local cache. This is a no-brainer. However, it's important to know the following:

- Minimum number (*min*) of entries required to show a usable and meaningful UI
- Time it takes to load M entries from local cache (let's call it *tl*)
- Time it takes to get latest M entries from remote server (let's call it *tr*)
- Maximum number (*max*) of entries you will ever keep in memory at any given point in time for speedier access, especially during fast swipes and scrolls

If we cannot load M entries in 3 seconds, the user experience degrades significantly.[4]

These values will help define a concrete strategy for data retrieval during app startup.

Consider the following few scenarios:

1. *tl* = 3 seconds, *tr* = 1 second
2. *tl* = 1.5 seconds, *tr* = 1.5 seconds
3. *tl* = 1 second, *tr* = 3 seconds

Let *min* = 5 and *max* = 20. We will discuss varying values of M for these timings.

In our case study, our view hierarchy is as shown in Figure 5-5, and we will measure time against the same.

---

4 J. O'Dell, VentureBeat, "This Is Why Users Think Your Mobile App Sucks: A 3-Second Response Time" (*http://bit.ly/1Br2yID*).

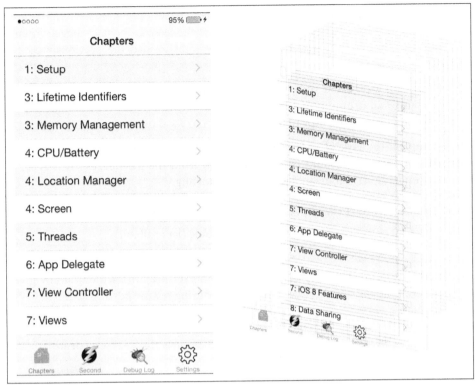

Figure 5-5. View controller structure

Note that the actual container hierarchy is `window.HPMainTabBarViewController`, the root view controller, contains three child controllers: `HPChapterViewController`, `HPDebugLogViewController`, and `HPSettingsViewController`. Figure 5-5 only shows the currently visible view controller. The children are present, just not visible.

Scenario 1

In the case where the time to sync from the remote server is orders of magnitude faster than loading from the local cache, you should trigger the sync task as early as possible. In the typical MVC style that Cocoa promotes, the corresponding `UIView Controller` will be responsible for the trigger because it is the view controller that knows what data it needs to plumb into the UI. It is very likely that the service will be set up in the app delegate and injected into the view controller, but it is the view controller that will, in general, trigger the service. However, to save those extra milliseconds, there is no harm in triggering the sync from the app delegate. Setting up the view controller and loading even the shell UI can take some time.

This may not be too complex to implement, especially with the ReactiveCocoa framework. We can create a signal and pass it on to the view controller, which can pass it downstream if needed. The view controller will be notified once the data is available. Additionally, there is no need to worry about using the local cache except for the special case when there is no network available.

In the first subscenario, it is assumed that the time corresponds to retrieving a large number of entries, equal to or exceeding the minimum required to give a good user experience. What this means is that we are sure that there is no further juggling required once the data is available. It can be directly pushed into the app and a refresh can happen.

Example 5-4 demonstrates how we can make use of a *promise* that is started in the app delegate but made use of in the view controller. This approach seems to violate the MVC principle, so many people disagree with it. Taking a different outlook, it is merely a dependency injection. The promise is the data source injected into the view controller.

Example 5-4. View controller with data source injection

```
//HPAppDelegate.m
-(BOOL)application:(UIApplication *)application
    didFinishLaunchingWithOptions:(NSDictionary *)launchOptions {

    //validate access token, user login, etc.
    RACSignal *feedSignal = [[[HPSyncService sharedInstance]
            fetchType:@"feed"]] replay]; ❶

    HPUserFeedViewController *viewController =
        (HPUserFeedViewController *) self.window.rootViewController;

    viewController.feedSignal = feedSignal; ❷
}

//HPUserFeedViewController.m
-(void)viewDidLoad {
    @weakfily(self);
    [[self.feedSignal ❸
        deliverOn:[RACScheduler mainThreadScheduler]] ❹
        subscribeNext:^(HPUserFeed *feed) {
            @strongify(self);
            [self updateWithFeed:feed]; ❺
            self.feedSignal = nil; ❻
        } error:^(NSError *) {
            //handle error
        }];
}
```

❶ Create the signal.

❷   Assuming that the `rootViewController` is `HPUserFeedViewController` and that there is a property `feedSignal`, set it to the signal obtained earlier.

❸   The controller attaches the subscriber to the signal. Because this operation is done in `viewDidLoad`, it is guaranteed to be executed only once.

❹   A helper call for the response to be delivered on the main thread.

❺   Trigger a UI update.

❻   Free the `feedSignal`. This will reduce the reference count by one and eventually help get it `dealloced`.

In the other subscenario, where the number of entries obtained is not enough to provide a good user experience, pick one of the alternatives:

- Make your service more performant in order to return enough entries.
- If you are, for some reason, stuck with a service not under your control, you will need to think outside the box. See if the same content can be rendered in a manner that takes up more space, so that you can reduce the number of entries to be fetched. You do not need to add padding to create more whitespace.

  For example, if there is an image shown as a small thumbnail, it can be shown larger to give a better summary view. Keep in mind that these new designs can, in fact, result in a better user experience. Figure 5-6 shows screenshots from Facebook and Yahoo Finance. Compare the older screenshots on the left to the ones taken from the newer versions of the apps on the right. Notice how in the more recent images a single entry not only takes up more space (the information is less dense) but also provides better visual appeal.

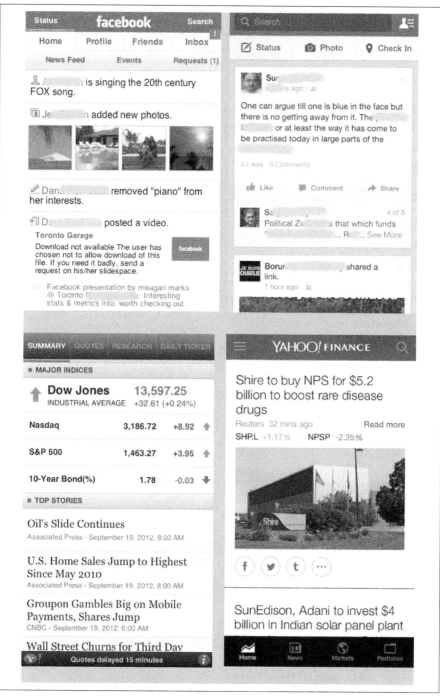

Figure 5-6. Facebook and Yahoo Finance, then and now

Scenario 2

In the case where the time to load from the local cache is comparable to the time taken to retrieve from the server, it's advisable to trigger both the operations simultaneously.

As an example, a mail app may be opened after a substantially long period. In addition to loading from the local cache, it also must synchronize with the server. The time it takes to load messages locally will likely be comparable to the time needed for retrieving new messages.

As before, the fetch should be triggered as early as possible. Inject the signals into the view controller and let it pick up the values from there. The view controller will need to synchronize the update. It should also discard the local cache if values are available from the server—after all, they will be more recent.

With these changes, the view controller code will be similar to that shown in Example 5-5.

Example 5-5. View controller with multiple data source injections

```
@interface HPUserFeedViewController ()

@property (nonatomic, copy) BOOL updatedFromServer; ❶

@end

@implementation HPUserFeedViewController

-(void)viewDidLoad {
    self.updatedFromServer = NO;

    @weakify(self);
    [[self.cacheFeedSignal ❷
        deliverOn: [RACScheduler mainThreadScheduler]
        subscribeNext:^(HPUserFeed *feed) {
            @strongify(self);
            [self updateWithFeed:feed fromServer:NO];
            self.cacheFeedSignal = nil;
        } error:^(NSError *error) {
            //handle error
        }];

    [[self.serverFeedSignal ❸
        deliverOn: [RACScheduler mainThreadScheduler]
        subscribeNext:^(HPUserFeed *feed) {
            @strongify(self);
            [self updateWithFeed:feed fromServer:YES];
            self.cacheFeedSignal = nil;
        } error:^(NSError *error) {
```

```
            //handle error
        }];
}

-(void)updateWithFeed:(HPUserFeed *)feed
    fromServer:(BOOL)fromServer { ❹

    if(self.updatedFromServer) { ❺
        return;
    }
    //proceed with UI refresh
    self.updatedFromServer = fromServer; ❻
}

@end
```

❶ updatedFromServer is a *private* property to track whether the update that happened used data from the remote server.

❷ Add a subscription to the cacheFeedSignal, which will receive data from the local cache.

❸ Add a subscription to the serverFeedSignal, which will receive data from the remote server.

❹ The method to update the UI now takes an extra parameter—a flag that specifies whether the source of the data is the remote server or not.

❺ If the UI has already received updates from the server, there is no need for further updates. This may happen when the server response is available faster than loading from the local cache.

❻ Once the refresh is done, set the updatedFromServer flag indicating whether the refresh was using data from the server.

In the subscenario where the entries from an individual source are not enough to provide a good user experience, it may be preferable to combine the results from the two sources and present the final result. After all, the time taken to retrieve results is comparable, and the merging of the results will be transparent to the user.

Scenario 3

The most common scenario is when the time taken to load data from the local cache is orders of magnitude faster than the time taken to retrieve the latest data from the server. In this case, the stale data should be loaded and updated once the latest data is available.

From an implementation perspective, the solution will be similar to what we saw in scenario 2—two data sources injected into the view controller. The only difference is that the probability of the condition `if(self.updatedFromServer)` being executed in `updateWithFeed:fromServer:` is almost zero.

Warm Launch

Warm launch is about switching to an already-running app. The app may have become inactive because the user swiped down the status bar, or it may have been backgrounded because the user either pressed the home button or switched to another app.

There are two scenarios for warm launch:

- User taps the icon
- App receives a deep link

App relaunch

When the user taps the app icon, generally there is nothing special to be done.

In cases where the app is either very secure or runs heavy animations, it may monitor background and foreground notifications. In the former case, the app may show a login each time it comes into the foreground, while in the latter case, animations or game state may have been suspended and require a resume. Figure 5-7 illustrates how the apps Temple Run and Intuit Mint handle this scenario.

Other than that, it is mostly no different than the user continuing to interact with the app.

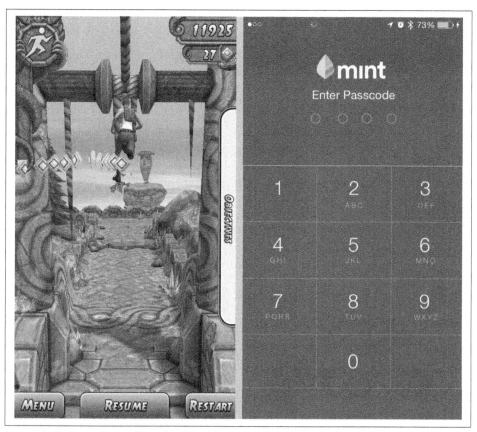

Figure 5-7. App warm relaunch—TempleRun and Mint (TempleRun pauses the game and expects the user to resume it while Mint secures the access with a passcode)

Deep links

When your app receives a call to `application:openURL:sourceApplication:annota tion:`, the expectation is that the user will be taken to the specific screen in the app that completes his original intent. However, the target app may already be loaded in a specific state.

If the deep link requires fetching data from the server, you can either show stale state associated with the deep link or show only a progress bar while it refreshes with the latest data from the server.

To help the user complete his intent, you can follow these best practices:

- Support deep links by providing an option to "go back" to the source app. The simplest way to do this is to accept a parameter in the incoming URL that will be the destination URL once the action in this app is complete.

As an example, the Facebook app allows you to deep link into the Messenger app with an option to return to the Facebook app once you are done messaging.

- Prefer implementing the app as a simplified finite state machine. This allows you to push the new screen and pop it once the interaction is completed.

Using the previous example, if you open the Messenger app, there is no "back" button to take you to the Facebook app. The state is "pushed" onto the app if you deep link into the Messenger app.

Here, the intent is to "chat with a friend." Once the intent is complete, there is nothing better than providing an option to go back to where the user started. Note that for this communication, both apps must support deep links.

iPhones still do not have a hardware Back button, which means that the app must accommodate the UI itself. Figure 5-8 shows examples of two more apps: the Chrome browser and Google Maps. Notice that the UI to take the user back into the original app is very different in each and highly tied to that of the destination app.

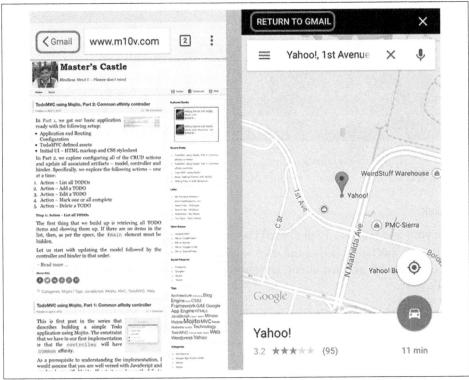

Figure 5-8. Deep links with "Back" navigation support

Launch After Upgrade

An app's first launch after upgrade will follow one of the following scenarios:

- There is no local cache, or the app discards it completely.
- The local cache can be used, either as is or migrated, by the upgraded version of the app.

If there is no local cache or the app decides to discard it (e.g., if the data is unusable or if synchronizing from the server is faster), no special processing is required.

Inform the user about what is about to happen to the local data. The following best practices can be applied to keep the user happy:

- When the local cache can be used, inform the user about it. Do not inform the user if there is no migration required because then the use of the local cache is implicit.
- If the data must be migrated and the process may take several minutes, give an option to postpone it.
- When the local cache must be discarded because it is easier and faster to retrieve data from the server, inform the user about it.

  A case in hand is when migrating several records, say in a mail app, to the updated schema in the newer version of the app may be more complex than retrieving them from the server.

Push Notifications

Notifications are an integral part of a content-driven app. The content may be curated like news or user-generated like email. It is assumed that you are aware of the callbacks `application:didReceiveRemoteNotification:` and `application:didReceiveLocalNotification:` in the app delegate.

It is important to know the order in which the methods are called and how the user interaction drives other method calls. It impacts the sequence of initialization that your app follows and what subcomponent initialization you can place in specific callbacks to minimize resource utilization and maximize the quantum of tasks to be accomplished.

Remote Notifications

Figure 5-9 shows the delegate callbacks received for notifications.

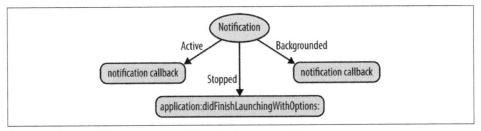

Figure 5-9. App delegate complete lifecycle for notifications

The lifecycle on iOS 8 can be described as follows:

- If the app is active, it receives the notification via the `didReceiveRemoteNotifica` `tion` callback.

  No other callbacks are invoked. No UI is presented to the user to avoid any distraction.

- If the app is backgrounded or stopped, only the silent push notification callbacks are triggered.

  Based on the notification settings, non-silent push notifications may appear in the notification center or as alerts and/or update the app icon's badge counter.

- When the user opens a notification by interacting with it using the notification center or an alert, one of the following may happen:

  — If the app was backgrounded, the notification callback method is invoked.

  — If the app was stopped, the notification object (`NSDictionary`) is available in the `launchOptions` parameter to the method `application:didFinishLaun` `chingWithOptions:`.

As you might have noticed, the lifecycle is not very clean and is highly dependent on the application state, which forces you to have handler blocks at multiple places in your code.

A typical outline for handling notifications is similar to the one given in Example 5-6.

Example 5-6. Handling notifications

```
-(void)application:(UIApplication *)application
    didReceiveRemoteNotification:(NSDictionary *)userInfo { ❶
    //See the next method
}

- (void)application:(UIApplication *)application
    didReceiveRemoteNotification:(NSDictionary *)userInfo
    fetchCompletionHandler:(void (^)(UIBackgroundFetchResult))completionHandler { ❷
    //process remote notification - app running ❸
```

```
        if(application.applicationState == UIApplicationStateInactive) { ❹
            //user tapped the notification in notification center or the alert
            [self processRemoteNotification:userInfo];
        } else if(application.applicationState == UIApplicationStateBackground) {
            //App in background, no user interaction - just fetch data
        } else {
            //app is already active - show in-app update
        }
}

-(void)application:(UIApplication *)application
    didFinishLaunchingWithOptions:(NSDictionary *)launchOptions { ❺
    id notification = [launchOptions
        objectForKey:UIApplicationLaunchOptionsRemoteNotificationKey];

    if(notification != nil) { ❻
        NSDictionary *userInfo = (NSDictionary *)notification; ❼
        [self processRemoteNotification:userInfo];
    }
}

-(void)processRemoteNotification:(NSDictionary *)userInfo { ❽
}
```

❶   iOS 7 callback.

❷   iOS 8 callback. If implemented, this is called instead of the method `applica`
    `tion:didReceiveRemoteNotification`.

❸   The callback is called if and only if the app is running. The callback will not be
    invoked if the app is not running.

❹   If the app is active, it is preferred to not immediately switch the UI—a subtle
    indicator (e.g., in-app banner) in the app should be preferred. If backgrounded,
    this callback was invoked because the user tapped on the notification—feel free to
    switch the UI.

❺   This is where all the magic happens.

❻   When the user checks for the presence of the key `UIApplicationLaunchOptions`
    `RemoteNotificationKey`.

❼   If present, this is where the remote notification data is available. Process it.

❽   Central place to process notification.

Let's look at some of the best practices that you can follow to manage this lifecycle so
that your app will provide the best user experience possible:

- When the app receives a notification in the active state, either discard it or show subtle feedback. For example:
  — In case of a mail app, if the notification is about a new mail, update the badge for the folder that the mail belongs to. If the notification is about a new mail in the thread that is currently open, a better option may be to update the thread and show an indicator that a new mail is available. Similarly, if the new message is for a different chat session, you can perhaps show an in-app banner, such as the one shown in Figure 5-10. The banner placement should be such that it does not obstruct the user from completing the current task.
  — In the case of a messaging app, if the notification is about a new message in the currently open chat session, show the message inline, updating the thread. (It is not a good idea to use push notifications for all messages, because delivery is not 100% guaranteed.)

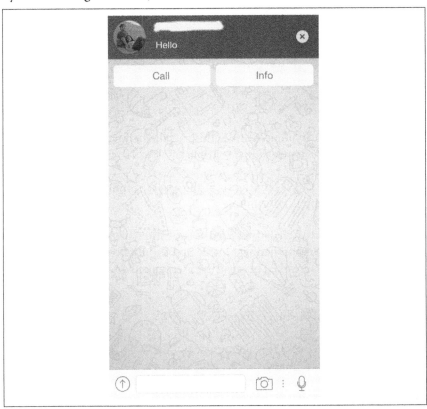

Figure 5-10. WhatsApp showing in-app banner for a new message in a different chat session

- When the app receives a notification in the inactive state, it is because the user tapped on the notification. But because the user was already in the middle of doing something else, you may want to push the new UI with support to "go back" to the previous UI. The exact semantics of the user experience will depend on the app and the action.

  For example, in the case of a financial app, if the current screen being shown is the account summary and the notification is about the transaction just completed, show the user the corresponding details with the "back" navigation taking the user back to the account summary.

- When the app receives details about the notification object in the `applica tion:didFinishLaunchingWithOptions:` callback, take the user directly to the UI related to the notification.

Note that `application:didReceiveRemoteNotification:` is called only when an app is in the foreground, whereas `application:didReceiveRemoteNotification:fetch CompletionHandler:`, if implemented, can be called even if the app is in the background and can even start the app if it is not already running. Such notifications are known as *silent push notifications*.

It is also important to note that the latter method may be called twice:

- First when the notification is received and the payload contains the key `content-available` with value 1[5]

- Second when the user interacts with the notification, either in the notification center or an alert

To distinguish between the two, use the application state, as illustrated in Example 5-6.

Notifications should be meaningful. The payload should have appropriate text to be shown to the user and also data to be used in the callback to decide whether a background fetch should be triggered.

Local Notifications

Unlike remote notifications, local notifications will not show any UI when the app is in use.

Great. So the question are as follows:

---

5 Stack Overflow, "didReceiveRemoteNotification:fetchCompletionHandler Not Being Called When App Is in Background and Not Connected to Xcode" (*http://stackoverflow.com/a/20851481/332210*).

- If the app is in use, why would you show a local notification?
- And if the app is not in use, it is suspended—in which case, how can you show a local notification?

The answer lies in *silent remote notifications*. If the remote notification payload has the property `content-available` set to a value of 1, it tells the OS that the remote notification should not be shown to the user but must be directly passed on to the app. Like a regular push notification, it may wake up the app, if need be.

The app can then process the data, trigger a remote fetch if needed, and create a local notification. The advantage of this approach is that by the time the user interacts with the notification, the data may have already been downloaded, processed, and made available in a usable form. As such, the response time to show the details about the notification is short and the user feels happy about the fast and responsive app.

The `application:didReceiveRemoteNotification:fetchCompletionHandler:` app delegate callback (or the `application:didReceiveLocalNotification:` callback, if that is not implemented) is called when the app is in the foreground or when the user taps on the notification when the app is in the background, whereas the `application:handleActionWithIdentifier:forRemoteNotification:completionHandler:` callback is called when the user uses the custom action in the notification.

 Use local notifications in conjunction with silent push notifications to make the app responsive and usable faster on the next launch.

Background Fetch

Background fetch was introduced in iOS 7 and is a great option to periodically sync data from the server. There are three basic steps to enable background fetch:

1. Enable the capability in your project settings.
2. Set the refresh interval, preferably in `application:didFinishLaunchingWithOptions`. Use the `-UIApplication setMinimumBackgroundFetchInterval:` method to request that the refresh be done at the specified frequency.
3. Implement the `application:performFetchWithCompletionHandler:` app delegate method. If the task is not complete within 30 seconds, the OS will schedule the method execution less frequently.

On a practical note, the typical time that the app may get is much smaller, generally in the range of 2–4 seconds. The Apple developer website lists 30 seconds as the upper-bound limit.[6]

Background fetch and push notifications can be used to create amazing and delightful experiences for the user. Let's look at some guidelines that you can follow to make a great impression:

- Use background fetch to periodically sync data with the server. Consider it like batch operations that you want to perform.

- Do not overly rely on the regularity of the execution of the background task. The OS will schedule it at periodic, though not regular, intervals.

During daytime hours, this interval will generally be in the range of 10–20 minutes (see Figure 5-11). The number varies based on how often the app completes the response with `UIBackgroundFetchResultNoData` or `UIBackgroundFetchResultNewData`, the average time it takes to complete the operation, network conditions, estimated available bandwidth, CPU and memory available, and more. The interval may increase to well over a few hours in the evening.

```
15:43:14.388 HPerf Apps[20551:8463048] [W] [performFetchWithCompletionHandler] called
15:43:14.389 HPerf Apps[20551:8463048] <HPInst> App Fetch
15:43:14.703 HPerf Apps[20551:8463048] [W] [shouldSaveApplicationState] called
15:43:14.705 HPerf Apps[20551:8463048] [W] [willEncodeRestorableStateWithCoder] called
16:03:38.540 HPerf Apps[20551:8463048] [W] [performFetchWithCompletionHandler] called
16:03:38.541 HPerf Apps[20551:8463048] <HPInst> App Fetch
16:03:38.769 HPerf Apps[20551:8463048] [W] [shouldSaveApplicationState] called
16:03:38.771 HPerf Apps[20551:8463048] [W] [willEncodeRestorableStateWithCoder] called
16:13:14.042 HPerf Apps[20551:8463048] [W] [performFetchWithCompletionHandler] called
16:13:14.043 HPerf Apps[20551:8463048] <HPInst> App Fetch
16:13:14.369 HPerf Apps[20551:8463048] [W] [shouldSaveApplicationState] called
16:13:14.370 HPerf Apps[20551:8463048] [W] [willEncodeRestorableStateWithCoder] called
16:28:14.453 HPerf Apps[20551:8463048] [W] [performFetchWithCompletionHandler] called
16:28:14.454 HPerf Apps[20551:8463048] <HPInst> App Fetch
16:28:14.726 HPerf Apps[20551:8463048] [W] [shouldSaveApplicationState] called
16:28:14.759 HPerf Apps[20551:8463048] [W] [willEncodeRestorableStateWithCoder] called
```

Figure 5-11. Background fetch interval tracker (highlighted in red)

- Use push notifications to wake up or start the app.

- Use `content-available = 1` in the payload so that the notification handler method can also synchronize data with the server.

Try to keep this synchronization only for the items related to the notification item rather than a complete resync.

---

6 iOS Developer Library, "UIApplicationDelegate" (*http://apple.co/1eMyYY0*).

Because the background fetch takes your app out of the suspended state, any suspended queues may resume. If the other layers of the app are not made aware of the fact that the task queues may soon be paused again, it can lead to a catastrophic crash.

Use `NSNotifications` to notify different components of the app to terminate any ongoing operations, because the app has been awakened for a background fetch operation and will soon be suspended again (30 seconds being upper limit).

It will be of added benefit to use `NSURLSession` with an `NSURLSessionConfiguration` object configured using `backgroundSessionConfigurationWithIdentifier`. This allows out-of-process execution of such long-running tasks, managed by an OS-level daemon. In a case where the app is killed or crashes, such *background network sessions* will continue.

For non-networking operations, you will have to implement such a system on your own.

Smart Silent Notifications

One of the apps I worked with in the past had strong security requirements. Specifically, the access token generated after a successful login had an expiration period of 24 hours. The app could auto-login without requiring the user to reenter credentials, but after 24 hours, the session would expire and need to be re-created—needless to say, this did not make for a very good user experience.

To resolve this problem, we used background fetch, which did nothing more than refresh the session.

However, we realized that when we added this feature, there were more frequent app crashes. Investigation revealed that the suspended operation queues were resuming, not knowing that the app would soon be suspended again. One of these operations was to synchronize data with the server, but because the sync could not complete, strange things happened—the connection timed out because of no activity; the server rarely received complete data; and if the server responded with the data, the client would rarely process the complete data, leaving the app in an inconsistent state.

We had to fix the app-sync layer so that it could be made aware of the application state before firing the sync operation.

We quickly switched to silent notifications. The server would send a silent push notification during the evening. This would wake up the app, which would in turn check whether the device was on WiFi and if it had enough battery (or, if not, whether it was in the process of charging). If so, it would do a preemptive session refresh.

As such, the following day, whenever the user would interact with the app, there would not be unexpected latencies.

Summary

Knowing about the application lifecycle and how it impacts the user's perception of your app is key to creating apps that users love.

At times, actual performance may be less important than the *perceived performance*. Using silent notifications and background fetches to *warm up* the app to keep it ready for the next use is a smart way to achieve a positive perception of your app.

Now that we've covered optimization techniques for various scenarios, including first launch, cold start, warm start, and launch after upgrade, you should be able to minimize the startup time and make your app usable as quickly as possible.

CHAPTER 6

User Interface

Only the baker knows what went wrong with the cake.

—Anonymous

Most users first notice performance issues when interacting with the user interface. An app might be termed sluggish if it takes a long time to synchronize data and refresh, or when the user interaction is jittery.

Factors such as power consumption, network usage, local storage, and the like are mostly invisible to the user. Although these factors do contribute to performance issues, it is the user interface that is the gateway to the app, and its sluggishness directly impacts user feedback.

There are external factors that you cannot control. Examples of external factors include:

Network
Poor network conditions increases the time taken to synchronize.

Hardware
Better hardware makes for better performance—newer iPhones running newer versions of the OS will see faster execution as compared to older iPhones. The app may run on CPUs varying from 32-bit 1.3 GHz to 64-bit 1.8 GHz, or RAM ranging from 1 GB to 2 GB.

Storage
The app may run on devices with varying storage ranging from 16 GB to 128 GB, which limits the offline cache that your app can store.

The app, however, can make decisions based on the conditions under which it is executed to keep the user interaction fluid.

In this chapter, we discuss ways to minimize the time taken to update the user interface. At the end of this chapter, you should be able to find ways to tune your app to be able to run at 60 frames per second (fps). That means the app has 16.666 milliseconds (ms) to do all the processing it needs to complete the next frame of the transition. And if it takes 1×10^{-9} seconds to execute one instruction, the app can essentially execute about 10 million instructions in that time. On a different scale, if it takes ~30 nanoseconds (ns) to invoke a simple no-op method (including time to set up the stack frame, push parameters, execute, and finally clean it up), there is enough time to execute over half a million methods. And that is a lot of methods that can be executed.

Frame Rate

The human eye and its brain interface, the human visual system, can process 10 to 12 separate images per second, perceiving them individually. The threshold of human visual perception varies depending on what is being measured.

When looking at a lighted display, people begin to notice a brief interruption of darkness if it lasts about 16 ms or longer.

There are ways to optimize the frame rate, depending on the device's capabilities. For example, when running on a device with less RAM, load less data in memory. As another example, minimize use of animations on a slower CPU.

In this chapter, we look at the following components:

- The view controller and its lifecycle
- View rendering
- Custom views
- Layouts
- App extensions (widgets)
- Animations
- Interactive notifications

We study insights into these components, ways to optimize the execution, and tricks to have a better *perceived experience* if there is nothing more we can do to optimize execution.

View Controller

The view controller serves as the glue between data services and the view. Data services may not only provide access to in-memory data but also request updates from or post updates to the server or a local database.

The lifecycle of a view controller is tied to its `view` property—it determines when the view is created, shown, removed, and destroyed. Figure 6-1 shows the view controller lifecycle.

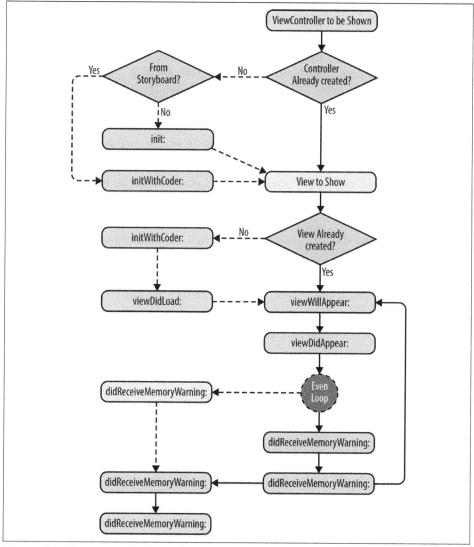

Figure 6-1. View controller lifecycle

App development generally starts with a lean view controller, which is good. But over time, these view controllers slowly turn into the dumping ground for all business logic and grow to several thousand lines of code. Although the total "volume" of logic may be unavoidable, there will always be a good case to refactor the code into smaller, reusable methods. This not only provides decoupling but also helps you uncover unused or duplicate code.

Let's begin with basic best practices to follow when structuring view controllers:

- Keep the view controller lightweight. In an MVC app, the controller is only glue. This is not where the entire business logic lies. It does not even belong to the model. The business logic belongs to the service or business logic component. Keep it there.

  The view controller should bind the service component to the views by means of what can be termed *action delegates* or *service providers*, which should preferably be injected into the controller (see "Dependency Injection" on page 75).

- Do not write animation logic in the view controller. This may be in an independent animation class that accepts views to apply animations on. View controllers *attach* the animations to the views or transitions.

  Special-purpose views may *own* their own animations. For example, a custom spinner controller will have its own animation.

- Use data source and delegate protocols to separate the code pertaining to data retrieval, update, and other business logic. View controllers are restricted to picking correct views and connecting them to the feeders.

- View controllers respond to events from the views—for example, button click or table cell selection—and connect them back into data sinks.

- View controllers respond to UI-related events from the OS—for example, orientation changes or low-memory warnings. This may trigger relayout of the views.

- Do not write custom `init` code. Why? Well, what if your view controller is repurposed to an XIB or storyboard? The `init` method will never be called.

- Do not handcraft the UI in the view controller using code. Do not implement all UI, view creation, and view layout logic in the view controller. Use nibs or storyboards.

  Handcrafted code does not last long, especially as the app grows and designs change. It is faster to redesign using Interface Builder than to hand code pixel coordinates.

  In addition, the app may run on devices with different sizes and form factors. It is difficult to scale custom code to work with all form factors, handle rotation during orientation changes, and keep pace with new design paradigms that evolve every couple of years or so.

Also, when you have the design separated out in independent nibs and storyboards, you will have the flexibility to run A/B testing where it is easy to choose between different layouts.

- Prefer creating a base view controller with common setup and have other view controllers inherit from this.

  This technique is not always possible, because there may be a need to inherit from different view controllers at different parts of the app. For example, you should use `UITableViewController` for the contacts list and `UIViewController` for the user profile.

  However, if you have multiple places where you need to show content in a `UIWeb View`, a base view controller will work well. If you need to display the privacy policy URL or terms and conditions page, you do not need to subclass. However, if you need to show an image or video that a user shares (in a messaging app), you can create subclasses that can define custom chrome or control overlays.

- Use categories for creating reusable code across view controllers. In case a parent view controller does not suffice (for example, because you need different *types* of view controllers in your app), create categories and add your custom methods or properties there.

  That way, you are not restricted to using a predefined base class and still get the benefit of reusability.

Now that we are aware of some best practices for writing view controllers, let's explore what to do and what not to do as far as the `UIViewController` lifecycle methods are concerned.

View Load

Two methods that participate in view initialization are `loadView` and `viewDidLoad`.

If you recollect the template code generated by Xcode when you add a new view controller, it has only the `viewDidLoad` method. `loadView` is called by the view controller when its `view` is requested, but is `nil` because it has not been created yet.

There are three ways in which the view can be loaded:

- From the nibs
- Using a storyboard (using `UIStoryboardSegue`)
- Using custom code to create the user interface

If you create a custom UI by overriding the `loadView` method, keep the following in mind:

- Do set the `view` property to the root of the view hierarchy.
- Ensure that the views are now shared with any other view controllers.
- Do not call [`super loadView`].

Use this method to change the view states, specifically if they were loaded from the nib files. We focus our discussion on `viewDidLoad`.

`viewDidLoad` is called exactly once, after the view hierarchy is ready but before the view is presented to the user. This is the place to do one-time initialization.

Common tasks that should be done in the `viewDidLoad` method include:

- Configuring data sources to populate data.
- Binding data to views.

  This is a debatable item. Depending on the use case, you may bind data once and have a refresh button, or bind each time `viewWillAppear` is called. The upside of doing the latter is that the UI always has the latest data. The downside is that if the data does not update frequently (e.g., in a news app), the user may see an unnecessary refresh each time (say, when the `UITableView` rebinds).

- Binding view event handlers, data source delegates, and other callbacks.
- Registering observers on data.

  Depending on where you bind data to the views, observers on data may also change.

- Monitoring for notifications from the notification center.
- Initializing animations.

During execution, time spent in the `viewDidLoad` method should be as minimal as possible. Specifically, the data to be rendered should either be already available or be loaded in another thread. Any delay in completion of `viewDidLoad` will result in delayed presentation of the UI associated with the view controller. The user will be stuck at app launch or with the previous view controller.

View Hierarchy

The UI presented is comprised of hierarchical views nested in a tree structure and positioned using constraints when using Auto Layout or programmatically otherwise. View construction and rendering involves the following steps:

1. Construct subviews.
2. Compute and apply constraints.

3. Perform steps 1 and 2 recursively for the subviews.

4. Render recursively.

As the view hierarchy gets complex, it takes longer to construct and render the view. Consider a simplistic flat hierarchy:

- `UILabel`
- Custom view
- `UIImageView`
- `UILabel`

On an iPhone 6 using iOS 8.1, the time taken from view controller load (`initWith Coder:`) to just before render (`viewWillAppear:`) is about 15 ms on average. And this does not take into account the one-time cost of loading the layout from the disk (storyboard/nib file). The method `viewDidAppear:` is called after about 300 ms but that is because of the transition animation.

Figures 6-2 and 6-3 show the UI for the view hierarchy and logged times, respectively.

The simple UI shown in Figure 6-2 took about 15 ms to load, leaving about 1.6 ms for other operations in order to achieve 60 fps rendering. As the UI grows in complexity and requires more data processing, it becomes even more important to optimize for execution.

If this simplistic example can take that long to load (not render) the UI, leaving you with just about 1 ms to do all the other operations, one can extrapolate the amount of effort needed to contain all execution within 16.66 ms for 60 fps rendering.

Frame Rate Versus Dropped Frames

Because there is very little that you can do about initial nib/storyboard load and view construction times, you'll need to go back to the drawing board and determine what makes users unhappy. Is it because the app cannot run at 60 fps or because it has jitter?

If the app drops 1 frame every second and runs at 59 fps, it will still be smooth. However, if it runs at 60 fps for 5 seconds and then drops 5 frames in the 6th second, that is where the user notices the jitter.

Although it's a few years old and mostly about Android, it's still worthwhile to have a bedtime reading of Andrew Munn's "Follow up to 'Android Graphics True Facts,' or The Reason Android is Laggy" (*http://bit.ly/1ABwcgB*).

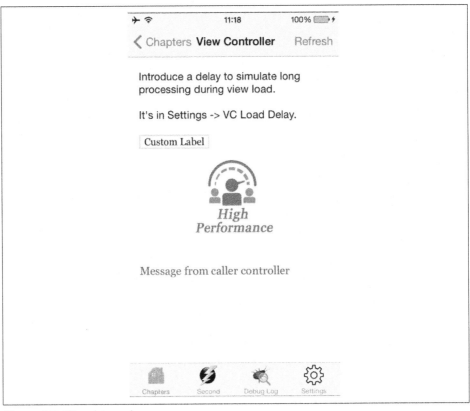

Figure 6-2. View hierarchy

```
-14 11:28:08.570 HPerf Apps[1788:541924] [I] [VC::initWithCoder]: 0.000410
-14 11:28:08.571 HPerf Apps[1788:541924] [V] prepareForSegue[HPCVC] destination: ident=segue_ch07_al_vc cls=HPChap
-14 11:28:08.572 HPerf Apps[1788:541924] [I] [VC::setMessage]
-14 11:28:08.586 HPerf Apps[1788:541924] [I] [MV::didAddSubview] time=8750ns for UILabel
-14 11:28:08.588 HPerf Apps[1788:541924] [I] [MV::didAddSubview] time=1000ns for HPCustomLabel
-14 11:28:08.590 HPerf Apps[1788:541924] [I] [MV::didAddSubview] time=750ns for UIImageView
-14 11:28:08.590 HPerf Apps[1788:541924] [I] [MV::didAddSubview] time=583ns for UILabel
-14 11:28:08.591 HPerf Apps[1788:541924] [I] [MV::didAddSubview] time=416ns for _UILayoutGuide
-14 11:28:08.592 HPerf Apps[1788:541924] [I] [MV::didAddSubview] time=791ns for _UILayoutGuide
-14 11:28:08.594 HPerf Apps[1788:541924] [I] [VC::p:viewDidLoad]: 0.024300
-14 11:28:08.595 HPerf Apps[1788:541924] [I] [VC::viewDidLoad]: 0.025468
-14 11:28:08.595 HPerf Apps[1788:541924] [I] [VC::viewWillAppear]: 0.025855
-14 11:28:08.596 HPerf Apps[1788:541924] <HPInst> SCR_ViewController
-14 11:28:08.611 HPerf Apps[1788:541924] [I] [MV::layoutSubviews] time=2420416ns
-14 11:28:08.615 HPerf Apps[1788:541924] [I] [MV::drawRect] time=1083ns
-14 11:28:09.124 HPerf Apps[1788:541924] [I] [VC::viewDidAppear]: 0.554471
-14 11:28:09.126 HPerf Apps[1788:541924] [I] [MV::layoutSubviews] time=74250ns
```

Figure 6-3. Logged times

Our focus now will be not only to get as much as possible of the main thread execution done within 16 ms, but also to minimize the number of frames dropped (or bulk drop of frames, to be more explicit).

View Visibility

The view controller provides four lifecycle methods to be notified about view visibility:

viewWillAppear:

> This method is called when the view hierarchy is ready and the view is about to be brought into the viewport. This happens when the view controller is about to be presented or the earlier pushed (modal or otherwise) view controller has popped out.
>
> The transition animation is yet to start at this point in time and the view is not yet visible to the end user. Do not start any view animations—they will be of no use.

viewDidAppear:

> This method is called after the view has been presented to the viewport and after the transition animation is complete.
>
> Because the animation can take about 300 ms, expect a big time difference between viewDidAppear: and viewWillAppear: as compared to viewWillAppear: and viewDidLoad:.
>
> Start or resume any view animations that you want to present to the end user here.

viewWillDisappear:

> This is an indication that the view is about to be hidden from the screen. This may be because another view controller is trying to take over the screen or because this view controller is about to be popped out.
>
> As you may notice, when the method is called, there is no direct way to know if the current view controller is about to be popped out or another view controller has pushed in.
>
> The only way to distinguish is to scan the viewControllers property of the navigationController for the current view controller. Example 6-1 provides skeleton code for this.

Example 6-1. Detect view controller push versus pop

```
-(void)viewWillDisappear:(BOOL)animated {
    NSInteger index = [self.navigationController.viewControllers
        indexOfObject:self];
    if(index == NSNotFound) {
        //about to be popped out, tear down
    } else {
```

```
        //just save state, pause
    }
    [super viewWillDisappear:animated];
}
```

Using unwind segues is the preferred option when using segues and storyboards. Technical Note TN2298 from Apple[1] provides a good overview of using unwind segues.

viewDidDisappear:

This method is called after the transition animation to the previous/next view controller is complete. As with viewDidAppear:, there is about a 300 ms gap from the viewWillDisappear: event.

Remember the lifecycle diagram presented in Figure 6-1? Flip back and you will notice that these lifecycle methods can be called multiple times, and depending upon the user interaction, there may be an infinite cycle of these events.

 The lifecycle methods related to view visibility are not called when the app is backgrounded or foregrounded, which is notified to UIAppDelegate. View controller lifecycle methods are called only when the app is active, not even during any transitions.

Register for UIApplicationDidBecomeActiveNotification, UIApplicationWillResignActiveNotification, and UIApplicationWillEnterForegroundNotification notifications in the view controller in combination with the view visibility callbacks. And do not forget to unregister in dealloc.

Some best practices for effectively using these lifecycle events are given next:

- Do not override loadView. Enough said.

- Use viewDidLoad as the last checkpoint to see if the data from data sources is available. If so, update the UI elements.

- Use viewWillAppear: to update the UI elements—but only if you really want to always show the *latest* details.

  For example, in a messaging app, if the user returns to the message list in the chat session after watching a shared video, you would want to refresh it with the latest messages.

  However, in a news app, you may not want to immediately refresh the list with all the new articles, lest the user lose the context. In the latter case, the *table view*

---

1 iOS Developer Library, "Technical Note TN2298: Using Unwind Segues" (*http://apple.co/1Hk6LP5*).

view controller will generally listen to the events from the *data source* and prefer to make subtle and infrequent updates to the list of new articles.

- Use `viewDidAppear:` to start animations. If you have streaming content such as video, play that. Subscribe to application events to detect if the animation/video or any other processing that continuously updates the video should continue or not.

  It is not advisable to update the UI here with the latest data. If you do so, the final effect will be that the user transitions into an old UI followed by an update after the transition animation is complete, which may not be a great experience.

  Having said that, there may still be use cases that force you to perform UI updates in `viewDidAppear:`. If the user experience is acceptable, go ahead with it.

- Use `viewWillDisappear:` to pause or stop animations. Again, do nothing more.

- Use `viewDidDisappear:` to tear down any complex data structures that you may have held in memory.

  This is also a good time to unregister for any notifications from the data sources that the view controller may be bound to and also with the notification center for the app events that will have been connected to animations, data sources, or other UI updates.

 If all other steps to optimize load time fail, add a subtle animation to your app. It may just give you the additional tens of milliseconds you need to complete the tasks without a noticeable delay when using the app. Note that prolonged animations will, not surprisingly, irritate the users, and you may end up losing them permanently. This should therefore be used as a last resort and with caution.

View

The most challenging part of optimizing views is that there are very few techniques that can be applied universally to all the views. Each view has its unique purpose, and most of the optimization techniques are bound to the specific view and the API it exposes.

But before we discuss them individually, let's review some basic rules to follow:

- Minimize work done in the main thread. Any extra code to be executed means higher chances of dropping a frame. Too many frames dropped will introduce jitter.

- Avoid *fat* nibs or storyboards. Storyboards are great, but the entire XML must be loaded (I/O) and parsed (XML processing) before it can really be used. Minimize the number of units that go into storyboards.

  If needed, create multiple storyboards or nib files. This will ensure that all the screens are not loaded in one go during app launch, but are loaded as needed. This not only helps the app start-up time but also keeps the overall memory requirement lower:

  > When a nib file is loaded into memory, the nib-loading code takes several steps to ensure the objects in the nib file are created and initialized properly.

  > When you load a nib file that contains references to image or sound resources, the nib-loading code reads the actual image or sound file into memory and caches it. … In iOS, only image resources are stored in named caches.[2]

- Avoid multiple layers of nesting in the view hierarchy. Try to keep it as flat as possible. Nesting is a necessary evil, but still an evil.

  Each time a view is added anywhere in the hierarchy, its ancestor tree receives a `setNeedsLayout:` with a value of `YES` that causes `layoutSubviews:` to be invoked when the event queue is processed. This is an expensive call because the view has to recompute the positions of the subviews using the constraints, and it happens for each level in the ancestor tree.

  The Twitter team posted that for a tweet, instead of using a composite view comprising a `UIImageView` and a few `UILabel` elements, they created a custom view and preferred to have a simplistic and optimized implementation of `drawRect:`.[3]

- Lazy-load the views and reuse them wherever possible. The more views you have, the longer it takes to not only load but also render them, which impacts both memory and CPU usage.

  If needed, create your own view cache. This may be over and above the cell-reuse support already provided in `UITableView` and `UICollectionView`. These containers will let the view be `dealloced` when not in the viewport. If the view construction is complex and takes time, implementing a custom view cache is advisable.

  What if you use `UIScrollView`? Definitely lazy-load. Load only the views required for scroll position `0`, and then mimic `UITableView` behavior by building your own view cache. Use `delegate`'s `scrollViewDidScroll:` in conjunction with the `contentOffset` (scroll position) property to know which views are to be rendered.

---

2 iOS Developer Library, "Resource Programming Guide: Nib Files" (*http://bit.ly/1CwoRy5*).

3 Twitter Blog, "Simple Strategies for Smooth Animation on the iPhone" (*http://bit.ly/1M74uh6*).

As a general practice, render elements up to the screen height beyond the view-port to avoid any jitter during scroll since they need to be rendered in quick succession as the scrolling starts.

And keep this at the back of your mind: `UITableView` inherits from `UIScroll View`, which means if `UITableView` can do smart view caching, so can your custom code.

- Prefer custom drawing for complex UIs. It results in one view to be drawn instead of multiple subviews, and avoids costly `layoutSubviews` and `drawRect:` calls.

  In addition, you avoid the cost of using general-purpose, feature-rich components by using optimized views for optimized direct drawing.

  For example, if you need to display plain text, you do not need the heavy lifting of `UILabel` (see Figure 6-4 later).

Now that we've covered these basic foundational rules, let's explore some of the more common views and take a deep dive into performance tips associated with each.

UILabel

This is probably the most common view used on iOS. However simple it may seem, rendering it is not trivial. There are a few complex steps involved:

1. Using the font family, font style, and text to be rendered, compute the number of pixels it requires. This is an extremely costly process and it should be done as sparingly as possible.[4]
2. Check against the `width` of the available `frame` to render.
3. Check against the `numberOfLines` to compute the number of lines to show.
4. Was `sizeToFit` called? If so, compute the height.
5. If `sizeToFit` was not called, check if content can be shown for the given `height` of the `frame`.
6. If the `frame` is not sufficient, use `lineBreakMode` to determine the wrap or truncation location.
7. Take care of other configuration options, as seen in Figure 6-4 (e.g., if it is plain text or attributed, shadows, alignment, autoshrink, etc.).
8. Finally, use the font, style, and color to render the *final* text to be shown.

---

4 Required size computation has to be done in the main thread.

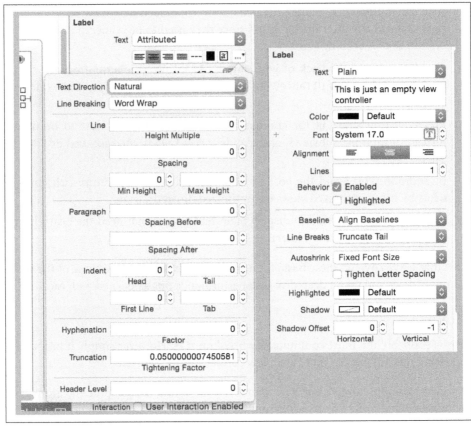

Figure 6-4. UILabel options

Specifying each `UILabel` is a lot of work. With fewer labels, the efforts are manageable, but with many labels, be careful of how you create, configure, and reuse them.

If you dynamically compute the width of a label as a fraction of the container's width, ensure that the width is evenly divisible by that percentage. For example, if two labels each occupy 50% of the width of the container, let the width of the container be even. Avoid calls like `width/2`. If the width is a fraction, everything will work great except that the rendering requires anti-aliasing, which is an expensive operation.

UIButton

Buttons are almost everywhere—the navigation items in a navigation controller, the "Send" button in a messaging app or in custom forms, and so on. So, unless your app has only animations and custom rendering, there will be a button somewhere in the app.

There are four ways to render a button:

- Default rendering with custom text
- Button with full-sized assets
- Resizable assets
- Using CALayer and Bézier paths for custom drawing

We will not go into the details of what goes into each but will primarily focus on the advantages and disadvantages of each option. The first option is very straightforward and the remaining are discussed in "Designing for iOS: Taming UIButton" (*http://bit.ly/1NE5yXs*).

Table 6-1 presents the pros and cons of working with each option for rendering a button.

Table 6-1. Button rendering options

Option	Advantages	Drawbacks
Custom text	• Simplest, uncomplicated, and most straightforward to use	• Generally dull, unfancy buttons
Full-size assets	• Customizable backgrounds • No-code implementation possible • A/B testing possible—images can be downloaded when running experiments	• Images are bundled with the app, resulting in a larger bundle size
Resizable-size assets	• Customizable backgrounds • No-code implementation possible • A/B testing possible—images can be downloaded when running experiments • Relatively less increase in bundle size	• Any change in an asset may require recomputing/resetting the UIEdgeInsets values
Custom drawing using CALayer/Bézier path	• Total custom drawing	• Any change or upgrade in format may require an update to the app

You will need to weigh the pros and cons of these options, and choose the one that suits your needs. A button is an otherwise simple component to render—it will rarely need any performance boost. However, if you intend to make it more beautiful, colorful, and fancy, you will need to explore the many other available options.

UIImageView

No app is complete without images—they're what make apps beautiful.

However, images are one of the most expensive UI elements to be rendered. And they are mostly dumb—once created, they cannot be changed. To show an image variation, another image has to be loaded. Animated GIFs are still not natively supported on iOS. You will have to create an array of `animationImages` that are subsequently animated. Other options include writing custom code or using a third-party library such as ImageMagick (*http://www.imagemagick.org/*) or `AnimatedGIFImageSeriali zation` (*https://github.com/mattt/AnimatedGIFImageSerialization*).

Follow these best practices to maximize performance when working with `UIImage` and `UIImageView`:

- For *known* images, use the `imageNamed:` method to load the images. It ensures that the content is loaded in memory only once and repurposed across multiple `UIImage` objects.

- Use an asset catalog for loading bundled images with the `imageNamed:` method. This is especially useful if the app has a bunch of icons, each one of which may be small in size. Feel free to create multiple catalogs of related images (i.e., images that are generally used together).

  When iOS loads from the disk, there is an optimal buffer size that can be used to load multiple images in a single read. Also, opening multiple I/O streams has overheads as compared to opening one stream and reading multiple images from there. It is generally faster to read one combo file that is 32 KB in size than 16 files that are each 2 KB in size.

  However, if you want to load a large image that will be used only once, or at best very sparingly, consider using `imageWithContentsOfFile:` (*http://bit.ly/image WithContentsOfFile*) instead of using an asset catalog and the `imageNamed:` method, because the asset catalog caches the images (which is not needed in this case).

  In an app that I worked on, the team saw a reduction of about 300 ms in initial load time by choosing to bundle the images for the initial two screens in one asset catalog.

- For other images, use a high-performing image cache library. `AFNetworking` and `SDWebImage` are great libraries to use.

  When working with an in-memory image cache, be sure to configure memory usage parameters correctly. Do not hardcode. Make it adaptive—a percentage of available RAM is a good way to configure it.

- Load the image of the same size as the `UIImageView` to be rendered. You get the maximum performance when the dimensions of the image parsed and of the `UIImageView` are the same—resizing images is an expensive operation, and it is even costlier if the image view is contained in a `UIScrollView`.

  If the image is downloaded from the network, try to download the image that matches the view size. If that option is not available, preprocess the image to resize it appropriately.

- If there is a need to apply effects like blur or shades, create a copy of the image contents, apply the effects, and use the final bitmap to create the final `UIImage`. That way, the effects are only applied once and the original image can be used for other displays if needed.

- Whatever technique you use to load the images, execute it off the main thread, preferably in a dedicated queue.

  Specifically, decompress JPG/PNG images off the main thread.

- Last but not the least, determine whether you really need the images. If you were to show a rating bar (*http://stackoverflow.com/questions/27600288/rating-bar-like-android-in-codename-one*), you might be better off with a custom view with direct drawing than using multiple images with transparency and overlays.

UITableView

`UITableView` is the most common view used to show data, whether it is for a news app, a mail app, a photo feed, or anything else. `UITableView` provides a great option to show a list of entries that can be either homogeneous or heterogeneous.

`UITableView` binds with two protocols:

`UITableViewDataSource`

The `dataSource` property must be configured to the data source. The data source, as the name says, is the source of the data to be fed into the table cells.

`UITableViewDelegate`

The `delegate` property must be configured to the delegate that receives the callbacks when the user interacts with the table or its cells.

A partial logical relationship between these protocols and `UITableView` is shown in Figure 6-5.

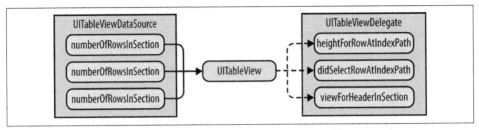

Figure 6-5. UITableView, UITableViewDataSource, and UITableViewDelegate

Here are some best practices to keep in mind when working with UITableView:

- In the dataSource method tableView:cellForRowAtIndexPath:, use table View:dequeueReusableCellWithIdentifier: or tableView:dequeueReusable CellWithIdentifier:forIndexPath: to *reuse cells instead of creating new cells each time.*

  Cell creation has a performance cost. The cost grows multifold if several cells have to be created in a short span of time—for example, when the user scrolls the table view. Also, as cells go out of scope, they are dealloced, resulting in a double whammy. Reusing cells means the only overhead will be to render the cells.

- Avoid dynamic-height cells as much as possible. Fixed, predetermined heights means less computation. With dynamically configured content, not only must the height be computed when required, but the cell contents have to flow and lay-out must be performed each time the view is rendered. That can be a big performance hit.

  Figure 6-6 shows examples of UITableView with fixed- and variable-height cells. If you intend to use variable-height cells, taller cells may prove to be beneficial because the heights will have to be computed for fewer cells, reducing the computation.

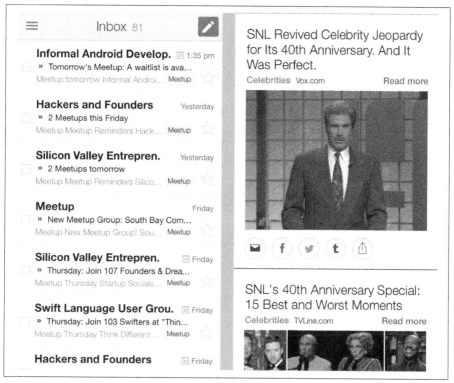

Figure 6-6. UITableView (left with fixed-height and right with variable-height cells)

- If you really need dynamic-height cells, define a rule to mark the cells dirty. If a cell is dirty, compute the height and cache it. Continue to return the cached height in the `tableView:heightForRowAtIndexPath:` callback of the `delegate` until the cell is not dirty.

  If the model to render is immutable, a simple rule that can be used is to check if the model currently being rendered is the same as the one at the corresponding `indexPath`. If so, the same values will be rendered and hence it requires no further processing. If not, recompute the values and attach the new object (model) to the cell.

- When reusing the cells using custom views, avoid laying them out each time by calling `layoutIfNeeded` it is requested.

  Even if a cell is fixed-height, it is possible that the individual elements within the cell may still be configurable to be of varying height—for example, `UILabel` supports multiline content and `UIImageView` can work with varying-sized images.

  Avoid that. Fix the size of each element. This ensures minimal time needed to render the cells.

- Avoid nonopaque cell subviews. Whenever you create a `UITableViewCell`, try to only have opaque elements in it. Translucent or transparent elements (views with `alpha` less than 1.0) may look great but have a performance hit.

  For aesthetic reasons, you may still want to have `alpha` set to a value less than 1.0. If that is case, be aware of the costs.

- Consider using shell interfaces when fast-scrolling (see Figure 6-7). When the user fast-scrolls the table view, it is possible that even with all your optimizations, the view reuse and rendering will still take well over 16 ms and there will be occasional frame drops that may result in a jittery experience.

Figure 6-7. Using shell interfaces

A good option in these situations is to use a shell interface, which can be defined as a predefined interface whose only purpose is to indicate to the end user that there is some data to be shown. As the scrolling velocity drops down below a threshold, flush in the final view and populate it with the data.

You can get the velocity using the `panGestureRecognizer` property associated with the table view (see Example 6-2).

Example 6-2. UITableView velocity

```
-(void)scrollViewDidScroll:(UIScrollView *)scrollView {
    CGPoint velocity = [tableView.panGestureRecognizer
                          velocityInView:self.view];
    self.velocity = velocity;
}

-(UITableViewCell *)tableView:(UITableView *)tableView
    cellForRowAtIndexPath:(NSIndexPath *)indexPath {
    if(fabs(self.velocity.y) > 2000) {
        //return shell cell
    } else {
        //return real cell
    }
}
```

- Avoid gradients, image scaling, and any offscreen drawing. These effects are a drain on the CPU as well as the graphics processing unit (GPU).

UIWebView

UIWebView is the most common view used to render *unknown* or *dynamic* content. Typically, you would have either some embedded HTML or a web URL and point the web view to it.

The following are some common scenarios where you would invariably use UIWeb View even if your app is all native otherwise:

- In any app, for user login. Apps such as Spotify, Mint, and LinkedIn use the native UI to render the login form. However, this has constraints.

  For example, if you want to screen for spam robots by using a CAPTCHA, you need to either build support for all formats (*http://bit.ly/google-capt*) and bundle it into the app or point the user to the web-login URL and let the server generate any complex UI as needed.

- In any app, for showing the privacy policy or terms of use. Because these change over time and require a lot of formatting (text styles, numbered lists, cross-references to other content), using native views is not an option.

- In a news or article reader, because most of the articles are created for the Web and hence are in HTML.

- In a mail app—for example, to render a message or thread and to compose a reply when the initial mail is in HTML.

If you have minimal rich content to be shown, use `NSAttributed String` with `UILabel`.

There is no CSS or JavaScript support. It is a string with associated sets of attributes (e.g., font and kerning) that apply to individual characters or ranges of characters in the string.

The following are some best practices to keep in mind while working with `UIWebView` (note that because there is very little to be done about it, not all of these concern performance; instead, the focus here is on presenting the HTML content in the most appropriate manner):

- `UIWebView` can be bulky and sluggish. Reuse web view objects as much as possible. `UIWebView` is also known to leak memory. So, one instance per app should be good enough.

  Whenever you want to present a new URL to the user, reset the content to empty HTML. This ensures that the web view does not show previous content to the end user. Use `loadHTMLString:baseURL:` followed by `loadRequest:` to accomplish this.

- Attach a custom `UIWebViewDelegate`. Implement the `webView:shouldStartLoad WithRequest:navigationType:` method. Watch out for the URL scheme. If it is anything other than `http` or `https`, beware: your app knows how to handle it or warn the user that the site is trying to let her out of the app.

  This is a great option not only to ensure that the user does not abruptly land in another app, but also for safeguarding against malicious content, especially if you happen to show content from an unknown URL—say, in a mail or messaging app.

- You can create an app-to-JavaScript bridge by using the `stringByEvaluatingJa vaScriptFromString:` method to execute JavaScript in the currently loaded web page. To call a method into a native app, use custom URL schemes and refer to the preceding bullet point on how to handle them.

- Implement the method `webView:didFailLoadWithError:` of the delegate to keep a close track of any and all errors that may occur.

- Implement the `webView:didFailLoadWithError:` method to handle specific errors, as shown in Example 6-3. The `NSError` object has meaningful insights if the `domain` equals `NSURLErrorDomain`.

Example 6-3. Handling errors with UIWebView

```
-(void)webView:(UIWebView *)webView
    didFailLoadWithError:(NSError *)error {
```

```
    if([NSURLErrorDomain isEqualToString:error.domain]) {
        switch(error.code) {
            case NSURLErrorBadURL:
                //handle bad URL
                break;
            case NSURLErrorTimedOut:
                //handle timeout
                break;
            //... etc.
        }
    }
}
```

- UIWebView will not notify of any HTTP protocol errors like a 404 or 500
  response. As shown in Example 6-4, you will have to make a double call, first
  using a custom NSURLConnection call and then by the web view. Provide a delegate to the NSURLConnection and implement connection:didReceiveResponse:
  to get response details.

Example 6-4. UIWebView and HTTP errors

```
@interface HPWebViewController() <UIWebViewDelegate,
                                  NSURLConnectionDataDelegate>

@property (nonatomic, assign) BOOL shouldValidate;

@end

@implementation HPWebViewController

-(BOOL)webView:(UIWebView *)webView
    shouldStartLoadWithRequest:(NSURLRequest *)request
    navigationType:(UIWebViewNavigationType) navigationType {

    if(self.shouldValidate) {
        [NSURLConnection connectionWithRequest:request delegate:self];
        return NO;
    }

    return YES;
}

- (void)connection:(NSURLConnection *)connection
    didReceiveResponse:(NSURLResponse *)response {

    NSInteger status = [(NSHTTPURLResponse *)response statusCode];
    if(status >= 400) {
        //Bingo! An error.
```

```
            //Show alert or hide web view - don't show bad page.
        } else {
            self.shouldValidate = NO;
            [self.webView loadRequest:connection.originalRequest];
        }
        [connection cancel];
    }

@end
```

Because this technique requires a double loading of the web page, it is not recommended. It is OK for the web view to show an error when loading the page. After all, the user requested it, perhaps by tapping on a link in a message he received.

- The container where you embed the UIWebView should provide the following:

    — Navigation buttons (back and forward)

    — Reload button

    — Cancel button to cancel the page currently being loaded

    — UILabel to show the title of the page

    — Close button to move out from the web view, unless that is the only UI that you have in your app—for example, in a hybrid app

Hybrid apps are HTML apps embedded within UIKit—specifically, UIWebView or the new WKWebView. This book does not discuss the performance of hybrid apps (that would be another book in itself).

New in iOS 8: WebKit

iOS 8 features WebKit (*http://bit.ly/ios-dev-webkit*), which is more performant than UIWebView. If you are writing a new app from the ground up, prefer using WKWebView over UIWebView. However, if you choose to use WKWebView, remember that you will need a fallback to UIWebView for iOS 7 devices.

The basic rules for using WKWebView are the same as those for UIWebView, which we discussed earlier. As a side note, there is an app (*http://bit.ly/wk-webview*) that you can download to test the difference between the two.[5]

---

5 Disclaimer: I do not endorse this app.

Custom Views

Writing custom views from the ground up is not common in a non-gaming or non-animation-centric app. The more commonly used option is to create *composite* views using Interface Builder and custom nib files.

Although this is a great preliminary technique, once you create a more complex UI or use these composite views in table views, you will begin to notice performance degradation.

The Twitter team ran into this problem early in the development of their app and moved from using a composite view to one with direct drawing, thus minimizing the overall compositing required to render the view.[6]

Figure 6-8 shows the UI rendered for a tweet.

Figure 6-8. Tweet to render

A basic implementation of the UI might include the following elements (see Figure 6-9):

1. `UIImageView` for the avatar image

2. `UILabel` with `NSAttributedText` for the username

3. `UITextView` with `detectorType = UIDataDetectorTypeLink` for the tweet content, because it may have links

4. `UILabel` for the date

---

6 Twitter Blog, "Simple Strategies for Smooth Animation on the iPhone" (*http://bit.ly/1M74uh6*).

Figure 6-9. Naïve tweet view

Each view burdens Core Animation with extra compositing. In addition, creating a nested hierarchy results in `layoutSubviews` being called multiple times as the content of each subview changes.

To optimize performance, the team created a custom view wherein a single `dra wRect:` draws everything, as shown in Figure 6-10.

Figure 6-10. Custom tweet view—direct drawing

Suppose we have a mail app and for the inbox, we need to show a summary of the mails with the following details:

- Sender's name/email ID
- Date or time it was sent
- Subject
- Snippet of the body (a few leading characters)
- An indicator of whether the mail is new, has been read, or has been replied to
- A selector (maybe just a checkbox) to select multiple mails
- An indicator whether the mail has any attachments

The final layout should something like Figure 6-11.

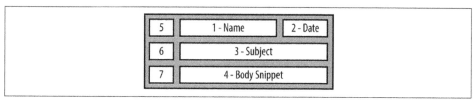

Figure 6-11. Mail summary

We'll create this view in both styles (composite and custom views) and measure the performance of both views (the time it takes to create one cell and the time it takes to render). We will also analyze other pros and cons of working with each style.

Composite view

Creating a composite view is straightforward. You simply need to create a new view class that inherits from `UITableViewCell`.

These are the steps you'll need to follow:

1. Navigate to File→New→File.
2. Select iOS→Source→Cocoa Custom Touch.
3. The class name is `HPMailCompositeCell` and it is a subclass of `UITableViewCell`.
4. Select the option "Also create XIB file."
5. Click Finish.

Add four `UILabel`, two `UIImage`, and one `UIButton` element, and arrange them so that the final structure matches what is shown in Figure 6-12.

 For a complex view, use view rasterization during animations, including but not limited to scrolling.

If the view layout does not change, which will generally be the case during scrolling, set the value of the `UIView`'s `layer`'s property `shouldRasterize` to `YES` during animation and to `NO` after the animation completes.[7]

---

7 Stack Overflow, "When Should I Set layer.shouldRasterize to YES?" (*http://stackoverflow.com/a/19408290*).

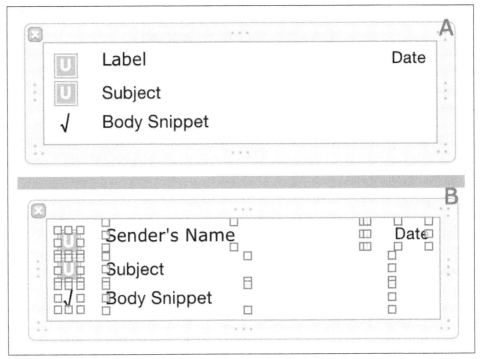

Figure 6-12. Composite view—layout (A) and individual (B) views

Direct drawing

For creating a custom view with direct drawing, we again create a new class that inherits from `UITableViewCell`, except that we do not select the option to create an XIB file.

We name this class `HPMailDirectDrawCell`.

We will need properties to support the details, as discussed earlier. And finally, we will override the method `drawRect:` to custom-render the elements.

Example 6-5 shows representative code to render all the elements.

Example 6-5. Custom view with direct drawing

```
//HPMailDirectDrawCell.h
typedef NS_ENUM(NSInteger, HPMailDirectDrawCellStatus) {
    HPMailDirectDrawCellStatusUnread,
        HPMailDirectDrawCellStatusRead,
        HPMailDirectDrawCellStatusReplied
};

@interface HPMailDirectDrawCell : UITableViewCell
```

```objc
@property (nonatomic, copy) NSString *email;
@property (nonatomic, copy) NSString *subject;
@property (nonatomic, copy) NSString *date;
@property (nonatomic, copy) NSString *snippet;
@property (nonatomic, assign) HPMailDirectDrawCellStatus mailStatus;
@property (nonatomic, assign) BOOL hasAttachment;
@property (nonatomic, assign) BOOL isMailSelected;

@end

@implementation HPMailDirectDrawCell
//Override all initializers - omitted for brevity

//Override drawRect method
-(void)drawRect:(CGRect)rect {
    {
            UIImage *statusImage = nil;
            switch(self.mailStatus) {
                    case HPMailDirectDrawCellStatusRead:
                            statusImage = [UIImage imageNamed:@"mail_read"];
                            break;
                    case HPMailDirectDrawCellStatusReplied:
                            statusImage = [UIImage imageNamed:@"mail_replied"];
                            break;
                    case HPMailDirectDrawCellStatusUnread:
                    default:
                            statusImage = [UIImage imageNamed:@"mail_new"];
                            break;
            }

            CGRect statusRect = CGRectMake(8, 4, 12, 12);
            [statusImage drawInRect:statusRect];
    }

    {
            UIImage *attachmentImage = nil;
            if(self.hasAttachment) {
                    attachmentImage = [UIImage imageNamed:@"mail_attachment"];
     CGRect attachmentRect = CGRectMake(8, 20, 12, 12);
     [attachmentImage drawInRect:attachmentRect];
            }
    }

  {
            UIImage *selectedImage = [UIImage imageNamed:
          (self.isMailSelected ? @"mail_selected": @"mail_unselected")];
       CGRect selectedRect = CGRectMake(8, 36, 12, 12);
    [selectedImage drawInRect:selectedRect];

       //Alternatively, can use Core Graphics to draw vector images
       }
```

```
CGFloat fontSize = 13;
CGFloat width = rect.size.width;
CGFloat remainderWidth = width - 28;
{
        CGFloat emailWidth = remainderWidth - 72;
        UIFont *emailFont=[UIFont boldSystemFontOfSize:fontSize];
        NSDictionary *attrs = @{ NSFontAttributeName: emailFont };

        [self.email drawInRect:CGRectMake(28, 4, emailWidth, 16)
    withAttributes:attrs];
}

{
        UIFont *stdFont = [UIFont systemFontOfSize:fontSize];
        NSDictionary *attrs = @{ NSFontAttributeName: stdFont };
        [self.subject drawInRect:CGRectMake(28, 24, remainderWidth, 16)
    withAttributes:attrs];
        [self.snippet drawInRect:CGRectMake(28, 44, remainderWidth, 16)
    withAttributes:attrs];
}

{
        UIFont *verdana = [UIFont fontWithName:@"Verdana" size:10];
        NSDictionary *attrs = @{ NSFontAttributeName: verdana };
        [self.date drawInRect:CGRectMake(width - 60, 4, 60, 16)
    withAttributes:attrs];
}
}
@end
```

There are two aspects to compare now: runtime performance and code maintenance.

The runtime performance, as can be expected, is better in a custom view with direct draw. What is the difference? Well, let's look at the numbers in Figure 6-13.

```
0.177 HPerf Apps[3307:891359] [I] [prepareForSegue] i=ch_08_10_cpsv, row=3
0.226 HPerf Apps[3307:891359] [I] [cell 0]: Time=17675125 ns
0.232 HPerf Apps[3307:891359] [I] [cell 1]: Time=1980958 ns
0.237 HPerf Apps[3307:891359] [I] [cell 2]: Time=1913166 ns
0.241 HPerf Apps[3307:891359] [I] [cell 3]: Time=1937208 ns
0.245 HPerf Apps[3307:891359] [I] [cell 4]: Time=1838375 ns
0.249 HPerf Apps[3307:891359] [I] [cell 5]: Time=1976000 ns
0.253 HPerf Apps[3307:891359] [I] [cell 6]: Time=1944208 ns
0.257 HPerf Apps[3307:891359] [I] [cell 7]: Time=1852250 ns
0.785 HPerf Apps[3307:891359] <HPInst> SCR_Views_Custom_Composite
3.290 HPerf Apps[3307:891359] [I] [cell 8]: Time=6602208 ns
3.341 HPerf Apps[3307:891359] [I] [cell 9]: Time=9596000 ns
3.352 HPerf Apps[3307:891359] [I] [cell 10]: Time=130708 ns
3.380 HPerf Apps[3307:891359] [I] [cell 11]: Time=79916 ns

4.383 HPerf Apps[3307:891359] [I] [prepareForSegue] i=ch_08_10_cpsv, row=4
4.397 HPerf Apps[3307:891359] [I] [cell 0]: Time=359041 ns
4.398 HPerf Apps[3307:891359] [I] [cell 1]: Time=177416 ns
4.400 HPerf Apps[3307:891359] [I] [cell 2]: Time=199041 ns
4.401 HPerf Apps[3307:891359] [I] [cell 3]: Time=125625 ns
4.401 HPerf Apps[3307:891359] [I] [cell 4]: Time=110541 ns
4.403 HPerf Apps[3307:891359] [I] [cell 5]: Time=215166 ns
4.403 HPerf Apps[3307:891359] [I] [cell 6]: Time=120583 ns
4.405 HPerf Apps[3307:891359] [I] [cell 7]: Time=222458 ns
4.924 HPerf Apps[3307:891359] <HPInst> SCR_Views_Custom_Composite
5.649 HPerf Apps[3307:891359] [I] [cell 8]: Time=293375 ns
5.680 HPerf Apps[3307:891359] [I] [cell 9]: Time=133250 ns
5.713 HPerf Apps[3307:891359] [I] [cell 10]: Time=59208 ns
5.730 HPerf Apps[3307:891359] [I] [cell 11]: Time=28083 ns
```

Figure 6-13. Composite view versus direct drawing—comparing initialization and reuse

Table 6-2 summarizes the times by tasks for composite view and direct draw for the code given in Example 6-5.

Table 6-2. Comparision by numbers

Task	Composite view	Direct draw
First init	17.6 ms	0.36 ms
Subsequent inits	1.8–1.9 ms	0.1–0.2 ms
First init after scroll	6.6 ms	0.3 ms
Second init after scroll	9.6 ms	0.13 ms
Reuse	0.08–0.13 ms	0.03–0.08 ms

As you may notice, there is a staggering performance difference of a factor of 2x–20x. The initial load is blazingly 50x faster when using direct draw.

And that is when the code for direct draw is not even optimized.

Thus, from a performance perspective, direct drawing should offer better performance at times—orders of magnitude better than composite views.

However, from a maintenance perspective, the code can be difficult to maintain and evolve. Once you have stabilized the app, there will be a definitive case to move away from a composite UI to direct drawing.

Additionally, if you create a view comprised of only standard controls, it is easier to do A/B testing by sending a new nib file across to the device and loading the UI from there. That way, you can play around with different layouts without releasing a newer version of the app.

Auto Layout

iOS 6 introduced Auto Layout, which alleviates the headache of aligning elements in a fairly complex screen. Auto Layout lets you describe the positions of views relative to each other and the container and the sizes through what is known as *constraints*. Constraints can describe an element's distance (horizontal or vertical) from another element, its size (width or height), or its alignment with another element (horizontal or vertical).

It is assumed that you have working knowledge of Auto Layout. If not, you should review the official reference in the iOS Developer Library (*http://apple.co/1Qt4FlD*) or Matthijs Hollemans's "Beginning Auto Layout Tutorial in iOS 7: Part 1" (*http://bit.ly/ rw-autolayout*).

Though Auto Layout is a great option, allowing you to leave the element positioning and sizing to the core engine rather than doing it all in your code, it comes with performance overhead. Implementing Auto Layout involves *solving linear equations that satisfy the constraints*. It uses the Cassowary (*http://bit.ly/casso-cocoa*) constraint solver toolkit. And as is the case with any *generic equation solver*, the complexity is $O(N)$, where N is the number of constraints and not the number of elements. This means that in general, there may be about $4N$ equations to be solved to determine the position and size of all the elements in the view, and also that the time taken to solve the equations increases disproportionally with the number of elements and constraints involved.

In a test done by Florian Kugler,[8] if the number of views grows to a few hundred, Auto Layout can take over tens of seconds or more, while directly setting frames can be done in milliseconds. In general, directly setting the frames is around 1,000x faster than using Auto Layout. The result of Kugler's test is shown in Figure 6-14. The source code of the app on which the test was done is available on Github (*https:// github.com/floriankugler/AutoLayoutProfiling*).

---

8 Florian Kugler, "Auto Layout Performance on iOS" (*http://bit.ly/1EPflLq*).

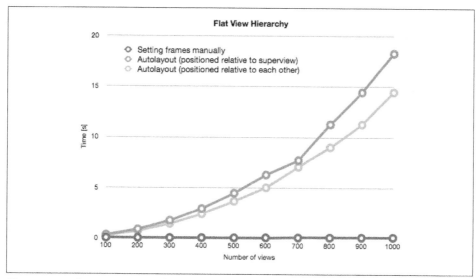

Figure 6-14. Auto Layout performance

It is interesting to note here that Auto Layout using *local constraints* (i.e., elements positioned relative to each other) is faster than using *global constraints*, where the elements are positioned relative to the superview.

Any custom code will have specialized knowledge of the view, and as such the rendering will be faster than using a generic equation solver to place and size the views.

Having said that, when Kugler measured the numbers for a more real-world app, even though Auto Layout was slower, it was not slower by a factor of 10x or 100x, as in the test app. For an app such as that shown in Figure 6-15, Auto Layout took about 180 ms while custom code took about 120 ms. So, even though Auto Layout takes about 50% more time, it is still not that bad a choice.

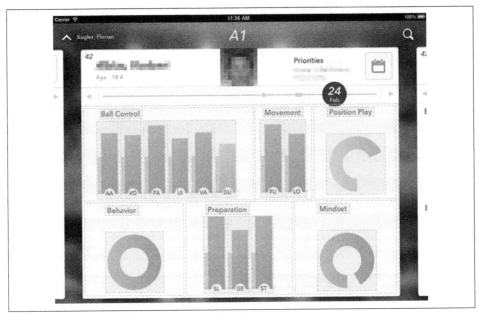

Figure 6-15. Real-world app for testing Auto Layout

What is the final verdict on Auto Layout? Use your discretion. Do measure the time it takes to bring up the view and render it. If it is beyond a threshold, explore the option of using custom code. The threshold is very much specific to the app. Keep in mind that when using Auto Layout, there is always room to improve the layout and rendering performance.

With custom code, there is always the burden of carrying and testing the custom code each time the layout is updated. This also means that you may be forgoing the possibility of running A/B tests using custom templates.

Size Classes

Until the iPhone 4S, app development was straightforward—there was only one size and resolution to develop for. The iPhone 5 and 5S came with increased vertical size. The iPhone 6 and 6 Plus added more pixels horizontally as well as vertically. In the iPad series, the iPad 4 doubled the resolution of the previous generation. The pixels per inch (ppi) increased by 3x, and as a result, app designers and developers have twice as many images to bundle (which makes the bundle heavier to download), not to mention the greater number of pixels to worry about when direct drawing.

Table 6-3. iOS devices—screen resolution and densities[a]

Device	Screen resolution	Pixel density (ppi)
iPhone 3G	320x480	163
iPhone 4	640x960	326
iPhone 4S	640x960	326
iPhone 5	640x1136	326
iPhone 5S	640x1136	326
iPhone 6	750x1334	326
iPhone 6 Plus	1080x1920*	401
iPad 2	1024x768	132
iPad (3rd Gen)	2048x1536	264
iPad (4th Gen)	2048x1536	264
iPad Air	2048x1536	264
iPad Air 2	2048x1536	264
iPad Mini	1024x768	163
iPad Mini (Retina)	2048x1536	325

[a] The hardware pixels. The software pixels are actually 1242x2208 at 461 ppi (*http://bit.ly/curious-case-iphone6*).

iOS rendering features the concept of *points*, which is the density-independent resolution. Note that ppi is not a point-to-pixel ratio. Consider point as a scale factor given by iOS so that you do not have to worry about scaling per se. So, a 10 pt view may correspond to 10 px on the iPhone 3G, 20 px on the iPhone 4 and 5S, and 30 px on the iPhone 6 Plus. When you define the constraints, they are in points, as shown in Figure 6-16. The font sizes are also in points.

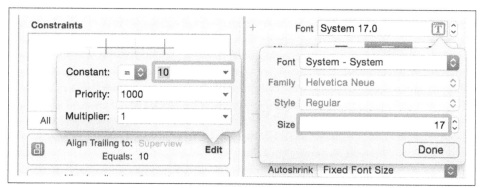

Figure 6-16. View constraints

When creating custom views with direct drawing, the `drawRect:` method gives the scaled `CGRect` dimensions. For the custom cell that we created earlier, notice that the size presented is 320x64 on the iPhone 5S as well as iPhone 6.

Instead of exposing exact pixel dimensions to the developer, Apple has done a great job of abstracting out the configurations through what it calls *size classes*. A size class identifies a relative amount of display space for the height and for the width.

The size class available for a view controller is based on the following three factors:

- Screen size

- Device orientation

- Part of the screen available to the view controller (note that when using a split view controller to display master and detail controllers, none of the controllers has access to the entire screen)

When designing a view controller in interface builder, use the *size class controller* near the layout toolbar at the bottom to select a class, as shown in Figure 6-17.

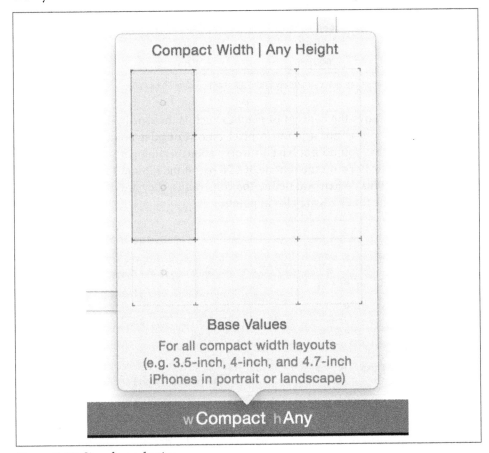

Figure 6-17. Size class selection

iOS defines two size classes: compact and regular. The compact size class kicks in when using *constrained space*, whereas regular is used for *expansive space*. As illustrated in Figure 6-17, you choose a horizontal and a vertical size class to configure the final UI.

The iOS Developer Library article "iOS Human Interface Guidelines" (*http://bit.ly/ios-adaptivity-and-layout*) provides details of which class is selected for different device and orientation combinations. Figure 6-18 maps the devices and orientations to the size classes.

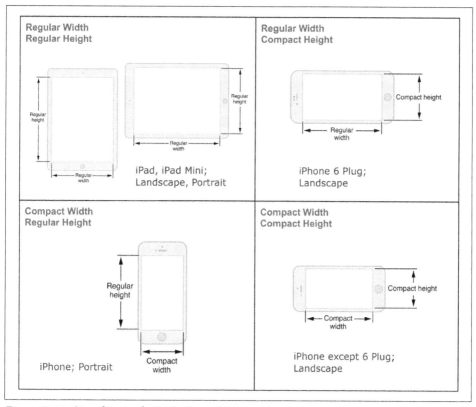

Figure 6-18. Size class to device/orientation mapping

For any view, you will be able to change all parameters that affect its final position and size. These include constraints in all views as well as font size wherever applicable. Figure 6-19 shows how you can add constraints for a specific size class.

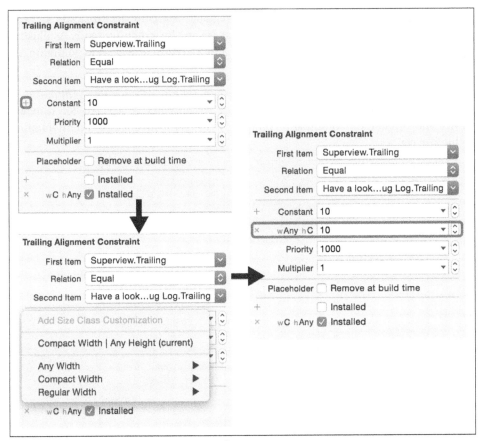

Figure 6-19. Configuring size class–specific parameters

Size classes provide a *segmented* approach to classify the UI without having to create independent layouts for simplistic scenarios such as orientations. Use them wherever possible—the whole reason the infrastructure has been created is to ease development.

From a performance perspective, there is minimal impact when loading the storyboard or the XIB file. The good part is that the total contribution of these class-based constraints to the final XIB file is a small fraction. In addition, if the app supports multiple orientations, the XIB file is loaded only once, giving a big leg-up for the app when the orientation change occurs. And note that loading the XIB file is a one-time cost when running the app.

Size classes require Auto Layout. If you choose not to use Auto Layout for performance reasons, you will not be able to use size classes.

New Interaction Features in iOS 8

iOS 8 introduced two fantastic features for letting the user interact with an app:

- Interactive notifications
- App extensions

The following two subsections explore these options. We will begin by looking at the basic setup for each of these features, and then look at how can they be used to provide the best user experience possible.

Interactive Notifications

You can use interactive notifications to allow the user to provide a quick response to an input.

Up to iOS 7, a user tapping on a notification (or swiping on the lock screen) would only result in the app being launched. Subsequent actions were required to be performed in the app. Starting in iOS 8, developers can give users the ability to perform predefined actions from notifications.

You determine what to do in the app based on which notification the user swiped by using the value from `launchOptions` when `application:didFinishLaunchingWithOptions:` is called.

This works great, except when a notification expects a user to respond and there is more than one possible response option available, or if the response can be obtained faster than launching the app and taking the user to a specific view controller—which is a very cumbersome and time-consuming process for the user.

With iOS 8, it's possible to add a *category* to a notification, which can have one or more *actions* associated with it. The user can take one of the available actions.

Here are a few examples of possible actions when using interactive notifications:

- Mail: reply, mark spam
- Messaging: remind, reply
- Comment to your post in a social app: reply to comment, like the comment
- Tasks and reminders: snooze, mark complete

Figure 6-20 shows an example of providing a fast-action interface to respond using interactive notifications. The example here is a reminder notification. When swiped left, the user is presented with two action options: Snooze and Complete. If the user selects Snooze, the reminder will pop up again after a while. If the user selects Complete, the task is marked complete.

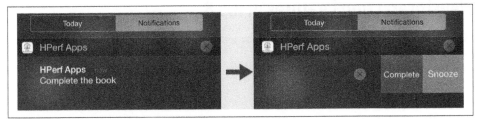

Figure 6-20. Interactive notification—task reminder

The benefit is that the user does not need to open the app to take further action. The notification is handled by the `application:handleActionWithIdentifier:forLocal Notification:` callback in the `UIAppDelegate` protocol implementation class.

The user can also respond to the notification when logged into the device using the pull-down banner. The UI is slightly different, as shown in Figure 6-21.

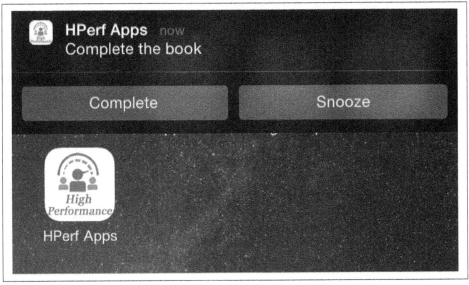

Figure 6-21. Interactive notification banner

App Extensions

The Apple developer website (*https://developer.apple.com/app-extensions*) describes app extensions as follows:

> App extensions give users access to your app's functionality and content throughout iOS 8 and OS X Yosemite. For example, your app can now appear as a widget on the Today screen, add new buttons in the Action sheet, offer photo filters within the iOS Photos app, or display a new system-wide custom keyboard. Use extensions to place the power of your app wherever your users need it most.

iOS 8 introduced *app extensions* that can be added to an app. Figure 6-22 shows the Xcode menu for adding new extensions to the host app.

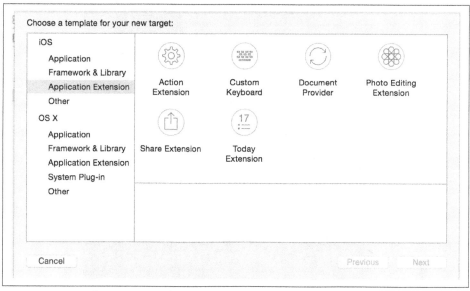

Figure 6-22. Xcode menu to add app extensions

The app extensions available in iOS 8 are:

Today (more commonly referred to as Widget)
    Helps you get a quick update or perform a quick task in the Today view of Notification Center (see Figure 6-23 for an example).

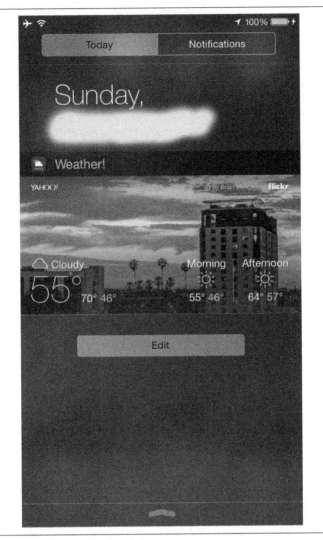

Figure 6-23. Widget from Yahoo Weather app

Custom Keyboard

Allows you to use your favorite keyboard in any and all apps, including Search (see Figure 6-24). It is great to finally have the freedom to replace the iOS system keyboard with a custom keyboard for use in all apps.

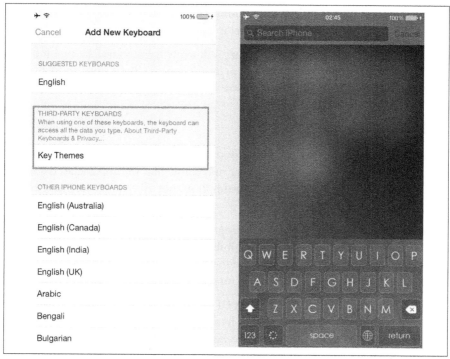

Figure 6-24. Custom keyboards

Share

Allows sharing data across apps in a more seamless manner. Deep linking also allows sharing data, but the user is forced to change the context to the target app.

Action

Helps the user to view or transform content that originates in a host app. For example, you may want to view video in your favorite media player rather than the mail/messaging app where you actually received it.

Photo Editing

Allows users to edit a photo or video within the Photos app. So, you can now download an app such as Adobe Photoshop Express and use it to edit all your photos, without needing to manually open the photo to be edited in that app; you can now launch the editor from within Photos.

Document Provider

Allows other apps to access the documents managed by your app. The document provider acts as a local repository for a particular type of document, letting the user gather all those documents into one place.

These extensions are bundled as subbundles within the host app and are governed by the same lifecycle and rules of app development.

The extension-specific best practices are still evolving. It may take two full cycles of app releases before patterns and best practices merge. Right now, most of these are general guidelines no different than those for any iOS app.

Summary

With an understanding of the view controller lifecycle, you can now tune the perceived performance of your app. A user may know that the app caches data for faster load times or is great on network consumption, but all that is secondary if the final user interface is poorly implemented.

Choosing between a declarative or programmatic UI is a decision that should be based on performance as well as extensibility. This chapter's in-depth analysis of common views should empower you to use them wisely, while the alternatives for custom views give you options to choose from for a given scenario in your app.

Note that when rendering or updating UI elements and performing animations (e.g., scrolling or otherwise) at 60 fps, you have about 16 ms available to perform all the required operations. This may include network or disk I/O, view content updating, layout, and final rendering. Divide the tasks into subtasks in such a manner that they consume minimal cumulative time on the main thread in one event cycle.

CHAPTER 7

Network

With the necessity to use networking in an app and with limited choices for minimizing latency (e.g., using CDNs or edge servers or using smaller payload formats like Protobuf or data compressions), everything gets down to best utilizing the available network conditions and planning ahead for varying scenarios.

In this chapter, we look at the factors that impact the overall latency and how you can make best use of the information available to maximize performance.

Metrics and Measurement

Most of the work done in networking is outside of your control, so it is important to identify the metrics to measure. We will discuss some of the more important performance-related metrics in this chapter. Note that this is not intended to be a comprehensive list, but just to point out the more important ones to measure in relation to optimizing performance.

Figure 7-1 shows a bird's-eye view of a typical request over the network.

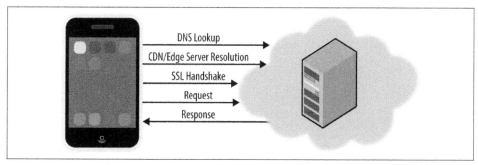

Figure 7-1. Network—device to server

The general structure of the discussions that follow is a description of the metric of concern, one or a couple of examples, followed by best practices.

DNS Lookup Time

The first step to initiating a connection is DNS lookup. If your app is network heavy, DNS lookup times can slow it down. In a rigorous statistical sample of two locations, DNS lookup time to the host *www.google.com* from Sunnyvale, California, took 2,846 ms while it took 34 ms from New Delhi, India (see Figure 7-2).

The lookup time is a function of the performance of the primary DNS server configured. The final connection time is a function of the route traced to the destination IP address.

Using content delivery networks (CDNs) to minimize latency is a common practice. You will notice in Figure 7-2 that the IP address resolved for the domain *www.google.com* is different in the two sites—the one resolved to in Sunnyvale is a server in the United States while the one resolved to in New Delhi is in India. But because DNS lookup is done for every unique subdomain, having multiple CDN hostnames can result in slowdown of the app.

Figure 7-2. DNS lookup times for www.google.com from Sunnyvale, CA (top) and New Delhi, India (bottom)

To minimize the latencies that arise from DNS lookup times, follow these best practices:

- Minimize the number of unique domains the app uses. Multiple domains are unavoidable because of the way routing works in general. Most likely, you will need one each for the following:

1. Identity management (login, logout, profile)

2. Data serving (API endpoints)

3. CDN (images and other static artifacts)

   There may be a need for other domains (e.g., for serving video, uploading instrumentation data, subcomponent-specific data serving, serving ads, or even country-specific geolocalization). If the number of subdomains goes up to double digits, that can be cause for worry.

- Connection to all domains may not be required at app startup. During app launch, identity management and data for the initial screen might be all that the app requires. For subsequent subdomains, try to have preemptive DNS resolution, a.k.a. *DNS prefetch*. There are two options for accomplishing this.

  If you have subdomains and hosting under your control, you can configure a predetermined URL to return a HTTP 204 status code with no content and make an early connection to this URL.

  The second option is to use `gethostbyname` to perform an explicit DNS lookup. However, the host may resolve to a different IP for different protocols, such as one address for HTTP requests and another for HTTPS requests. Though not very common, Layer 7 routing can resolve the IP address based on the actual request—for example, one address for images and another for video. For these reasons, resolving DNS before connecting is often unhelpful and a dummy call to the host is more effective.

SSL Handshake Time

For reasons of security, it can be assumed that all the connections in your app are over TLS/SSL (using HTTPS). HTTPS calls start with an *SSL handshake*, which involves validating the server certificate and sharing a randomly generated key for communication. While this might sound simple, it is a multistep process and can take a lot of time (see Figure 7-3).

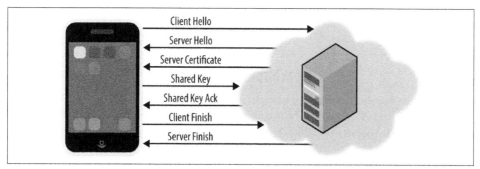

Figure 7-3. SSL handshake

You should adhere to the following best practices:

- Minimize the number of connections that the app makes. As a corollary to this, minimize the number of unique hostnames the app connects to.

- Do not close HTTP/S connections after the request is complete.

  Add the header `Connection: keep-alive` for all HTTPS calls. This ensures that the same connection can be reused for the next request.

- Use domain sharding. This allows you to use the same socket even if the connections are for multiple hostnames, as long as they resolve to the same IP and the same certificates can be used (e.g., in wildcard domains).

  Domain sharding is available in SPDY or its successor, HTTP/2 (*https:// http2.github.io*). You will need a networking library that supports either of the two formats.

 iOS 9 has native support for HTTP/2.

For iOS 8 and earlier, you will need a third-party library such as CocoaSPDY from Twitter. This is available on GitHub (*https:// github.com/twitter/CocoaSPDY*). You can use it by including the CocoaPod `CocoaSPDY`.

Network Type

As users drifted from desktop devices, they gave up always-connected, high-speed broadband networks for either similar-quality WiFi networks or intermittently connected, varying-bandwidth mobile networks. Even more challenging is the scenario where the user is mobile—the network and quality change as the device switches between mobile towers. A device can go from an LTE network to GPRS or a no-signal zone at any time, and there is absolutely nothing that either you or the user can do about it.

Reachability to a Host

You can use Apple's Reachability library (*http://bit.ly/apple-reachability*) or Tony Million's drop-in-replacement (*https://github.com/tonymillion/Reachability*) of the same with additional support of callback invocation whenever the reachability status to a host changes.

 If the device is idle for more than a few seconds (the exact value is nonndeterministic, but those few seconds can turn into minutes as well), the network radio could have been turned off, resulting in an extra Radio Resource Controller (RRC) latency that can run into the hundreds or thousands of milliseconds.

Ensure that your app is ready to handle such scenarios by first determining the host's reachability.

In general, iPhones and iPads can use any of the following networks to connect to the Internet:

WiFi

If the WiFi network is a private network (e.g., your home or office connection), you can expect to have good, continuous connectivity to the Internet.

However, being on a WiFi network does not guarantee Internet connection. For example, if the device is connected to a public hotspot (e.g., in a hotel or shopping mall), it will not have Internet access if the user fails to provide appropriate credentials.

And even if the device is connected to the Internet, there might be restrictions regarding which domains and/or ports it can connect to. As an example, the *www.google.com* or *www.yahoo.com* domains might be allowed, but not *mail.google.com* or *mail.yahoo.com*.

4G: LTE, HSPA+ (the high-speed data networks)

These are the latest-generation data networks. Typical latency overheads range from 100 ms to 600 ms before the first real business-related byte may be sent over. These networks allocate radio-related resources dynamically in submillisecond intervals and send bursts of data.

Theoretically, speeds vary from 100 Mbps for high-mobility communication such as from cars and trains to 1 Gbps for low-mobility communication, such as by pedestrians or stationary users.

3G: HSDPA, HSUPA, UMTS, CDMA2000 (the medium-speed data networks)
These are the previous generation of data networks, but may be used more frequently than LTE.

Speeds on 3G can vary from 200 Kbps to well over 50 Mbps. The speeds may not be symmetric. HSDPA has high download speeds while HSUPA has high upload speeds.

2G: EDGE, GPRS (the low-speed data networks)
The network of the '90s still refuses to die. These were the initial digital networks (1G networks used analog signals) and provide low bandwidths. EDGE has a theoretical limit of 500 Kbps while GPRS can only go up to 50 Kbps.

The Reachability library can give you details of which network the host is reachable from. Use that information to determine the type of content to transfer (e.g., text versus image versus video), batch size for multiple items to transfer, and so on.

0.2% Data Transfer; 46% Power Consumption!

In 2011, the University of Michigan and AT&T published "Profiling Resource Usage for Mobile Applications" (*http://bit.ly/usage-mobile-app*), a research paper that analyzes mobile apps for network use and power consumption efficiency.

The paper discusses Pandora, which serves as a great case study for the inefficiency of intermittent network transfers on mobile networks. Although the problem has since been fixed, the case study is still worthwhile reading.

Whenever the app plays a song, it downloads the song in its entirety, which is the correct behavior: burst as much data as possible and let the radio be turned off for as long as possible.

However, after the transfer, the app would send periodic instrumentation events every 60 seconds. These events accounted for just 0.2% of the total transferred bytes but a whopping 46% of the app's total power consumption.

The event data is generally minimal, but because the radio was kept active for significantly longer, it ended up nearly doubling the app's battery consumption.

By batching this data into fewer requests or sending it when the radio is already active, the unnecessary energy tails can be eliminated and high power efficiency can be achieved.

To ensure that your app is not part of a similar case study, follow these best practices when developing network-centric apps:

- *Design for variable network availability.* The only aspect that is consistent in mobile networks is variance in network availability. For media streaming, prefer

HTTP Live Streaming (HLS) or any of the available adaptive bitrate streaming technologies, as these will allow dynamic switching across the best streaming quality for the available bandwidth at the moment, resulting in smooth video play.

For non-streaming content, you will need to implement strategies on how much data should be downloaded in a single fetch—and this has to be adaptive. For example, you may not want to fetch all 200 new emails since the last update in one go. It may be prudent to start by downloading the first 50 emails and then progressively download more.

Similarly, do not turn on the video autoplay on low-speed networks or those that may cost a lot of money for the user.

For custom non-streaming data fetch, keep intelligence on the server. Let the client send network characteristics and the server decide the number of records to return. This will allow you to make adaptive changes without having to release a new version of the app.

- In case of failures, *retry after a random and exponentially growing delay.*

  For example, after the first failure, the app might retry after 1 second. On the second failure, it would then retry after 2 seconds, followed by a 4-second delay. Do not forget to have a maximum automatic retry count per session.

- *Establish a minimum time between forced refreshes.* When the user asks for explicit refresh, do not fire off the request immediately. Instead, check if either a request is already pending or the time gap from the last attempt is less than a threshold. If so, do not send the request.

- *Use reachability* to discover any changes to the network state. As shown in Figure 7-4, use indicators to show any unavailability to the user. After all, it is not your fault that the device does not have Internet access. By letting users know about potential connection issues, you will avoid blame being placed on your app.

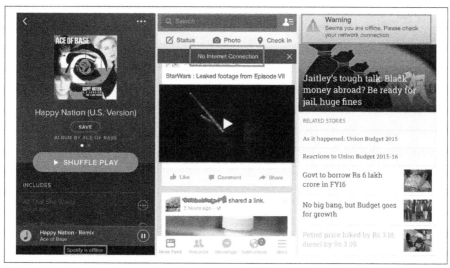

Figure 7-4. Spotify, Facebook, and TOI apps with offline network status indicators

- *Do not cache the network state.* Always use the latest value for network-sensitive tasks, either through a callback to know when to trigger a request or an explicit check before a request is made.
- *Download content based on the network type.* If you have an image to show, do not always download the original, high-quality image. Always download the image that is suitable for the device—the image size requirements for an iPhone 4S can be very different from those of an iPad 3rd Generation.

If your app has video content, it is a good idea to have a preview image associated with it. If the app supports an autoplay feature, use the preview image to be shown on non-WiFi networks, as they are known to cost a lot of money to the user.

In addition, include an option for turning off autodownload and/or autoplay of heavy content such as images, audio, and video. Figure 7-5 shows an example of such a setting in the WhatsApp app.

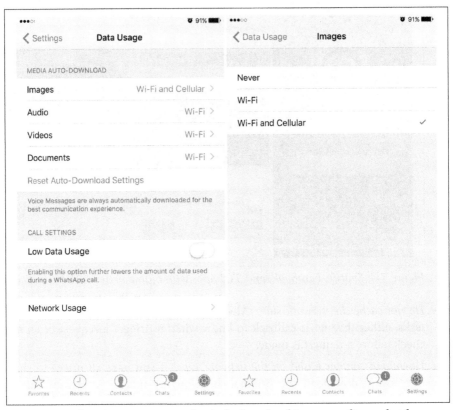

Figure 7-5. *WhatsApp settings to selectively download image, audio, and video content*

- *Prefetch optimistically.* When on a WiFi network, prefetch content that you think the user will need after some time. Use this cached content subsequently. Prefer downloading in bursts and let the network radio be shut down after use. This will help save battery.

Prefetch will always be a point of contention. There is always a tug-of-war between downloading minimal data and prefetching all content that *may* be needed in the near future.

There is no golden rule to follow. A lot depends on the median data size, number of downloads to perform, expected usage pattern, and network conditions. If the network is choppy and you need to perform minimal data transfers, see if you can batch the requests.

- If applicable, *support offline storage* with sync when the network is available. More often than not, the network cache should suffice. But if you need more structured data, using local files or Core Data is always a preferred option.

For a game, cache the last level-up details. For a mail app, storing a few of the latest emails with attachments is a great option.

Depending on the app, you may allow users to *create* new content offline that can be synchronized with the server when network connectivity is available. Examples include composing a new email or responding to one in a mail app, updating a profile photo in a social app, and capturing photos or videos to be uploaded later.

Always decouple networking and communication from the user interface. If the app can perform operations offline, notify the user that it can. Otherwise, notify the user that it cannot. Do not let the user start an interaction with the app and then lead to a point of no return—this is a poor user experience.

 Do not add an option for making offline transactions in a financial, banking, or stock trading app, or any app that requires syncing with the server—the updated data may not be available in offline mode.

Figure 7-6 shows the Facebook and E*Trade apps working in offline mode. The Facebook app notifies the user about network unavailability, but allows posting comments or status updates. These are synchronized later, when the network is available. The E*Trade app, on the other hand, also allows users to interact with the app, but they reach a dead end when searching for a stock quote, resulting in a poor user experience.

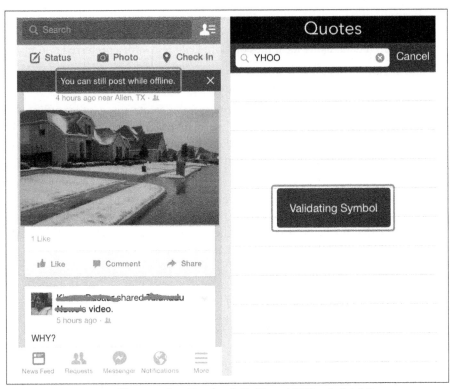

Figure 7-6. Apps in offline mode—Facebook (left) and E*Trade (right)

Note that network conditions will always be beyond the app's control, but the user experience you provide within those constraints is always controlled by the app. Make the best of the available options, including offline storage, network reachability, and network type, to perform (or not perform) networking operation, and notify (or do not notify) the user about them.

Latency

Latency is the extra time spent in the network transmission when requesting a resource from the server. It is important to set up a system for measuring network latency.

Network latency can be measured by subtracting the time spent on the server (in computation and serving the response) from the total time spent during the request:

```
Round-Trip Time = (Timestamp of Response - Timestamp of Request)
Network Latency = Round-Trip Time - Time Spent on Server
```

The *time spent on server* can be computed by the server. The *round-trip time* is accurately available to the client. The server can send the *time spent* in a custom header in the response that can then be used on the client side to compute the latency.

Example 7-1 shows sample code for computing latency. The code assumes the response includes a custom header X-Server-Time that contains the time spent on the server in milliseconds.

Example 7-1. Computing network latency

```
//server - NodeJS
app.post("/some/path", function(req, res) {
    var startTime = new Date().getTime();
    //process
    var body = processRequest(req);
    var endTime = new Date().getTime();
    var serverTime = endTime - startTime;
    res.header("X-Server-Time", String(serverTime));
    res.send(body);
});

//client - iOS app
-(void)fireRequestWithLatency:(NSURLRequest *)request {

    NSDate *startTime = nil;
    AFHTTPRequestOperation *op =
        [[AFHTTPRequestOperation alloc] initWithRequest:request];
    [op setCompletionBlockWithSuccess:^(AFHTTPRequestOperation *op, id res) {

        NSDate *endTime = [NSDate date];
        NSTimeInterval roundTrip = [endTime timeIntervalSinceDate:startTime];
        long roundTripMillis = (long)(roundTrip * 1000);

        NSHTTPURLResponse *res = op.response;
        NSString *serverTime = [res.allHeaderFields objectForKey:@"X-Server-Time"];
        long serverTimeMillis = [serverTime longLongValue];

        long latencyMillis = roundTripMillis - serverTimeMillis;

    } failure:^(AFHTTPRequestOperation *op, NSError *error) {
        //Process error. Present error to the user, if need be.
    }];

    startTime = [NSDate date];
    [op start];
}
```

The code presented in Example 7-1 is mostly accurate about network latency, except that it includes the time taken to flush the data to the wire on the server side and the time to parse the response on the client side. If that can be separated out, it will provide the true network latency time, including any device overheads.

While you have the data to analyze any patterns in latency, additionally keep track of the following data:

Connection timeouts

It's important to keep track of how many times the connection timed out. This metric will provide you details of geographic distribution categorized by network quality—either poor infrastructure or lower capacity—which in turn will help you plan sync-time spread. For example, instead of syncing at a specific time across a time zone, the sync can be spread over a short duration of time, say, a few minutes.

Response timeouts

Capture the number of times the connection succeeded but the response timed out. This will help you plan datacenter capacity based on geographic location and times of the day and year.

Payload size

The request as well as the response size can be measured completely on the server side. Use this data to identify any peaks that can slow down your network operations and determine options for either reducing the total data footprint by selecting appropriate serialization format (JSON, CSV, Protobuf, etc.) or splitting the data and using incremental syncs (e.g., by using smaller batch sizes or sending partial data in multiple chunks).

Maximizing the Capacity of a Bad Network

I once worked on a fantasy sports app where the engineering team were noticing longer latencies and more timeouts (connection as well as response timeouts). We also realized that the server would typically send over 200 KB of compressed JSON data for initial consumption—and we had to do this within about 20 minutes of match commencement.

On a match night, it was typical for there to be well over 10,000 users connecting to one cell tower, for a total of 50,000–80,000 users overall, causing a mobile data network choke.

Although we could not do anything to improve connectivity, we used some tricks to improve the experience. To start with, we sent push notifications to the devices. The first push notification, which asked users if they were going to the match or not, was sent a few hours before it began. Not all of the users responded, but a fairly large number did (we used gamification to incentivize). That gave us data about not only estimated traffic but, more importantly, which users would require notifications.

The second push notification was sent only to users who indicated that they would be going to the match. This push notification was sent out in batches during the first 20 minutes of the match. If there were 1,000 users in the stadium, 100 of them would receive the notification during the initial two minutes, the next 100 in the following two minutes, and so on.

The notificaton would wake the app, which would use geolocation to decide whether or not to get the data. Now, instead of 1,000 people connecting simultaneously, connections would be made in groups of 100 users at a time.

For obvious reasons, you cannot expect each user to open the app immediately, but that one push notification would serve to wake up the app and have it sync data. Any further interaction with the app was then much smoother.

Networking API

While performing any network operation, what becomes important is the API that you choose.

Earlier versions of iOS provided NSURLConnection to execute network requests. It was the app developer's job to manage connection pools and deal with app backgrounding, suspension, and resumption of the requests.

NSURLSession was introduced in iOS 7 and should now be the de facto choice for performing any network operation. Let's take a look at some of the advantages of using NSURLSession:[1]

- NSURLSession is a configurable container for putting related requests into. As an example, all calls to your servers can be configured to always include an access token.

- You get all the benefits of background networking. This helps with battery life, supports UIKit multitasking, and uses the same delegate model as in-process transfers.

- Any networking task can be paused, stopped, and restarted. Unlike with NSURL Connection, there is no need for NSOperation subclasses.

- You can subclass NSURLSession to configure a session to use private storage (cache, cookie jar, etc.) on a per-session basis.

- When using NSURLConnection, if an authentication challenge was issued, the challenge would come back for an arbitrary request and you wouldn't know

---

[1] For tips on usage, see Ken Toh's "NSURLSession Tutorial: Getting Started" (*http://www.raywenderlich.com/51127/nsurlsession-tutorial*).

exactly what request was getting the challenge. With `NSURLSession`, the delegate handles authentication.

- `NSURLConnection` has some asynchronous block–based methods, but a delegate cannot be used with them. When a request is made, it either succeeds or fails, even if authentication was needed.

  With `NSURLSession`, you can take a hybrid approach—that is, you can use the asynchronous block–based methods and also set up a delegate to handle authentication.

App Deployment

With the statistics for these metrics, you can better plan app deployment. That includes not only the servers, their locations, and their capacities, but also the clients and how to get the best in a given scenario.

In this section, we look at important components of our end-to-end app from a networking perspective—the components that are under our control.

Servers

As we look at geographical distribution of network latencies, we can use this information to select an appropriate location for the datacenters. If you use a hosted datacenter provider, select one that has multiple locations, such as Amazon AWS or Rackspace Cloud. If you own the datacenters, you should ensure that they are geographically spread out.

It is a no-brainer that your servers should be situated in multiple locations so that you can better serve content locally.

Here are some best practices that you should follow:

- *Use multiple datacenters*, so that your servers are spread out geographically, closer to your users.
- *Use CDNs* to serve static content such as images, JavaScript, CSS, fonts, and so on.
- *Use edge servers (http://serverfault.com/a/67489)* in proximity to serve dynamic content.
- *Avoid multiple domains* (DNS lookup times can be long and diminish the user experience).

Note that the second and fourth points are competing requirements—you will need to make a trade-off. For information on minimizing DNS lookup times when using CDNs, see the best practices discussed in "DNS Lookup Time" on page 224.

Request

In order to properly set up networking, it's important to correctly configure your HTTP/S requests. You should follow these best practices:

- Instead of making one request for each unit of operation, *make batch requests*. Even if you have to implement multiple backend subsystems to do so, consolidating batches of requests provide enough of a performance gain that it's usually worthwhile.

  The client can post a multiplexed request with data for multiple backends and the server can respond with a multipart/mixed response. The client will have to demultiplex the response. Figure 7-7 shows an outline of how this can be achieved.

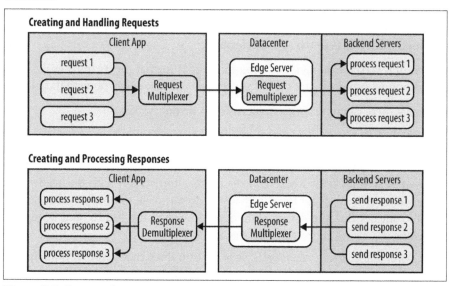

Figure 7-7. Request demux system

- *Use persistent HTTP connections*, also known as HTTP keep-alive. They help minimize TCP and SSL handshake overheads, and reduce network congestion.

  Alternatively, use WebSockets. Libraries like SocketRocket (*https://github.com/square/SocketRocket*) from Square can help you get started with using WebSockets on iOS.

- *Use HTTP/2 (https://http2.github.io/) whenever available.* HTTP/2 supports true multiplexing of HTTP requests over a single connection, coalescing requests across multiple sub-domains into one if they resolve to one IP address, header compression, and much more. The benefits of using HTTP/2 are enormous. And the best part is that the protocol remains unchanged as far as the message structure is concerned, which continues to be comprised of headers and body.

- *Use HTTP cache headers for the correct level of caching.* For standard images that you intend to download (e.g., theme backgrounds or emoticons), the content can have an expiry date far ahead in the future. This ensures not only that the networking library caches them locally, but also that other devices benefit from intermediary servers (ISP servers or proxies) caching them locally. The response headers that affect HTTP caching are `Last-Modified`, `Expires`, `ETag`, and `Cache-Control`.

Data Format

Choosing the correct data format is as important as choosing the network parameters. A choice as simple as PNG versus WEBP for lossless image compression can make a big difference to the app's performance.

If your app is data oriented, choosing the proper format for its transfer is key. There are additional protocol-supported features that can also help you with it.

Note that there can be security concerns even if you use SSL.

You should follow these best practices when choosing a data format:

- *Use data compression.* This is particularly important when transferring text content such as JSON or XML. `NSURLRequest` automatically adds the header `Accept-Encoding: gzip, deflate` so that you do not have to do that yourself. But this also means that the server should acknowledge the header and send the data using the appropriate `Transfer-Encoding`.

- *Choose the correct data format.* It is a no-brainer that verbose, human-readable formats such as JSON and XML are resource intensive—serialization, transport, and deserialization takes much longer than using a custom-crafted, binary, machine-friendly format. We will not discuss media compression (i.e., image compression and video codecs), but rather focus on text data formats.

  The most commonly chosen data formats for native apps happen to be JSON and XML. And the only reason is that the web services/APIs were written for the Web and repurposed for mobile.

  However, if you aren't already, you need to start thinking mobile first. The previously mentioned formats are handy to handcraft but resource intensive for machine operations. Prefer a more optimized format from both a size and a serialization/deserialization perspective.

The most popular binary format to transport records is Protocol Buffers, a.k.a. Protobuf. Other protocols include Apache Thrift and Apache Avro. In general, Protobuf is known to outperform the others, but a lot can depend on the type of data being used. If the data is largely strings, you should find ways to optimize their loading, as they are not compressed by any of these formats. Compress the data using `deflate`, `gzip`, or any lossless compression algorithm.

Tools

With the basic foundation laid correctly, you will need a little support from some tools to levitate the execution.

Network Link Conditioner

The Network Link Conditioner is available on iOS devices as well as the Simulator. You can access it via the Developer menu in the Settings app. Figure 7-8 shows how to get to the Network Link Conditioner and the settings.

You can either choose one of the predefined profiles or create a new profile. The Network Link Conditioner allows you to simulate varying network conditions by controlling important parameters:

Inbound traffic
Bandwidth, packet loss, and delay (the response latency)

Outbound traffic
Bandwidth, packet loss, and delay

DNS
Lookup latency

Protocol
IPv4, IPv6, or both

Interface
WiFi, cellular, or both

You should use the Network Link Conditioner to test how your app behaves in extreme scenarios. You may not do these tests on a regular basis, but you should do them at least once before every new release.

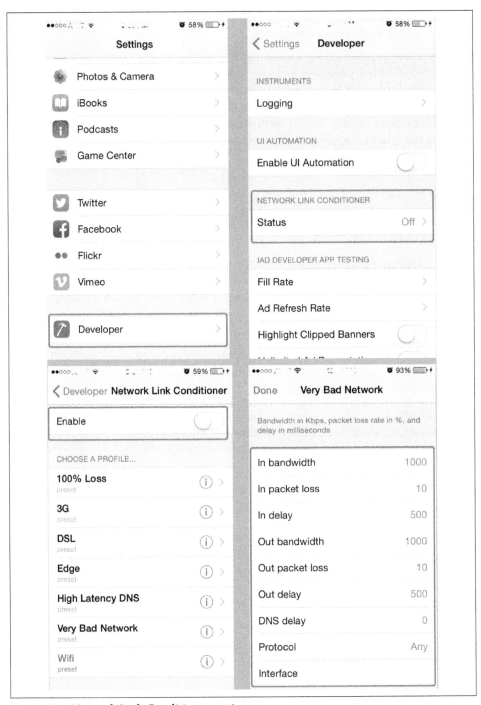

Figure 7-8. Network Link Conditioner settings

AT&T Application Resource Optimizer

Although the official documentation (*http://bit.ly/att-docs*) states that the AT&T Application Resource Optimizer (ARO) (*http://developer.att.com/campaigns/application-resource-optimizer*) tool allows you to optimize the performance of *mobile web applications*, it can be used for native apps as well.

To use the tool, you will need to configure your iPhone/iPad development and debugging (using Xcode) so that you can see the Developer menu that we discussed earlier, and you need administrative privileges on the Mac machine.

You can enable the Developer menu by following these steps:

1. Connect the iOS device to the Mac OS X device.
2. Open Xcode.
3. Navigate to Window → Devices.
4. Select the iOS device and select "Use for Development."

The ARO tool comprises two steps: *data collection* and *data analysis*. To collect data, follow these steps:

1. Navigate to Menu Bar → Data Collector → Start Collector.
2. Run the app on the device.
3. Navigate to Menu Bar → Data Collector → Stop Collector.

The Data Analyzer evaluates the data collected from your app against a set of Best Practices tests. Results are presented in a summary screen (Figure 7-9).

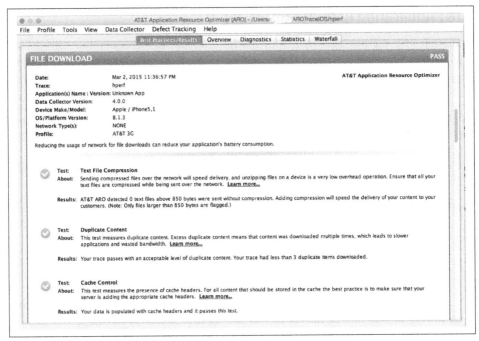

Figure 7-9. ARO Data Analyzer: summary

The tool collects the data in *~/AROTraceIOS/{name}/*. In the overall statistics collected, the following are of importance:

- Device details (model, OS version, screen dimensions, etc.)
- Traffic details via pcap interface
- Battery consumption

Figure 7-10 shows the network analysis summary graph in the ARO tool.

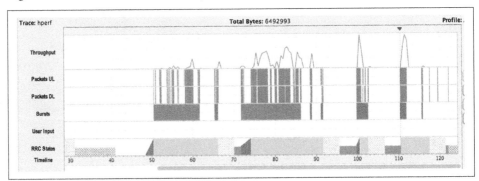

Figure 7-10. ARO Data Analyzer: network usage diagnostics

This analysis is presented in an easy-to-understand manner, but the raw data can be analyzed programmatically for more detailed reports, and more importantly, historical data can be used to analyze the performance changes over time.

Charles

Charles (*http://www.charlesproxy.com*) is a very powerful web debugging proxy. You can configure it to do the following:

Monitor HTTP requests

You can monitor HTTP traffic, including request and response data and HTTP headers. Figure 7-11 shows a sample request from the Facebook app. Figure 7-12 shows the response to the same request. The response is JSON content and can be formatted without using any external tool.

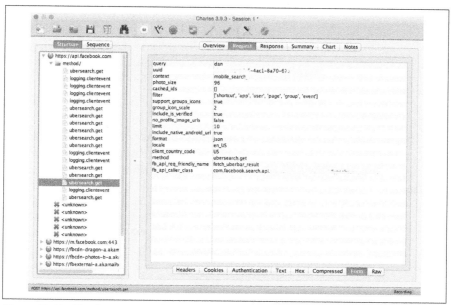

Figure 7-11. Charles: request details

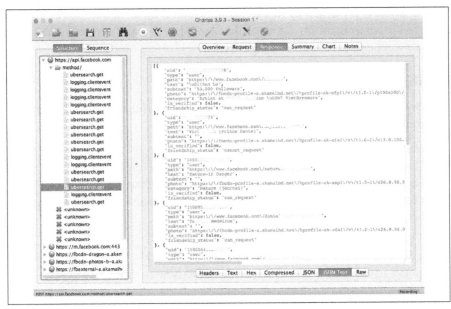

Figure 7-12. Charles: response details

Monitor HTTPS requests

This requires setting up a certificate. You can either create your own self-signed certificate or use the default available from the website (*http://charlesproxy.com/charles.crt*), as seen in Figure 7-13. Install the certificate on the device, and you can now watch HTTPS requests as well.

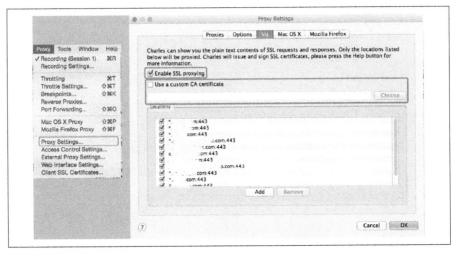

Figure 7-13. Charles: SSL settings

Use the keys from the website only on test devices. Both the private and the public key are in the public domain. If you use them on your personal device, you are subject to a big risk—all communications can be monitored.

Send a custom response

This is a very useful feature to test various possible scenarios without disturbing the production servers. To test performance, send a large volume of data. To test stability, send a large volume of data as well as invalid inputs.

You can go to Tools → Rewrite → Enable Rewrite → Add, as shown in Figure 7-14, and configure the response against a URL, as in Figure 7-15.

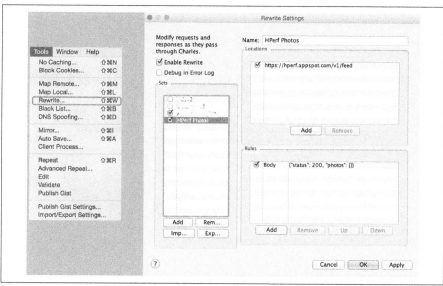

Figure 7-14. Charles: enable custom response

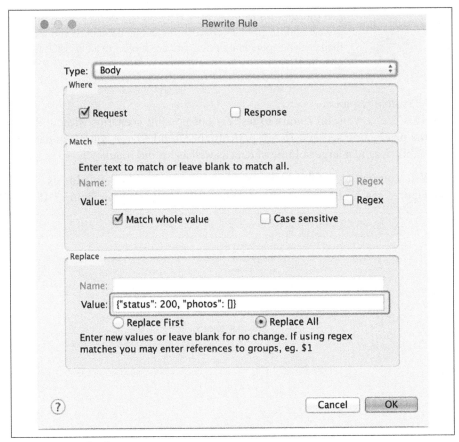

Figure 7-15. Charles: set up custom response

From a development, debugging, and testing perspective, keep in mind that the session log can be saved and distributed to the team for analysis.

Summary

An understanding of the important metrics related to networking and techniques for measuring them will empower you to develop apps that can be optimized to minimize any resource utilization for a better user experience.

More often than not, you'll need to make trade-offs, as the requirements to optimize against multiple parameters will be competing and there will be a need to strike a balance. Examples include using SSL for security versus memory utilization and execution speed, CDNs for cacheable static content for speed versus a single hostname for speed, and so on.

Do not rely on the network state, as it can change at any time. The best you can do is ensure that your networking tier is adaptive to the network type and state. Specifically, for media streaming, use adaptive multibitrate HLS. For non-media content, perform batch operations and try to prefetch as much as possible. It's critical that you serve data suitable for the device—you'll need to take device capability, size, and form factor into account.

Tools should help you test your app in varying network conditions and with different data responses. Use these tools to test various corner cases related to networking, requests, and responses to harden the app.

CHAPTER 8

Data Sharing

At times, you will want to share data with another app or get access to shared data from another app installed on the device. For example, a few use cases for sharing data include the following:

- Integrating with other apps (e.g., giving users the ability to sign into your app using their Facebook login)
- Releasing a suite of complementary apps such as those offered by Google (i.e., Gmail, Google Calendar, Google Hangouts, and Google+)
- Moving user data from a unified app to multiple special-purpose apps, detecting their presence and transferring controls when required (e.g., the Facebook app splits into Messenger, Pages, and Groups apps for messaging, pages management, and groups management, respectively)
- Opening a document in the best available viewer (e.g., opening a PDF file for viewing in a native viewer or a photo for editing in Photoshop Express)

Each technique for sharing data has specific constraints on what can be shared. As an example, using the clipboard may consume a lot of RAM, whereas document sharing uses device storage (both RAM and device storage must be cleared after use). Similarly, using deep linking has overheads of data serialization and parsing.

In this chapter, we discuss various data sharing options from a performance perspective and identify best practices when working with a specific option.

Deep Linking

In the context of the mobile apps, deep linking consists of using a uniform resource identifier (URI) that links to a specific location within a mobile app rather than simply launching the app.

Deep linking provides a decoupled solution to sharing data across apps. Similar to HTTP URLs to access websites, deep linking in iOS is available through what is known as a *custom URL scheme*. You can configure your app to respond to a unique scheme and the OS will ensure that whenever that scheme is used, it is handled by your app. The app can respond to any number of schemes.

There is a reserved list of URL schemes that an app cannot respond to:

`http, https`
> Standard schemes for browsing the Web; handled by Safari. An exception is for YouTube links, which are opened by the YouTube app, if installed (this is due to a partnership with Google formed before Apple created its own video player).

`mailto`
> Scheme to send emails; handled by the Mail app. Example: `mailto:email@domain.com`.

`itms, itms-apps`
> Used to take a user to an app install screen; handled by the App Store application. These were the only options available until Store Kit (*http://bit.ly/ios-store-kit*) was introduced in iOS 6.

`tel`
> Used to call a phone number; handled by the Phone app. Example: `tel://` `1234567890`.

`app-settings`
> New in iOS 8, this scheme takes you to the Settings app and directly into the app settings.

Choosing Unique Schemes

The URL scheme that you choose must be unique across all the apps installed, or else the behavior is undefined.[1]

You can use one or more of the following approaches to create unique schemes:

---

[1] On Android, if multiple apps respond to a scheme, the OS prompts the user to select one. A similar feature will hopefully be introduced in iOS in the future.

Reverse DNS notation

For example, `com.yourdomain.appname` if you own the domain `yourdomain.com`.

Bundle ID

Because the bundle ID must be unique across all the apps submitted to the App Store, you can use this ID.

Prefixed app ID

Each app is given a unique numeric ID on the App Store. You can prefix it with a few characters, and you should come up with a fairly unique ID. For example, if your app ID is `1234567890`, you can choose the scheme `ios1234567890` or `app1234567890`.

Whatever option(s) you use, you can only hope there is not another app with the same scheme, which may go undetected. Any mischievous app can use the same scheme, and unless you know that such an app exists, it may continue to intercept links meant for your app.

And unless you choose a scheme that you can argue to be *owned* by you, you may find it difficult to file a complaint with Apple Support. So, choose a scheme that you can defend. Using a scheme such as `com.yourdomain.appname` is a better, more defensible choice than `mail` or `song`.

iOS 9 introduces *universal links* to allow handling `http` or `https` by the app that can verify the domain ownership. We discuss this in "Universal Links" on page 404.

There are three steps that drive the life of a deep link:

1. *Detect if the scheme can be handled.* The `-[UIApplication canOpenURL:]` method allows you to check if a specific scheme can be handled by at least one of the apps installed on the device. Choosing a unique scheme can help you detect if a specific app is installed or not.

Custom URL schemes can be used to detect if an app is installed or not by using the uniqueness of the scheme. You can use version suffixes to detect if a particular version is installed or not.

For that, the app can support multiple schemes. For example, Yelp (*https://www.yelp.com/developers/documentation/v2/iphone*) uses three schemes, `yelp5.3`, `yelp4`, and `yelp`, for app versions 5.3.0 or later, 4.0.0 or later, and 2.0.0 or later, respectively. So, if `canOpenURL:` returns `YES` for `yelp4`, you know that version 4.0.0 or higher is installed on the device, and this can help you choose different URLs for a better user experience.

Similarly, you may choose to use `com.yourdmain.appname+v1` and `com.yourdomain.appname+v2` with versions 1 and 2 of your app, respectively.

2. *Open the URL into the app.* Once the app's presence has been detected, the next step is to create the final URL and open the app, using the `-[UIApplication openURL]` method to launch it.

URL Format

There is no standard or even a convention on how the URL should be formatted. Apps have used various styles. A general URL format is `scheme://host/path?query#fragment`, where `path` can have forward slashes to represent a nested path.

A few styles that are used are:

Path-only URLs
> The idea is to use only the path for all the details needed to process the data. Examples include `fb://profile/{id}`, used by the Facebook app to show a user's profile.
>
> It has the advantage of being simple and mostly human-readable.

Path and query-based URLs
> This is the more generalized and widely used format. Examples include `yelp:///search?term=burritos`, used by the Yelp app to search for a specific term.
>
> `x-callback-url` (*http://x-callback-url.com/*) proposed a standard to use URLs of the format `{scheme}://{host}/{action}?{x-callback parameters}&{action parameters}`, with host always being `x-callback-url`. Tumblr, Google Maps, Google Chrome, and a few other apps (*http://x-callback-url.com/apps/*) support this format.

It has the advantage of programmatic simplicity of creation and parsing. Standards like RFC 6874 (*http://bit.ly/rfc-6874*), RFC 3986 (*http://bit.ly/rfc-uri*), and RFC 1738 (*http://bit.ly/rfc-1738*) exist for generalized URL formats. Standard parsers exist to parse more complex query strings that may have escape sequences.

3. *Handle links in the target app.* When the app receives the URL, the UIAppDele gate gets a notification via the callback method -[UIAppDelegate applica tion:openURL:sourceApplication:annotation:]. Parse the incoming URL, extract the parameters/values, process, and proceed.

Responding to a deep link can take the user to another section of the app, so you should include an option for the user to go back to the *previous* section in the app. A good option for implementing this is to use a finite state machine.

Example 8-1 shows an example of deep linking—the source and the target.

Example 8-1. Deep linking

```
//Source application - some view controller
-(void)openTargetApp {
    NSURL *url = [NSURL URLWithString:
        @"com.yourdomain.app://x-callback-url/quote?ticker=GOOG\
            &start=2014-01-01&end=2014-12-31"]; ❶
    UIApplication *app = [UIApplication sharedApplication];
    if([app canOpenURL:url]) { ❷
        [app openURL:url]; ❸
    }
    //else show error
}

//Target application - app delegate
-(BOOL)application:(UIApplication *)application
    openURL:(NSURL *)url
    sourceApplication:(NSString *)sourceApplication
    annotation:(id)annotation { ❹

    NSString *host = url.host; ❺
    NSString *path = url.path; ❺
    NSDictionary *params = [self parseQuery:url.query]; ❺
    if([@"x-callback-url" isEqualToString:host]) { ❻
        if([@"quote" isEqualToString:path]) { ❻
            [self processQuoteUsingParameters:params]; ❼
        }
```

```
    }
    return YES;
}

-(NSDictionary *)parseQuery:(NSString *)query {
    NSMutableDictionary *dict = [NSMutableDictionary new];
    if(query) {
        //parse with '&' and '=' as delimiters
        NSArray *pairs = [query componentsSeparatedByString:@"&"];  ❽

        for(NSString *pair in pairs) {
            NSArray *kv = [pair componentsSeparatedByString:@"="];
            NSString *key = [kv.firstObject stringByRemovingPercentEncoding];
            NSString *value = [kv.lastObject stringByRemovingPercentEncoding];
        }

        [dict setObject:value forKey:key];
    }
    return [NSDictionary dictionaryWithDictionary:dict];
}

-(void)processQuoteUsingParameters:(NSDictionary *)params {
    NSString *ticker = [dict objectForKey:@"ticker"];
    NSDate *startDate = [dict objectForKey:@"start"];
    NSDate *endDate = [dict objectForKey:@"end"];  ❾
    //validate and process
}
```

❶ Construct the URL.

❷ Check if the app is installed.

❸ Launch the target app.

❹ The delegate callback in the target app that receives the URL.

❺ Extract the necessary details from the URL, including host, path, and query.

❻ Process the URL—check for the host and path in this example.

❼ In this example, process the quotes.

❽ Query string parsing. This code is not optimized, as it does double parsing of the string.

❾ Process the values extracted. Do not forget to validate.

Deep linking will probably be the most often used option for sharing data to and from your app, and it is important to optimize the creation and parsing time. The following list covers some of the best practices you can follow to achieve optimum performance:

- Prefer shorter URLs, as they are faster to construct and faster to parse.
- Avoid regular expression–based patterns.

  If you use the Button Deep Link SDK (*http://www.usebutton.com/sdk/deeplinks/*), it uses path-based URLs and regular expressions based on that. For example, the path pattern {scheme}//say/:title/:message (*http://bit.ly/ex-button-config*) requires two regular expressions—one for the slash-delimiter and one for extracting parameter names.

- Prefer query-based URLs for standard parsing. Parsing using character-based delimiters is faster than using regular expressions.
- Support deep-linking callbacks in your URLs to help the user complete the intent. A good idea is to support three options: success, failure, and cancel.

  For example, if you have a photo editor app, it will be great to let the user go back to the photo app with the edited photo. As another example, if your app is used for authentication, provide an option to take the user back to the source app with details of whether the login was successful, was cancelled, or failed.

  The x-callback-url specification provides support for these callbacks.

- Prefer deep-linking continuation in your URLs to help the user define a workflow that may require coordination across multiple apps.

  For example, the user may want to accomplish the following:

  1. Capture a photo.
  2. Edit the photo.
  3. Mail the updated photo to family and friends.
  4. Share the updated photo on social media.
  5. And finally, return to the photo app to capture the next photo.

     The first app can define the list of apps to deep link into and a final done deep link to be called after the entire process is complete.

- Do not put any sensitive data in the URLs. Specifically, do not use any auth tokens. These tokens could be hijacked by an unknown app.
- Do not trust any incoming data. Always validate the URLs. As an additional measure, it may be a good idea to expect the app to sign the data before passing it on and to validate the signature before processing. However, for this to happen securely, the private key must be kept on the server, and as such it requires network connectivity.

- Use `sourceApplication` to identify the source. This is very useful in the event that you have a whitelist of apps from which you can always trust the data. Use of `sourceApplication` is not orthogonal to signature validation. This can be the first step before URL processing commences.

Pasteboards

The official documentation describes pasteboards as follows:

> A pasteboard is a secure and standardized mechanism for the exchange of data within or between applications. Many operations depend on the pasteboard, [notably] copy-cut-paste. ... But you can also use pasteboards in other situations where sharing data between applications is desirable.[2]

Pasteboards are available through the `UIPasteBoard` class, which accesses a *shared repository* where a writer and a reader object meet for data exchange. The writer is also known as the pasteboard owner and *deposits* the data on a pasteboard instance. The reader *accesses* the pasteboard to copy the data into its address space.

Pasteboards can be either public or private. Each pasteboard must have a unique name.

A pasteboard can hold one or more entities, which are known as pasteboard *items*. Each item can have multiple representations.

Figure 8-1 shows a pasteboard with two items, each with multiple formats:

- A text item that has content in two standard formats (RTF and plain text)
- An image item that has image content in two standard formats (JPG and PNG) and one private format (`com.yourdomain.app.type`), known privately to specific apps

---

2 iOS Developer Library, "Pasteboard" (*http://bit.ly/ios-dev-uipb*).

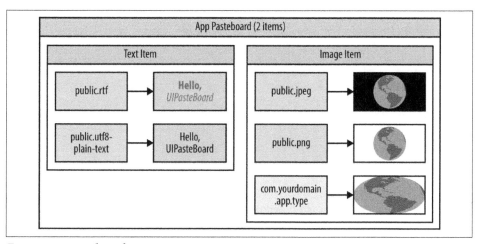

Figure 8-1. Pasteboard item representations

Example 8-2 shows sample code to share the data.

Example 8-2. Using a pasteboard to share data

```
//Sharing to public pasteboard
-(void)shareToPublicRTFData:(NSData *)rtfData text:(NSString *)text {
  [[UIPasteboard generalPasteboard] setData:rtfData forPasteboardType:kUTTypeRTF]; ❶

  [[UIPasteboard generalPasteboard] setData:text forPasteboardType:kUTTypePlainText];
  [UIPasteboard generalPasteboard].string = text;
  [UIPasteboard generalPasteboard].strings = @[text]; ❷
}

//Data assumed to be of UTI type "com.yourdomain.app.type"
-(void)shareToPublicCustomData:(NSData *)data {
  [[UIPasteboard generalPasteboard]
    setData:data
    forPasteboardType:@"com.yourdomain.app.type"]; ❸
}

//Sharing to custom named pasteboard
-(void)sharePrivatelyCustomData:(NSData *)data {
  UIPasteboard *appPasteboard = [UIPasteboard
      pasteboardWithName:@"myApp"
      create:YES]; ❹

  [appPasteboard
    setData:data
    forPasteboardType:@"com.yourdomain.app.type"]; ❺
}

//Reading from public pasteboard
```

```
-(NSArray *)readSharedStrings {
  return [UIPasteboard generalPasteboard].strings; ❻
}

//Reading from named pasteboard
-(NSData *)readPrivateData {
  UIPasteboard *appPasteboard = [UIPasteboard
        pasteboardWithName:@"myApp"
        create:YES];

  return [appPasteboard
      dataForPasteboardType:@"com.yourdomain.app.type"]; ❼
}
```

❶   Set binary data for a known type kUTTypeRTF.

❷   Plain text string can be set for type kUTTypePlainText as well as using string property. It can also be made available using strings property which is an array of NSString objects.

❸   Set binary data for a custom type.

❹   Get a pasteboard with the given name. Create one if none exists.

❺   Set the data for the custom pasteboard.

❻   Retrieve array of strings stored in the strings property.

❼   Retrieve data for custom type in a custom pasteboard (non-public).

A pasteboard has the following benefits over deep linking:

- It has the capability to support complex data like images.
- It has support to represent data in multiple forms which can be used based on the target's app capabilities. For example, a messaging app can use plain-text format, whereas a mail app can use rich-text format from the same pasteboard item.
- The pasteboard content can persist even after app shutdown.

However, compared to deep linking, one big drawback of using a pasteboard is that the format of the data shared is not in any standard format. As such, it cannot be used for general-purpose sharing without being able to define the data contract between the two applications.

Also, as shown in Example 8-2, plain-text data can be shared using multiple options; at times, it may get confusing as to which format to use.

In addition, unlike deep linking, a pasteboard cannot be used to detect if the target application is installed or not. This information helps create a better user experience —for example, by prompting the user to install the app if it is not already installed.

Furthermore, unlike deep links, a pasteboard can be accessed by any application, so it comes with deep security concerns.

When working with pasteboards, you should follow these best practices:

- A pasteboard is essentially an interprocess communication mediated by the pasteboard service. All security rules of IPC apply (i.e., do not send any secure data, do not trust any incoming data).

- Because you do not control which app accesses the pasteboard, using it is always insecure unless the data is encrypted.

- Do not use large amounts of data in a pasteboard. Although pasteboards have support for exchanging images and for multiple formats, keep in mind that each entry not only consumes memory but also takes extra time to write and read.

- Clear the pasteboard when the app is about to enter the background by using either a `UIApplicationDidEnterBackgroundNotification` notification or a `UIApplicationWillResignActiveNotification` notification. Better still, you could implement the corresponding callback methods of `UIApplicationDelegate`.

  You can clear the pasteboard by setting the `items` to `nil`, as shown here:

  ```
  myPasteboard.items = nil;
  ```

- To prevent any kind of copy/paste, subclass `UITextView` and return `NO` for the `copy:` action in `canPerformAction`.[3]

Sharing Content

The first two options that we explored—custom URL schemes and pasteboards—are completely machine driven and are not human controlled. The end user cannot choose which app to go into and/or which app to make use of the data with.

To fill this gap, iOS provides several options for sharing documents with a specific app. The source app produces the data to be shared and the user chooses the app to consume the data in. Figure 8-2 shows the WhatsApp and Photos apps using document sharing options. The list of apps available depends on the option chosen, as we will explore next.

---

3 Stack Overflow, "How to Disable Copy, Cut, Select, Select All in UITextView" (*http://stackoverflow.com/a/1429320*).

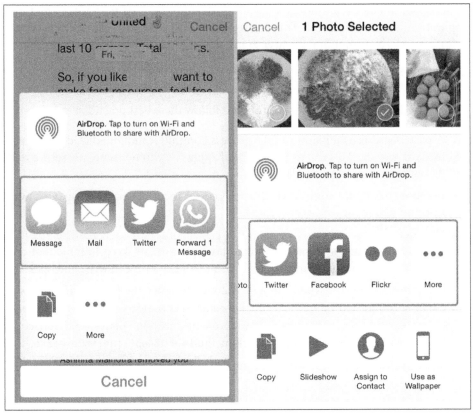

Figure 8-2. WhatsApp and Photos sharing a message and a photo, respectively

Document Interaction

The `UIDocumentInteractionController` class, available since iOS 3.2, allows apps to open documents in other apps installed on the device. It also supports previewing, printing, emailing, and copying of documents.

> `UIDocumentInteractionController` is not a subclass of `UIView`
> `Controller`. You have to configure a view controller to use to pre-
> view the document.

There are two sides to using the controller: the publisher and the consumer.

As a publisher, your app publishes the document to be viewed. It is the controller's responsibility to load the target app, make the content available to the consumer app, and finally take the user back to the host app. The following subsection presents representative code for the publisher.

As a consumer, your app's responsibility includes processing the document (and rendering the result). It is also responsible for performing some cleanup, as shown in "Consumer" on page 267.

Figure 8-3 illustrates the steps that occur during document sharing.

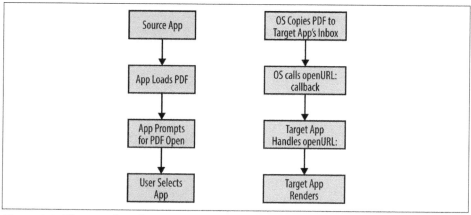

Figure 8-3. The complete document sharing process

Publisher

As a publisher, the app can either *preview* or *open* a document. The UIDocument InteractionController operates via a UIDocumentInteractionController Delegate delegate for the host app to specify the parent view controller to show the preview window in. The view controller also requires the path to the document and the uniform type identifier associated with the document type.

Uniform Type Identifier

A uniform type identifier (UTI) is a text string used to uniquely identify the type of an item. There are built-in UTIs to identify common system objects. Examples include public.document for documents, public.jpeg for JPEG images, and public.plain-text for plain text.

There is also a provision to allow third-party developers to add their own UTIs for app-specific or proprietary uses. Examples include com.adobe.pdf for PDF documents and com.apple.keynote.key for Apple Keynote documents.

The delegate gets a callback to determine if a specific *action* can be performed. The actions include copy:, print:, and saveToCameraRoll: by default. It also gets a callback before the preview/open UI is about to be presented and after it has been presented.

Example 8-3 shows sample code for sharing a document for *preview* and *open*.

Example 8-3. Document interaction—publisher

```
#import <MobileCoreServices/MobileCoreServices.h> ❶

@interface HPDocumentViewerViewController
    <UIDocumentInteractionControllerDelegate> ❷

@property (nonatomic, strong) UIDocumentInteractionController *docController;

@end

@implementation HPDocumentViewerViewController

-(UIViewController *)documentInteractionControllerViewControllerForPreview:
    (UIDocumentInteractionController *) controller { ❸
    return self;
}

-(NSURL *)fileInDocsDirectory:(NSString *)filename {
    NSArray *paths = NSSearchPathForDirectoriesInDomains(NSDocumentDirectory,
        NSUserDomainMask, YES);
    NSString *docsDir = [paths firstObject];
    NSString *fullPath = [docsDir stringByAppendingPathComponent:filename];

    return [NSURL fileURLWithPath:fullPath];
}

-(void)configureDIControllerWithURL:(NSURL *)url
    uti:(NSString *)uti { ❹

    UIDocumentInteractionController controller = [UIDocumentInteractionController
        interactionControllerWithURL:url]; ❺
        controller.delegate = self;
        controller.UTI = uti; ❻
        self.docController = controller; ❼
}

-(IBAction)previewDocument {
    NSURL *fileURL = [self fileInDocsDirectory:@"sample.pdf"]; ❽

    if(fileURL) {
        [self configureDIControllerWithURL:fileURL uti:kUTTypePDF];
        [self.docController presentPreviewAnimated:YES]; ❾
    }
}
```

```
-(IBAction)openDocument {
    NSURL *fileURL = [self fileInDocsDirectory:@"sample.pdf"];

    if(fileURL) {
        [self configureDIControllerWithURL:fileURL uti:kUTTypePDF];

        [self.docController presentOpenInMenuFromRect:self.view.frame
            inView:self.view animated:YES]; ❿
    }
}
@end
```

❶ The `UIDocumentInteractionController` class and related types and constants are defined in `MobileCoreServices`.

❷ The controller needs the `UIDocumentInteractionControllerDelegate`. Let the view controller implement the protocol.

❸ Although all the methods are options, you must implement the method `documen tInteractionControllerViewControllerForPreview:`—this provides the `UIViewController` on which the child view controller is presented.

❹ Helper method to configure the controller with the content URL and UTI type.

❺ Get a reference to the controller referring to the URL.

❻ Specify the delegate and UTI type.

❼ Set a strong reference to the controller, which ensures that the controller is not dealloced prematurely.

❽ Note that the URL referenced by the `UIDocumentInteractionController` object must be reachable by the OS. It is a good idea to download the contents of the file, if need be, and refer to it using the local (file) URL.

❾ Use `presentPreviewAnimated:` to preview the document. Figure 8-4 shows the view controller in animation when being presented in our app.

❿ Use `presentOpenInMenuFromRect:inView:animated:` to show the "Open in…" menu and let the user choose the app to open the document. Figure 8-5 shows the menu from within our app.

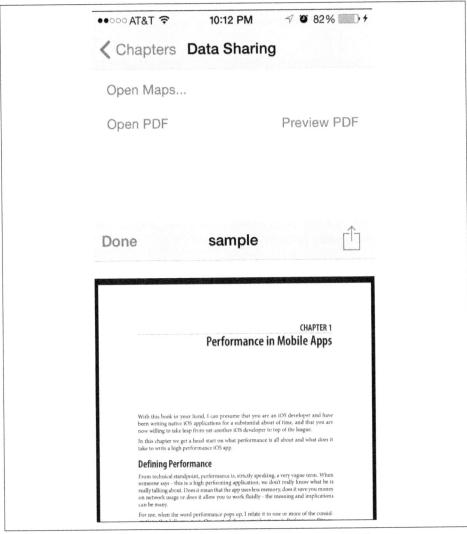

Figure 8-4. Preview a PDF document (view controller being presented)

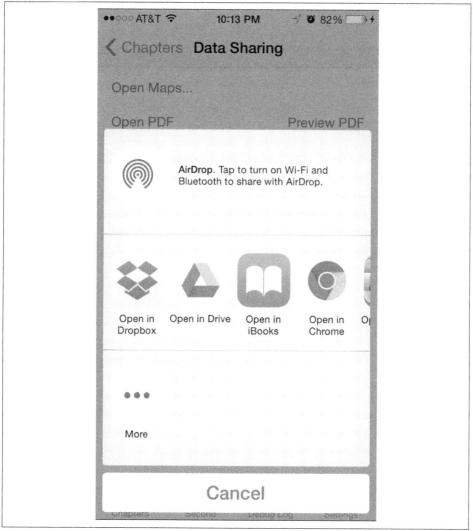

Figure 8-5. "Open in..." menu for a PDF document

 UIDocumentInteractionController requires an NSURL to read contents and it must refer to a local file using the file scheme. Any other scheme will cause an exception to be raised, which can ultimately result in an app crash.

Consumer

Being a consumer requires two basic steps: registering file types supported by the app, and then processing the document content. You can either support one or more of the system-defined types in iOS or register a new type, which is useful for sharing within a suite of apps from the same company or otherwise.

To register a file type supported by your app, the following details must be configured in the Document Types section of your app's *Info.plist*:

Name
> The human-readable name that you want to give.

Types
> One of the standard uniform type identifiers[4] (e.g., `com.adobe.pdf`), or a custom UTI.

Icon
> An icon associated with the document, if different from the app icon.

Properties
> Optionally, you can configure additional document type properties.

Figure 8-6 shows the Document Types section filled in for our app. Notice that Types has been set to `com.adobe.pdf`, a predefined type. Feel free to choose a custom name to share custom types within the suite of your apps. The same value must be used as the `UTI` property of the `UIDocumentInteractionController` object.

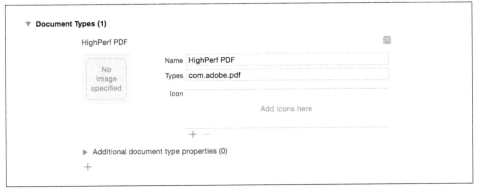

Figure 8-6. Configure Document Types to handle PDF documents

With this setting, if you open the *https://bitcoin.org/bitcoin.pdf* URL in Safari and tap on the "Open in…" menu, it shows our app (see Figure 8-7).

---

4 For the full list, see the iOS Developer Library (*http://bit.ly/ios-uti*).

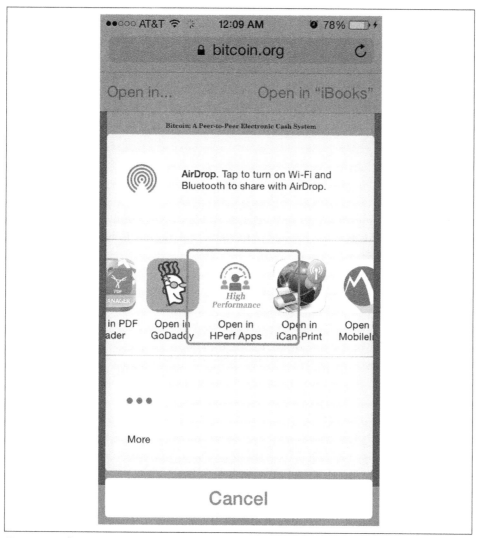

Figure 8-7. "Open in…" menu in Safari when viewing a PDF document

Now, we must handle the `application:openURL:sourceApplication:annotation:` app delegate callback. As noted in Figure 8-3, the shared document is copied into the app's *Inbox* folder. The `url` passed to the callback is a `file` URL referring to the file. If a user shares the same document multiple times with the same app, the OS creates multiple copies of the document and a new URL is made available each time. Example 8-4 shows representative code to process the document.

Example 8-4. Document interaction—consumer

```
@implement HPAppDelegate

-(BOOL)application:(UIApplication *)application
    openURL:(NSURL *)url sourceApplication:(NSString *)src
    annotation:(id)annotation {

    DDLogDebug("%s src: %@, url: %@", __PRETTY_FUNCTION__, src, url);
        return YES;

}

@end
```

If you look at the logs from the app delegate in Figure 8-8, you will notice that even though the same document is opened in the same app, the url is different each time.

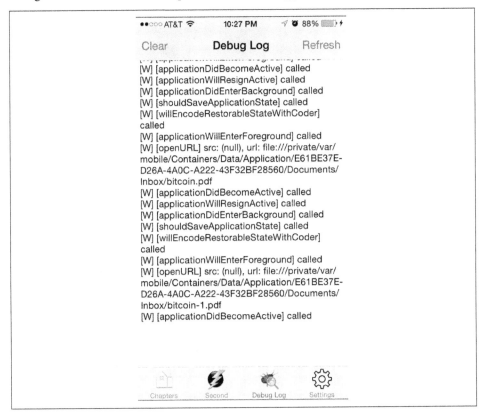

Figure 8-8. App delegate callback debug log

Sharing documents using `UIDocumentInteractionController` should follow similar best practices as the previous sharing options that we have discussed so far. Additionally, there is one more concern at hand.

As mentioned, using `UIDocumentInteractionController` results in the document being copied into the app's *Inbox* folder. It is thereafter the app's responsibility to delete the file and clean up the folder. The resultant file is *owned* by the consumer app. Don't forget to delete the file once you are done.

Activities

UTIs have worked well in the past. However, the rise of cloud services and social media has prioritized remote entities over local files. As such, a tension exists between UTIs and remote URLs.

`UIActivityViewController` provides a unified services interface to share and perform actions on data within an app. It was introduced in iOS 6.

Using `UIActivityViewController` is easier and more flexible than using `UIDocument InteractionController`. Unlike with `UIDocumentInteractionController`, which allows only `file` URLs, using `UIActivityViewController` you can share one or more of the following types:

NSString
: Any string can be shared.

NSAttributedString
: Useful to share formatted or rich text.

NSURL
: Any URL can be shared. It is up to the target app to make use of the URL. Mail or messaging apps may choose to share the URL as is, whereas a reader or a cloud service app may attempt to fetch the contents and process them.

UIImage
: An image, if provided, can also be saved to Camera Roll, assigned to a contact, or printed.

ALAsset
: This represents a photo or video managed by the Photos app, which can be shared with the target app.

UIActivityItemSource
: Any object that conforms to this protocol can be shared. This helps in creating custom objects that can be shared across apps.

To save a `UIImage` to Camera Roll or work with an `ALAsset`, the app needs permission to access Photos. If the app has never asked before, the user will be prompted to grant permissions. If the user has denied or granted access earlier, the permission prompt will never appear.

There are two types of activities: *actions* and *shares* (see Figure 8-9). Shares bring up the UI from third-party apps (e.g., Facebook, Twitter, Vimeo, etc.), whereas actions are mostly about built-in apps (Photos, printer, clipboard/copy, Safari, Contacts, etc.). In addition, there is AirDrop support for images. A complete list of built-in action types is available on the Apple developer website (*http://bit.ly/ios-activity-types*).

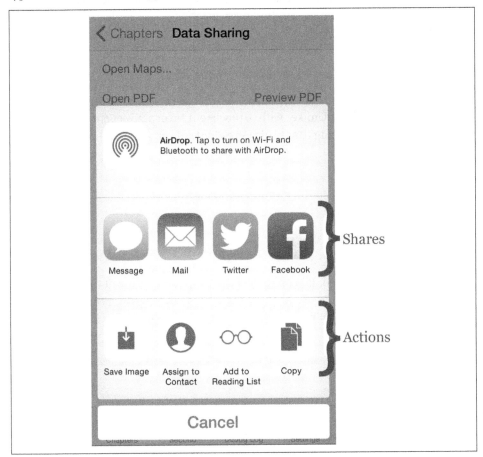

Figure 8-9. Using UIActivityViewController—action and share activities

Example 8-5 shows representative code for enabling the activity view controller in an app. You have the option to *exclude* one or more activities. In addition, you can let the user share content into the same app by having a custom implementation of UIActiv ity, an abstract class that must be subclassed.

Example 8-5. Using UIActivityViewController to share data

```
-(void)shareSomeContent {
    NSString *text = @"Text to share";
    NSURL *url = [NSURL URLWithString:@"http://github.com"];
    UIImage *image = [UIImage imageNamed:"blah"]; ❶

    NSArray *items = @[text, url, image];
    UIActivityViewController *ctrl = [[UIActivityViewController alloc]
        initWithActivityItems:items
        applicationActivities:nil]; ❷

    ctrl.excludedActivityTypes = @[ UIActivityTypePostToFacebook ]; ❸
    [self presentViewController:ctrl animated:YES completed:nil]; ❹
}
```

❶ A few items to share—a string, a URL, and an image.

❷ Instantiate UIActivityViewController with activity items. In this example, there are no applicationActivities configured. If you need them, they must be UIActivity subclassed objects.

❸ Exclude disallowed activity types—here, *posting to Facebook* has been excluded.

❹ Finally, present the view controller, either modally (as demonstrated here) or using navigationController.

Activities are a very flexible, extensible, and powerful option for sharing content with another app. The performance and security concerns here are a union of the concerns that we have discussed with other data sharing options so far.

Shared Keychain

A shared keychain is another option for sharing data among your apps securely. Only the apps that belong to the same group ID and are signed using the same certificates can share the data.

The only way to implement single sign-on across all your apps is using a shared keychain.

This is also the only option for sharing data across apps from the same publisher (same signing certificate) that does not require invoking another app from the one being used by the user.

Because the data is encrypted, it should be the place to store secure information such as credentials, credit card number (though without CVV), and so on. Avoid flushing in a lot of generic, nonsecure data because the access is slower than to non-encrypted data.

iOS 8 Extensions

iOS 8 introduced four new options for sharing content across apps under the broader category of what is known as *application extensions* (described briefly in Chapter 6).

If you open the project and click the plus icon (+) to add a target (see Figure 8-10), you should find a new Application Extension entry under iOS, which should present you with the options shown in Figure 8-11.

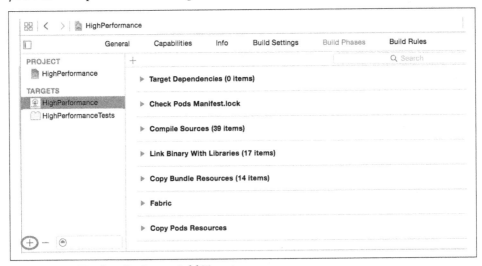

Figure 8-10. Xcode → Project → Add Target

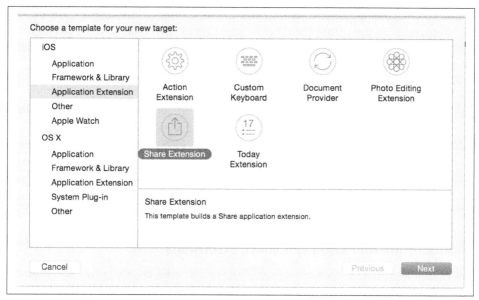

Figure 8-11. Select iOS → Application Extension

Of all these options, the following are of interest for the purpose of sharing data:

- Action extension
- Share extension
- Document Provider extension
- App groups

From an implementation perspective, they are not really *new* to us. We have already discussed sharing via actions and shares using `UIActivityViewController` and sharing documents using `UIDocumentInteractionController`, in the previous section.

Most of the newness lies in the overall plumbing, the ease of implementation, and the options made available to the end user.

But before we explore these extensions for sharing data, let's explore some new classes that were added in iOS 8:

`NSExtensionContext` *(http://apple.co/1HejEzB)*
Represents the host app context from which the extension is invoked. It provides an array of `inputItems` (i.e., the data shared to the app).

`NSExtensionItem` *(http://apple.co/1BFpuls)*

Represents an item from the array of `inputItems`. An `NSExtensionItem` object is an immutable collection of values representing different aspects of the item, available via the `attachments` property.

`NSItemProvider` *(http://apple.co/1ECgC4H)*

Represents a data object that can be found in an `NSExtensionItem` object's `attachments` property, such as text, images, and URLs. Use the method `hasItem ConformingToTypeIdentifier:` to check the UTI type it represents. To retrieve the data for the corresponding type, use the method `loadItemForTypeIdenti fier:options:completionHandler:`. The callback method can be invoked in any thread—do not forget to switch context to the main thread to make any UI changes.

Configuration for Action and Share Extensions

For Action and Share extensions, apart from specific artifacts, these two are common for all templates:

Metadata (Info.plist)

The two most important entries are the bundle display name, which is the name that appears next to the item, and `NSExtensionItem`, which provides metadata of when to show this action in the list. Xcode sets the value of `NSExtension` → `NSEx tensionAttributes` → `NSExtensionActivationRule` to `TRUEPREDICATE` (type `String`), which essentially indicates that the action is always available. You can change it to type `Dictionary` and provide more fine-grained control, using the keys listed in Table 8-1.

Table 8-1. App extension keys

Key	Description
`NSExtensionActivationSupportsText`	App supports text (`NSString` or `NSAttributedString` values)
`NSExtensionActivationSupportsFileWithMaxCount`	App supports handling of any file (`NSURL` with `file` scheme)
`NSExtensionActivationSupportsWebURLWithMaxCount`	App supports web URLs (`NSURL` with `http` or `https` scheme)
`NSExtensionActivationSupportsWebPageWithMaxCount`	App supports web pages
`NSExtensionActivationSupportsImageWithMaxCount`	App supports images (`UIImage` value)
`NSExtensionActivationSupportsMovieWithMaxCount`	App supports videos
`NSExtensionActivationSupportsAttachmentsWithMin Count`	Minimum number of attachments required for the extension to be activated (defaults to 1)

Key	Description
NSExtensionActivationSupportsAttachmentsWithMax Count	Maximum number of attachments the extension supports (defaults to Long max value)

A positive value indicates the maximum number of entries that can be shared for the specific type. For example, a value of 2 for `NSExtensionActivationSupport sImageWithMaxCount` means that a maximum of two images can be shared. A missing key or zero value means that the extension does not support that specific type. To declare a more complex definition, you can use an `NSPredicate`-compilable structure. See the section "Declaring Supported Data Types for a Share or Action Extension" in the App Extension Programming Guide (*http:// apple.co/1LDgW9X*).

Target product name
   A new target is created with the name as provided in the Product Name field when creating a new extension.

Action Extensions

Action extensions allow you to add your view controller to be added to the action section when using `UIActivityViewController`. While iOS 7 came bundled with a predefined list of actions from other apps and there was no way to add more, this changed in iOS 8.

When you create an Action extension, Xcode will create the following additional artifacts:

Storyboard `MainInterface`
   The storyboard UI to be shown when the user selects the action.

Class `ActionViewController`
   The view controller class backing the storyboard.

   Being a view controller, it goes through the usual lifecycle (recall Figure 6-1, which we studied earlier).

Example 8-6 shows typical code for rendering the image shared by the source app.

Example 8-6. Action—render image from shared data

```
- (void)viewDidLoad {
    [super viewDidLoad];
        BOOL imageFound = NO;
        for(NSExtensionItem *item in self.extensionContext.inputItems) { ❶
            for(NSItemProvider *itemProvider in item.attachments) { ❷
            if([itemProvider
```

```
                hasItemConformingToTypeIdentifier:(NSString *)kUTTypeImage]) { ❸
                    [self processItem:itemProvider];
                    imageFound = YES;
                    break;
                }
        }
            if(imageFound) {
                break;
            }
        }
    }
}

-(void)processItem:(NSItemProvider *)itemProvider {
    UIImageView __weak *imageView = self.imageView;
    [itemProvider loadItemForTypeIdentifier:(NSString *)kUTTypeImage
    options:nil
    completionHandler:^(UIImage *image, NSError *error) { ❹
            if(image) {
                    [[NSOperationQueue mainQueue] addOperationWithBlock:^{
                            [imageView setImage:image];
                    }]; ❺
            }
    }];
}
```

❶ Scan through all the extension items.

❷ For each item, scan through all the attachments.

❸ Check if the attachment is of type image.

❹ If so, retrieve the content.

❺ Because the retrieval callback can be called on a non-main thread, switch the context to update the `UIImageView` with the `UIImage` content.

Share Extensions

A share extension is slightly different from a share activity in that it is a system-provided UI and cannot be customized by the receiving app:

> Users get access to Share extensions in the system-provided UI. In iOS, users tap the Share button and choose a Share extension from the sharing area of the activity view controller that appears.[5]

---

5 iOS Developer Library, "Share" (*http://bit.ly/ios-share*).

When you create a Share extension, Xcode will create the following additional artifacts:

Storyboard MainInterface

This is of no significance, at least until iOS 8.2. In the future, Apple might decide to allow apps to provide a custom UI.

Class ShareViewController

This is a subclass of SLComposeServiceViewController introduced in iOS 8. Although it is a view controller, the UI configured by the controller is completely ignored.

The class provides hooks to the following lifecycle events:

Content validation

The first method called is isContentValid. Validate the incoming values (see Example 8-6) using NSExtensionContext and return YES if the data is valid or NO if it is invalid. The activity will always be shown, irrespective of the value, but the Post button will be disabled if the content is invalid (Figure 8-12).

Figure 8-12. Share activity, with valid content (left) and with invalid content (right)

viewDidLoad

Called after initial content validation, after the view is loaded. Use the textView property to get access to the UITextView editor to make changes to the text, if need be.

Get configuration items

After the view load, the method configurationItems is called to retrieve any configuration items. It returns an array of zero or more SLComposeSheetConfigura tionItem (subclassed) entries.

The SLComposeSheetConfigurationItem object provides a title and value to be displayed beneath the share editor (see Figure 8-12) using a standard UITable View.

The SLComposeSheetConfigurationItem object also provides a tapHandler, which is called when the user taps on the configuration item. The tapHandler can push a view controller that can show options to change the value. For example, the Facebook app allows changing album, location, and privacy values for an image (see Figure 8-13).

Figure 8-13. Facebook share—activity (left) and album configuration (right)

View controller lifecycle methods
The methods viewWillAppear and viewDidAppear are called subsequently.

Content validation
The last leg of content validation is performed immediately after the view is shown.

Content validation on change
Whenever the user changes the content in the editor, isContentValid is called. The extension can call the validateContent method to trigger revalidation or

the `reloadConfigurationItems` method to reload configuration items. It can also implement the `charactersRemaining` method to return a nonnegative value indicating the number of characters remaining (Figure 8-14 shows a Twitter share showing the value).

Figure 8-14. Twitter share, with number of characters remaining

Cancel notification

The method `didSelectCancel` is called if the user taps the Cancel button.

Post notification

The method `didSelectPost` is called if the user taps the Post button.

Here are some important points to keep in mind when working with a Share extension:

- All of these methods are called *after* the user selects the activity.

- For cancel and post notifications, call the `NSExtensionItem` method `completeRequestReturningItems:completionHandler:` to indicate that the activity's interaction is complete. Otherwise, you will leave the source app in an unusable state.

- As a best practice, build your app against iOS 8 or later. When you want to use an activity in the app, detect if the app is running on iOS 7 or earlier. If so, use a custom activity view controller. If not, let the OS choose the activities for you.

Document Provider Extension

Document providers are an iOS 8 extension version of the document interaction API. To read the contents of a shared document, use `UIDocumentPickerViewController`. To present a UI to share a document, `UIDocumentPickerExtensionViewController` should be subclassed.

Working with a document provider requires iCloud entitlements. Go to Project → App Target → iCloud and select iCloud Documents, as shown in Figure 8-15.

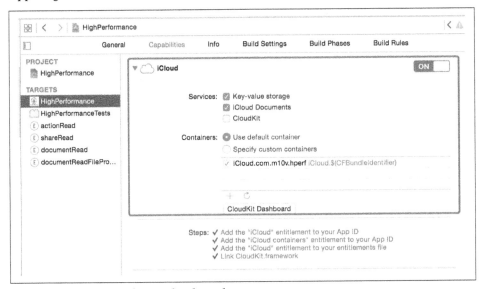

Figure 8-15. App manifest—iCloud entitlements

Open/import document

`UIDocumentPickerViewController` (which is often referred to as the *document picker*) provides a hook to interface with other document providers installed on the device. The document picker can work in either open/import mode or export mode.

The approach is similar to that of the document interaction provider except that this is from the other end of the "Open in…" menu. As a result, instead of now going into the apps that are the source of the document (e.g., browser, Google Drive, Dropbox, etc.), the user can be in the app of interest and import documents and proceed.

Figure 8-16 shows the changes in steps to edit a document using document interaction versus the document picker.

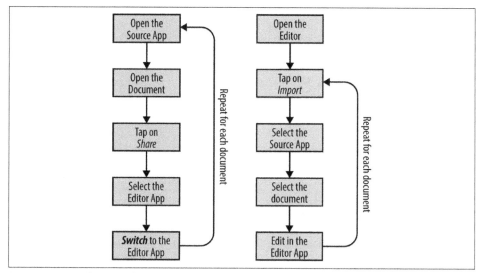

Figure 8-16. Editing a document using activity or document interaction (left) and using document picker (right)

A `UIDocumentPickerViewController` object needs to be configured with:

Document types
The UTI types that the editor app can support.

Mode
Must be configured to `Open` or `Import`.

Delegate
The delegate, of type `UIDocumentPickerDelegate`, responds when the user selects a document. It may additionally (optionally) respond when the user cancels the selection.

Example 8-7 shows representative code for opening/importing a document from another document provider.

Example 8-7. Document provider—open/import

```
@interface HPDocumentEditorViewController
    : UIViewController <UIDocumentPickerDelegate> ❶
@end

@implementation HPDocumentEditorViewController
-(IBAction)openButtonWasClicked:(id)sender {
    NSArray *types = @[
        (NSString *)kUTTypeImage
        ]; ❷
```

```
         UIDocumentPickerViewController *dpvc =
         [[UIDocumentPickerViewController alloc]
                         initWithDocumentTypes:types
             inMode:UIDocumentPickerModeImport]; ❸
         dpvc.delegate = self; ❹
         [self.navigationController presentViewController:dpvc
         animated:YES completion:nil]; ❺
}

-(void)documentPicker:(UIDocumentPickerViewController *)controller
    didPickDocumentAtURL:(NSURL *)url { ❻
    NSData *data = [NSData  dataWithContentsOfURL:url]; ❼
    //process data, render in editor, let user edit
}

-(void)documentPickerWasCancelled:(UIDocumentPickerViewController *)controller { ❽
    //maybe show a message that the user did not select a document
}

@end
```

❶ The editor app's view controller conforms to the `UIDocumentPickerDelegate` protocol.

❷ The UTI types the editor can handle.

❸ The `UIDocumentPickerViewController` object is configured using the UTI types and in `UIDocumentPickerModeImport` mode.

❹ Specify the `delegate` (this is a mandatory step).

❺ Present the view controller.

❻ The delegate callback method invoked when the user selects a document.

❼ The `url` is a local `file` URL. The contents of the document are copied in your app's *tmp/DocumentPickerIncoming* folder.

❽ The delegate callback method invoked when the user cancels selection of a document.

The user navigation when using the document picker is as shown in Figure 8-17.

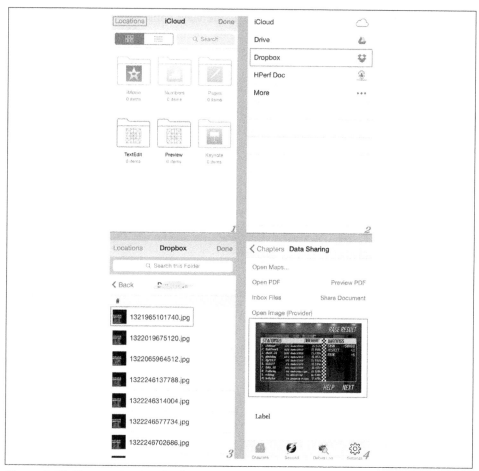

Figure 8-17. User navigation for document import: (1) iCloud opens by default—select Locations to select a provider; (2) select a provider; (3) select a document; (4) process the document in the editor app

Provide document

To act as a data source to provide a document, you need to:

1. Create the UI to help the user select the document.
2. Pass on the contents of the document to the editor app.

To create the UI, the view controller must be a subclass of `UIDocumentPickerExten sionViewController`. The UI presented by this view controller is made available in the editor app when the user selects this app as the location (refer to Figure 8-17).

When the user selects the document to use, the view controller must download the contents from the server if needed and make the document available to the editor app as a `file` URL. Example 8-8 shows representative code for a picker extension.

Example 8-8. Picker extension—view controller

```
@interface HPDocumentPickerViewController
    : UIDocumentPickerExtensionViewController ❶

@end

@interface HPEntry ❷
@property (nonatomic, copy) NSString *filename;
@property (nonatomic, copy) NSString *serverPath;
@property (nonatomic, assign) NSUInteger *size;
@property (nonatomic, copy) NSString *uti;
@property (nonatomic, copy) NSURL *iconURL;
@end

@implementation HPDocumentPickerViewController

-(void)viewDidAppear:(BOOL)animated {
    [super viewDidAppear:animated];
    //retrieve the files' metadata from server and update
    //UITableView is a good option ❸
}

- (void)tableView:(UITableView *)tableView
    didSelectRowAtIndexPath:(NSIndexPath *)indexPath { ❹

    HPEntry *selected = [self.allFiles objectAtIndex:indexPath.row];
    //download the contents from server, if needed ❺

    NSURL* localFileURL = [self.documentStorageURL
        URLByAppendingPathComponent:selected.filename]; ❻
    [self dismissGrantingAccessToURL:localFileURL]; ❼
}

@end
```

❶ View controller class, a subclass of `UIDocumentPickerExtensionViewControl ler`; provides list of available documents and destinations to the user.

❷ Model class representing a remote file entry.

❸ Retrieve list of files from the server, update UI, wait for the user to respond, show a loading indicator or progress bar in the interim—all the fancy stuff of the UI.

❹ Assuming that `UITableView` was used, the delegate callback when the user selects a file.

❺ The file contents, if on the server, must be downloaded by the app extension. The final contents *must* be from a local `file` URL.

❻ Save the contents into the folder `self.documentStorageURL`, which is appropriately set when using a file provider.

❼ OK—everything is good to go. Notify the OS that the editor app must be given permissions to work with the file. The OS copies the file into the editor app's corresponding folder. The document picker (mediator) in the editor app is notified. We have already discussed the other side of the story, in Example 8-7.

App Groups

App extensions are a very interesting feature. Though an extension is always *bundled* with the app, it runs in its own process and has its own data sandbox.

In a typical scenario, the host app will connect with the app extension, which *can* connect with the container app, as shown in Figure 8-18.

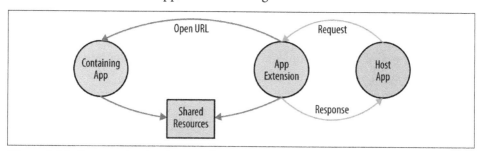

Figure 8-18. Communication between host app, app extension, and containing app (original image courtesy of Apple)

All the options that we have discussed so far have been for sharing data across multiple apps. However, because an app extension runs in its own sandbox, it cannot directly access data (user defaults, documents folder, cache folder, Core Data, SQLite, etc.) that is stored by the container app directly. The sandbox structure is similar to that shown in Figure 8-19.

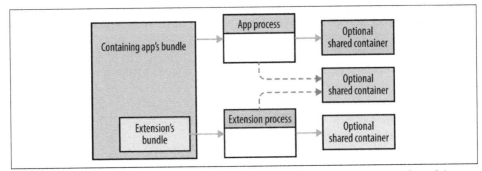

Figure 8-19. App versus app extension container (original image courtesy of Apple)

The app groups feature, introduced in iOS 7, allows creating a shared sandbox that can be accessed by the container app as well as the app extensions. Additionally, app groups support sharing data across multiple apps—however, similar to with a shared keychain, the apps must be signed using the same certificate.

The app group must be configured for not only the container app but also bundled *all* app extensions that need a shared container. Multiple app groups can be configured for appropriate data isolation.

To set up an app group, go to the project manifest, select the target, and under Capabilities, set the App Groups option to ON (Figure 8-20). Finally, add one or more group IDs that you want to use.

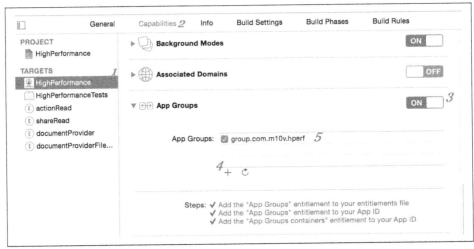

Figure 8-20. Xcode settings to enable app groups

You can now use NSUserDefaults or NSFileManager to work with shared data, as shown in Example 8-9.

Example 8-9. Sharing data using app groups

```
-(void)sharedDataUsingAppGroups {
    NSString *sharedGroupId = @"group.com.m10v.hperf"; ❶

    NSUserDefaults *defs = [[NSUserDefaults alloc]
            initWithSuiteName:sharedGroupId]; ❷

    NSFileManager *fileMgr = [NSFileManager defaultManager];
    NSURL *groupFolder = [fileMgr
        containerURLForSecurityApplicationGroupIdentifier:sharedGroupId]; ❸
}
```

❶ The group ID; must match that provided in the manifest (see Figure 8-20).

❷ NSUserDefaults; use initWithSuiteName: initializer.

❸ NSFileManager; get shared folder using containerURLForSecurityApplication GroupIdentifier: method.

> If you need to access the network, use NSURLSession so that the container app as well as the app extension can access the transferred data and shared network preferences, specifically the cookie jar.

Summary

In this chapter, we explored several options for sharing data across apps. Of all the available options, the custom URL scheme is the only one that allows sharing data from the Web (via the Safari browser or an embedded UIWebView) to native apps. Others, however, provide a richer UI. Activities present a share sheet and let users choose their favorite app to process the data—a very useful option for social sharing.

We also noted that a shared keychain is a powerful option for sharing data within apps from the same company, signed using the same certificate.

Toward the end of the chapter, we looked at the app extensions introduced in iOS 8 and how they help extend document interaction and activities across apps. App groups allow easy access to shared data across the app and extensions.

CHAPTER 9

Security

With your app running in an unknown execution environment and exchanging data over unknown transmission networks, it is important to always keep security as one of your top priorities so that you can protect users' as well as the app's sensitive data.

Risks exist on jailbroken as well as regular devices. For example, a YouTube video from JosiahsTech (*https://youtu.be/1NTpi4NjkCE*) demonstrates how simple it can be to modify the popular game Temple Run.

Security: Enough Is Not Enough

Security is a vast area, and a few pages in a book definitely do not suffice to do the topic any justice. For a deeper study, you may prefer more specialized literature:

- *Hacking and Securing iOS Applications: Stealing Data, Hijacking Software, and How to Prevent It* (*http://amzn.to/1bnf44K*) by Jonathan Zdziarski (O'Reilly)

- *iOS Hacker's Handbook* (*http://amzn.to/1BnavNd*) by Charlie Miller et al. (Wiley)

- *iOS Application Security: The Definitive Guide for Hackers and Developers* (*http://amzn.to/1Hq15sc*) by David Thiel (No Starch Press)

Each additional layer of security causes app slowdown, either through code execution (e.g., moving from 1,024-bit DSA key encryption keys to 2,048-bit RSA encryption keys), or through user intervention (e.g., introducing two-factor authentication or an app PIN). There will therefore be a trade-off required as to how many layers of security you wish to add vis-à-vis delay introduced in letting users complete their intent.

In this chapter, we explore key aspects of security in the app. We will not do a deep dive on pen testing. We take a categorical approach to security, looking at it from the following perspectives:

App access
How to make access to your app secure, how to manage identity, and other related topics.

Network security
This includes everything that you do talking to the servers.

Local storage
All about data on the device.

Data sharing
Getting data into and out of your app from and to other apps.

App Access

Your app may or may not implement authentication. For most games, news, utility, and other similar apps, there may not be any need for authentication.

This section discusses options for identifying a device, a user, multiple users on the same device, or the same user across multiple apps on the same or multiple devices.

Anonymous Access

Your app may or may not require authentication. As an example, a news app that does not require subscription may never require authentication. To allow personalized news or ads, however, as in the Yahoo! Digest News app, there will be a need to have a unique identifier for the device.

There are two options available for identifying a device: Identifier for Vendor (IDFV) or Identifier for Advertiser (IDFA). Let's take a closer look at each of these.

The IDFV (*http://apple.co/1xxe8oK*) is a persistent unique identifier for each app on a device that identifies the device to the app's vendor. A part of the app's bundle ID is used to generate the IDFV, so even if the apps are from the same company, the IDFV *can* be different.

Use the -[UIDevice identifierForVendor] method to get the IDFV. It may be nil if the user has not unlocked the device after a restart but the app has been woken up during background task execution or on a push notification. Try again after a delay, if that is the case. Example 9-1 shows some simple code for retrieving the IDFV. Do not execute this on the main thread as is.

Example 9-1. Retrieving the IDFV

```
-(NSString *)idfv {
    UIDevice *device = [UIDevice currentDevice];
    NSUUID *rv = device.identifierForVendor;
    while(!rv) {
        [Thread sleepForTimeInterval:0.005];
        rv = device.identifierForVendor;
    }
    return rv.UUIDString;
}
```

In iOS 6, the IDFV is created from the first two parts of the bundle ID. So, for the bundle ID com.bundle.id.app1, only com.bundle will be used.

In iOS 7, there was a bug where it was found that two apps with bundle IDs com.bun dle.id.app1 and com.bundle.id.app2 could have different IDFVs even if they were from the same vendor (using the same certificate to sign the apps). Instead of fixing the bug, Apple updated its documentation.

In iOS 7 and later, the entire bundle ID except for the last part is used to generate the IDFV. As a result, the table for IDFV generation is as given in Table 9-1.

Table 9-1. Part of bundle ID used in IDFV generation

Bundle ID	iOS 6	iOS 7 or later
com.bundle.id.app1	com.bundle	com.bundle.id
com.bundle.id.app2	com.bundle	com.bundle.id
com.bundle.id.suite.app1	com.bundle	com.bundle.id.suite
com.bundle.id.suite.app2	com.bundle	com.bundle.id.suite
simpleid[a]	simpleid	simpleid

[a] Not a recommended bundle ID.

The change in iOS 7 means that you now have two options for keeping a unique device ID and tracking across multiple apps. One option is to keep the bundle IDs unique except for the last part. But if that is not possible, you can use the second option, which is to share the key obtained by the first installed app using a shared keychain.

The IDFV is reset when all apps from the same vendor are uninstalled from the device. So, if you have only one app, uninstalling and reinstalling it multiple times will generate different IDs.

If you cannot use a shared keychain or the same bundle ID up to the last part, you have no way to identify the device uniquely across multiple apps.

The IDFA is a resettable identifier that is unique across all the apps on the device. Because it is unique across apps, it is a *truly unique* ID. However, it is resettable by the user. In addition, Apple places a restriction on its use and you must vouch for using it when submitting your app to iTunes Connect for review. This ID should only be used by the ad serving system. It also comes with a flag indicating whether the user wants this ID to be used. Per the documentation (*http://apple.co/1OyHGYa*), if the flag is not enabled, the IDFA can only be used for *frequency capping, attribution, conversion events, estimating the number of unique users, advertising fraud detection, and debugging.*

That is, you can use it to estimate the number of unique users of your app but not to identify a particular user. Example 9-2 shows sample code to retrieve the IDFA. Do not call the API on the main thread because the value returned may be `nil`, resulting in the need to retry. As with the IDFV, this can happen, for example, if the device has been restarted but the user has not yet unlocked the device.

Example 9-2. Retrieving the IDFA

```
-(NSString *)idfa {
    ASIdentifierManager *mgr = [ASIdentifierManager sharedManager];
    if(mgr.isAdvertisingTrackingEnabled) {
        UUID *rv = mgr.advertisingIdentifier;
        while(!rv) {
            [Thread sleepForTimeInterval:0.005];
            rv = mgr.advertisingIdentifier;
        }
        return rv.UUIDString;
    }
    return nil;
}
```

Still Using UDID?

The *unique device identifier* (UDID) is now deprecated (as of iOS 6). If you haven't already done so, you should remove any references to it.

Authenticated Access

When you need to identify a user, you need authenticated access. That does not mean that the authentication has to be done within your app. Some of the available options for authentication include:

App passcode
    Also known as the app PIN, this is the *local* credentials that you may want to add to your app irrespective of whether there is a set of credentials to *log in* to the

app. Essentially, it is a password that is stored only locally on the device. For example, an *expense management* app may never store any data on the server but still want to protect access on the device. On the other hand, a medical records app may use a passcode as a second layer of security. So, the user first logs in with the required credentials (typically, username/email and password), and local security is added as an additional layer.

Figure 9-1 shows two apps, one with only local credentials and the other using the app PIN as a secondary security measure.

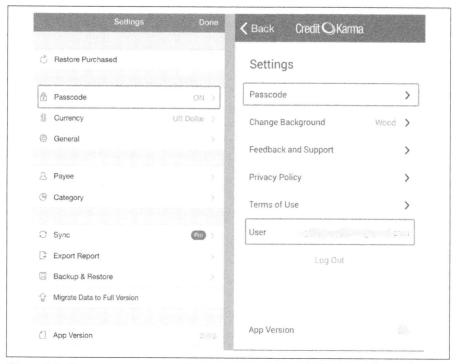

Figure 9-1. Expense report app without remote credentials (left) and the Credit Karma app with remote credentials using app PIN as a second layer of security (right)

 Store the password locally using a keychain. Do not store it unencrypted in a file or database.

Game Center

This option is available exclusively for games. Use GameKit to connect with the Game Center, which will take care of authenticating the users using their credentials. Game Center has access to the user profile, personal records, and more, but shares only what is required to uniquely identify the user (i.e., the user ID).

Example 9-3 show template code to get the user's identity after Game Center login.

Example 9-3. Using Game Center to log in

```
#include <GameKit/GameKit.h>  ❶

@implementation HPLoginViewController

-(void)authWithGameCenter {
    GKLocalPlayer __weak *player = [GKLocalPlayer localPlayer];  ❷
    if(!player.authenticated) {  ❸
        player.authenticateHandler = ^(UIViewController *vc,
                                        NSError *error) {  ❹
            if(error) {
                //handle error
            } else if(vc) {  ❺
                [self presentViewController:vc animated:YES completion:^{
                    //verify again if the user is now authenticated
                }];
            } else {
                GKLocalPlayer *lp = player;
                if(lp) {
                    [self verifyLocalPlayer:lp];  ❻
                }
            }
        };
    } else {
        [self verifyLocalPlayer:lp];
    }
}

-(void)verifyLocalPlayer:(GKLoalPlayer *)player {
    [player generateIdentityVerificationSignatureWithCompletionHandler:
        ^(NSURL *publicKeyURL, NSData *signature,
          NSData *salt, uint64_t timestamp,
          NSError *error) {  ❼

        if(error) {
            //handle error!
        } else {
            //player id = player.playerID
            //verify using the data  ❽
        }

    }];
```

```
}

@end
```

❶ Include GameKit headers. Do not forget to link with `GameKit.framework`.

❷ `GKLocalPlayer` represents the authenticated player running the game. At any given time, only one player may be authenticated on the device.

❸ Check if the player is authenticated.

❹ Setting the `authenticateHandler` property will trigger the authorization.

❺ If the user had not earlier authorized connecting with GameKit, the view controller returned in the callback method must be shown.

❻ If there is no view controller and no error, it's all good. But some more work needs to be done to get the user's details.

❼ Use the `generateIdentityVerificationSignatureWithCompletionHan dler:` method to get the signature to authenticate the local player.

❽ The actual task of verification should happen on your servers (*http://bit.ly/ ios-gk-player-id*), as described next.

For local player verification (server side), follow these steps:

1. Use the `publicKeyURL` to get an X.509 certificate. The URL must be an `apple.com` domain `https` URL. This key must be signed by Apple.

2. Concatenate `player.playerID`, the app's bundle ID, the `timestamp` in big-endian UInt 64 format, and the `salt`, in that order.

3. Generate the SHA-1 hash of the concatenated data.

4. Verify the signature against this hash using the public key downloaded in step 1.

5. If they match, all is good. The user did authenticate and the `player.play erID` is OK to use.

Third-party authentication

The semantics are similar to Game Center authentication in that you own the user and login experience. Specific SDKs are not covered here, but feel free to explore the ones from Facebook (*https://developers.facebook.com/docs/ios*), Google+ (*http://bit.ly/gp-signin*), or Twitter (*https://dev.twitter.com/twitter-kit/ios/ twitter-login*).

Your own authentication

Most apps choose to retain full control of the registration and login process, which requires a custom authentication mechanism. Using an email/username with a password as the credentials is the most popular mechanism for authenticating. We briefly discuss key measures to take when implementing this:

- Enforce strong passwords, at least six characters long with a mix of upper- and lowercase characters (if applicable, like in the Roman alphabet), numbers, and special characters.

  Some apps set limits on the maximum length, but this is not a good idea. It is like saying to your user, "Hey! Sorry, but we cannot allow more security than that."

  In addition, it is important to note that longer but easy-to-remember passwords may be harder to crack than shorter and obfuscated passwords. However, because it is tedious to key in longer passwords on mobile devices, shorter and more complex passwords are typically preferred.

- Provide a list of active sessions and allow users to invalidate any existing session on another device or location.

- Support two-factor authentication (2FA) and use it whenever you encounter unusual behavior. Examples include login from a new location or from a new device at an unusual time.

- For financial or money-related apps, enable session timeouts (i.e., if the app is in the background for a certain amount of time—say, longer than 5 or 10 minutes—it's appropriate to invalidate the session). This is similar to enabling the Remember Me option on websites.

- Optionally, use a shorter app PIN for local authentication while the user is perpetually logged in with a nonexpiring access token. Figure 9-1 shows the Credit Karma app with a local app PIN.

- For perpetual login, ensure that the access token (akin to cookies in a browser) is stored in the keychain locally.

- Enable CAPTCHA (you may choose to use this in a limited way—for example, you might enable it after 3 or 5 invalid attempts in a row).

- Optionally, use local authentication to integrate Touch ID with a keychain for passwordless login.

- Follow the best practices discussed in "Network Security" on page 299 and "Local Storage" on page 305.

Use of cryptographic options such as a keychain or Touch ID adds overheads, causing a delayed response to the user.

Touch ID has been found to be slow and unreliable even with latest updates. In particular, it can result in nonrecognition of the fingerprint, resulting in multiple retries.

Network Security

An in-depth discussion of the network was provided in Chapter 7. In this section, we discuss security best practices in any communication with a remote device, be it a server or a peer.

Use HTTPS

Assuming that you use HTTP as the underlying messaging protocol (TCP being the transport-layer protocol), you *must* use it over TLS/SSL—that is, you should always use HTTPS. However, there are a few concerns with using HTTPS. If these potential risks are not addressed, HTTPS may be compromised.

CRIME attacks

Do not use SSL/TLS compression. If you use it now, turn it off immediately before proceeeding. You are at a big risk. With TLS compression (`gzip`, `deflate`, or any other format), any request is subject to a CRIME (Compression Ratio Info-leak Made Easy) attack. The risk can be mitigated by turning off TLS compression and sending an anti-CRIME cookie, which can simply be a unique random cookie, with every response.

BREACH attacks

If you use request/response body compression (`Transfer-Encoding = gzip` or `deflate`), your communication is subject to BREACH (Browser Reconnaissance and Exfiltration via Adaptive Compression of Hypertext) attacks, a type of attack first noted in September 2012. The risk applies when the following criteria are satisfied:

- The app uses HTTP compression.
- The response reflects user input.
- The response reflects a secret.

There is no single way to mitigate this risk. The Breach Attack (*http://www.breachat tack.com*) website lists the following approaches, in order of effectiveness:

- Disable HTTP compression. This increases the amount of data to be transported, and may not be a practical solution.

- Separate secrets from user input. Keep authorization codes away from the request body.
- Randomize secrets per request. But, because the secrets are randomized per request, multiple parallel requests may no longer be possible.
- Mask secrets. Do not send them raw.
- Protect vulnerable HTML pages with CSRF. On mobile native apps, there is no need for CSRF unless using mobile web.
- Hide length. A good way to do that is to use chunked transfer encoding in HTTP responses.
- Rate-limit the requests (this should only be used as a last resort).

Use Certificate Pinning

HTTPS is not a cure-all—adopting it will not magically make all your communications secure. The basis of HTTPS is the trust in the public key that is used to encrypt the initial message (during the SSL handshake). A man-in-the-middle (MITM) attack involves being able to capture the key used to encrypt the messages.

Figure 9-2 shows an outline of a MITM attack where the mediator (say, the WiFi hotspot that your device is connected to or the proxy server being used) intercepts the requests from the device. When the device sends a request for the server's certificate, the mediator sends the request on to the server and captures its reply. Then, instead of returning that key to the device, it returns its own key. This is the same technique used by the Charles proxy server (see "Charles" on page 245).

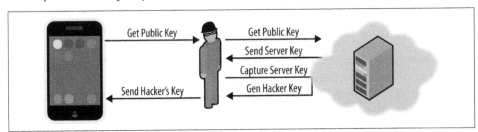

Figure 9-2. Man-in-the-middle attack

All that is required for the request not to be invalidated is the *trust* that the network library puts in the certificate received. The certificates are nothing but signed public keys. So, if the network library trusts the signer, it trusts the public key provided by the host. A hacker supplying a fake *root certificate* is all that is needed for all security measures to fall apart.

It is not uncommon to find personal devices that are used for development and have the Charles certificate installed. And because both the private key and the certificate are available in the public domain, it is not uncommon to use this certificate as the starting point for an attack.

How many of the secondhand devices available in the market can really be trusted? It is fairly easy to jailbreak an iOS device.

The solution to this problem is what is known as certificate pinning (*http://bit.ly/cert-plan*). The way this works is that the app creates a custom *trust level* by trusting only one or a few certificates that can be the root certificates for your app. This allows trusting only the certificates from a whitelist, which ensures that an unknown certificate that would allow network monitoring cannot be installed on the device.

When working with `NSURLConnection`, you can provide an `NSURLConnection Delegate` that can perform the certificate validation.

Example 9-4 shows representative code[1] that you can use to implement certificate pinning in your app.

Example 9-4. Certificate pinning

```
typedef void(^HPResponseHandler)(NSURLResponse *, NSError *error);

@interface HPPinnedRequestExecutor ❶

@property (nonatomic, readonly) NSURLRequest *request;
@property (nonatomic, copy) HPResponseHandler handler;

@end

@interface HPPinnedRequestExecutor () <NSURLConnectionDelegate>

@property (nonatomic, readwrite) NSURLRequest *request;

@end

@implementation HPPinnedRequestExecutor

-(instancetype)initWithRequest:(NSURLRequest *)request {
    if(self = [super init]) {
        self.request = request;
    }
    return self;
}
```

---

1 Adapted from OWASP (*http://bit.ly/cert-key*).

```
-(void)executeWithHandler:(HPResponseHandler)handler {
    self.handler = handler;
    [[NSURLConnection alloc] initWithRequest:self.request delegate:self];
}

- (void)connection:(NSURLConnection *)connection
    didReceiveResponse:(NSURLResponse *)response {
    //Do regular stuff, send result using handler
}

-(BOOL)connection:(NSURLConnection *)connection
    canAuthenticateAgainstProtectionSpace:(NSURLProtectionSpace*)space {
    return [NSURLAuthenticationMethodServerTrust
        isEqualToString:space.authenticationMethod];  ❷
}

- (void)connection:(NSURLConnection *)connection
    didReceiveAuthenticationChallenge:(NSURLAuthenticationChallenge *)challenge {  ❸

    void (^cancel)() = ^{
        [challenge.sender cancelAuthenticationChallenge:challenge];
    };

    if([NSURLAuthenticationMethodServerTrust
        isEqualToString:challenge.protectionSpace.authenticationMethod]) {

        SecTrustRef serverTrust = challenge.protectionSpace.serverTrust;
        if(serverTrust == nil) {
            cancel();
            return;
        }

        OSStatus status = SecTrustEvaluate(serverTrust, NULL);
        if(status != errSecSuccess) {
            cancel();
            return;
        }

        SecCertificateRef svrCert = SecTrustGetCertificateAtIndex(serverTrust, 0);
        if(svrCert == nil) {
            cancel();
            return;
        }

        CFDataRef svrCertData = SecCertificateCopyData(svrCert);
        if(svrCertData == nil) {
            cancel();
            return;
        }

        const UInt8* const data = CFDataGetBytePtr(svrCertData);
```

```
const CFIndex size = CFDataGetLength(serverCertificateData);
NSData* cert1 = [NSData dataWithBytes:data length:(NSUInteger)size];

if(cert1 == nil) {
    cancel();
    return;
}

NSString *file = [[NSBundle mainBundle]
    pathForResource:@"pinned-key"
    ofType:@"der"];
NSData* cert2 = [NSData dataWithContentsOfFile:file];

if(cert2 == nil) {
    cancel();
    return;
}

if(![cert1 isEqualToData:cert2]) {
    cancel();
    return;
} ❹

[challenge.sender
    useCredential:[NSURLCredential credentialForTrust:serverTrust]
    forAuthenticationChallenge:challenge]; ❺
    }
}

@end
```

❶ Implement the NSURLConnectionDelegate protocol.

❷ The connection:canAuthenticateAgainstProtectionSpace: method checks whether the delegate is able to respond to a protection space's form of authentication. We return YES for SSL (server trust).

❸ The connection:didReceiveAuthenticationChallenge: method processes the challenge and can either cancel the authentication (invalidate) or use the credentials (validate).

❹ Invalidate the certificate if anything fails, like when no certificate is found or when it does not match against the bundled key.

❺ Validate the certificate if everything succeeds.

Notes for iOS 8 and Later

The delegate callback methods `connection:canAuthenticateAgainstProtection
Space:` and `connection:didReceiveAuthenticationChallenge:` are deprecated in
iOS 8 in favor of the `connection:willSendRequestForAuthenticationChallenge:`
callback.

Depending on the validation result, the delegate is expected to call one of the following on the `NSURLAuthenticationChallengeSender` protocol (use the `chal
lenge.sender` object):

`useCredential:forAuthenticationChallenge:`
   Validation succeeded. Use the certificate.

`cancelAuthenticationChallenge:`
   Validation failed. Cancel the request.

`continueWithoutCredentialForAuthenticationChallenge:`
   Proceed without the certificate (never do this).

`performDefaultHandlingForAuthenticationChallenge:`
   Let the request proceed through the default route provided by the system.

`rejectProtectionSpaceAndContinueWithChallenge:`
   Reject the currently supplied protection space. Very rarely, if at all, used for SSL
   certificate validation.

A similar approach can be implemented for an `NSURLSession` object.[2] This allows
control at the session scope without having to worry about each request that the app
creates.

You do not have to maintain the hefty code. Libraries like `RNPinned
CertValidator` (*https://github.com/rnapier/RNPinnedCertValida
tor*) can help you reduce the code to a few lines (*http://
robnapier.net/pinning-your-ssl-certs*).

If you use the `AFNetworking` library, you may have to write different code. There are, however, tutorials available on the Internet[3] to
help you out with that.

---

2 iOS Developer Library, "Authentication Challenges and TLS Chain Validation" (*http://apple.co/1ElV6Ud*).

3 For example, Eric Allam's "AFNetworking SSL Pinning with Self-Signed Certificates" (*http://bit.ly/afn-certpin*).

Local Storage

Similar to the data that is exchanged over the network, the data that is stored on the device is not tamper-proof, and an intruder can either read or modify the data if it is not handled carefully. The following are a few points to keep in mind and best practices to follow to safeguard local storage:

Local storage is not secure

It is very easy to get into the local storage on a jailbroken device. If you watched the video that was referenced at the start of this chapter, you will notice that the files can be replaced or modified with ready-to-use tools.

"That is only one device and the data tampered with is for the user on that device," you may say. And I agree. But knowing the side effects in the overall app ecosystem because of that type of tampering is important.

For example, in a mail app, the device may be injected with the data for sending mails, resulting in a very easy way to send mass mails using the app. Even if the user is blacklisted or blocked later, the damage may already have been done. Servers should implement additional security, rate-limiting techniques, and enhanced DDoS protection solutions to safeguard.

Encrypt local storage

Local storage can be encrypted by the OS through the data protection capability.

To enable data protection, go to Xcode and select the target. Under the Capabilities tab, look for Data Protection and turn it ON (see Figure 9-3). This will add the data protection entitlement to the app ID.

Figure 9-3. Enabling data protection in Xcode

By default, when data protection is enabled, all local storage used by the app is encrypted using the device passcode. This means that the data is inaccessible until the device is unlocked.

You can configure the security level on the Apple Developer portal by navigating to Certificates, Identifiers & Profiles → Identifiers. Go to the App IDs subsection and select the app ID to configure. You should notice that data protection is enabled (see Figure 9-4).

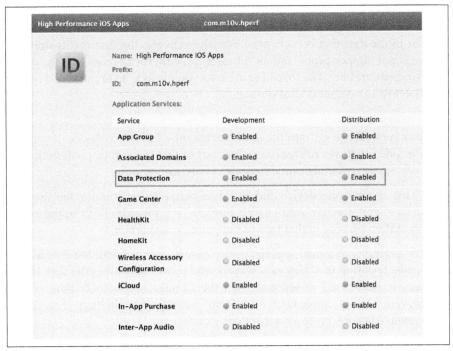

Figure 9-4. Apple Developer → App Capabilities Configuration → Data Protection

Clicking the Edit button will allow you to configure the capabilities. Figure 9-5 shows the security levels data protection capability.

Figure 9-5. Security levels for data protection

The sharing and permissions options are as follows:

- Complete Protection: This requires the device to be unlocked anytime the file must be accessed for reading or writing. Shortly after the device is locked (after 10 seconds if the Require Password setting is set to Immediately), the encryption keys are discarded, resulting in all data being inaccessible until the device is unlocked again.

- Protected Unless Open: This requires the device to be unlocked when creating a handle to the file, but once the handle is available, the contents can be written even when the device is locked. This is useful when the app needs write capabilities to the file even when the device is locked. For example, downloading an attachment in a mail app can be triggered by the user when the device is unlocked, and the app can trigger a background operation to continue downloading it long after the device is locked.

- Protected Until First User Authentication: This requires the device to be unlocked once after reboot. After the first unlock, the app can access all files without any restrictions.

Note that whatever the security level is, once data protection is enabled, the files cannot be accessed immediately after a reboot—the user must unlock the device at least once. This also means that if an app receives a push notification and tries to read/write a file, it will result in an error if the device was never unlocked after reboot.

For per-file protection, you can use the method -[NSData writeTo File:options:error:] with options set to NSDataWritingFileProtection Complete for complete protection, NSDataWritingFileProtectionCompleteUnlessOpen for protected unless open, or NSDataWritingFileProtectionCompleteUntilFirstUserAuthenti cation for protected until first user authentication. Note that if data protection is enabled at the app level, the default value is as set on the Developer Portal.

Alternatively, you can use the method -[NSFileManager createFileAt Path:contents:attributes:] with the attributes dictionary set to @{NSFi leProtectionKey: <required-level>} (along with other attributes if needed), where the required-level can be NSFileProtectionComplete, NSFileProtectionCompleteUnlessOpen, or NSFileProtectionCompleteUn tilFirstUserAuthentication.

In addition, use the property -[UIApplication protectedDataAvailable] to determine if the protected files can be accessed. The value is set to YES if the device is unlocked or if data protection is not enabled. When the value of this property is NO, files with the NSFileProtectionComplete or NSFilePro tectionCompleteUnlessOpen attribute cannot be accessed until the device is unlocked, and files with the NSDataWritingFileProtectionCompleteUntil FirstUserAuthentication attribute cannot be accessed until the device is rebooted and unlocked.

User defaults (`NSUserDefaults`) are not safe

> More often than not, we treat user defaults as being kept in a safe place. In fact, they are simple. *plist* files kept alongside other app files.[4]

App Bundle (`NSBundle`) values are not safe either

> Ouch! The app bundle settings are considered to be bundled with the app and never modified. This is only partially correct, because the *.plist* file that contains the values can actually be tampered with.

Don't completely rely on the keychain

> The keychain's security can be broken. Attackers will definitely be unable to access critical information while the device is locked. However, it is important to not rely overly on the keychain. The reason is that the encryption key is generated by a predetermined formula using the device passcode, which is merely four digits long. This provides a maximum of 10,000 combinations—and we know that when it comes to security, 10,000 combinations is not a great deal of security at all. Taking into consideration that an iOS device will not allow a login attempt for one minute after six wrong attempts (*https://support.apple.com/en-us/ HT204306*), running 10,000 combinations manually can be done in a few hours.

> However, generally speaking, the attacker does not have to go so far. As per a report published a few years back (*http://bit.ly/iphone-pws*), the top 10 passcodes represent 15% of all passcodes in use.

> Thankfully, recent versions of iOS do have an option for enabling stronger passwords. You can go to Settings → Touch ID & Passcode, and you will notice that the Simple Passcode option is selected (Figure 9-6).

---

4 Prateek Gianchandani, InfoSec Institute, "iOS Application Security Part 20 - Local Data Storage (NSUser-Defaults, CoreData, Sqlite, Plist Files)" (*http://bit.ly/1HdOp4y*).

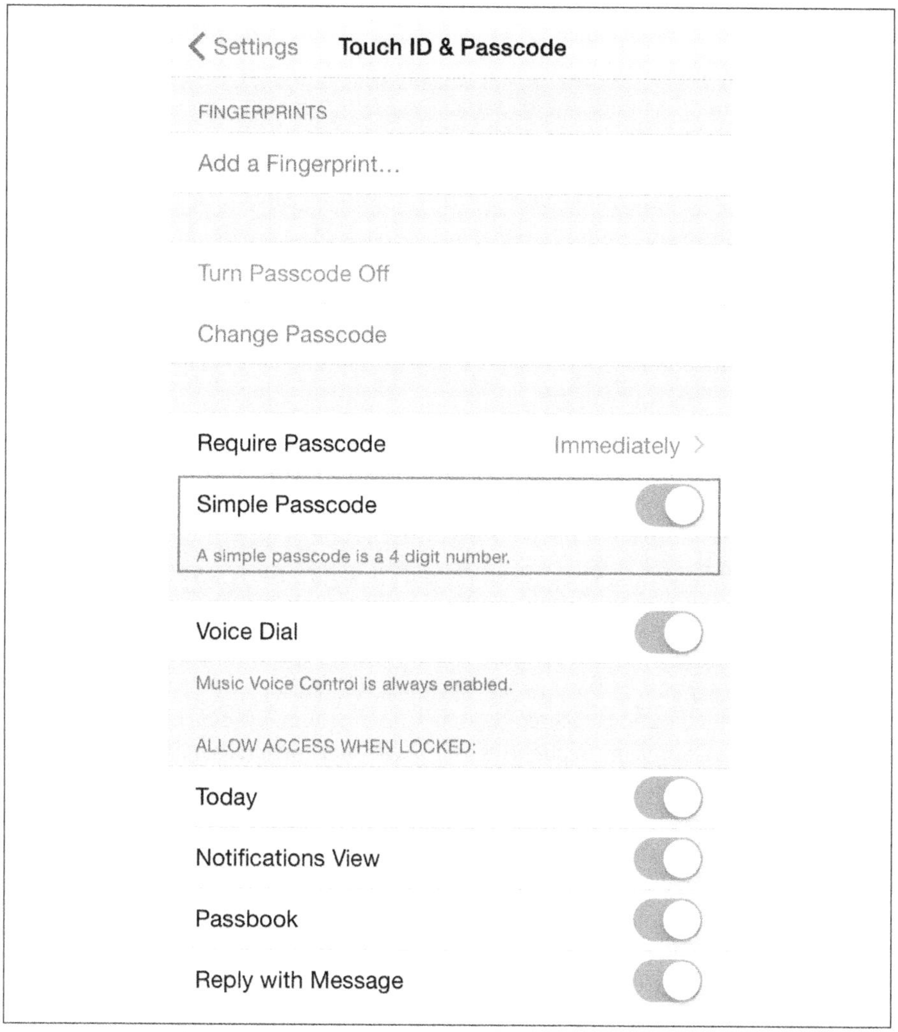

Figure 9-6. Simple passcode

As simple passcode is comprised of exactly four digits, whereas a non-simple passcode can be arbitrarily long and can include alphanumeric characters as well as special characters. As illustrated in Figure 9-7, the keyboards for each of these options are different. Though using an alphanumeric passcode is a great option, the total number of users that will have this option enabled is very small, so you can't rely on it.

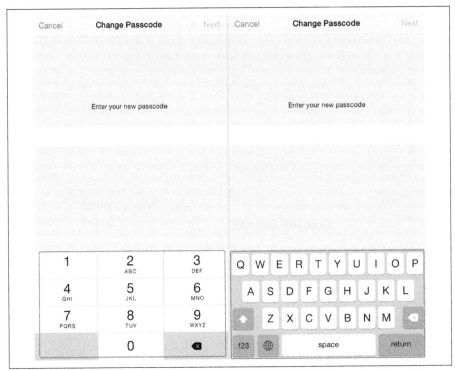

Figure 9-7. A simple passcode uses four digits (left), whereas a complex passcode allows for alphanumeric and special characters (right)

As a practice, encrypt the data stored in the keystore and store only minimal data. The keys may be generated per device and stored locally. Again, note that the best that you can do is make it a little harder for an attacker to locate and decrypt the data. If the attacker has physical access to the device, there is only so much that you can do.

Be careful what you log

It is very common to log using the built-in NSLog function because that's the way the developers are taught.[5] The official documentation (*http://bit.ly/ios-nslog*) states that the function "Logs an error message to the Apple System Log facility." It is not console logging. There is no iOS device console. The logs can be seen even days after they are actually logged.

From Xcode, navigate to Window → Devices—you should see a list of connected devices and simulators, as shown in Figure 9-8.

---

5 Technically, this is not data storage. But device logs are akin to data stores, automatic and perpetual.

Figure 9-8. Devices summary

If you click the View Device Logs button, you should be able to see all the logs, as shown in Figure 9-9. This includes the output from NSLog.

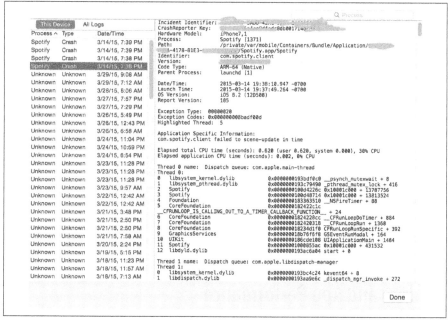

Figure 9-9. Device logs

As a best practice, do not use NSLog in non-debug builds at all. A good way to do that is to use a wrapper function and a macro as demonstrated in Example 9-5. An even better option is to use a third-party library like CocoaLumberjack. We discussed logging in depth in "Logging" on page 20.

Example 9-5. Logging using NSLog

```
@implementation HPLogger

+(void)log:(NSString *)format, ... {

#ifdef _DEBUG ❶
    va_list args;
    va_start(args, format);
    NSLogv(format, args);
    va_end(args);
#endif

}
```

❶ Emit the logs only in debug mode. Feel free to use some other condition (rather than the `#ifdef _DEBUG` used here), as suitable to your app.

The bottom line is, if someone has the device and it is unlocked, all data is accessible. Even if it is locked, most (or probably all) of the data can be accessed.

It is a race between the police and the thief. One can only expect the tools to get more advanced and smarter on both sides, but the race to supremacy will never end. It all comes down to who leads and who plays the catch-up role.

Data Sharing

One simple, basic rule to follow when sharing data and processing incoming data is this: do not trust the other side.

When receiving data, always validate. The only assumption that the app should make about the data is that it may be invalid and wrong. For additional security, ask for the data to be signed.

Similarly, because you do not know which app will process it, never send out sensitive data. If you really need to share sensitive data, deliver a token and then ask the other app to request the data from your app (or server).

Security and App Performance

Every extra layer of encryption or safety measures that you add counts toward the overall memory consumed and processing time. There is no way that you can optimize across all dimensions. You will have to make some trade-offs.

At times, using a 2,048-bit RSA key may not be what you require. A 1,024-bit DSA key may be good enough. At other times, a symmetric encryption algorithm like Rijndael is all that may be needed to secure the data.[6]

Retrieving initial values from the keychain can lead to prolonged load time. You should be prudent and cautious.

Certificate pinning has its own cost and can slow down all your network operations.

Creating and validating data signatures requires computing the content hash, which means one additional pass over the content. This can take a lot of time depending upon the content size, not to mention the additional time taken to compute and validate the digital signature.

All of these steps add up pretty quickly. You may have the safest and most secure app in the world, but if it takes 30 minutes just to load, no one will be interested in using it. For that matter, even 5 seconds may negatively impact the user experience and you may lose the users forever, particularly if there are other apps that fulfill the same need.

Checklist

The list of malicious attacks and other areas of concern that you need to safeguard your app against is possibly endless. When testing your iOS app for security, you should run through the checklist in Table 9-2.

Table 9-2. Security checklist

Description	Status
Static Code Analysis	
Is NSLog used?	Yes/No
If so, NSLog is used only in debug builds	Yes/No
All URLs are HTTPS	Yes/No
Paths to local files are not hardcoded	Yes/No
Dependencies are checked for the latest versions and patches	Yes/No
No private APIs are used	Yes/No
No private keys or secrets are embedded in the code	Yes/No
No private keys or secrets are embedded in the resources	Yes/No
There is no unreachable or dead code	Yes/No
Entitlements are correct (none missing, none extra)	Yes/No

---

6 Note that using cryptography makes the approval process for the app to go live in the App Store longer since there may be export restrictions to the API that you use.

Description	Status
If using the `connection:willSendRequestForAuthenticationChallenge:` method, there is no direct branch (without any code) to `useCredential:forAuthenticationChallenge:`	Yes/No
App uses IDFV	Yes/No
App uses IDFA	Yes/No
Correct provisioning profile/certificate is configured for app signing	Yes/No
There are checks against SQL injection	Yes/No
Runtime Analysis—Log	
Logging is done only to file	Yes/No
Log files are deleted periodically	Yes/No
Log rotation is implemented	Yes/No
There are no secrets or sensitive information in the log	Yes/No
No sensitive information is logged when stack trace is printed[a]	Yes/No
Runtime Analysis—Network	
Only HTTPS URLs are used	Yes/No
Server has implementation against CRIME attack	Yes/No
Server and client app have implementation against BREACH attack	Yes/No
Client app uses certificate pinning	Yes/No
Correct caching policy is set up	Yes/No
Runtime Analysis—Authentication	
App uses third-party authentication	Yes/No
App uses custom authentication	Yes/No
Third-party auth SDK is well audited against the remainder of this checklist	Yes/No
Login UI masks password	Yes/No
Password is not copyable	Yes/No
Access token is stored in keychain	Yes/No
App implements passcode	Yes/No
Passcode is stored in keychain	Yes/No
It is possible to change authentication workflow through a server config[b]	Yes/No
Runtime Analysis—Local Storage	
App uses local storage	Yes/No
Any sensitive information is encrypted	Yes/No
Storage is cleaned up periodically	Yes/No
Runtime Analysis—Data Sharing	
App uses shared keystore to keep common settings	Yes/No
Deep link URLs are validated	Yes/No
Any incoming data is validated	Yes/No
No sensitive data is shared to an unknown app	Yes/No

Description	Status
Correct group IDs are configured when using the app extensions	Yes/No

[a] When handling exceptions or otherwise.

[b] If the login process is breached, it should be possible to change the authentication flow—for example, trigger a 2FA, add a CAPTCHA, or, in an extreme case, switch to web login from the native login UI.

This checklist has been compiled from working on security in the past and from the following sources:

1. iOS Security by Apple (*http://apple.co/1I6xVi1*)
2. OWASP Mobile Security Project - Security Testing Guide (*http://bit.ly/1MrVEwp*)
3. OWASP iOS Application Security Testing Cheat Sheet (*http://bit.ly/1HZr3mw*)
4. OWASP iOS Developer Cheat Sheet (*http://bit.ly/1alk6P5*)
5. Stack Overflow, "Security Analysis Tools for iOS 6" (*http://bit.ly/1BLbHLr*)
6. Penetration Testing of iPhone Applications: Part 1 (*http://bit.ly/19uvlDJ*) and Part 2 (*http://bit.ly/1CG7j4h*)

Summary

Reading a single chapter will never be sufficient to fully understand security. This chapter presented a brief summary of key security aspects from a few perspectives. We looked at what it takes to implement security measures and how that impacts the overall experience of the app.

The checklist at the end of this chapter should be followed to ensure that the commonly found security loopholes are closed and at least well-defined measures are implemented—in the app, on the server, and in the layer between the two.

PART IV

Beyond Code

Il meglio è l'inimico del bene.

Perfect is the enemy of good.

—Anonymous

Having investigated the app in depth from within, it is time to think out of the box. Literally.

In this part of the book, we cover application testing, tools, and monitoring the app in the wild. We'll discuss how to make use of the data that we get or the instrumentation data that the app generates to track app performance and improve subsequent releases.

CHAPTER 10

Testing and Release

Testing a feature, a component, or an app is as important as implementing it.

The development team writes code to cover various scenarios, and the quality assurance team asserts that the code works as intended. Frequently, there is overlap between the quality assurance team and the development team—for example, in startups and smaller companies, development and quality assurance tasks are often performed by the same person or people.

In this chapter, we study the fundamentals of test cases, various test case types, testing frameworks to support them, test automation, and continuous integration.

It can be assumed that the team follows some development methodology, which can even be cowboy coding, and you indeed need to write test cases to formally test the app.

Test Types

A test's *type* refers to the categorical purpose of what it intends to do. For example, if the purpose is to test a method, a class, or a component, it may be a unit test. Similarly, if the purpose is to test the app from installation or deployment to all the functions, it may be classified as an acceptance or end-to-end test.

Instead of presenting all of the dozen or more different test types, we focus our discussion on the following broad categories that are critical to any user-facing app in general and an iOS app in particular:

Unit testing
Testing an isolated method in a simulated environment to ensure validity

Functional testing
> Testing a method in a real-world scenario for accuracy

Performance testing
> Testing a method, a module, or a complete app for performance

Definitions

The following definitions will come in handy as we discuss testing:

Test case
> A scenario that needs to be tested. It includes a condition under which a method, feature, or application will execute; a set of inputs, as required in the scenario being tested; and an expected behavior, including an output and/or changes to the system.

Test fixture
> Represents the preparation needed and any associated cleanup to be done to perform one or more test cases. This may involve object creation, dependency setup, database configuration, and more.

Test suite
> A collection of test fixtures with the test cases, test suites, or both. It is used to aggregate tests that should execute together.

Test runner
> A system that executes the tests and provides the results. For our purposes, Xcode is the graphical test runner. The command-line utilities also enable a CLI that is useful in test automation.

Test report
> The summary of which tests executed successfully and which failed, along with the error messages if available.

Test coverage
> Measures the amount of testing performed by a test suite and is useful to find untested parts of the app. When testing at code level, a test coverage report summary comprises a percentage result indicating how many lines of code have been tested (see Figure 10-1). A detailed report may indicate which parts of the code are untested.

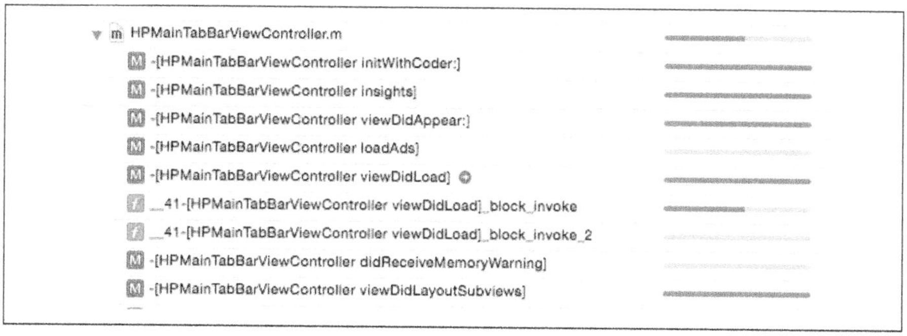

Figure 10-1. Test coverage report

TDD

Test-driven development is a software development process that uses a repetitive but very short development cycle. The steps include writing automated test case(s), writing minimal code to pass these tests, and refactoring the code to acceptable standards and quality.

Unit Testing

Unit testing checks individual methods, or sets of one or more modules, together with associated data in isolation for validity. To achieve isolation, the dependencies are mocked to provide the desired behavior for the scenario being testing.

Although it can be tedious to test all the methods (including the property getters or setters), it is worthwhile—if a call fails, you'll know exactly which one failed, and the developer will probably know what might have gone wrong.

Xcode comes with built-in support for the XCTest (*http://apple.co/1PlWsUa*) unit testing framework.

Setup

Unit testing requires a test target to be set up. If your project does not yet have a test target, you'll need to create one by following these steps:

1. Open the test navigator.
2. Click on the + sign.
3. Select the New Test Target option.
4. Type in the details for the new target, as shown in Figure 10-2.

Choose options for your new target:

Product Name: | HighPerformance Tests
Organization Name: | Gaurav Vaish
Organization Identifier: | com.m10v
Bundle Identifier: | com.m10v.HighPerformance-Tests
Language: | Objective-C
Project: | HighPerformance
Target to be Tested: | HighPerformance

Cancel   Previous   Finish

Figure 10-2. Adding the test target

Xcode should have configured the project in a few places.

First, verify that it has created a new target in the project (see Figure 10-3).

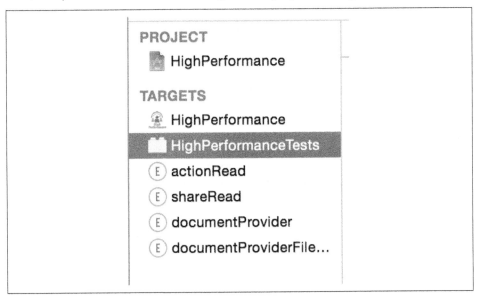

Figure 10-3. Verifying the test target

Second, if you open the project's scheme in Xcode (by navigating to Product → Scheme → Manage Schemes → Select project → Edit), you should notice that under Test → Test there is an entry with the name that was provided as the Product Name when creating the test target earlier (HighPerformanceTests, in our case; see Figure 10-4).

Figure 10-4. Test setup on the product scheme

Writing Unit Tests

With the target set up, we are ready to write our first unit test.

XCTest requires creating a subclass of XCTestCase to represent a test fixture (it's not a test case per se), and in that subclass you write the test cases. The test suite (all test fixtures) execution invokes the methods in a particular order:

+[setUp]
> This is the test fixture setup method and is called before any test case in the class executes. All common initializations for the test fixture go here. Note that this is a class method.

-[setUp]
> This is the test case setup method and is called before each test case executes. All common initializations for each test case go here. This is an instance method.

`-[testXXX]`

> All the instance methods of the test fixture whose names start with `test` and that do not take any parameters are the test cases that get executed.

`-[tearDown]`

> This is the test case cleanup method and is called after each test case executes. This is an instance method.

`+[tearDown]`

> This is the test fixture cleanup method and is called after all test cases in the class execute. This is a class method.

A test case is successful if there is no error or exception when executing the test method. You can also check for more complex scenarios such as testing for `nil`, testing for equality, and so on using assertion macros provided in the SDK. The macros are named `XCTAssert<AssertionType>`[1] (e.g., `XCTAssertEqual` for testing equality of two values or objects).

Figure 10-5 shows a visual representation of the execution lifecycle. Note that the instance methods `-[setUp]` and `-[tearDown]` can be called multiple times.

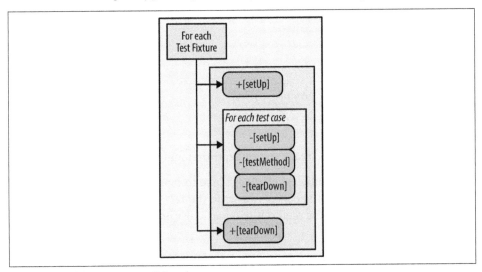

Figure 10-5. Test execution lifecycle

As an example, let's write some tests for the class `HPAlbum` that we introduced earlier, in Example 4-9.

---

1 iOS Developer Library, "Assertions Listed by Category" (*http://apple.co/1N2sS6g*).

Example 10-1. Unit tests for HPAlbum

```
@implementation HPAlbumTest ❶
- (void)testInitializer { ❷
    HPAlbum *album = [[HPAlbum alloc] init];
        XCTAssert(album, @"Album alloc-init failed"); ❸
}

- (void)testPropertyGetters { ❹
        HPAlbum *album = [[HPAlbum alloc] init];
        album.name = @"Album-1";
        NSDate *ctime = [NSDate date];
        album.creationTime = ctime;

        HPPhoto *coverPhoto = [[HPPhoto alloc] init];
        coverPhoto.album = album;

        album.coverPhoto = coverPhoto;
        NSArray *photos = @[coverPhoto];
        album.photos = photos; ❺

        XCTAssertEqualObjects(@"Album-1", album.name);
        XCTAssertEqualObjects(ctime, album.creationTime);
        XCTAssertEqualObjects(coverPhoto, album.coverPhoto);
        XCTAssertEqualObjects(photos, album.photos); ❻
}

@end
```

❶ The test fixture. General convention is to name the test class as *ClassName*Test.

❷ The test case is an instance method with its name prefixed by test. Name the method to indicate what it actually tests.

❸ XCTAssert method to assert that the object is not nil.

❹ Another test case, to test the property getters. Do not test multiple methods in one test case.

❺ Object setup and code to be executed before testing the state.

❻ Assertions to test object equality. If the assertion fails, the test case fails. There is a bug and the code must be fixed.

Code Coverage

Writing unit tests is important. But at the end of the day, how do we know what part of the code has been tested and what remains untested? *Code coverage* refers to the percentage of code tested, using automated unit or functional tests.

The code coverage files can be generated directly using the Apple LLVM code generator, and you can set that option from within Xcode. There are two ways to do that—one allows report visualization from within Xcode and the other generates XML/HTML-based reports.

Integrated coverage report

A developer can run the test cases and visualize the reports from within Xcode itself.

To see code coverage reports from within Xcode, enable test coverage data on the main target. Go to the menu entry Product → Scheme → Edit Scheme (⌘ <). In the scheme editor dialog, go to the Test entry on the left and select "Gather coverage data," as shown in Figure 10-6. To save your changes, click Done.

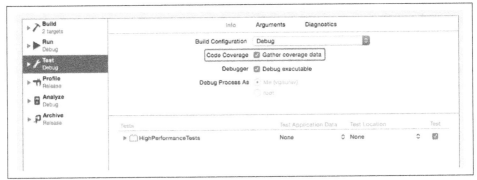

Figure 10-6. Xcode settings to enable coverage data collection

Run the test cases. With these settings, Xcode will collect coverage details when executing the test cases. To see the coverage report, follow these steps:

1. Go to Report Navigator in the Navigator pane (see Figure 10-7).

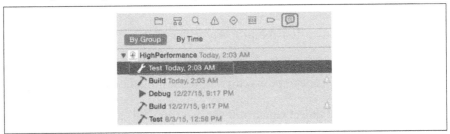

Figure 10-7. Report Navigator

2. Select the latest Test run.

3. Go to the Coverage tab.

You should see the coverage report as shown in Figure 10-8.

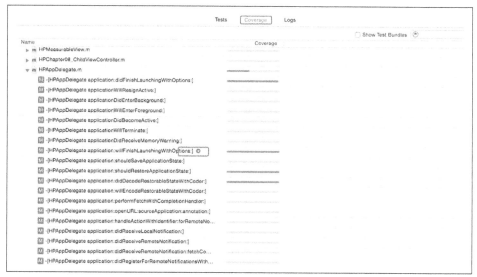

Figure 10-8. Xcode integrated test coverage report

If you tap on the little right arrow next to any method (see Figure 10-8), it will take you to the source code, where you can see the exact lines that have been tested (covered) or are left to be tested (not covered) in the test run (see Figure 10-9).

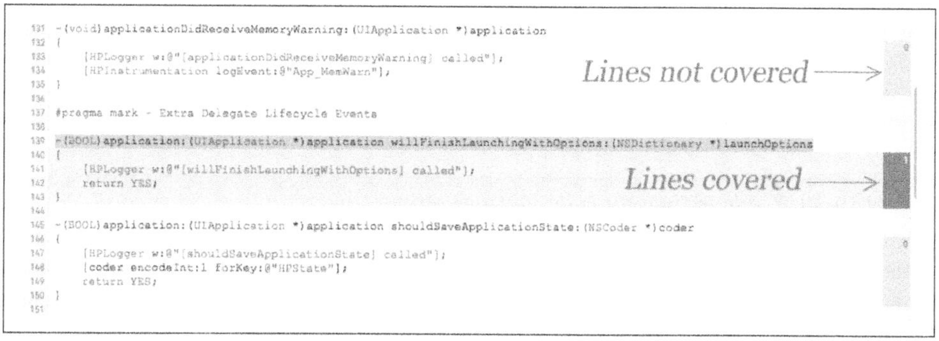

Figure 10-9. Xcode—coverage report integration with source code

External coverage report

You can also generate reports in XML or HTML formats. This is useful when you use continuous integration and tests run on a non-developer machine, or when you want to preserve the reports for later.

To generate the files that will contain coverage data, turn on the following flags:

Generate Debug Symbols
   Will emit the debug symbols in the compiled binary

Generate Test Coverage Files
   Will generate the binary files that contain the coverage data

Instrument Program Flow
   Will instrument the app as the test cases execute

It is recommended to create a custom build configuration to isolate the coverage from regular builds, as the former can be slow for regular testing. Figure 10-10 shows where you can find these settings.

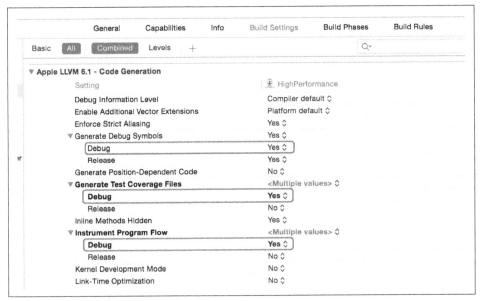

Figure 10-10. Xcode settings for code coverage setup

This will generate the *.gcno* and *.gcda* files in the derived data folder of the project. The *.gcno* file has details to reconstruct the basic block graphs and assign source line numbers to blocks. The *.gcda* file contains the ARC transition count.

The next step is to use these files to generate the report that can be exported to either XML or HTML format.

For us, the following two tools are useful:

lcov
   Lets us collect coverage data from multiple files into a unified file known as the *INFOFILE*.

genhtml

Generates the HTML report using the *INFOFILE* generated by the lcov tool.

These tools are not installed on Mac OS X by default, nor do they come bundled with the Xcode command-line tools. Use MacPorts (*https://www.macports.org*) or Homebrew (*http://brew.sh*) to install the lcov package.

To generate the report, add a New Run Script Phase in the build phases in Xcode with the code shown in Example 10-2.

Example 10-2. Code coverage report generation from within Xcode

```
lcov --directory "${OBJECT_FILE_DIR_normal}/${CURRENT_ARCH}"
    --capture
    --output-file "${PROJECT_DIR}/${PROJECT_NAME}.info"

genhtml --output-directory "${PROJECT_DIR}/${PROJECT_NAME}-coverage"
    "${PROJECT_DIR}/${PROJECT_NAME}.info"
```

Build the project. You should see the coverage report in the folder named *<your_project_name>-coverage* in the project folder. If you open the main file, *index.html*, you should see a report similar to the one shown in Figure 10-11.

LCOV - code coverage report

			Hit	Total	Coverage
Current view:	top level - Core				
Test:	HighPerformance.info	**Lines:**	69	178	**38.8 %**
Date:	2015-04-04 23:08:50	**Functions:**	15	49	**30.6 %**

Filename	Line Coverage ⬍			Functions ⬍	
HPCache.m		76.0 %	19 / 25	58.3 %	7 / 12
HPInstrumentation.m		63.6 %	7 / 11	66.7 %	2 / 3
HPLocationManager.h		0.0 %	0 / 1	0.0 %	0 / 2
HPLocationManager.m		0.0 %	0 / 41	0.0 %	0 / 14
HPLogger.m		55.8 %	43 / 77	54.5 %	6 / 11
HPUtils.m		0.0 %	0 / 23	0.0 %	0 / 7

Generated by: LCOV version 1.11

Figure 10-11. HTML coverage report

Asynchronous Operations

Suppose we want to test the HPSyncService class. It has methods that perform asynchronous network operations, and responses may not be available immediately. We need more elaborate techniques to test such methods.

The XCTestCase class comes with built-in support for testing asynchronous methods, so you do not need to write fancy code just for asynchronous operations.

The steps to test an asynchronous method are as follows:

1. Use the expectationWithDescription: method to get an XCTestExpectation instance. It also configures XCTestCase in what can be termed a *manual* mode. In this mode, the completion of the test method does not mark the success of the test case.

2. Use the waitForExpectationsWithTimeout:handler: method to wait for the operation to be complete. If the test case was not completed, the handler block will be invoked.

3. Use the XCTestExpectation object's method fulfill to indicate that the operation is complete and the wait can stop. This is the manual mode referred to in the first step.

Example 10-3 provides concrete code to test async operations.

Example 10-3. Testing async operations

```
@implementation HPSyncServiceTest

-(void)testFetchType_WithId_Completion {

    HPSyncService *svc = [HPSyncService sharedInstance];

    XCTestExpectation *expectation
        = [self expectationWithDescription:@"Test Fetch Type"]; ❶

    [svc fetchType:@"user" withId:@"id1"
        completion:^(NSDictionary *) { ❷

        //... validate data, apply assertions ❸
        [expectation fulfill]; ❹

    }];

    [self waitForExpectationsWithTimeout:1 handler:^{ ❺
        [svc cancelAllPendingRequests]; ❻
    }];
}
```

@end

❶ Get an expectation to be fulfilled. We are now in the manual mode of test case validation.

❷ Execute the method to test, with appropriate setup and parameter values.

❸ As earlier, validate the data using XCTAssertXXX macros.

❹ Once done, mark the expectation to be fulfilled.

❺ Wait for the expectation fulfillment. In this case, wait for 1 second.

❻ If the expectation was not fulfilled, perform cleanup. In this case, cancel any pending operations.

Xcode 6 Bonus: Performance Unit Tests

You can also run performance tests within the gambit of unit tests.

The XCTestCase class provides a method measureBlock (*http://apple.co/1SHL41A*) that can be used to measure the performance of a block of code.

Example 10-4 shows a test case using measureBlock to test performance.

Example 10-4. Performance in unit tests

```
-(void)testObjectForKey_Performance {
    HPCache *cache = [HPCache sharedInstance];

    [self measureBlock:^{
            id obj = [cache objectForKey:@"key-does-not-exist"];
            XCTAssertNil(obj);
    }];
}
```

Figure 10-12 shows output when the test in Example 10-4 is executed.

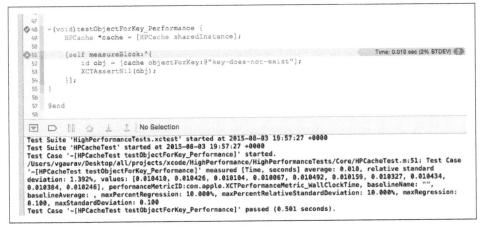

Figure 10-12. Output of the performance unit test

Xcode emits the average time for execution as well as the standard deviation. You can also set a baseline to test variations against.

To do so, just click on the tick-box next to the line that has the `measureBlock` class, as shown in Figure 10-13.

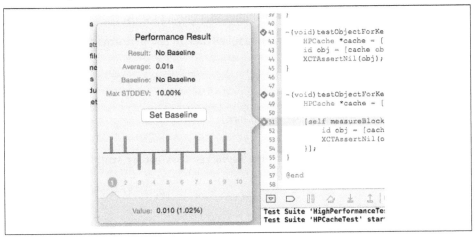

Figure 10-13. Configure baseline for performance unit tests

Once the baseline is set, the output will show not just the average and standard deviation but also the worst performance against the baseline, as shown in Figure 10-14.

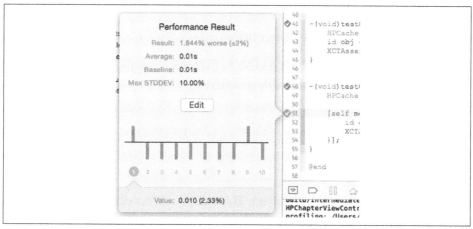

Figure 10-14. Measurements against the baseline

Dependency Mocking

The class that we put to test earlier, HPAlbum, is one of the simplest classes in our app to test. It does not have dependencies on any other subsystems like networking or persistence. In general, there are a whole bunch of questions that a test writer has in mind.

What if we wanted to test the HPUserService class (see Example 4-11), and specifically the method userWithId:completion:? It interacts with the class HPSyncService, wherein the method fetchType:withId:completion: makes a network call to fetch the data from the server. Questions to consider include:

1. Should the app really make a network call?

2. How do we tell the server what response to send, if we want to test out various scenarios?

3. Should we set up another server with fake responses? If so, how can the networking layer be made configurable to talk to various servers depending on the environment it is being used in (i.e., production versus test)?

   Even if we make it configurable, how do we ensure that configuration does not make its way into the production app, even accidentally?

There are more questions that you may have. This is where we need a system that should be able to *mock* the dependencies. This is how a test case with dependency mocking would work:

1. Configure the dependency to work in a prescribed manner, return a specific value, or change to a specific state when provided a particular input.

2. Execute the test case.

3. Reset the dependency to work normally.

The -[setUp] method is where dependencies will be configured, while they will be reset in the -[tearDown] method of the test fixture.

Vocabulary

Let's look at some vocabulary before we proceed further into concrete frameworks and code:

Dummy/double
> A general term for a fake test object. There are four types of doubles:

> *Stub*
>> Provides canned answers to calls made during the test. It does not interact with other parts of the app or make changes to other states. Stubs are useful when the components have been designed for dependency injection. When testing, the stubbed dependency, configured to work in a specific manner, can be *injected* into the component.

> *Spy*
>> Captures and makes available parameter and state information. It keeps track of the methods invoked with their parameters and helps verify correct method invocations. When testing, obtain the *original* object and create a spy for it that will monitor the method invocations. At the end, verify the behavior.

> *Mock*
>> Mimics the behavior of a real object in a controlled manner. A mock object is configured for only the methods that a test case interacts with.

> *Fake*
>> Works identically to the original object, except that it fakes out the underlying implementation.[2] An example of this is a fake database that may store data in memory and perform lame searches rather than using an actual database engine.

BDD
> Behavior-driven development, developed by Dan North, is an extension of TDD. Like TDD, BDD tests a specific functionality, but it also verifies underlying behavior.

---

2 See Martin Fowler, "Mocks Aren't Stubs" (*http://martinfowler.com/articles/mocksArentStubs.html*).

For example, you may want to check login functionality that tests against a set of credentials. Given correct credentials, the function should succeed, and it should fail otherwise. A TDD approach will help you test this, but if you want to *verify the behavior* (i.e., that the component actually makes calls to a database or web service), BDD kicks in. Dummy objects that can mimic or fake the underlying behavior and be used to verify it are a key part of BDD.

Mocking framework

A framework that allows creation of dummies. This includes provision for creation of mock objects at the least, but it is usually expected to provide spy objects as well.

OCMock (*http://ocmock.org*) is a great mocking framework that supports both mock and spy objects. Without getting into deeper discussion, let's look into key aspects of using the framework:

Create mock object

Use the `OCMClassMock` macro to create a mock instance of a class.

Create spy object

Use the `OCMPartialMock` macro to create a spy or partial mock of an object.

Stub functionality

Use the `OCMStub` macro to stub the function to either do nothing or return a value.

Verify behavior

Use the `OCMVerify` macro to verify if an underlying subsystem was interacted with in a specific manner (i.e., whether a specific method was called with particular parameters).

Example 10-5 shows a sample test case using the OCMock framework.

Example 10-5. Using OCMock to write an advanced test case

```objc
#include <OCMock/OCMock.h>
#include <OCMock/NSInvocation+OCMAdditions.h>  ❶

@implementation HPUserServiceTest

-(void)testUserWithId_Completion {
    id syncService = OCMClassMock([HPSyncService class]);  ❷
    OCMStub([syncService sharedInstance]).andReturn(syncService);  ❸

    NSString *userId = @"user-id";
    NSString *fname = @"fn-user-id",
        *lname = @"ln-user-id",
            *gender = @"gender-x";
        NSDate *dob = [NSDate date];

    data = @{
        @"id": userId,
        @"fname": fname,
        @"lname": lname,
        @"gender": gender,
        @"dateOfBirth": dob
    };  ❹

    [OCMStub([ssvc fetchType:OCMOCK_ANY
        withId:OCMOCK_ANY
        completion:OCMOCK_ANY
    ]) andDo:^(NSInvocation *invocation) {  ❺

        id cb = [pinvocation getArgumentAtIndexAsObject:4];
        void (^callback)(NSDictionary *) = cb;
        callback(data);  ❻
    }];

    HPUserService *svc = [HPUserService sharedInstance];
    [svc userWithId:userId completion:^(HPUser *user) {  ❼
        XCTAssert(user);
        XCTAssertEqualObjects(userId, user.userId);
        XCTAssertEqualObjects(fname, user.firstName);  ❽
        //... other state validations
    }];

    OCMVerify([ssvc sharedInstance]);
    OCMVerify([ssvc fetchType:@"user" withId:userId completion:[OCMArg any]]);  ❾
}

@end
```

❶ *OCMock.h* is the main header file to include. We use *NSInvocation+OCMAdditions.h* because we need specific functionality to implement.

❷ Mock an object of the `HPSyncService` class.

❸ Stub the class method `sharedInstance` to return the mock object obtained earlier.

❹ Input for the test case.

❺ Stub the instance method `fetchType:withId:completion:` to behave in a particular manner.

❻ For the test case, we do not make any network calls or perform database searches or cache lookups—instead, we execute code based on input data.

❼ After all the setup, the actual method to be tested, `userWithId:completion:`, is now invoked.

❽ Validate the state after execution.

❾ Verify that the methods were called with specific parameter values.

The concept behind unit tests is to treat the method to be tested as a black box. Testing it includes providing it with required input and validating actual output against an expected output without knowing the implementation of the function. This is achieved in step 8 in Example 10-5, and is the concept behind *test-driven development*.

Step 9 is getting deeper into the method to test and verify if it interacts with its dependencies in a specific manner (i.e., invokes the functions with specific parameter values). This is what constitutes a *behavior* and is key to *behavior-driven development*.

Other Frameworks

OCMock is just one of the several frameworks available. Table 10-1 shows a summary of other popular frameworks that you can choose from.[3]

---

3 Source: Mattt Thompson, "Unit Testing" (*http://nshipster.com/unit-testing/*).

Table 10-1. Unit testing frameworks for iOS

Framework type	Name	Maintainer	GitHub URL
Mock objects[a]	OCMock	Erik Doernenburg	https://github.com/erikdoe/ocmock
	OCMockito	Jon Reid	https://github.com/jonreid/OCMockito
Matchers[b]	Expecta[c]	Peter Jihoon Kim	https://github.com/specta/expecta
	OCHamcrest	Jon Reid	https://github.com/hamcrest/OCHamcrest
TDD/BDD frameworks	Specta	Peter Jihoon Kim	https://github.com/specta/specta
	Kiwi	Allen Ding	https://github.com/kiwi-bdd/Kiwi
	Cedar	Pivotal Labs	https://github.com/pivotal/cedar
	Calabash	Xamarin	http://calaba.sh

[a] For creating mock objects.

[b] For creating match rules declaratively.

[c] Think `expect(album.name).to.equal(@"Album-1")` rather than `XCTAssertEqualObjects(@"Album-1", album.name)`.

Functional Testing

Unit tests are great in that they help test individual methods. However, because we test these methods in isolation, setting up a clean configuration before each test case execution, they do not really help test the app as whole.

And that is where *functional test* comes into the picture. As the name implies, this involves making sure the app functions as expected. Here, we are not talking about units of technical operations but units of human operations. For example, instead of saying "test the `authenticateWithCredentials:` method," we prefer to say "test the authentication functionality," which may involve data input, network operation, UI updates, and other component interactions.

Functional testing is more about UI testing, and we treat the app as a black box. There is no mocking, no stubs or spies or mock objects—this is the real app in action.

Instruments provides support for functional testing through *UI automation*, which is the abbreviated name for *automated UI testing*.

Setup

Instruments provides a profiling template named Automation that can be used to create new functional tests (or import existing tests).

From Xcode, launch Instruments by navigating to Xcode → Open Developer Tool → Instruments. Select Automation and click Choose (see Figure 10-15).

Figure 10-16 shows the Instruments window for UI Automation. Configure the following (see Figure 10-16 for reference):

1. Select your app on the device or the simulation. As mentioned earlier, this is about running the actual app rather than mock or isolated code as in unit tests.

2. Switch to Display Settings.

3. Rename the test to something more meaningful. For example, if we intend to test our code of composite custom views, we may want to name it `Test_Custom Views_Composite`.

Figure 10-15. Instruments—Automation

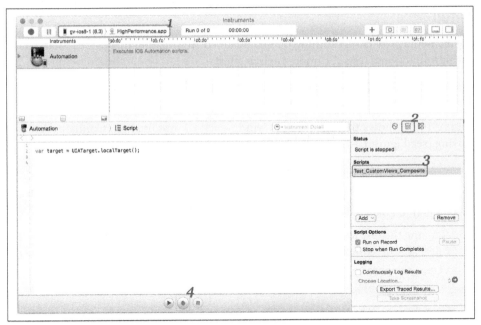

Figure 10-16. UI Automation—Setup

The next step is to enable it on the device. By default, for security reasons, UI Automation is disabled on the real devices. To enable it, navigate to Settings app → Developer → UI Automation → Enable UI Automation. Figure 10-17 shows you where to locate the setting.

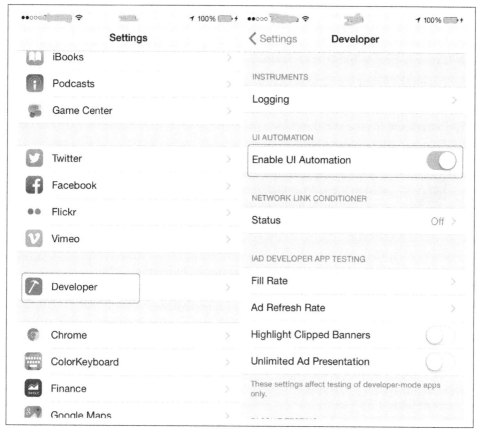

Figure 10-17. Enable UI Automation on device

With these steps completed, we are ready to write our functional tests.

Writing Functional Tests

There are two options for writing functional tests. The first option is to write all of the code by hand. Alternatively, you can generate code using the recorder and then customize it, which is the option we'll use here.

To start recording, click the Record button (see step 4 in Figure 10-16). This will start the app on the target device/simulator.

Run your app through the scenario you want to test. Once done, click the Stop button.

Try creating a test script for the following scenario:

1. Launch the sample app.

2. In the Chapters section, tap Threads.

3. Enter "1000" for the number of iterations.

4. Tap anywhere to hide the keyboard.

5. Tap on the Compute Thread Creation Time button.

6. Verify the result. It should be of the format "Average Creation: <time> µsec".

7. Extract and log the creation time.

 The UI Automation test cases are written in JavaScript, so you'll need to become familiar with it if you aren't already. The API reference is available under the topic "UI Automation JavaScript Reference for iOS" (*http://apple.co/1KhVvXa*) in the iOS Developer Library.

The autogenerated code looks similar to that shown in Example 10-6.

Example 10-6. UI Automation—default code using recorder

```
var target = UIATarget.localTarget(); ❶

target.frontMostApp().mainWindow()
    .tableViews()[0].tapWithOptions({tapOffset:{x:0.45, y:0.62}}); ❷
target.frontMostApp().mainWindow()
    .textFields()[0].tap();
target.frontMostApp().keyboard()
    .typeString("1000"); ❸
target.tap({x:111.50, y:308.50}); ❹
target.frontMostApp().mainWindow()
    .buttons()["Compute Thread Creation Time"].tap(); ❺
```

❶ Grab the target, which is either a device or a simulator.

❷ Tap the corresponding cell.

❸ Enter the iteration count.

❹ Tap anywhere to hide the keyboard.

❺ Tap the corresponding button.

Great, we now have working code that we can further enhance. Let's update the code as follows:

- Instead of the table view being tapped using *x/y* coordinates, we want it to be more deterministic and tap on a specific cell. For our specific case, we tap on the seventh cell. We'll use the `cells()` method of the `UIATableView` object to get all the cells, and tap the one at row 7 (index 6).

- We need to verify the results and log creation time. To do this, we'll use `UIALog ger`, which logs messages and tracks successes and failures.

Without diving deep into the API, the updated code is provided in Example 10-7.

Example 10-7. UI Automation—updated code with deterministic taps and result validation

```
var target = UIATarget.localTarget();

target.frontMostApp().mainWindow()
    .tableViews()[0].cells()[6].tap(); ❶
target.frontMostApp().mainWindow()
    .textFields()[0].tap();
target.frontMostApp().keyboard().typeString("1000");
target.frontMostApp().mainWindow()
    .buttons()["Compute Thread Creation Time"].tap();

var msg = target.frontMostApp().mainWindow()
    .staticTexts()[0].label(); ❷

var l = msg.length;
if(msg.indexOf("Average Creation: ") != 0) { ❸
    UIALogger.logFail("Did not find average creation at the start"); ❹
} else if(msg.indexOf(" µsec") != (l - 5)) {
    UIALogger.logFail("Did not find µsec at the end"); ❹
} else {
    var t = msg.substring(18, l - 5);
    UIALogger.logMessage("Thread creation took " + t + " µsec"); ❺
    UIALogger.logPass("Hurray! Success."); ❻
}
```

❶ Tap the cell at index=6.

❷ Grab the `label` of the first of the static texts. You can use `accessibilityLabel` instead of index for a more complex UI.

❸ Validate the value of the `label`.

❹ Log a failure if the `label` does not look right.

❺ If all good, log the computation time, and…

❻ ... mark the test case a success/pass.

Stop the app. Run the test case. Look at the Editor Log section (see Figure 10-18). It should report all the steps executed and the log messages, including the final failure/pass.

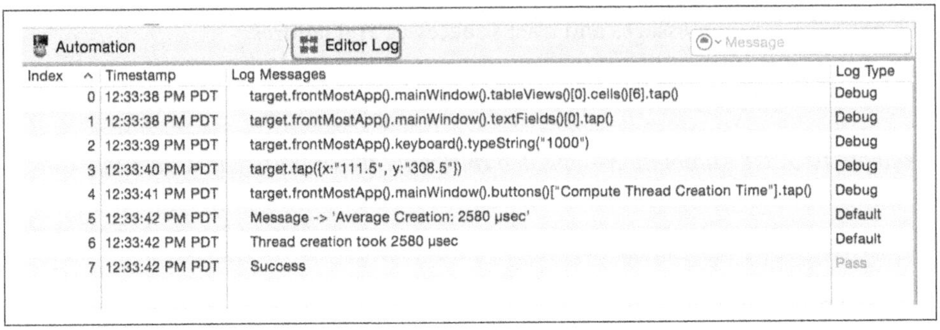

Automation		Editor Log	⊙∨ Message	
Index ∧	Timestamp	Log Messages		Log Type
0	12:33:38 PM PDT	target.frontMostApp().mainWindow().tableViews()[0].cells()[6].tap()		Debug
1	12:33:38 PM PDT	target.frontMostApp().mainWindow().textFields()[0].tap()		Debug
2	12:33:39 PM PDT	target.frontMostApp().keyboard().typeString("1000")		Debug
3	12:33:40 PM PDT	target.tap({x:"111.5", y:"308.5"})		Debug
4	12:33:41 PM PDT	target.frontMostApp().mainWindow().buttons()["Compute Thread Creation Time"].tap()		Debug
5	12:33:42 PM PDT	Message -> 'Average Creation: 2580 µsec'		Default
6	12:33:42 PM PDT	Thread creation took 2580 µsec		Default
7	12:33:42 PM PDT	Success		Pass

Figure 10-18. UI Automation—Editor Log

Project Structure

As you may have noticed, you can end up with either one huge JavaScript file or several of them, each for a particular scenario. The preferred approach is to use one scenario per file. However, keep in mind that only one file can be executed by Instruments at a time. This means that if you have to run multiple scenarios, you may end up launching the app several times.

An ideal way to manage all the test cases is to:

1. Create a folder called *tests* to store all the test cases.
2. In the folder, have just one file. Let's name it *allTests.js*.

   This file has no code of its own. It just does an #import on other files.
3. Create subfolders for scenario groups.

   Have one file per scenario in these folders.
4. Invoke *allTests.js* from Instruments.

Instruments provides a command-line interface to execute functional tests. It is very useful in the continuous integration and automated build pipeline that we briefly discuss in "Continuous Integration and Automation" on page 349. A typical execution command will be similar to that shown in Example 10-8.

Example 10-8. Instruments—command-line interface

```
$ instruments
    -t '/Applications/Xcode.app/Contents/Applications/Instruments.app/Contents/
       PlugIns/AutomationInstrument.xrplugin/Contents/Resources/
       Automation.tracetemplate' ❶
    -w '{device-uuid}' ❷
    -e UIASCRIPT '/path/to/project/tests/allTests.js' ❸
    -e UIARESULTPATH '/path/to/projet/test-results/' ❹
```

❶ Path to `Automation` template.

❷ Device UUID or simulator identifier. Execute `instruments -s` to get a list of simulators.

❸ Path to the UI Automation JavaScript file.

❹ Folder where the test results will be saved.

Dependency Isolation

When running unit tests, it is always advisable to isolate and mock the dependencies. This lets your tests get away with any variations related to the dependencies.

When running functional tests, `OCMock` is not available. As such, you cannot use the usual mocking frameworks. When running functional or performance tests, you will need to make those subsystems pluggable to be able to reset the state before each test and to isolate any variations due to networking, Core Data operations, and so on.

We introduced an `HPSyncService`, earlier (in Example 4-11) that was central to syncing data with the server. All we need to do now is to make it configurable so that `sharedInstance` returns an object that returns the results for a given scenario.

There are two approaches to this:

- Create a subclass that returns appropriate data for the scenario under test. Then, either use method swizzling or create a method `setSharedInstance` to direct all operations to an object of this subclass.

  The advantage of this approach is that all operations happen in-process and everything is under your control.

- Create a server that returns data for a specific scenario. Let's call it the *scenario server*. Before running the test case, configure the server against the scenario to be tested.

  The advantage of this approach is that it requires only a minimal configuration change to the app, namely the hostname/IP address to connect to.

Note that the server can be an embedded in-process server. For an embedded HTTP server, you may want to use CocoaHttpServer (*https://github.com/robbie hanson/CocoaHTTPServer*).

Both these approaches require a custom binary using a build target or scheme. In the former case, there will be a lot of custom code for various scenarios and a need for a custom scheme that builds using extra code and data for individual scenarios. In the latter case, the server's IP address needs to be configured appropriately, which can be set for debug builds using simple preprocessor macros.

Additionally, the UI Automation runtime does not have an API to talk to the scenario server. This is where you will need higher-level frameworks like Appium (*http:// appium.io*) or Calabash (*http://calaba.sh*).

Calabash uses Ruby. If you plan to use it, learn Ruby. It also requires a custom target that runs the Calabash server.

Appium, however, can work with a variety of languages (*http:// bit.ly/appium-lang*) and also does not require a custom target. It uses the WebDriver protocol to talk to the app.

Example 10-9 shows representative code that you can use to configure the scenario server based on the build configuration and execute your test cases.

Example 10-9. Using a scenario server to serve scenario-driven responses

```
//HPSyncService.m

#define MACRO_STRING_(msg) #msg
#define MACRO_STRING(msg) MACRO_STRING_(msg) ❶

#ifndef HP_CUSTOM_REMOTE_SERVER ❷
NSString *host = @"https://my-real-server.com"; ❸
#else
NSString *host = @MACRO_STRING(HP_CUSTOM_REMOTE_SERVER); ❹
#endif

//someTest.js for Appium - using Chai/Mocha style ❺
describe("login", function() { ❻
    before(function() { ❼
        //configure the WebDriver
    });

    after(function() { ❼
        //shut down the WebDriver
    });

    it("should succeed with valid credentials", function() { ❽
```

```
        http.get('scenario-server.com/setup?scenario_id=valid_login'
            + '&client_id=some-unique-id'); ❾
        driver.elementByName('username').text('testuser'); ❿
        driver.elementByName('password').text('testpass');
        driver.elementByName('Login').click();

        driver.waitForElementByName('profileImage').should.be.ok; ⓫
    });
});
```

❶ A helper macro to concatenate literals.

❷ Check if a remote server has been defined.

❸ If no remote server has been defined, use the default (production).

❹ If a remote server has been defined, use that.

❺ Functional test using Appium and JavaScript.

❻ The test suite. This suite tests all login scenarios.

❼ The before and after methods for the suite are called once per suite. Use befor
    eEach and afterEach to configure before and reset after each test case.

❽ it defines one test case, and one scenario.

❾ Configure the scenario server to respond using a specific scenario. http is the
    HTTP module. The URL to the server is only indicative, but you get the idea.

❿ Set up the app's UI. The elementByName method searches for a UIView object
    with the given accessibilityIdentifier (*http://apple.co/1At24WP*).

⓫ Verify that the profileImage has been loaded.

Example 10-9 is only representative code, but it should help you speed up writing
functional test cases.

Testing and Component Design

Testing and the testing framework may impact component design.

As an example, the instrumentation subsystem may be a singleton and will have
abstracted out several configuration steps. And rightly so. However, when you want
to test, you will want it to be customized to use a test-app ID rather than mess up
production app analytics. Also, for unit testing, you may want to reset all initializa-

tion, which in a real app is done only once. As such, you want your component to be resettable.

For other components, like the sync service, you may want to configure them using a different host. For each request that goes out to the scenario server, you may want to attach a scenario ID so that the server can respond appropriately (the scenario ID can be added by using a custom header, say, `X-Test-Scenario-ID`, or modifying the request itself).

One option is to use mocks or method swizzling. However, this requires knowing the component internals. Also, as more methods require mocking or swizzling based on the scenarios, this approach can soon get bloated and unmanageable.

That brings us to the second option for making all components configurable: prefer to use resettable components or the builder pattern with dependency injection (DI).

A resettable component means that either the component is not singleton, so that it can be created multiple times without any side effects, or, if it is a singleton, along with the `sharedInstance` method there is either a `setSharedInstance` or a `tearDown` method that can be called after each test case to reset the shared state. This method may be declared in a private header file that is not distributed to the developers using the class or the SDK.

If the component has a few dependencies, it should not use them directly by creating an instance or using a singleton but should instead provide a custom initializer or use the builder pattern where the dependencies can be injected.

For instance, instead of writing code like that shown in Example 10-10, prefer using code similar to what is given in Example 10-11.

Example 10-10. Dependency without injection

```
-(instancetype) init {
    if(self = [super init]) {
        self.logger = [Logger sharedInstance];
        self.instrumentation = [Flurry sharedInstance];
    }
    return self;
}
```

Example 10-11. Dependency with injection

```
-(instancetype) initWithLogger:(Logger *)logger
    instrumentation:(Flurry *)flurry {
    if(self = [super init]) {
        self.logger = logger;
        self.instrumentation = flurry;
    }
```

```
    return self;
}
```

If you have dependencies on other systems, you may want to create wrappers. This helps in completely mocking out the dependencies during testing. It may also help you in creating replaceable dependencies. For example, instead of taking Flurry as a dependency (as shown previously), define a protocol (say, Instrumentation) with appropriate methods. In production, you may create an implementation for Flurry named FlurryInstrumentation. Tomorrow, if you switch to MixPanel, you can create another implementation, MixPanelInstrumentation.

The protocol Instrumentation may be defined as follows:

```
@protocol Instrumentation <NSObject>

-(void)logEvent:(NSString *)eventName params:(NSDictionary *)params;

@end
```

In short, when you want to make your code and app testable and want more automated test cases than manual, you need to think about the component design ahead of time. It is possible that the app and component designs may be impacted by the choice of testing framework you intend to use, so choose carefully and plan well in advance.

Continuous Integration and Automation

Continuous integration (CI) is all about keeping the code sane and making sure that builds are up to date.

A typical development cycle (see Figure 10-19) involves developers writing code that is pushed to a version control system (e.g., Git or Mercurial). Each commit triggers the build pipeline, followed by all tests (unit, functional, performance, integration, etc.). The functional tests may run on a simulator or a variety of devices. For example, when testing a memory- and CPU-intensive game, you want to not only test it on an iPhone 6 Plus running iOS 8.x but also an iPhone 4S running iOS 7.x. A successful execution of all tests will result in the binary being distributed internally for manual testing of the cases that could not be automated. If everything is good, the QA team may certify the build for release/publishing to the App Store.

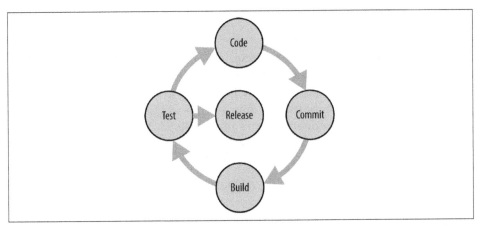

Figure 10-19. Continuous integration

In addition to automated unit tests and integration tests, CI will run on build servers and execute processes that run additional static and dynamic code analysis, measure and profile performance, create documentation from the source code, and facilitate manual QA processes.

There are several open source, commercial, and hosted solutions that will help you to implement CI for your app. Of the available options, I recommend using Travis (*https://travis-ci.com*) or Jenkins (*http://jenkins-ci.org*).

Travis is a commercial solution with a free plan for open source projects hosted on GitHub. Setup is a breeze—all you have to do is add a Travis configuration file with references to the workspace/project file, scheme, and iOS version, and point the Travis build engine to the repo.

Travis uses `xctool` (*https://github.com/facebook/xctool*) to build the project and execute tests, and provides integration for CocoaPods for project dependencies.

The downside of using Travis is that it may not provide the complete matrix of device and OS combinations. At the time of writing, for real devices, it provides support only for iOS 8.1.

Jenkins, on the other hand, is an open source, general-purpose job execution pipeline with a primary focus on building and testing software projects continuously and monitoring execution of externally run jobs such as cron, procmail, and so on. You will need the Xcode plug-in to build iOS apps.

The upside of using Jenkins is that you are in total control of the pipeline. You can choose to use the `instruments` command-line interface or the more advanced `xctool`. You can attach the machine you're running Jenkins on to physical devices and run the jobs.

Continuous integration is a large topic in itself and requires a separate discussion. For more information on Jenkins, check out John Ferguson Smart's *Jenkins: The Definitive Guide* (O'Reilly).

You should also explore Xcode Server as an option for continuous integration.[4]

 Because `xcodebuild` generates coverage and other intermediate files in the derived data folder of the project and its information is available only during build time, it needs extra steps to integrate with the CI tool.

For Jenkins, you can do the following:[5]

1. In Xcode, add a build phase that will copy the derived data path to a predetermined file.

2. In Jenkins, add a build step to use this folder to generate the coverage. Use XML format.

Best Practices

As with everything else, unit testing also has a few best practices to follow. After all, it's code to test another piece of code (don't ask who will test the test cases).

When writing unit tests, you should follow these best practices:

- Test all code, including all initializers.
- Test against all combinations of the parameter values.

  For example, if a method accepts three parameters and each parameter can have two variants in values (invalid and valid, for simplicity), you should have $2 \times 2 \times 2 = 8$ test cases in total. Well, there are 8 scenarios at the end.

  You can get the data from a central database or generate random data to cover various scenarios. Using this technique of a combination of human-crafted and machine-generated data is more formally known as *fuzzy testing*.

- Do not test private methods. Consider the method being tested as a black box.
- Prefer to stub out any external dependencies. This ensures that you can drive various scenarios easily.
- Set up the state before each test run and clear it after execution.

---

4 iOS Developer Library, "About Continuous Integration in Xcode" (*http://apple.co/1Kt4iXu*).

5 For further details, see Stack Overflow, "Generating gcda Files to View the Code-Coverage from XCTests in iOS with Jenkins" (*http://bit.ly/gen-gcda*).

Ensure that the outcome of one test case does not impact another.

- Each test case should be repeatable. Identical inputs should yield identical results.
- Each test case must have assertions to validate or invalidate the code being tested.
- Enable code coverage for the complete run. This gives you a glimpse of what code has been tested and what has not, and which components have better coverage and which need focus.

In addition to these guidelines, you should also not forget to apply all the other best practices of writing code. Unit tests are code too.

Now apply the same best practices to functional testing as well. The only difference here is that instead of testing a method in a class, you are now writing a test case to test a business use case, a user scenario.

Additionally, for functional testing, you should test various device and OS combinations. For example, test an iPhone 5S running iOS 7 as well as an iPhone 4S with iOS 8.3 and an iPhone 6 with iOS 8. The more combinations you can test, the better device coverage your functional tests will have, which will ultimately ensure that your app has accounted for various hardware- and OS-related scenarios.

Performance Testing

In the pursuit of testing functional aspects of the code, we tend to forget testing its qualitative aspects, especially performance.

Sadly, as of today, there is very little focus on app performance testing per se. Large companies invest quite heavily in performance. There are a bunch of toolkits and libraries available to test the server-side performance, but none for testing client-side performance. A quick web search for the phrase "ios app performance testing" will result in a lot of irrelevant ads.

Most companies create in-house tools to measure and improve performance. The best tool you have for this is Instruments. Use it to do memory, CPU, and energy profiling; identify memory leaks; and so on. But when you want to test performance at the unit level, you will have to write custom code.

XCTest does provide the `measureBlock` method to do basic performance testing of any block. But then, the reports from the test cases are only for pass/fail and coverage. The report generators do not account for performance aspects of method execution.

Even if you do measure performance when running unit tests, you may or may not get real numbers depending upon how the dependencies have been mocked.

In a nutshell, to test performance of your code, you will have to write custom code specific to what you want to measure.

To compute execution speed, you can use a simplistic timer. Example 10-12 provides a timer that you can use to time execution. The timer supports nesting so as to be able to identify bottlenecks in the call stack.

Example 10-12. Timer to track execution speed

```
@interface HPTimer ❶

+(HPTimer *)startWithName:(NSString *)name;

@property (nonatomic, readonly, assign) uint64_t timeNanos;
@property (nonatomic, readonly, copy) NSString *name;

-(uint64_t)stop;
-(void)printTree;

@end

@interface HPTimer ()

@property (nonatomic, strong) HPTimer *parent;
@property (nonatomic, strong) NSMutableArray *children;
@property (nonatomic, assign) uint64_t startTime;
@property (nonatomic, assign) uint64_t stopTime;
@property (nonatomic, assign) BOOL stopped;
@property (nonatomic, copy) NSString *threadName;

@end

@implementation HPTimer

+(HPTimer *)startWithName:(NSString *)name { ❷
    NSMutableDictionary *tls = [NSThread threadDictionary];
    HPTimer *top = [tls objectForKey:@"hp-timer-top"; ❸

    HPTimer *rv = [[HPTimer alloc] initWithParent:top name:name];
    [tls setObject:rv forKey:@"hp-timer-top"];

    rv.startTime = mach_absolute_time();
    return rv;
}

-(instancetype)initWithParent:(HPTimer *)parent
    name:(NSString *)name {
    if(self = [super init]) {
        self.parent = parent; ❹
        self.name = name;
        self.stopped = NO;
        self.children = [NSMutableArray array];
        self.threadName = [NSThread currentThread].name;
```

```
            if(parent) {
                [parent.children addObject:self];
            }
        }
        return self;
    }

    -(uint64_t)stop {
        self.stopTime = mach_absolute_time();
        self.stopped = YES;
        self.timeNanos = [HPUtils
            nanosUsingStart:self.startTime end:self.stopTime]; ❺

        NSMutableDictionary *tls = [NSThread threadDictionary];
        [tls setObject:self.parent forKey:@"hp-timer-top"]; ❻

        return self.timeNanos;
    }

    -(void)printTree {
        [self printTreeWithNode:self indent:@""];
    }

    +(void)printTreeWithNode:(HPTimer *)node
        indent:(NSMutableString *)indent { ❼
        if(node) {
            DDLogDebug(@"%@[%@][%@] -> %lld", indent, self.threadName,
                self.name, self.timeNanos);
            NSArray *children = node.children;
            if(children.count > 0) {
                indent = [indent stringByAppendingString:@" "];
                for(NSUInteger i = 0; i < children.count; i++) {
                    [self printTreeWithNode:[children objectAtIndex:i] indent];
                }
            }
        }
    }

    @end

    //Usage
    -(void)someMethodA {
        HPTimer *timer = [HPTimer startWithName:@"method-A"]; ❽
        [obj someMethodB];
        [timer stop]; ❾
        [timer printTree]; ❿
    }

    //in some other place
    -(void)someMethodB {
        HPTimer *timer = [HPTimer startWithName:@"method-B"]; ⓫
        //do stuff
```

```
    [timer stop]; ⓬
    //optionally, printTree ⓭
}
```

❶ The public API of the class, HPTimer.

❷ startWithName creates a marker, a new timer *context*.

❸ The timer context is local to the thread. Once created, the timer can be stopped, in our implementation, from any thread. The implementation can be changed to not make the timer thread sensitive and/or to restrict the usage of the stop method to the thread where the timer was created.

❹ Initialization—this sets up the call hierarchy tree for visualization later.

❺ We use the helper method that we created earlier to compute the time difference in nanoseconds.

❻ Pop the current timer from the thread-local storage (TLS).

❼ Pretty-print the timer tree.

❽ To use the timer, call the startWithName: method. Give the timer a meaningful name.

❾ After execution, call stop.

❿ Print the time taken to execute, including any nested timers.

⓫ In a nested method call, create another timer.

⓬ Stop the timer, as before.

⓭ You may or may not print the nested call tree.

Summary

Testing your app is as important as implementing it. Unit testing helps you test at the finest level, while functional testing monitors your app in a real execution environment. Enabling code coverage is a recommended step, as this helps you keep a check on what parts of the code have been left untested.

Continuous integration is an integral part of the overall release cycle today. Automated testing eases the job of the engineering team, especially when integrated with the CI process. This helps avoid any manual errors in application testing.

With this background on testing and continuous integration, you are now ready to make quality an integral part of your app development and build and release process. Minimizing any human intervention cuts down on errors creeping in and frees up the quality assurance team to perform other tasks.

CHAPTER 11

Tools

Now that we have reviewed most of the important aspects of implementing efficient and performant apps, in this chapter we explore a few tools to help analyze and debug various issues.

In the previous chapter, we learned that the validity and isolated functional performance of the app can be tested using code. However, specialized tools are required to analyze certain tasks. Some of these tasks include:

- Identifying and verifying accessibility tags
- Analyzing runtime execution performance of the app in terms of resource utilization
- Analyzing network and Core Data usage
- Analyzing rendering performance
- Performing user interactions through automated code
- Analyzing crash logs

There are many tools available, but we will focus on the following ones in this chapter:

- Apple's Accessibility Inspector
- Apple's Xcode Instruments
- Square's PonyDebugger
- XK72's Charles

Let's start with Accessibility Inspectors.

Accessibility Inspector

To reach a larger audience and to win accolades, you should make your app accessible. In addition, you might be legally required to make your app accessible. For example, in the United States, Section 508 may require your entire app (or certain parts of it) to be accessible. In other cases, the target audience may dictate the requirements (e.g., a travel or medical app should be accessible).

Each `UIView` (or its subclass) object can be provided an `accessibilityLabel` and `accessibilityHint`, apart from several other attributes. These values control what is provided to people with disabilities.

The `accessibilityLabel` provides the *help text* that is presented to the user. For example, it may be read aloud when VoiceOver is enabled. The `accessibilityHint` provides additional information about the UI element in case the `accessibilityLabel` does not suffice.

To analyze the app for the correct values, use an Accessibility Inspector.

Accessibility Inspectors provide accessibility information about each element in an app. There are two inspectors available: the first is integrated with Xcode for Mac OS X, and the second is available in the iOS Simulator.

To launch it from Xcode, navigate to Xcode → Developer Tools → Accessibility Inspector. To start the inspector in the Simulator, launch the Settings app, go to General → Accessibility, and turn on Accessibility Inspector (see Figure 11-1). Note that in both cases, you can only test simulator.

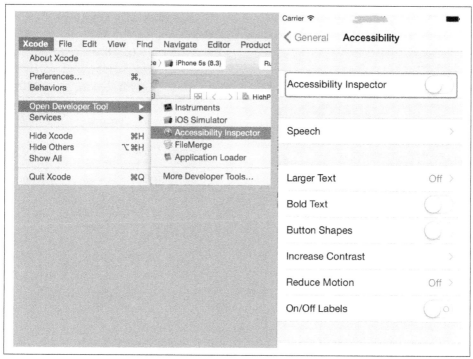

Figure 11-1. Starting the Accessibility Inspector in Xcode (left) and iOS Simulator (right)

Xcode Accessibility Inspector

The Accessibility Inspector built into Xcode is meant to provide accessibility details for any app running on Mac OS X. However, for most of the common elements, it works just as well with iOS Simulator. After all, Simulator is rendered natively on OS X.

Figure 11-2 shows the Xcode Accessibility Inspector in action. In the figure, the high-lighted element is the button with label "Permissions (Tap to Request)". Notice in the Inspector that the `accessibilityTitle`[1] property's value is the same as that of the UIButton's `titleLabel` property. For a UILabel, it is the value of its `text` property.

A custom UI element must provide its own `accessibilityLabel`.

---

1 This is a discrepancy in the tool vis-à-vis the documentation. It is documented as `accessibilityLabel` in AppleKit. See the Mac Developer Library (*http://apple.co/1MnmG46*).

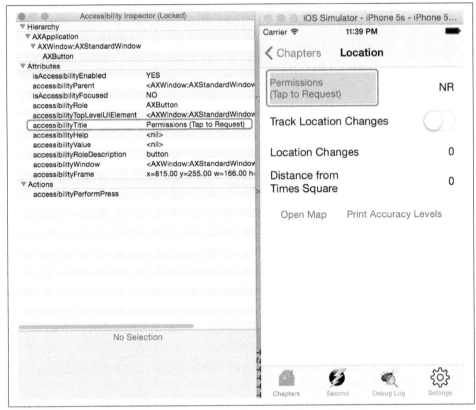

Figure 11-2. Inspecting iOS Simulator using the Xcode Accessibility Inspector

iOS Accessibility Inspector

When you turn on the Accessibility Inspector in the iOS Simulator, you will see a floating window (see Figure 11-3).

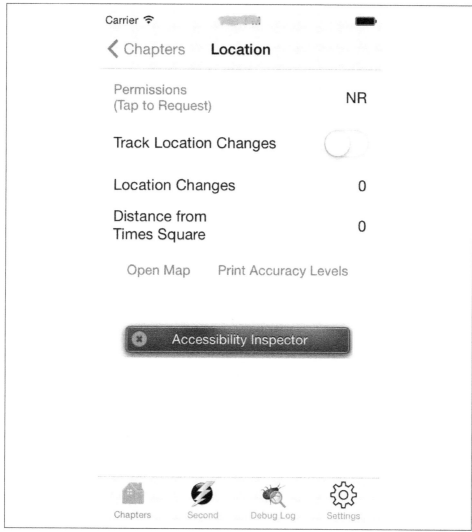

Figure 11-3. iOS Simulator—Accessibility Inspector: collapsed

If you tap the X icon and then tap on any UI element, the Inspector will show the accessibility info of the element. If you look at Figure 11-4, after the button was tapped (part 1 in the figure), the Inspector shows the accessibilityLabel (shown as Label in part 2) and the bounds. Along with this, it also shows the Traits value (*http://apple.co/1HLcHl1*), which indicates how the accessibility element behaves or should be treated. It is configured using the accessibilityTraits property (*http://apple.co/1JrQJb6*).

Figure 11-4. iOS Simulator—Accessibility Inspector: expanded

The Accessibility Inspector helps you to perform a quick accessibility analysis of the app.

Use UI Automation to automate testing for accessibility properties associated with each element[2] in the UI.

---

2 Use the `elements` property of any `UIAElement` object, specifically the `UIAWindow` object representing the main window of the topmost app. See the iOS Developer Library (*http://apple.co/1eQy25x*).

Instruments

Instruments is the de facto tool for most of the diagnosis, profiling, and analysis of the app at runtime. We looked at this tool briefly when we explored functional testing in the previous chapter.

It is now time to explore it in depth. Instruments can be launched from within Xcode by navigating to Xcode → Open Developer Tool → Instruments, as shown in Figure 11-5.

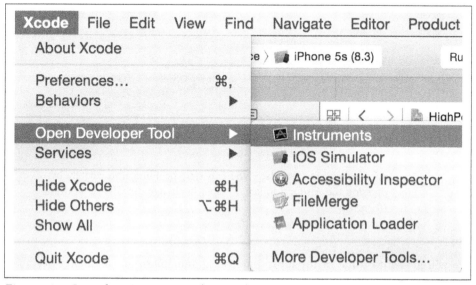

Figure 11-5. Launching Instruments from within Xcode

This will open a menu displaying a variety of templates that you can choose from, as shown in Figure 11-6. The Instruments bundled with Xcode 6.3.2 comes with about 20 different trace templates that help diagnose apps and devices from various perspectives.

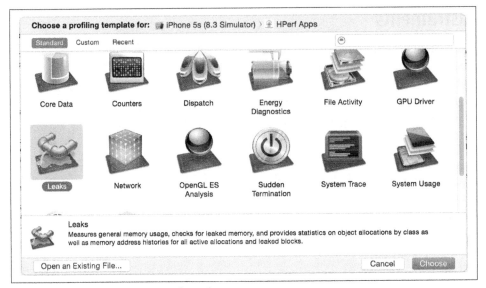

Figure 11-6. Instruments—template chooser

After selecting a template, you can start profiling immediately by pressing the Alt/Option key, which will change the Choose button to Profile.

We will look into some of the more interesting and important templates here. For details on each template, see the "Instruments User Guide" (*http://apple.co/1RO7a6b*) in the iOS Developer Library.

Using Instruments

After opening a template, you will notice the Instruments window with appropriate tracker(s) already configured. You may want to add more items to track. Any item is formally known as an *instrument*.

This can be confusing. *Instruments* is the name of the tool. *Instrument* is the name for each item to be monitored. For example, "CPU" is an instrument, and so is "network." The name of the tool, hence, is appropriately chosen to be Instruments.

Using Instruments to profile an app and improve its performance is comprised of the following steps:

1. Open a template. You can use a predefined template or start with a blank template.

2. Optionally, add instruments.

3. Profile the app. This may start the app if required.

4. Collect data.

5. Analyze the data.

6. Update the app, if necessary.

7. Repeat until satisfied with the app's performance.

If you select the Blank template, you will see an empty Instruments window. Otherwise, there may be preselected instruments based on the template chosen.

Click the Library icon for the window that lists available instruments. You can then select one or more instruments to track. See Figure 11-7 for the main window reference; Figure 11-8 shows the instrument selector in the Library window.

Select the app to profile using the Target section. The Record button starts app profiling. Use the Pause/Resume button to pause or resume recording. Once complete, press the Stop button.

The lower-right section of the main window is the Inspector pane, where you configure the record and display settings.

The lower-left part of the window, the Detail pane, shows the data related to the instrument selected in the upper half.

Figure 11-7 shows the main window of the Instruments tool. Let's take a closer look at the various options shown in the screenshot:

1. Library icon (opens the instruments list, as shown in Figure 11-8)

2. Target selector (either select an individual app or the device; you can only select an app installed using one of the developer profiles available on your host Mac OS X device)

3. Record, Pause, Resume, and Stop buttons

4. Inspector pane

5. Inspectors: Record Settings, Display Settings, and Extended Detail

6. Instrument selector

7. Recording graph over time

8. Detail pane that shows details based on the instrument selected

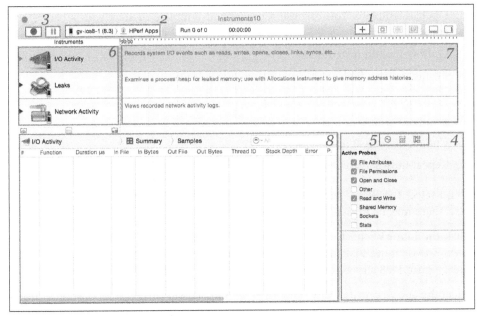

Figure 11-7. Instruments main window

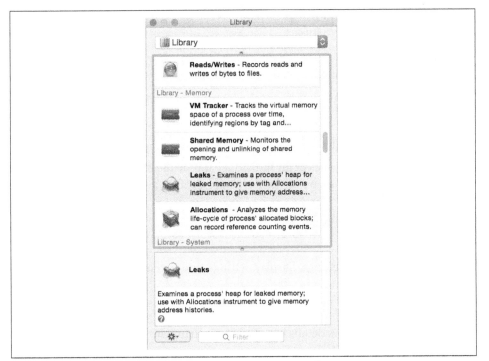

Figure 11-8. Instruments Library/instrument selector window

Activity Monitor

The Activity Monitor trace template monitors overall device activity (namely, CPU, memory, disk, and network). Use this to identify any excessive use of these resources in the app. Specifically, any surge for a long duration can be a cause of worry.

If a surge in use is found, it must be further diagnosed with other instruments.

This template can be used to collect a lot of device-level statistics. Before starting profiling, select the Record Settings in the Inspector pane and select the statistics that you are interested in collecting.

Figure 11-9 shows some of the available statistics. The section "Select statistics to list" (at the bottom) shows all the items that can be monitored, while "System statistics" (the second section from the top) displays the items that have been selected along with legends for the graph.

At the end of profiling, you should see results similar to those shown in Figure 11-10.

The top section shows the statistics over time. In Figure 11-10, it shows the Total Threads, % User Load, % Total Load, and % System Load statistics selected in Figure 11-9.

Because the Activity Monitor works at device level, the pie chart and line graphs shown in the Detail pane are snapshots. It shows four charts:

% CPU
Top 5 apps consuming maximum CPU.

CPU Time
Apps running for the longest duration. This section is generally worthless because the system apps will take the top slots.

Real Memory Usage (pie chart)
Top 5 apps in terms of total memory usage. You do not want your app to be in this list for an elongated duration.

Real Memory Usage (line graph)
This also visualizes the top 5 apps in terms of total memory usage, but in a line chart format.

Figure 11-9. Activity Monitor statistics selector

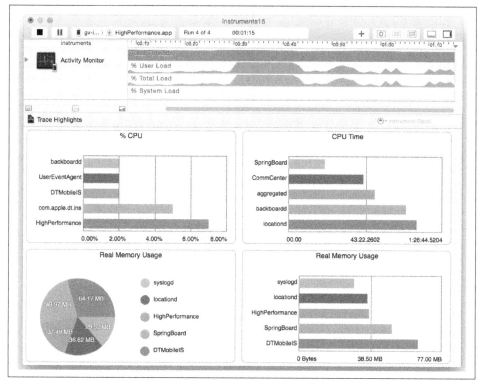

Figure 11-10. Instruments—Activity Monitor

Allocations

The Allocations trace template helps identify abandoned memory in the app. *Abandoned memory* is memory that has been allocated but is not needed anymore; it still *can* be deallocated.

Technically, abandoned memory is still legal because it is referenced by some part of the app—it's just that it is never actually used. Essentially, this is a memory leak, and you do not want that in the final release.

Allocating memory once and never using it may not be a big issue if the memory usage is not high. However, if the allocation is repetitive, it will all add up, resulting in memory hogging and leading to an app crash.

Examples include unfinished features that allocate memory for the feature object but do not ever use it. This is a trivial example, and it is far more complex to identify such scenarios in the real world.

Follow these steps to identify abandoned memory:

1. Choose the Allocations template to profile the app.

2. Identify an initial state to test.

3. Execute the steps that will take your app from the initial state to another and back.

   For example, the steps might be to log in, interact with the app, and then log out. In the case of a news app, you might go to a specific category, read an article, and then go back to the category screen.

4. Click the Mark Generation button in Display Settings (see Figure 11-11) to take a heap snapshot.

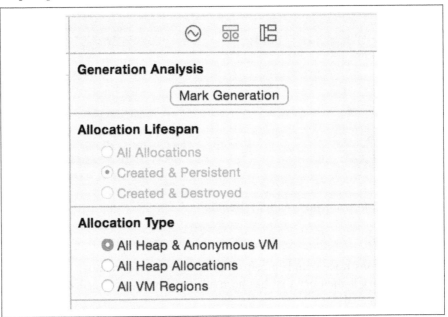

Figure 11-11. Allocations—Mark Generation button

5. Repeat steps 3 and 4 multiple times.

6. Analyze the objects captured in the snapshots to locate the abandoned memory.

On completion, you will have data similar to that shown in Figure 11-12.

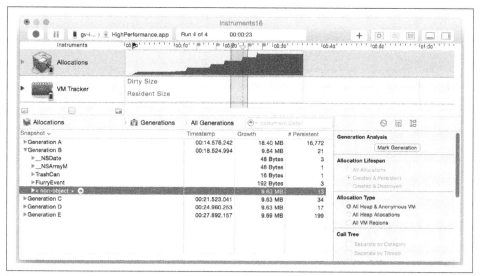

Figure 11-12. Allocations—summary

In Figure 11-12, the Allocations instrument shows a steady increase in memory usage over time (see the graph on the top). When the Mark Generation button is tapped, it creates snapshots that are available as Generations. The Details pane shows five generations, Generation A through Generation E.

In this specific case, generations B through E show a steady increase of about 9.5 MB each. On expanding Generation B, we can see that a strange <non-object> entry takes up over 99% of the extra memory. In a typical memory analysis, this may be hard to debug since its type is unknown and as such we may never know what to look for.

Clicking the arrow next to the item shows the details of the <non-object> allocation (see Figure 11-13).

Of all the <non-object> memory allocations, the one that we are interested is the one that contributes significantly to the extra memory consumed. In Figure 11-13, the data is sorted by Size in descending order. The first item shows that the memory was allocated in the method -[TrashCan init], reflected in the Responsible Caller column. The Extended Detail view in the Inspector pane on the right shows the complete stacktrace during the call, which reveals the call tree as given in Example 11-1.

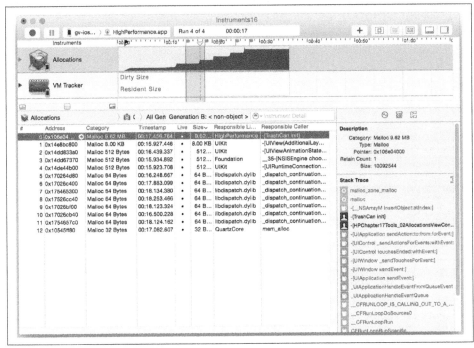

Figure 11-13. Allocation—details

Example 11-1. Stacktrace

```
malloc_zone_malloc
malloc
-[__NSArrayM insertObject:atIndex:]
-[TrashCan init]
-[HPChapter17Tools_02AllocationsViewCon...]
-[UIApplication sendAction:to:from:forEvent:]
```

The stacktrace reveals that an event was intercepted in the app that called a method in `HPChapter17Tools_02AllocationsViewController` that called the `-[TrashCan init]` method.

This is very useful information that can now help us fix the app.

Leaks

The Leaks trace template helps analyze general memory usage and checks for memory leaks—something that you will definitely want to safeguard your app against. It also provides statistics on object allocations by class as well as memory address histories for all active allocations and leaked blocks.

The Leaks template is comprised of the Allocations and Leaks instruments. We studied the Allocations instrument in the previous section.

The Leaks instrument finds memory references that are unreachable. Memory allocated for the Objective-C classes is reported with their names, whereas other references, like C structs, are reported as anonymous entities and appear in the report as Malloc-*size*.

Using the Leaks template is pretty straightforward. Just start it and it will start collecting the data.

Figure 11-14 shows results from a run that shows several memory leaks in the app.

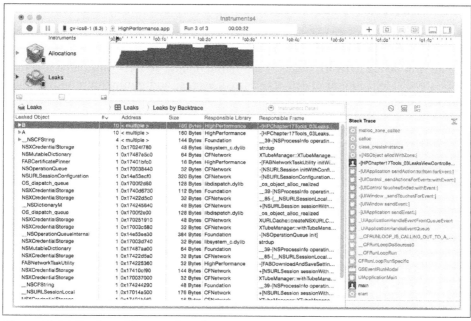

Figure 11-14. Leaks—objects and stacktrace

The Leaks instrument shows a few red bars at the top of the display. Those are the moments when the leaks happened. The higher the bar, the larger the leak. The Detail pane lists which objects leaked, with their total leak count and the size of the overall memory leak. The Extended Detail view in the Inspector pane shows the stacktrace, which is useful for debugging the app.

In a real-world app, catching memory leaks is a very tedious process and may require several hours of testing.

As a practice, continue to check for memory leaks for every update to the code. Divide your app into logical sections and run Leaks on each section.

Network

The Network trace template helps analyze network bandwidth connections made by the app. Excessive use of network, connections to multiple domains, downloading identical content multiple times, and using insecure connections are some of the concerns that, if found, must be addressed.

The template is comprised of the Connections instrument. Figure 11-15 shows results from using the Network trace template. The Details pane provides the details that you will need to debug network usage. It shows the remote address (hostname if reverse DNS is available), amount of data transferred, average and minimum roundtrip time, and other details.

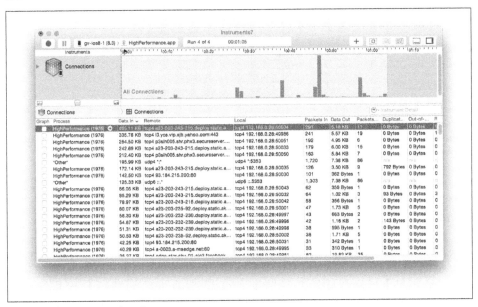

Figure 11-15. Network—Connections

Time Profiler

The Time Profiler trace template captures stacktrace details at regular intervals (sampling). It is comprised of one instrument of the same name.

As you interact with the app, it can record the number of times a method was on top of the stack. You can use this number to identify which methods are either being invoked several times or taking up a lot of the execution time. If a particular method was on the top in 100 out of 1,000 samples, it is fair to assume that it takes approximately 10% of the overall execution.

If a method is found to be under execution for large part of the app, it *may* be a cause of worry. The reasons may range from a need for continuous user interaction to excessive processing being done by the app. Depending upon the app, it may be an area of concern. For example, a gaming app may require continuous user interaction, but a utility app may not. Similarly, a video or running animation may be expected to perform excessive processing, but a mail app may not.

Figure 11-16 shows data captured using the Time Profiler trace template.

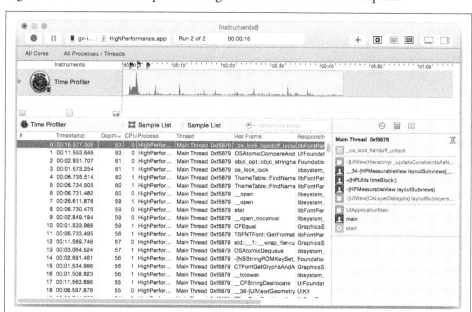

Figure 11-16. Time Profiler

In Figure 11-16, the stacktrace reveals that -[HPMeasurableView layoutSubviews] may be a possible culprit if the app is running slowly.

Xcode View Debugger

As more functionalities are added in an app and as the UI becomes more sophisticated, it not only adds complexities in design and implementation but also impacts rendering performance. As the rendered view hierarchy becomes more nested (or as the number of views in the hierarchy increases), the more time it takes to render, update, or apply animations, including showing options for a `UIPickerView` or scrolling in a `UIScrollView` or `UITableView`.

Xcode's view debugger helps you look at the view hierarchy when the app is running.

The view debugger can be activated by clicking the Debug View Hierarchy button in the Debug area toolbar. On clicking, the main thread is suspended and the primary view area in Xcode shows the current snapshot of the view hierarchy. You can drag around the snapshot to see a 3D perspective, as shown in Figure 11-17.

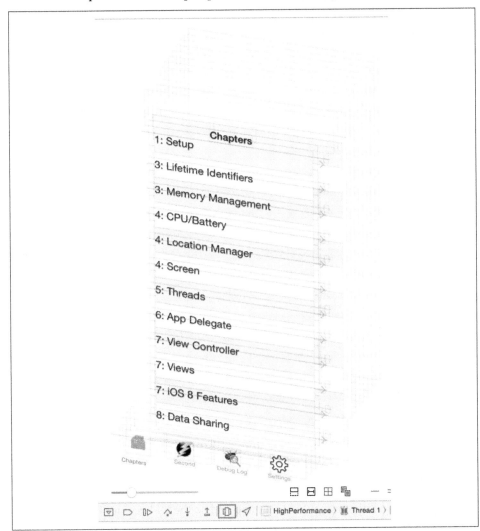

Figure 11-17. Xcode view debugger—view hierarchy

If you click on any UI element in the view hierarchy and open the Utilities area, you should be able to get more details about the view (see Figure 11-18).

Figure 11-18. View Debugger—details

PonyDebugger

When using the Xcode view debugger, the main thread is suspended when the debugger is in action. As such, you cannot track the view hierarchy without pausing an ongoing animation.

PonyDebugger (*https://github.com/square/PonyDebugger*) is a remote debugging toolset from Square Inc. that solves this problem. In addition, the device does not have to be physically connected to the development machine.

It is comprised of two components:

- A *gateway server* that forms the bridge between the app and the developer's view
- A *client* that connects to the gateway server

The gateway server is written in Python and can be installed using the commands given in Example 11-2.

Example 11-2. Installing the PonyDebugger gateway server

```
$ curl -s \
https://cloud.github.com/downloads/square/PonyDebugger/bootstrap-ponyd.py | \
  python - --ponyd-symlink=/usr/local/bin/ponyd ~/Library/PonyDebugger ❶
$ ponyd serve --listen-interface=192.168.0.1 ❷
```

❶ Download and install the ponyd daemon.

❷ Start the server. Use the IP address of your development machine. Configure the port using the `--listen-port` argument. It binds to `127.0.0.1:9000` by default.

Browse to *http://192.168.0.1:9000* to see the list of devices connected. You should see output similar to Figure 11-19.

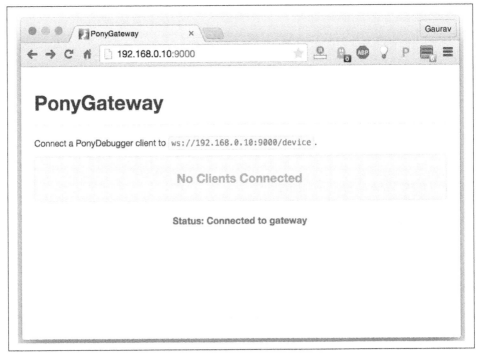

Figure 11-19. PonyDebugger—browsing the gateway server

The client API is available via CocoaPods for integration in the app. The name of the Pod is `PonyDebugger`. Example 11-3 provides representative code to integrate it in the app.

Example 11-3. PonyDebugger—client API

```
#import <PonyDebugger/PonyDebugger.h>

-(void)setupPonyDebugger { ❶
    PDDebugger *debugger = [PDDebugger defaultInstance]; ❷
    [debugger connectToURL:
        [NSURL URLWithString:@"ws://192.168.0.1:9000"]]; ❸

    [debugger enableRemoteLogging]; ❹
    [debugger enableNetworkTrafficDebugging]; ❺
        //[debugger forwardAllNetworkTraffic]; ❻
        [debugger enableViewHierarchyDebugging]; ❼
    [debugger enableCoreDataDebugging]; ❽
}
```

❶   Helper method to set up the client. Call this from the method `application:did
    FinishLaunchingWithOptions:` before any network call happens.

❷   `PDDebugger` is the object to configure.

❸   The URL to connect to. Must be `ws` (WebSocket protocol).

❹   Allows logs to be logged to the gateway. To enable logging, use the method `PDLog`
    instead of `NSLog`.

❺   Enables network logging, by swizzling `NSURLConnectionDelegate` classes.

❻   To let PonyDebugger find all such classes, use this method.

❼   Allows viewing the view hierarchy from the gateway.

❽   Allows viewing Core Data objects from the gateway. At the time of writing, it
    does not support updating records.

Because using PonyDebugger can leave your app open to all inter-
ceptions, enable it only in development/debug builds.

Once connected to the device, the browser shows data for all sections that have been
enabled.

The Elements tab shows the view hierarchy. Expanding the tree and selecting a node
highlights the corresponding view in the app. Figure 11-20 shows a `UITextField`

selected in the browser on the left and the corresponding view highlighted in the app on the right.

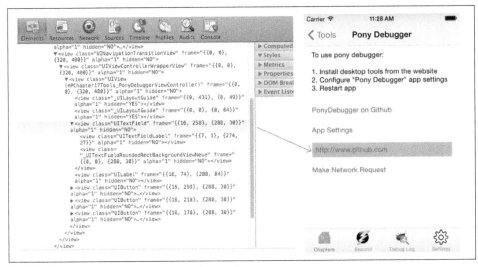

Figure 11-20. PonyDebugger—view hierarchy

In Figure 11-21, you can see the Network tab, which shows the list of all network requests in chronological order after app start. A few important things to keep in mind:

- The different domains to which connections are made
- Time taken for individual responses
- Data transferred for individual requests

Note that because the tool intercepts NSURLConnection delegate callbacks, it can handle only http and https requests. If you have connections using raw sockets or otherwise, PonyDebugger does not intercept them.

You can click on a request in the Network tab and get details of the specific request, similar to what is shown in Figure 11-22. You can see the request and response headers, response data, and any cookies sent and received. For POST or PUT requests, you can also see the request body.

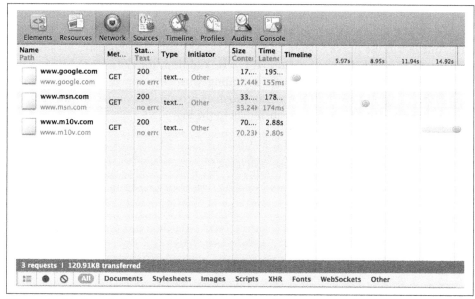

Figure 11-21. PonyDebugger—Network: viewing all requests

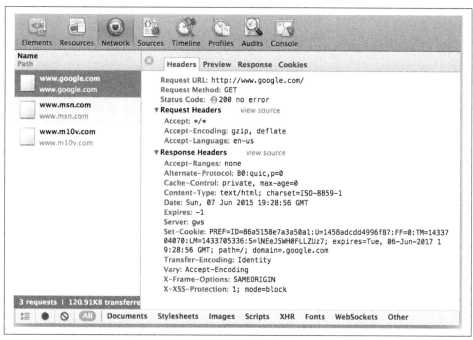

Figure 11-22. PonyDebugger—Network: debugging a single request

The Console shows the messages logged using calls to the NSLog method (see Figure 11-23). NSLog writes messages not only to the Xcode console during debugging, but also to the Apple System Logger (ASL). ASL calls are expensive because they require interprocess communication (IPC). In addition, the data logged is available through Xcode in non-debug builds, including when the app is installed from the App Store. Logging sensitive information, such as private keys or passwords, can pose security therats. Watch out for any such data in the log.

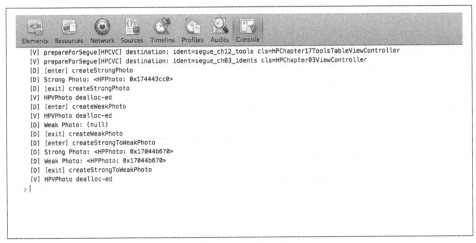

Figure 11-23. PonyDebugger—Console: remote logging

Using PonyDebugger's gateway server to monitor and analyze data is fairly straightforward. And because it is open source, you can update the code to hook into the socket to analyze data to automate testing.

Charles

The Charles proxy server from XK72 is a tool to monitor and manage http and https requests.

We briefly introduced this tool in "Charles" on page 245, but we will now discuss it in more depth.

The tool can *record* all the requests under what it calls a *session*. So, a session can have multiple requests. You can start or stop the recording by navigating to Proxy → Start Recording or Proxy → Stop Recording, respectively.

Each session can be provided with an inclusion and/or exclusion list of URLs that can be configured by navigating to Proxy → Recording Settings and selecting the Include or Exclude tab, respectively, as shown in Figure 11-24. A URL will be included in the session if either the Include list is empty or it is in that list but not in the Exclude list.

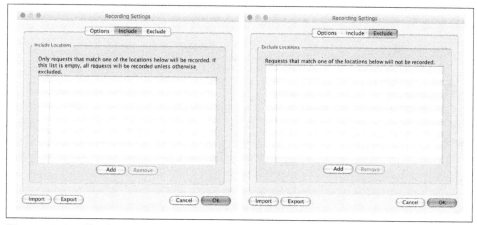

Figure 11-24. Charles—URL inclusion and exclusion lists

The URLs used in a session can be viewed in chronological order, as shown in Figure 11-25, or in a structured format as a tree with the domain at the top and path-separated child nodes, as shown in Figure 11-26. If you want to check the order of requests, the first format is useful. If you want to debug requests from a specific domain or path, the second format comes in handy.

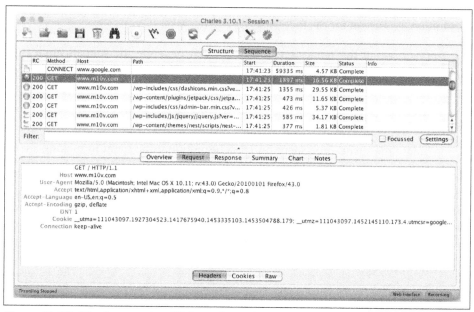

Figure 11-25. Charles—session URLs in chronological order (Sequence)

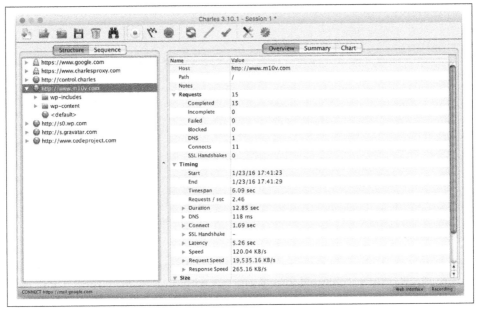

Figure 11-26. Charles—session URLs in a tree (Structure)

Using the structured format can give you a quick summary, as shown in Figure 11-26. In addition, it is useful for the following debugging tasks:

- You can see all the requests within a domain or a specific subpath under the domain in the Overview tab. http and https requests can be further drilled down into. Figure 11-27 shows an overview comprised of the following:

  — Requests (total requests made, completed and failed breakdown, server connects, and number of SSL handshakes)

  — Total time spent, time spent on DNS resolution, time spent in making a connection to the host, and SSL handshake time (if applicable)

  — Request (for POST and PUT requests) and response speeds in KBps

  — Request and response sizes in KB

- For time, speed, and size data, details are available as total, minimum, maximum, and average values, providing meaningful insights into the network requests made by the app.

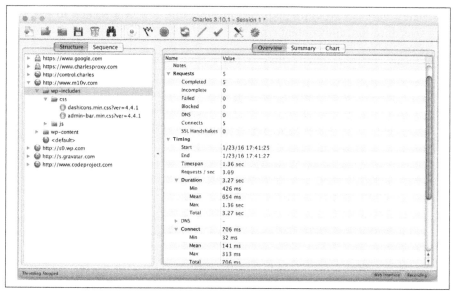

Figure 11-27. Charles—overview of requests and responses for a selected subpath

- The Summary tab provides the HTTP response code, content type (MIME type), header size, body size, and time taken to complete the request for each URL under the given subpath, as shown in Figure 11-28.

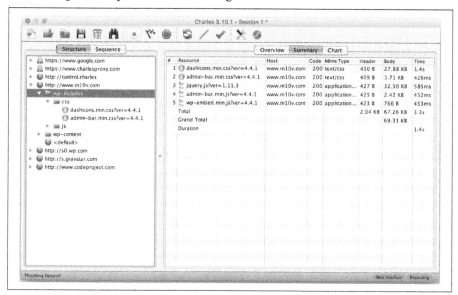

Figure 11-28. Charles—summary of all individual requests for a selected subpath

- The Chart tab provides graphical insights into the data related to the timeline, size, duration, and content type:

  1. The Timeline subtab shows relative time when the individual requests were made and how much time was spent making the connection, waiting for a response, and receiving the response (counting from the first byte received). This is shown in Figure 11-29. This data can be used to identify slow URLs or domains that take a long time to connect or respond.

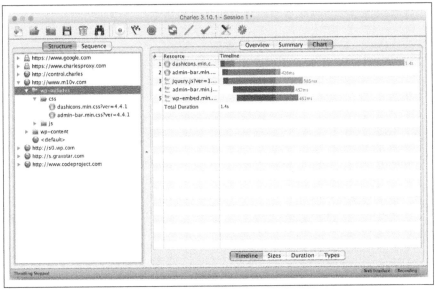

Figure 11-29. Charles—relative timeline of requests for a selected subpath

  2. The Sizes subtab shows a histogram of the response sizes, sorted with the largest on top (Figure 11-30). This data can be used to optimize response sizes or identify a need to increase server capacity or add edge servers for cached content.

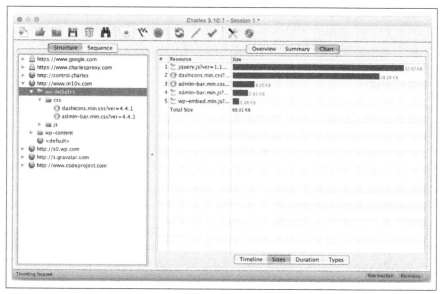

Figure 11-30. Charles—response sizes for the requests for a selected subpath

3. The Duration tab (Figure 11-31) provides response times for each request, sorted with the longest on top. This data can be used to identify slow requests/URLs and optimize the server accordingly.

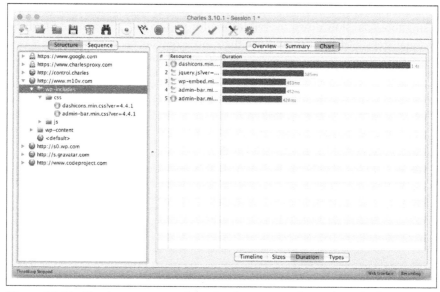

Figure 11-31. Charles—response times for the requests for a selected subpath

Charles is an exhaustive tool for monitoring networking from the app. It not only enables you to identify all the requests made, but also to drill down into individual requests to identify any bottlenecks in terms of time and size.

Summary

Tools are a developer's helping hand. When you use inline code to measure parameters such as memory and CPU usage, you may not get a true picture because the code will also use resources. Tools provide a nonintrusive option for measuring various aspects of performance.

With Apple's Accessibilty inspector, you can test the correctness of the accessibility-related attributes of the app.

With Instruments, you can monitor performance parameters such as memory used, check for possible memory leaks, see the view hierarchy and its complexity, and more. Any peak or trough in the related graphs should be an area of concern. Similarly, an ever-increasing memory-used graph is an indication of potential memory leaks.

Use PonyDebugger when you want to monitor and debug the view hierarchy without pausing the app execution. It can also help you monitor Core Data usage.

Network activities can be monitored extensively using Charles, especially when you want to test various scenarios without being intrusive to the app code.

Using tools can slow down overall testing for performance because it involves a lot of manual steps. Still, you should use them on a regular basis to keep the state of your app healthy.

CHAPTER 12

Instrumentation and Analytics

When we develop an app, the initial set of optimizations are based on best practices, guidelines, and the data collected from developer machines and/or the lab. However, that is only the first set of data available for analysis.

It isn't until the app is released that we begin collecting real data across devices and geographies that will help identify usage patterns and various scenarios that need tuning.

In Chapter 1, we looked at the parameters that we want to measure and fine-tune the app for, including the following:

- Memory usage
- Response time
- Network usage
- Local storage

Now that we have discussed various strategies for improving the user experience, and identified specific ways to make apps more performant, it's time to collect data from real users, analyze app usage, identify any bottlenecks, provide fixes and updates, and make users happier.

This chapter is about analyzing *production* data collected to identify app usage trends, user behavior, areas for improvement and optimization through instrumentation, analytics, and real user monitoring (RUM).

Vocabulary

Before we proceed further, let's look at some vocabulary that will be useful as we progress through this chapter:

Attribute
> A parameter whose value needs to be captured. Examples include app version, OS version, location, language, memory in use, and so on.

Event
> Anything that happens in the app, whether it is triggered by the user or the app itself.
>
> Examples of user-initiated events include logging in, watching a video, and so on. Examples of app-initiated events include cold start, background sync, fetching mail, and so on.
>
> An event is a collection of attributes comprising the OS Version, device type, time taken to cold start the app, bytes transferred in background sync, memory used in fetching mail, and so on.

Funnel
> A tool to measure how users move through a series of events.
>
> A funnel can be used to identify usage patterns and common places of task or app abandonment.

Instrumentation
> The ability to monitor or measure the level of performance and to diagnose errors. In the context of apps, it refers to sending corresponding events to the server for analysis.

Source code instrumentation
> Injecting code into the app to enable instrumentation.
>
> The injected code can be handcrafted by developers or generated automatically using tools at compile time, or you can use method swizzling to enable monitoring at runtime.
>
> To instrument an app in production running on a user's mobile device, source code instrumentation is the only option. Tools such as Instruments cannot be used because the mobile device is not connected to the development machine. Tools such as PonyDebugger or Charles cannot be used because the mobile device may not be in the same network as the engineering team, or might be behind a firewall or otherwise unreachable.

Analytics
> Discovery and communication of meaningful patterns in data.

In the context of apps, data is collected through app instrumentation.

Cohort
A group of users who share a common characteristic over a certain period of time.

Examples of cohorts include users of the same gender, users in the same city, and users who start using the app on a given date.

Cohort analysis
Performing analytics on the data segmented by cohorts.

Attribution
Assigning credit for sales and conversions to touchpoints in conversion paths.

A user may have multiple options to start to make a purchase or perform a task. The attribution model dictates what option or options will get the credit and hence the share of money spent in an ad campaign.

Real user monitoring
A passive monitoring technology that records all user interaction with the app, sends it to the servers, and helps monitor usage, trends, and any problems.

Instrumentation

There are several techniques available for instrumentation, including binary code rewriting, and in-place, on-the-fly, link-time, and source code instrumentation.

For our discussion, we are interested in source code instrumentation. This can help us perform app analysis, typically from user navigation and resource usage perspectives.

We first introduced instrumentation in Chapter 1. In Example 1-2, we created the class `HPInstrumentation`, which allowed us to log events (defined as occurrence or nonoccurrence of an expected behavior).

For example, if we want to track the performance of a *cache* component, in its method to retrieve a cached object, we can log either a `Cache Hit` event or a `Cache Miss` event.

Similarly, in the case of an ecommerce app, we might want to determine which screens the user viewed, the products that were viewed, how much time was spent on individual products, and so on.

Conceptually, instrumentation is no different from logging, except that with instrumentation the intent is to persist this data on the server for a substantially longer duration and use it for analysis, either later using offline batch processing jobs or in real time.

Let's now look into the three phases of instrumentation, namely planning, implementation, and deployment.

Planning

Instrumentation requires deep planning. The first step to planning is deciding whether to use a third-party library or to build one yourself.

When you're first starting out, it may be prudent to choose a third-party option. As the data, volume, and feature requirements grow, you can then invest in building your own library in-house.

Some of the popular third-party analytics SDKs for iOS include the following:

Flurry (http://developer.yahoo.com/flurry)
One of the more popular SDKs. Always free. Supports WatchKit.

Mixpanel (https://mixpanel.com)
Supports more complex features, such as A/B testing, without writing code and surveys. Free for up to 25,000 data points per month.

Appsee (https://www.appsee.com)
Supports interaction heat maps (see Figure 12-1) and video recordings of the app under use. No free setup.

Upsight (http://www.upsight.com/analytics)
Supports attribution and cohort analytics. Has free and paid editions.

Google Analytics (http://bit.ly/google-analytics-sdk-ios)
Offers more features from the social and ecommerce perspectives. Free for up to 200,000 hits per user per day and 500 per session. These limits apply to the premium account as well.

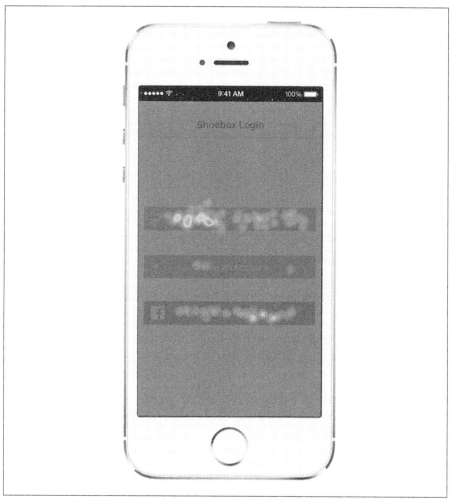

Figure 12-1. Heat map of user interaction in a view controller (image courtesy of Appsee)

There are several more in the market, but these serve as a good starter list.

These are some of the important features you will want in the analytics engine (it is assumed that logging an event by its name is always available and that basic data such as device info, locale, time zone, location, network/career, etc. can always be captured):

Extended events
Be able to add custom parameters or dimensions to any event.

Cohort analysis
Use dimensions from extended events, and be able to filter and analyze against specific values.

Timed events
Be able to time events to capture the duration.

Log all page views
Be able to instrument show/hide of view controllers.

User
Be able to set a user. That will provide the ability to track anonymous versus logged-in events.

Transaction
Be able to provide a monetary value for a transaction. Useful in ecommerce or apps with in-app purchases.

A/B testing
Be able to conduct experiments or A/B tests and monitor user behavior.

Real-time data
Be able to capture data in real time or near real time. Depending on the app, the acceptable delay in reporting the latest events may range from a few minutes to a few hours.

Security
Be able to monitor security. How secure is communication with the server, and how secure is data on the server?

Session playback
Be able to record videos and play them back for closer app-usage monitoring or to better identify erroneous scenarios and fix them faster.

Use this feature with caution, as this may have privacy and legal implications. The best place to use this feature is in private user study sessions.

If you intend to implement this option, make sure to include a prominent indicator to inform the user about the recording. In addition, you'll need to obtain explicit permission from the user before recording.

Heat maps
Be able to generate heat maps to identify hot spots and blind spots in the app.

Attribution

Be able to track click as well as app-install attributions.

Campaigns

Support managed versus self-directed campaigns. More useful for marketing analytics.

Funnels

Be able to define funnels using event flows.

Raw events

Last but not the least, the icing on the cake will be if raw data is available for more complex processing. This may be from an in-house solution.

Implementation

Once the instrumentation solution has been identified, the next step is the setup. For app instrumentation, you will need to:

Identify metrics

This comes from a collaboration of product, marketing, and engineering teams. The product manager will want user experience statistics, the marketing team will be interested in app usage and sections of user interest, while the engineering team will be eager to know about app performance.

Define events

Define the event names and related dimensions to support the key performance indicators (KPIs).

If the engineering team wants to know about average and peak memory usage data, the event (let's call it `Heap Size`) should contain data about used memory, free memory (recall the code from Example 2-40), and the time for which the app has been up and running.

Similarly, as another example, when the product manager wants to know if the new autocomplete feature has been well received, she may want not only the event where it was used but also how many times changes were made *after* auto-completion was used to measure its effectiveness.

You may want support for timing events. For example, in a news app, it may be of interest to note how much time a user spends on a particular news item or category listing. Depending upon the SDK that you use, you may have built-in support for timed events.[1] If not, you may have to implement a watch and monitor time yourself.

Write code

Once all the events have been identified and you have determined when each of them will be invoked, you need to write code.

As a good practice, start by creating a class with all the methods necessary for your app. Example 12-1 includes some of the common methods that your app will need. Start with the baseline and add as required over time.

Example 12-1. Instrumentation class—the methods

```
@interface HPInstrumentation

+(void)logEvent:(NSString *)name params:(NSDictionary *)params;  ❶

+(void)startTimerForEvent:(NSString *)name params:(NSDictionary *)params;
+(void)endTimerForEvent:(NSString *)name params:(NSDictionary *)params;  ❷

+(void)logViewControllerDidAppear:(UIViewController *)vc;  ❸

+(void)setLocation:(CLLocation *)location;  ❹
+(void)setUserId:(NSString *)userId;  ❺

+(void)logError:(NSString *)name
    message:(NSString *)message
    exception:(NSException *)e;  ❻

+(void)setMinimumTimeBetweenSessions:(NSInterval)interval;  ❼

@end
```

❶ Must-have method, logs generic event.

❷ Log timed events.

❸ Log that a view controller was viewed by the user.

❹ Set location information for all subsequent events.

❺ Set the user ID for all subsequent events. Useful for logged-in experience.

---

1 Flurry is one such SDK that supports timed events. See "Capture Event Duration" in the Flurry Developer Docs (*http://yhoo.it/1cTSpNL*).

❻ Special-purpose event to log errors.

❼ Special handling on how to count sessions, which impacts the daily active users (DAU) count. Should putting the app in the background and then in the foreground result in a new session, or should there be a minimum time gap between the two?

You can use the Aspects CocoaPod (*https://github.com/steipete/Aspects*) to set up tracking common events transparently. For example, if you want to track viewDidAppear: for all UIViewControllers, you can use the code given in Example 12-2.

Example 12-2. Using the Aspects CocoaPod for transparent method tracing

```
[UIViewController aspect_hookSelector:@selector(viewDidAppear:) ❶
 withOptions:AspectPositionAfter ❷
 usingBlock:^(id<AspectInfo> info, BOOL animated) { ❸
  NSDictionary *eventParams = @{
   @"ViewControllerClass": [info.instance class]
  }; ❹
  [HPInstrumentation logEvent:@"viewDidAppear"
  withParameters:eventParams]; ❺
} error:NULL];
```

❶ Attach a hook to the method viewDidAppear: of the UIViewController class.

❷ The hook (the custom code) must be called *after* the original method is invoked.

❸ Implement the hook. The parameters to this block are id<AspectInfo>, which provides the object in whose context the block has been called, and the parameters to the original method (viewDidAppear:, in this case).

❹ Set the parameters to the event being logged.

❺ Log the event.

There can be more methods defined for special-purpose needs—for example, methods that can describe transactional operations such as a purchase or a refund.[2]

---

2 The Google Analytics API supports tracking transactional events (*https://goo.gl/ibvYYt*).

Verify

Do not forget to test before release. Test not only for correctness but also for scale. Ensure that the third-party service that you are banking upon has enough capacity to not melt down under load from your app's events.

Deployment

The final stage is to deploy. It involves deploying servers to production (if using an in-house solution) and releasing the app to the App Store.

Using data to generate reports and identify patterns and trends is not part of instrumentation per se but is important in the analytics stage, which we discuss next.

Analytics

Analytics is about discovering and presenting meaningful patterns in data, and it generally favors *data visualization*—mostly graphs, geographical maps, and heat maps—to communicate the insights.

In the context of apps, analytics uses data from instrumentation events to work toward presenting insights against the KPIs planned for.

Analytics solutions will generally process a part of the data to provide high-level trends. The percentage sampling may be done either on the client side or on the server side. If done on the client side, it is possible that out of all the events, only a few of them are reported to the server. If done on the server side, the client may send all the data, but the server may process only a fraction of available events.

Analytics is very useful to identify trends and work in distribution KPIs. You can use it to identify average session duration or average transaction amount per user. But do not use this to track, for example, how many times your app has been installed. There are special-purpose APIs available for accurately tracking these statistics.

Top-Down Versus Bottom-Up Analytics

A *top-down* analytics system sits in the client app and actively monitors user behavior. Monitored activites may include how deep (vertically) a user goes in a content stream, the views that a user interacts with and the view controllers a user transitions across, time spent with a segment of the app, and so on.

A *bottom-up* analytics system looks at correlating server-side information to reconstruct user behavior and experience. For example, you can use the API calls to identify how may entries in a content stream were requested for a user and draw conclusions about the stream depth the user went to.

Both approaches have their own caveats.

A top-down approach can result in high network usage and loss of data if the connection is terminated or the network is unavailable, or increased local storage if a local persistent buffer is used for batch processing.

A bottom-up approach will not have real data but will only be an asymptotic reconstruction of the user behavior. You may never know how much time was spent viewing an item in a feed, but only know that the corresponding item was fetched.

Real User Monitoring

Real user monitoring is an approach to monitoring an app to capture and analyze *every transaction of every user*. It relies on in-app (server or client) monitoring services that monitor components in action, their functionality, the app's responsiveness, overall resource usage, and various other parameters.

It is also known by various other names, including end-user monitoring (EUM), real-user measurement, real-user metrics, and so on.

Analytics Versus Real User Monitoring

Analytics also provides these insights. Perhaps you're wondering what the big deal is about RUM. You might say, "It's all about instrumenting the app and analyzing the data."

Fair enough. Good point. Analytics and RUM serve identical purposes—that is, they both instrument the app, analyze data, and provide reports.

The big difference between analytics and RUM is that analytics works on partial data, referred to as *samples*, to provide high-level trends.

Various products to help instrument and analyze your app brand themselves as analytics rather than RUM products because they track only samples.

Using RUM

Because RUM is about tracking all events rather than samples, you should use it to monitor mission-critical events. Some examples of these include the following:

- Any errors, including app crashes or invalid state
- Quality changes in the app after a new release
- Behavioral changes related to new features
- Tracking all steps in a transaction

Summary

App instrumentation is as important as functional implementation. It is the gateway to insights into app quality, app health, user behavior, and more.

Use analytics tools to sift through enormous volumes of data to identify patterns to those insights. You can create a sequence of segues through the app usage to study user behavior, identifying common pain points or steps in the overall sequence where the user drops off. This is particularly useful in steps that ultimately lead to a monetary transaction, as you will be especially interested to learn common reasons for the drop-off in those cases.

RUM should be used to monitor mission-critical steps, including but not limited to app quality and user behavior.

Again, remember not to overwhelm the app. Overuse of instrumentation can put severe load not only on the client app on the device but also the server app trying to handle and process that data.

Instrumentation is not a replacement for debugging. Use debugging tools on development devices only.

iOS 9

iOS 9, released on September 9, 2015, brings in changes that can help improve app performance. This part discusses these changes and how you can use them effectively.

iOS 9

iOS 9 includes some important changes that can impact how your app works.

Apart from improving the performance of standard components and the operating system in general, several other features can boost your app's performance.

In this chapter, we discuss the following:

Application lifecycle
> New features have been introduced in iOS, and a few of the old features have been overhauled in ways that impact performance techniques.

User interface
> New views are available and may boost rendering performance. A completely new way of showing websites is also available.

Extensions
> Two new extensions have been introduced in iOS 9. If you implement them, you will need to take care of their performance.

App thinning
> You can now not only optimize your app manually, but also let Apple's app optimizer do it for you for the device on which it will be installed—something to look forward to.

A complete list of changes in iOS 9 is available on the Apple developer website (*http://apple.co/1Bn94oT*).

Application Lifecycle

iOS 9 provides new options to start and activate an app, and also imposes restrictions on existing ones.

Universal links now replace custom URL schemes for general use. Custom URL schemes are still available, but using the feature to detect the presence of an app is now highly restricted. You can no longer invade users' privacy to test hundreds of apps for their presence on the device.

The new Spotlight-integrated in-app search provides new options for users to discover your app, even if it is not installed on their device. This means incorporating new features, writing new code, and making it work well.

Universal Links

In iOS 8, the only way to launch another app, specifically from the Web, was using custom schemes (we discussed this in "Deep links" on page 167). This technique is still available, but with strong restrictions.

Your app can still use `canOpenURL:` to detect availability of an app on the device. However, to prevent abuse of this method,[1] iOS 9 restricted the invocation of this method to a maximum of 50 unique schemes only.

 If you compiled your app against iOS 8 or lower, the first 50 unique schemes will be tracked on the device. If you compiled your app against iOS 9, you *must* include the full list of schemes (maximum 50) that the app will open in its lifecycle.

iOS 9 introduces *univeral links*, which allow your app to handle `http` or `https` links that were previously available for launch only from Safari.

The general outline of the execution is:

1. Source app calls `openURL:` with an `http` or `https` URL.
2. OS detects if there is an app installed that can handle that specific URL:

   - If yes, launch the app.
   - If no, open the URL using Safari.

The advantage of this approach is that the URL can always be opened. Or in other words, `canOpenURL:` for these links will always return `YES`, and you do not have to worry about bifurcating the flow in your app.

---

1 For example, privacy concerns were raised after Twitter launched its "app graph" feature (*http://bit.ly/twitter-appgraph*) that collected lists of the apps installed on devices.

The mobile website can use Smart App Banners[2] to incentivize users to download the app.

To use this feature, you need to configure the following:

1. Add the `com.apple.developer.associated-domains` entitlement to the app, as shown in Figure 13-1.

Figure 13-1. Associated domains entitlement

The value must be `applinks:{domain-to-handle}`. Wildcard subdomains are not available. Each subdomain must be registered individually.

2. Add a signed JSON file *apple-app-site-association* with app and path associations that the app can handle.

    Use the same key as used to sign the app.

This establishes the trust between the app and the domain.

For example, for the entitlement `applinks:ios.mydomain.com`, and with the association file shown in Example 13-1, the app can handle `http[s]://ios.mydomain.com/mypath/` and `http[s]://ios.mydomain.com/basepath/` and its subpaths.

---

2 iOS Developer Library, "Promoting Apps with Smart App Banners" (*http://apple.co/1TzDzxp*).

Example 13-1. Universal links: app site association file

```
{
    "applinks": {  ❶
        "details": {  ❷
            "ABCDEFGHIJ.com.mydomain.bundleid": {  ❸
                "paths": [  ❹
                    "/mypath/",
                    "/basepath/*"
                ]
            }
        }
    }
}
```

❶ The service `applinks`. The same file is also used for `activitycontinuation`.

❷ The `details` section—must be named as is.

❸ The complete key for the app. The format is `{team-id}.{app-bundle-id}`.

❹ List of paths; can be wildcard.

Use the `openssl` command-line tool to sign the file (see Example 13-2).

Example 13-2. Universal links: signing the site association file

```
cat content.json | openssl smime
    -sign
    -inkey app-signer-private.key
    -signer app-signer-certificate.pem
    -noattr
    -nodetach
    -outform DER
    > apple-app-site-association
```

To handle the URL, implement the `application:continueUserActivity:restora
tionHandler:` method of the `UIApplicationDelegate` protocol. Example 13-3 shows
an example of how to handle the link.

Example 13-3. Universal links: handling the link

```
- (BOOL)application:(UIApplication *)application
    continueUserActivity:(NSUserActivity *)userActivity
    restorationHandler:(void (^)(NSArray * restorableObjects))restorationHandler {  ❶

    NSURL *url = userActivity.webpageURL;  ❷
    //process URL
```

```
    return YES;
}
```

❶   The app delegate callback.

❷   Use the `webpageURL` property to get the URL.

Search

App Search[3] provides new ways to search public information inside an app, even when it is not installed on the device. All such information can be surfaced to the users using Handoff, Siri Reminders, and Spotlight Search.

If the app is installed, it can be deep-linked into. If it is not installed, Safari can take the user to the web page. Universal links ensure that you need to provide only one URL.

Any content can be made available for indexing by Apple's servers. Local, on-device content is initially used during local searches only. As the content gains "popularity" across devices, it is sent to Apple's servers and indexed centrally to be made available across devices.

You can use App Search to help users with app discovery when the app is not installed and provide quick access to the contents when the app is installed. The user will install the app if it is not installed. If the app is installed, the user may be able to directly get to a specific result without you having to implement a custom search (moreover, the user won't need to go through a multistep navigation within the app, which adds to the overall user experience).

Now, as you use one or more of the available options, you will need to take care of the implementation performance within your app.

There are three ways in which the content can be surfaced:

- New methods and properties in the `NSUserActivity` class help you index items.
- The Core Spotlight framework helps add app-specific content to the on-device index and enable deep links into your app.
- Web markup lets you make your related web content searchable.

---

3 iOS Developer Library, "App Search Programming Guide" (*http://apple.co/1RZA8RN*).

NSUserActivity

NSUserActivity has new methods in iOS 9 to add the app states to the local index. The following new properties provide enhancements for local and public indexing:

- The property keywords can be used to link associated keywords.
- The property eligibleForSearch can be used to make the data available for local search.
- The property eligibleForPublicIndexing can be used to make the data available for public indexing (on Apple's servers) so that it can be used for search across devices.

Example 13-4 shows sample code to that effect.

Example 13-4. Adding to local index: NSUserActivity

```
NSUserActivity *activity = [[NSUserActivity alloc]
    initWithActivityType:@"com.mydomain.plist-activity-type"]; ❶

activity.title = @"iOS 9 Features"; ❷
activity.keywords = [NSSet setWithObjects:@"ios 9",
    @"new features", @"wwdc 2015", nil]; ❸
activity.userInfo = @{ ... }; ❹
activity.eligibleForSearch = YES; ❺
activity.eligibleForPublicIndexing = YES; ❻
[activity becomeCurrent]; ❼
```

❶ Create an activity with a registered activity type.

❷ Set the title, to appear in search results.

❸ Keywords associated with the data.

❹ Set an additional NSDictionary of data associated with the activity.

❺ Make the activity eligible for search.

❻ Mark the activity eligible for public indexing. The data will be sent to Apple's servers and indexed. It will appear in public Spotlight and Safari searches and be ranked based on *popularity index*.

❼ Mark the current state of the app (make the activity current). Once done, it is automatically added to the universal index (CSSearchableIndex).

Here are some tips for performance:

- Provide enough keywords to make the content searchable, but do not use too many keywords. Note that searches may be performed locally, and multiple keywords can not only dilute the ranking but also make search slower.

- userInfo can be used to store custom data associated with the activity. Because this data will be stored outside of the app, keep it minimal. This data will be serialized when creating the index and deserialized when the user lands on the search result. The more data there is, the longer it will take.

Core Spotlight

A new Core Spotlight[4] framework has been introduced in iOS 9. It helps your app participate in search by providing ways to index the content within your app and manage the on-device index. The content can be app provided or user generated.

Core Spotlight provides an API to make content searchable using a unique ID (unique per app) and perform update and delete operations. Once indexed, the data can be searched using Spotlight and Safari searches. If the item has an NSUserActiv ity associated with it, it can also be made available on the public index.

This framework provides more control over the structured data. Specifically, the requirement for a unique app ID makes the ultimate search for content in the designated app more streamlined.[5]

Example 13-5 shows sample code for using the Core Spotlight framework.

Example 13-5. Using Core Spotlight

```
//Adding content to index
#import <CoreSpotlight/CoreSpotlight.h> ❶
#import <MobileCoreServices/MobileCoreServices.h> ❷

-(void)addToIndex:(...) { ❸
    CSSearchableItemAttributeSet *attrs = [[CSSearchableItemAttributeSet alloc] ❹
        initWithItemContentType:(NSString *)kUTTypeText]; ❺

    attrs.title = @"Mango";
    attrs.contentDescription = @"King of Fruits";
    attrs.keywords = @["mango", "fruit", "vegetation"]; ❻

    CSSearchableItem *item = [[CSSearchableItem alloc]
        initWithUniqueIdentifier:@"mango"
```

---

4 iOS Developer Library, "Core Spotlight Framework" (*http://apple.co/1QFKy5I*).

5 Compare this with NSUserActivity, where a unique ID is not required. The developer may add it in the user Info dictionary, but it is optional.

```
            domainIdentifier:@"com.mydomain.item-domain"
            attributeSet:attrs]; ❼

    [[CSSearchableIndex defaultSearchableIndex] ❽
        indexSearchableItems:@[item] ❾
        completionHandler:^(NSError *e) { ❿
            if(e) {
                //handle error
            } else {
                //all is well
            }
    }];
}

//Handling search result link in AppDelegate
-(BOOL)application:(UIApplication *)application
    continueUserActivity:(NSUserActivity *)userActivity
    restorationHandler:(void (^)(NSArray *))restorationHandler { ⓫

    if([CSSearchableItemActionType isEqualToString:userActivity.activityType]) { ⓬
        NSDictionary *details = userActivity.userInfo; ⓭
        NSString *itemId = [details
                objectForKey:CSSearchableItemActivityIdentifier]; ⓮

        //process using the unique ID
    }

    return YES;
}
```

The Core Spotlight API is available in the *CoreSpotlight.h* ❶ header file.

We will need the *MobileCoreServices.h* ❷ header file to use the *UTI* type constants.

In this example, we have added a helper method, addToIndex, ❸ to add content to the index. The parameters to this method have been omitted for brevity.

The class CSSearchableItemAttributeSet ❹ can be used to define attributes related to the content to be indexed. Important attributes are title and contentDescrip tion, which define the output in search results. Figure 13-2 shows the search result in Spotlight for the content in the example. Depending upon the entity type, you may use one or more of the several other attributes available.[6]

In our example, we designate the content type of the item to be plain text ❺.[7]

It is important to add a title and, optionally, contentDescription ❻. They control the visualization of the search result (see Figure 13-2).

---

6 See the complete list on the Apple developer website (*http://apple.co/1SvhU5y*).

7 We discussed document types in "Sharing Content" on page 261.

Once the attributes are configured, it is time to use these attributes to make the final item, `CSSearchableItem` object, to be indexed **❼**. It requires a per-app `uniqueIdentifier`. The exact purpose of `domainIdentifier` is not known at the time of writing.[8]

`CSSearchableIndex` **❽** is the main class that helps in creating indexes. The `defaultSearchableIndex` is the global index on the device.

The method `indexSearchableItems:completionHandler:` allows indexing multiple items **❾** asynchronously.

The result of indexing is available in the completion handler **❿** provided. The completion handler must not be `nil`.

On the other side, when the user taps on the search result from the app, the app delegate method `application:continueUserActivity:restorationHandler:` **⓫** is called.

The `activityType` in this case is always `CSSearchableItemActionType`.

⓬ The `userInfo` **⓭** dictionary always has at least one entry. That entry, with the key `CSSearchableItemActivityIdentifier`, **⓮** provides the unique identifier used earlier when creating the `CSSearchableItem`. Use this value to look up the entity in the app and display the details.

You should follow these performance-related recommendations when using the Core Spotlight API:

- Provide enough details in the `title` and `description`, but do not make them overly long. In addition to the user not seeing the complete data, it also takes time to serialize/deserialize them.

- Do not overuse keywords. In addition to the possibility of being penalized for overuse, it may impact index creation and search performance.

- Minimize the content provided in the `userInfo` dictionary of the user activity. Keep just enough data to be able to quickly reach a specific result.

---

8 It can be merely metadata. It may also be used to further classify an item within the app so that the `uniqueIdentifier` essentially is per-app per-domain. This will allow multiple SDKs/components to work seamlessly within an app.

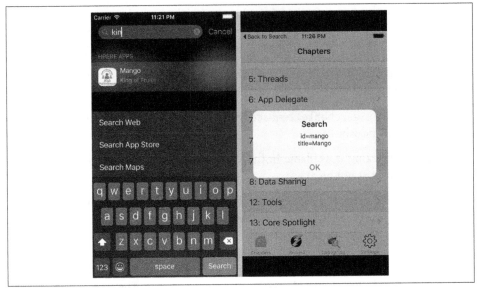

Figure 13-2. Spotlight search (left) and search result shown in app (right; alert for demo)

Web markup

Since iOS 6, Smart App Banners[9] have been the standard way to help increase app downloads if the user visits an app's website in Mobile Safari on iOS devices.

Apple has introduced new enhancements. Applebot (*https://support.apple.com/en-us/HT204683*) will now crawl the web pages looking for meta tags to feed data for the public indexes for searches in Spotlight and Siri. In WWDC 2015, Apple mentioned that it will support standard meta tags,[10] including but not limited to those defined at Schema.org and by the Open Graph protocol. And in specific scenarios where these open standards do not suffice, new tags have been provisioned by Apple.

For your app's content to appear in searches, you can use these tags to provide specific context of the page.

Search Best Practices

Universal links and search, though seemingly different, feed into each other. NSUser Activity and Core Spotlight help build the index using local content, making it available to the central Apple servers. Web markup helps Apple servers index (using Applebot) web content when it can link into the app.

---

9 iOS Developer Library, "Promoting Apps with Smart App Banners" (*http://apple.co/1NnawJc*).

10 iOS Developer Library, "Mark Up Web Content" (*http://apple.co/1qMnZ7L*).

However, these results will only surface *when they are popular enough*, apart from several other factors. Most of these other factors are currently unknown, but as an app developer, you must ensure that you provide enough information so as to enrich the indexes. This will ensure that users are able to discover your app, discover content within the app, and engage with it.

The following list includes some of my preliminary recommendations (note that this list of best practices is not yet battle tested; it is by no means comprehensive, and it will evolve as we get further into the adoption of the new techniques and study instrumentation data):

- Use universal links. The web page and app should show the same content for the same link.

- Use the same ID when providing content to index. This will ensure a higher engagement ranking for the same content.

- Use `description` for a better user experience.

- If applicable, provide a thumbnail image.

- Use keywords, and use them wisely.

  There is no reference available on how many keywords will result in a ranking penalty, but there are enough reasons to guess that there will be penalties for spamming with keywords.

- Implement your app as a finite state machine and ensure that the search results leading into the app are handled gracefully.

  The user may land into the same app multiple times with the same or different items or universal links to be viewed.

As you can see in Figure 13-2, the righthand screenshot that displays the app handling the result has a small Back to Search button that takes the user back to Spotlight. However, the only notifications that you get are those of `application WillResignActive` and subsequent events.

This means that, strictly speaking, you really do not know if the user got a call, tapped the Home button, or pressed the Back to Search button.

This also means that you do not know what to do with the last search result or universal link that was opened in the app once it is backgrounded. Should you leave it open? Should you take the app back to the previous state that it was in before opening the link?

The OS-provided Back button takes the user into the source app. The app gets an `applicationDidBecomeActive:` callback but cannot distinguish between app switching by the user and tapping of the Back button. As such, it is advisable to provide a custom Back button in the app itself, so that when the user returns to the app, the last result is still displayed but with an option to return to the previous state.

The next complexity to handle will be to manage multiple results/links that the app is linked into. The app may end up with several items to go Back from before the user can finally see its original state.

It will be a product decision whether or not to support multiple items in what can be called the *back stack*.

It will also be a product decision whether or not to provide a direct link to the original application state when multiple items exist in the back stack.

And the engineering will have to support it.

User Interface

There are a bunch of updates for the user interface tier of the application in iOS 9. Whether you decide to use them will impact your app's performance. For the purpose of discussion, they have been divided into two broad categories:

- UIKit framework changes
- Safari Services framework changes

Gaming frameworks—e.g., the GameplayKit, Model I/O, MetalKit, Metal, SceneKit, and SpriteKit frameworks—are not discussed.

UIKit Framework

iOS 9 features a new container view, `UIStackView` (*http://apple.co/1Noq1jW*), that helps with rendering views horizontally or vertically.

In cases where you need to create a more form-like UI with well-defined horizontally or vertically aligned views (which happens to be a more common case), `UIStackView` provides an easier and faster way out.

If you recollect the mail view that we discussed earlier (Figure 6-11 in "Custom Views" on page 203), it had seven subviews. Using Auto Layout meant multiple constraints to be handcrafted carefully and runtime overheads when solving the linear equations (refer to Figure 6-14 in "Auto Layout" on page 210).

The overheads of using Auto Layout occur not only at runtime but also at design time. Figure 6-11 has over 20 constraints. Crafting them to work across various screen sizes of iPhones and iPads is never easy.

Borrowing from Android

UIStackView is a welcome, long-awaited feature.

Android has had LinearLayout (*http://bit.ly/1fYQUzK*) since its early days. And it is good to see teams learning from one another to the benefit of app developers and, ultimately, the end users.

At Yahoo, we implemented our own version of linear layout and saw great improvements. For a view with 10–12 UI elements, we saw runtime improvement of 19% in view creation and layout time. As the views recycled in the UITableView, relayout also saw improvement by well over 10%.

During development, a complex view that would take up to three days to design across iPhones and iPads took only a few hours using the new component.

The Xcode 7 storyboard editor has support for *pushing* multiple views within a UIStackView. If you look at Figure 13-3, you will notice a new icon in its toolbar (bottom right). Select multiple views and click this Stack icon. All the selected views will be *pushed* inside a new UIStackView.

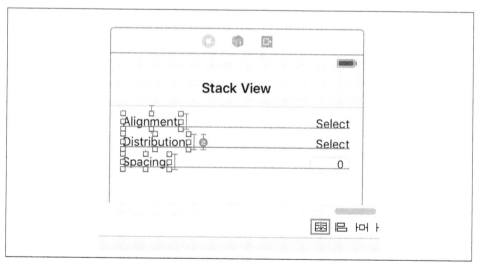

Figure 13-3. Storyboard—arranging views within a UIStackView

The following properties control the rendering of the arranged views of a UIStack View:

axis

> Defines the orientation of the layout. Can be UILayoutConstraintAxisHorizon tal or UILayoutConstraintAxisVertical.
>
> UILayoutConstraintAxisVertical indicates that the arranged views will be rendered vertically, with the view added later rendered beneath the view added previously. UILayoutConstraintAxisHorizontal causes the arranged views to be rendered horizontally, with the view added later rendered to the right of the view added previously.
>
> The default value is UILayoutConstraintAxisVertical.

alignment

> Controls how the arranged views are aligned. The alignment is on the axis perpendicular to the stack view's axis. The default value is UIStackViewAlignment Fill.

distribution

> Distribution controls how the arranged views are sized. This affects the size and positioning of the views *along* the stack view's axis. The default value is UIStack ViewDistributionFill.

spacing

> Specifies the distance, in points, between the adjacent edges of the arranged views. The default value is 0.

baselineRelativeArrangement

> Controls whether the *vertical* spacing between the views is measured from their baselines. If YES, the space is from the last baseline of a text-based view to the first baseline of the view below it.

layoutMarginsRelativeArrangement

> Determines whether the arranged views are laid out relative to the layout margins or bounds. Default is NO, meaning it uses bounds.

Figure 13-4 shows the relevance of these properties for the *horizontal* axis. For the *vertical* axis, rotate the relevance axis of these properties by 90 degrees.

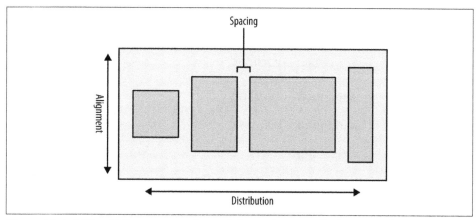

Figure 13-4. UIStackView—properties and their relevance (for horizontal axis)

 UIStackView is a subclass of UIView. However, it is a *nonrendering* subclass. Unlike other UIView subclasses, it does not draw on the canvas. So, if you were to override the drawRect: method, it would not affect the final rendering. Nor would changing other properties like backgroundColor.

UIStackView uses the concept of arrangedSubview+s for lay out. Use the method +addArrangedSubview rather than addSub view to add a view to the layout.

Alternatively, you can use insertArrangedSubview:atIndex: to insert a view at a non-tail position.

To remove a view, use removeArrangedSubview: on UIStackView as well as removeFromSuperview on the child view being removed.

Figure 13-5 shows the corresponding Xcode attribute editor for UIStackView.

For now, there are only a few best practices that can be associated with UIStackView:

- Use it whenever possible. It will not only reduce the time taken to design a view but also improve runtime performance.
- Use the properties to control the final layout.
- If you are not satisfied with its performance, maybe because the view is just too complex, use a custom layout.

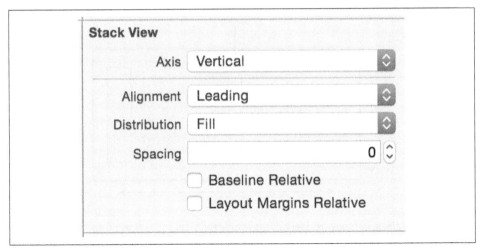

Figure 13-5. UIStackView—Xcode attribute editor

Safari Services Framework

The Safari Services framework was added in iOS 7, and went mostly unnoticed because the primary support provided by the API was to programmatically add URLs to the user's Safari reading list. iOS 9 adds the SFSafariViewController, which we'll look at in this section. In the past, apps have mostly used UIWebView (discussed in "UIWebView" on page 199) to render web content. In iOS 8, a *WebKit* framework was introduced that provided a better-performing WKWebView class, and several apps migrated from UIWebView to WKWebView.

The performance improved, but a few problems still remained unsolved:

- The rendering engine was always based on a version of WebKit (*https://www.webkit.org*) that was not the latest, and at least a few releases behind the one used in the Safari browser on the device. This meant that viewing the web content in Safari was always better than viewing it in the inline browser using UIWebView or WKWebView.

- There was no way to share cookies. So, if the user had logged into a website using the browser (Safari, Chrome, or any other), there was still a need to log in when using the inline browser. There were only two options: either take the user out from your app into Safari (or Chrome), or make the user log in again. Figure 13-6 shows the app settings from the HipChat app, as an example.

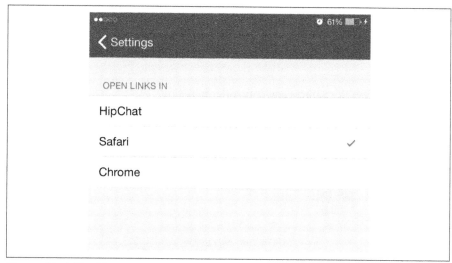

Figure 13-6. HipChat—options to open links

`SFSafariViewController` attempts to solve these problems. Note that it is not a view but a view controller. This means that you cannot control the UI chrome like the address bar and actions at the bottom of the screen surrounding the HTML content, as shown in Figure 13-7.

The view controller uses the cookies from the Safari browser and runs in a separate process. This means that if the user logged in using Safari, browsing can continue seamlessly.

> The cookies from your app are not shared to the Safari view controller, which means if the user was logged in only in your app, another login will be required.
>
> Once the user logs in, either using the view controller or using the Safari app, that session will continue.

Example 13-6 shows sample code for using the `SFSafariViewController`.

Example 13-6. Using SFSafariViewController

```
-(void)showURL:(NSURL *)url {
    SFSafariViewController *safari = [[SFSafariViewController alloc]
        initWithURL:url entersReaderIfAvailable:NO];

    safari.delegate = self;
    [self presentViewController:safari animated:YES completion:nil];
}
```

```
-(void)safariViewControllerDidFinish:(SFSafariViewController *)controller {
    //User tapped Done button
    [controller dismissViewControllerAnimated:YES completion:nil];
}
```

Figure 13-7 shows the Safari view controller in action.

Figure 13-7. Safari view controller

Note that the session from the Safari browser will not be carried over to the SFSafari
ViewController (see Figure 13-8).

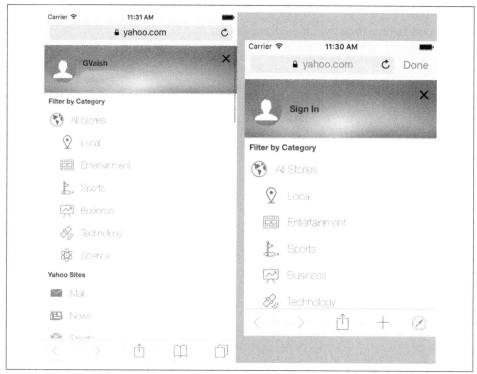

Figure 13-8. Even if the user is logged in in the Safari app (left), he will not automatically be logged in with the native app using SFSafariViewController (right)

I recommend using `SFSafariViewController`. However, because it is available in iOS 9 only, you will still need to provide a fallback to `WKWebView` for iOS 8 users and/or `UIWebView` for iOS 7 users.

Do not enable `entersReaderIfAvailable` when using the view controller. Let the user decide when to enter the reader mode.

Extensions

iOS 9 introduces two new extension points (see Figure 13-9) that impact how a user can engage with the app and what UI is shown to the user:

Content Blocker extension
    Allows restricting content viewing when browsing in Safari and when using the
    `SFSafariViewController`

Spotlight Index extension

Allows for updating the on-device index for App Search even when the app is not running

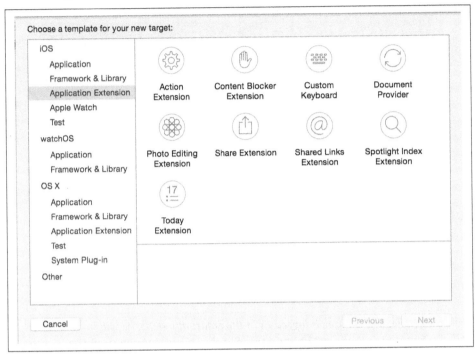

Figure 13-9. iOS 9 extensions

Depending upon the app, you may implement one or both of these extensions.

For example, you may create an app to protect children's privacy and restrict exposure to mature content when browsing. The Content Blocker extension is the option to implement such a plug-in for the Safari browser on the device.

Similarly, it will be a good idea to allow indexed content to be updated even when not being used for long. This will ensure that the outdated entries do not show up in the Spotlight search. The Spotlight Index extension will help you accomplish this.

Content Blocker Extension

Have you been using Adblock Plus (*https://adblockplus.org*) on your desktop machine to remove those nasty ads? If so, you've probably wished it was available for mobile too. The Content Blocker extension can help you with that.

This extension point integrates with Safari (*http://apple.co/1SvqjpG*) and allows filtering content viewed on a website.

If you go to Settings → Safari, you will notice a new entry called Content Blockers. You can have one or more content blockers installed on the device and selectively activate them.

The Content Blocker extension uses a JSON configuration file that controls what elements will be visible and what will be blocked. The specification of the JSON content is available on the WebKit website (*http://bit.ly/webkit-cb*).

Example 13-7 shows an example of Content Blocker extension. It requires a class to implement the NSExtensionRequestHandling protocol. It has just one method, begin RequestWithExtensionContext:, which calls the method -[NSExtensionContext completeRequestReturningItems:completionHandler:] with the filter definitions.

Example 13-7. Content Blocker extension

```
//Code
- (void)beginRequestWithExtensionContext:(NSExtensionContext *)context {

    NSURL *url = [[NSBundle mainBundle]
            URLForResource:@"blockerList" withExtension:@"json"]; ❶
    NSItemProvider *attachment = [[NSItemProvider alloc]
        initWithContentsOfURL:url]; ❷

    NSExtensionItem *item = [[NSExtensionItem alloc] init];
    item.attachments = @[attachment]; ❸

    [context completeRequestReturningItems:@[item] completionHandler:nil]; ❹
}
```

❶ The URL to the filter definitions (JSON content).

❷ Create an NSItemProvider. Here, we use the initWIthContentsOfURL initializer.

❸ Create an NSExtensionItem object with the NSItemProvider attachments.

❹ Last, filter the content by calling completeRequestReturningItems. See Example 13-8 for a sample filter definition.

Example 13-8. Sample filter definition

```
[{
    "trigger": {
        "url-filter": "webkit.org/images/icon-gold.png" ❶
    },
    "action": {
        "type": "block" ❷
    }
}]
```

❶ The `trigger` (when the filter should kick in). Here, based on the URL being processed.

❷ The `action` (what to do when the `trigger` criteria are satisfied). Here, *block* the content. Do not show it.

Figure 13-10 shows how you can configure the content blocker.

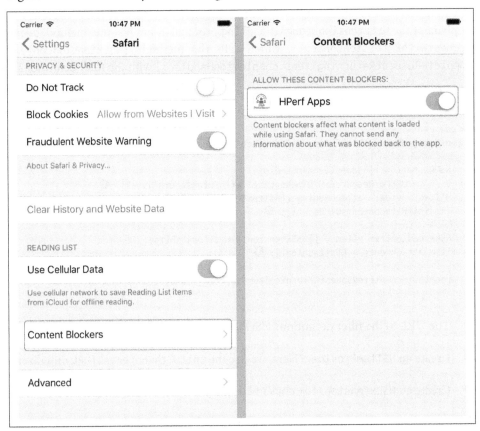

Figure 13-10. Safari content blocker settings

Figure 13-11 shows how the content blocker can affect the visible content on a given website (here, *http://www.webkit.org*). The screenshot on the left is when the content blocker is turned on while the one on the right is with the content blocker turned off. Notice that when the content blocker is turned on, it does not show the WebKit app logo.

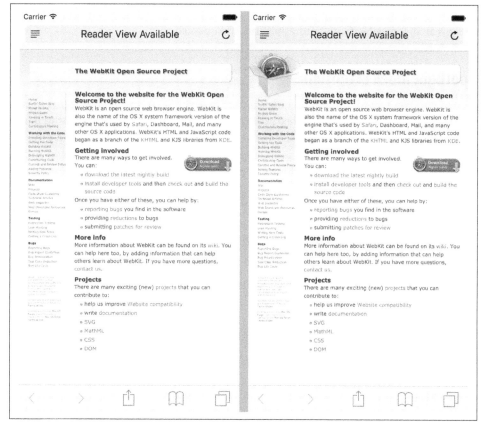

Figure 13-11. WebKit website with content blocker turned on (left) and with content blocked turned off (right)

Because this is the first time an extension has been made available to mobile Safari, best practices from the real world are yet to evolve. Here are a few basic recommendations:

- Try loading the file from the local filesystem rather than syncing from the network each time it is activated or used.

- For dynamic filters (Adblock Plus, for example, may want to implement this and update from the server[11]), use background fetch to periodically sync the file from the server.

- Minimize the number of entries in the filter. This will in turn minimize the time taken to parse and apply the filter on a complex web page.

---

11 Sebastian Noack, "Adblock Plus and (a Little) More" (*http://bit.ly/1GULO0e*).

- Do not abuse it. It is highly recommended to publish the file on your website and make it accessible from your app (hint: use openURL:).

Spotlight Index Extension

In general, you would update the indexes for Spotlight Search when the app is in use. However, using the Spotlight Index extension, you can create an index-maintenance extension that lets the OS coordinate with the app when it is not running and gives an opportunity to update the index and/or verify the validity of an item (for example, whether the item is still active and has not expired).

Working with the Spotlight Index extension requires a class that inherits from CSIn dexExtensionRequestHandler with implementation of the following methods:

searchableIndex:reindexAllSearchableItemsWithAcknowledgementHandler:
  Called to trigger indexing of all items on the device

searchableIndex:reindexSearchableItemsWithIdentifiers:acknowledgementHan dler:
  Called to trigger validation of specific items with the given uniqueIdentifiers

The best practices for implementing a Spotlight extension would be same as those for search that we discussed under "Search Best Practices" on page 412.

App Thinning

Prior to iOS 9, when you needed a universal binary to support multiple devices (iPod, iPhone, iPad, and now Apple Watch), you had to bundle all the resources together or run the risk of upsetting users if you downloaded them on first launch.

The asset catalog (see "UIImageView" on page 194) proved to be a very useful feature in that it not only optimized the image load but also helped organize different versions of an image for various devices. But this made the final binary that the user downloaded huge.

On the other hand, optimizing the use of resources (images, audio clips, and video clips) meant splitting them into two categories. The ones that were always needed were bundled with the app, while the ones that were only needed after some time were fetched from the server. This approach reduced the binary size by a few notches and avoid going heavy on network use.

However, this meant writing a lot of custom code, and maintaining your servers to fetch the assets when needed. This was especially painful for apps that support multiple skins or themes, with games being most affected.

iOS 9 introduces three features to address resource distribution–related problems:

- Slicing
- On-demand resources
- Bitcode

Slicing

As the developer, you continue to upload the universal (fat) binary uploaded to iTunes Connect, continuing executables and resources applicable for all devices. The App Store is responsible for creating multiple bundles for download based on the devices supported by the app.

This process, known as *slicing*, creates and delivers the variant of the app bundle applicable for the target device where the app gets downloaded and installed.

The variant contains only the specific executable architecture and resources that are needed for the target device:

- The executable downloaded is for the processor architecture.
- GPU resources are sliced based on device capabilities.
- Images are sliced based on device family and resolution.

The App Store sends the sliced bundle for devices running iOS 9 and later. For previous versions, the universal bundle is delivered.

For the images to be sliced, they *must* be in the asset catalog. Any other images are not sliced.

On Demand Resources

On-demand resources (http://apple.co/1YrrsmK) are the app contents that are hosted on the App Store separately from the downloaded app bundle.

Starting in iOS 9, you can *tag* certain resources, such as images and audio clips, and then manage those resources by tags.

Specifically, you can configure:

- Resources to be bundled with the app
- Resources to be installed after first app launch
- Installing all resources against a keyword
- Removing all resources against a keyword

The resources may also be sliced. This ensures that you only have the resources that are needed by the app and the app does not hog disk space. As a side effect of the smaller bundle size and minimal assets on the device, the app load time is also shorter.

For example, if your app has multiple skins or themes, the initial set of images bundled can just be the default theme. You may also choose to keep only a few of the most recent themes on the device, or only the themes accessed in the previous hour.

Figure 13-12 shows the lifecycle of an on-demand resource from App Store to device.

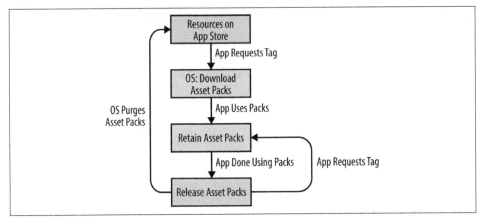

Figure 13-12. Lifecycle of on-demand resources

You must first set up the project to enable on-demand resources, as shown in Figure 13-13.

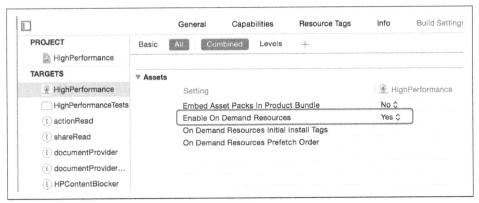

Figure 13-13. Xcode settings to enable on-demand resources

After on-demand resources have been enabled for the project, the next step is to manage the tags and assets associated with them. In Xcode 7, the project settings page now contains a new Resource Tags tab that can be used to do the tag management (see Figure 13-14). You can use the Asset Catalog editor to associate tags with an asset.

Figure 13-14. Xcode—Resource Tags tab

In Figure 13-14, there are three tags—namely, theme_default, theme_black, and theme_blue. The theme_default tag has been added under Initial Install Tags, meaning that the resources will be part of the app binary downloaded. There are no tags under Prefetched Tag Order, which contains the resources to be downloaded on first app launch. And finally, the theme_black and theme_blue are under Download Only On Demand, which indicates that those resources will not be downloaded until the app specifically requests them.

Figure 13-15 shows how to associate the tags with a specific asset catalog item.

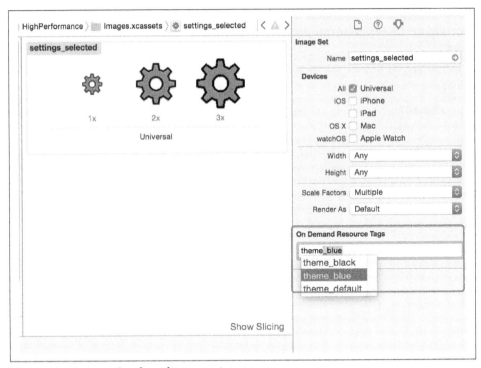

Figure 13-15. Asset Catalog editor associate tags

Once this is configured, you are all set to go. Well, mostly. The last step is to manage the on-demand tags.

Use the class `NSBundleResourceRequest` (*http://apple.co/1NuyYbs*) to manage the lifecycle of the on-demand tagged resources. Example 13-9 shows sample code to download or end access to these resources. Note that to use the resources, you will continue to use the same code as before (using `NSBundle` or `UIImage:imageNamed:`).

Example 13-9. Managing on-demand resource tags

```
NSSet *tags = [NSSet setWithArray: @[@"theme_blue"]];
NSBundleResourceRequest *req = [[NSBundleResourceRequest alloc]
        initWithTags:tags]; ❶

[req beginAccessingResourcesWithCompletionHandler:^(NSError *e) { ❷
    if(e) {
        //handle error
    } else {
        //process, for example
        UIImage *image = [UIImage imageNamed:@"settings"];
    }
}];
```

```
[req conditionallyBeginAccessingResourcesWithCompletionHandler:^(BOOL available) { ❸
    if(available) { ❹
        //Great. The resources are already available. Proceed.
    } else { ❺
        //Not available. May be never downloaded or purged. Download.
    }
}];

[req endAccessingResources]; ❻
```

❶ Create an `NSBundleResourceRequest` object for tags the app is interested in using.

❷ Request to download. Handle the scenarios where an error occurs or the download was successful.

❸ Check if the resources are already available on the device.

❹ If they are available, great. Use them as earlier.

❺ If they're not available, use the `beginAccessingResourcesWithCompletionHan dler:` method to enqueue download.

❻ Inform the system that you are done using the resources for the given tags.

Bitcode

Bitcode is an intermediate representation of a compiled program.

An app uploaded to iTunes Connect can contain executables in a bitcode format that are compiled to native format and linked with the final binaries in the App Store.

Using bitcode allows Apple to *reoptimize* the app binary in the future without any need to resubmit a new version to the store.

Figure 13-16 shows Xcode project settings to enable bitcode. The default option for a new Xcode 7 project is to enable bitcode.

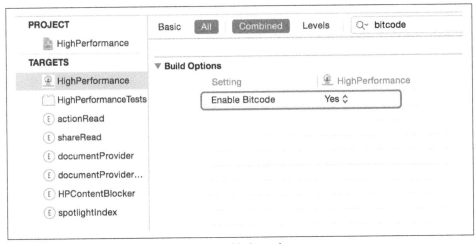

Figure 13-16. Xcode Project settings to enable bitcode

Bitcode is optional for iOS. However, it is *required* for watchOS.

Summary

iOS 9 has some really power-packed features that you should use to improve your app's lovability, real performance, and perceived performance. Use universal links to provide one URL that is universally accessible and sharable—no more custom schemes to manage nasty handoffs. Index the public contents of your app so that they are available in Spotlight Search. `SFSafariViewController` should be the preferred choice moving forward, but ensure that you provide a fallback for iOS 8 and older devices. Finally, app thinning is a feature that you must enable: specifically the on-demand resources if your application is resource heavy and you do not need all of them right when the app is installed.

Index

Numbers

A

About the Author

Gaurav Vaish was introduced to GW-BASIC when he was 12 years old and fell in love with its simplicity. Over 20 years later, he has programmed in most of the major languages, on every popular operating system, and probably for every device popular today.

He works in the Mobile and Emerging Products (MEP) group at Yahoo! headquarters —specifically, in the Mobile SDK team, whose charter is to create optimized reusable solutions that are incorporated across Yahoo mobile apps, run on dozens of types of devices, and are used by hundreds of millions of users every month, performing over a billion user interactions weekly and handling over a billion network connections daily.

Gaurav started his career in 2002 with Adobe Systems India, working in the Engineering Solutions group. In 2005 he started his own company, Edujini Labs, focusing on corporate training and collaborative learning.

Gaurav holds a B. Tech. in electrical engineering with a specialization in speech signal processing from IIT Kanpur, India.

He is the author of the books *Reflections by IITians* and *Getting Started with NoSQL*. He runs a personal blog at *http://www.m10v.com*.

Colophon

The animal on the cover of *High Performance iOS Apps* is a pomarine skua (*Stercorarius pomarinus*), a migrating seabird that can be found all over the world. It winters at sea in tropical oceans, and then returns north to lay its eggs on the arctic tundra during the summer. Although the name is unrelated to the Baltic Sea region of Pomerania, *Pomeranian skua* is a commonly used misnomer for these birds.

Full-grown pomarine skuas can range from 18 to 26 inches in length and weigh close to two pounds. Identification of this species of skua can be difficult due to its similarities to the parasitic jaeger (another kind of seabird) and the fact that adults are *polymorphic*, or come in three different color patterns. All three patterns contain various shades of brown, black, and white, often with white underbellies and a white wing flash.

Pomarine skuas feed on fish, carrion, smaller birds, and even rodents. They have been known to steal fish from gulls, terns, or gannets in mid-flight and are only preyed upon by adult white-tailed and golden eagles. Once females have nested in the arctic, they lay two to three olive brown eggs in grass nests on the ground. Skuas are known for their fierce defense of these nests; though they cannot do much damage, it is certainly a frightening experience to have an angry mother bird dive straight at your head!

Many of the animals on O'Reilly covers are endangered; all of them are important to the world. To learn more about how you can help, go to animals.oreilly.com.

The cover image is from Lydekker's *Royal Natural History*. The cover fonts are URW Typewriter and Guardian Sans. The text font is Adobe Minion Pro; the heading font is Adobe Myriad Condensed; and the code font is Dalton Maag's Ubuntu Mono.

Get even more for your money.

Join the O'Reilly Community, and register the O'Reilly books you own. It's free, and you'll get:

- $4.99 ebook upgrade offer
- 40% upgrade offer on O'Reilly print books
- Membership discounts on books and events
- Free lifetime updates to ebooks and videos
- Multiple ebook formats, DRM FREE
- Participation in the O'Reilly community
- Newsletters
- Account management
- 100% Satisfaction Guarantee

Signing up is easy:

1. Go to: oreilly.com/go/register
2. Create an O'Reilly login.
3. Provide your address.
4. Register your books.

Note: English-language books only

To order books online:
oreilly.com/store

For questions about products or an order:
orders@oreilly.com

To sign up to get topic-specific email announcements and/or news about upcoming books, conferences, special offers, and new technologies:
elists@oreilly.com

For technical questions about book content:
booktech@oreilly.com

To submit new book proposals to our editors:
proposals@oreilly.com

O'Reilly books are available in multiple DRM-free ebook formats. For more information:
oreilly.com/ebooks

Lightning Source UK Ltd.
Milton Keynes UK
UKOW05f1236160616

276391UK0000